ne American Bourgeoisie: Distinction and entity in the Nineteenth Century

Palgrave Studies in CULTURAL AND INTELLECTUAL HISTORY

Series Editors

Anthony J. La Vopa, North Carolina State University.

Suzanne Marchand, Louisiana State University.

Javed Majeed, Queen Mary, University of London.

The Palgrave Studies in Cultural and Intellectual History series has three primary aims: to close divi
between intellectual and cultural approaches, thus bringing them into mutually enriching interactions
encourage interdisciplinarity in intellectual and cultural history; and to globalize the field, both in g
graphical scope and in subjects and methods. This series is open to work on a range of modes of intellect
inquiry, including social theory and the social sciences, the natural sciences, economic thought, literatu
religion, gender and sexuality, philosophy, political and legal thought, psychology, and music and the a
It encompasses not just North America but Africa, Asia, Eurasia, Europe, Latin America, and the Mid
East. It includes both nationally focused studies and studies of intellectual and cultural exchanges betw
different nations and regions of the world, and encompasses research monographs, synthetic studies, edi
collections, and broad works of reinterpretation. Regardless of methodology or geography, all books in t
series are historical in the fundamental sense of undertaking rigorous contextual analysis.

Published by Palgrave Macmillan:

Indian Mobilities in the West, 1900–1947: Gender, Performance, Embodiment
By Shompa Lahiri

The Shelley-Byron Circle and the Idea of Europe
By Paul Stock

Culture and Hegemony in the Colonial Middle East
By Yaseen Noorani

Recovering Bishop Berkeley: Virtue and Society in the Anglo-Irish Context
By Scott Breuninger

The Reading of Russian Literature in China: A Moral Example and Manual of Practice
By Mark Gamsa

Rammohun Roy and the Making of Victorian Britain
By Lynn Zastoupil

Carl Gustav Jung: Avant-Garde Conservative
By Jay Sherry

Law and Politics in British Colonial Thought: Transpositions of Empire
By Shaunnagh Dorsett and Ian Hunter, eds.

Sir John Malcolm and the Creation of British India
By Jack Harrington

The American Bourgeoisie: Distinction and Identity in the Nineteenth Century
By Sven Beckert and Julia B. Rosenbaum, eds.

Nature Engaged: Science in Practice from the Renaissance to the Present (forthcoming)
By Jessica Riskin and Mario Biagioli, eds.

Character, Self, and Sociability in the Scottish Enlightenment (forthcoming)
By Thomas Ahnert and Susan Manning, eds.

The American Bourgeoisie: Distinction and Identity in the Nineteenth Century

Sven Beckert and Julia B. Rosenbaum

palgrave
macmillan

THE AMERICAN BOURGEOISIE: DISTINCTION AND IDENTITY IN THE NINETEENTH CENTURY

First published in 2010 by
PALGRAVE MACMILLAN®
in the United States—a division of St. Martin's Press LLC,
175 Fifth Avenue, New York, NY 10010.

Where this book is distributed in the UK, Europe and the rest of the world, this is by Palgrave Macmillan, a division of Macmillan Publishers Limited, registered in England, company number 785998, of Houndmills, Basingstoke, Hampshire RG21 6XS.

Palgrave Macmillan is the global academic imprint of the above companies and has companies and representatives throughout the world.

Palgrave® and Macmillan® are registered trademarks in the United States, the United Kingdom, Europe and other countries.

ISBN: 978–0–230–10294–1

Library of Congress Cataloging-in-Publication Data

The American bourgeoisie : distinction and identity in the nineteenth century / [edited by] Sven Beckert and Julia Rosenbaum.
p. cm.—(Palgrave studies in cultural and intellectual history)
ISBN 978–0–230–10294–1 (hardback)
1. Middle class—United States—History—19th century. I. Beckert, Sven, 1965– II. Rosenbaum, Julia B.

HT690.U6A46 2010
305.5'5097309034–dc22 2010023204

A catalogue record of the book is available from the British Library.

Design by Newgen Imaging Systems (P) Ltd., Chennai, India.

First edition: December 2010

10 9 8 7 6 5 4 3 2 1

›ntents

Part III The Public Sphere

List of Images

Acknowledgments

This volume could not have taken shape without with the initial and generous support of the Charles Warren Center for Studies in American History at Harvard University, the Leiden University Foundation, and the Goethe Institute, Boston. Their funding allowed for a two-day working conference that brought together scholars from across disciplines to present, discuss, and debate aspects of nineteenth-century class formation of the American bourgeoisie. We are particularly grateful to Elizabeth Blackmar, Sarah Burns, Ute Frevert, and Thimo de Nijs, the four moderators who helped make the sessions lively and stimulating conversations.

In transforming talks into texts for this collection of essays, we feel fortunate to have worked with a group of contributors as diligent and patient as ours. We thank Robert Johnston and Noam Maggor for their insightful comments on an earlier draft of the introduction. Paul Mathis provided essential research assistance, and in preparing the final manuscript we are indebted to Jesse Halvorsen and Barbara Ross.

Acknowledgments

[illegible]

Introduction

Sven Beckert and Julia B. Rosenbaum

Legacies of a nineteenth-century bourgeois world surround us, from the art collections we admire to the Newport mansions we visit to the foodstuffs we fancy. Our American cultural landscape has been shaped by the ethos, preferences, and practices of one of the world's most powerful nineteenth-century economic elites—the American bourgeoisie. The museums, philharmonic orchestras, and operas they created inspire to this day. The buildings they constructed continue to give shape to many of our cities. The institutional forms they developed and the host of institutions they established structure our public life. Most distinctively, the nineteenth-century American bourgeoisie combined familiar forms of economic might and political power with a new form of cultural clout: because of this, nowhere in the world did a bourgeoisie emerge as influential as that in American cities such as New York, Boston, Philadelphia, Chicago, and San Francisco.

Having accumulated fortunes in trade, manufacturing, and financial services, bourgeois Americans exerted tremendous influence on how their fellow citizens worked and lived, and how they governed. Investment in new manufacturing techniques and a shift to the factory as the most efficient locus of production weakened the making of home goods and artisanal work and gathered thousands and, eventually, millions of Americans into urban industrial centers. Investments in canals and railroads opened up western territories, changing the scale and location of American farming, as well as the possibilities for industrialization. Enabled by their private control of ever larger amounts of capital, bourgeois Americans also dramatically influenced how Americans lived: While most Americans since the nation's inception had been farmers who produced for their own subsistence and the market, in the course of the nineteenth century, ever larger numbers of Americans became wage earners, entirely dependent for their subsistence on their ability to find paid employment. In 1800, only 6.1 percent of Americans lived in towns and cities of more than 2,500 inhabitants; by 1900, that number had exploded to 39.6 percent, largely due to the shifting patterns of capital investments.[1] Such tremendous economic power became ever more concentrated in the hands of the few as select Americans—the Carnegies, Rockefellers, and Morgans, among others—accumulated some of the world's largest fortunes. As an economic elite, they also wielded enormous political power, swaying legislatures in their favor and defining agendas of political parties. Indeed, the American state was structured in ways that allowed the interests of the owners of capital to gain supremacy.[2] Along with the consolidation of economic and political power, their might as a social group depended on an ability, over the course of the nineteenth century, to establish a class *culture* and then to rigorously maintain it—to map the terms for intellectual and social practices and preferences.

How this economic elite emerged as consummate cultural arbiters and tastemakers is the subject of this volume.

But who, precisely, constituted the American bourgeoisie? No group of Americans during the nineteenth century specifically used the term "bourgeois" to name their own collectivity. If the term was used in public discourse, then it typically almost always described a group of capital-rich French men and women socially located between the aristocracy and the working class.[3] From our twenty-first century vantage point, however, the term bourgeoisie most precisely and effectively describes the group of people we are concerned with here—Americans who distinctively wedded culture to capital. In terms of capital, the American bourgeoisie controlled substantial wealth, did not work with their own hands, nor did they work for wages. The vast majority of Americans, which included wage workers and slaves, artisans and farmers, and even most small business owners, were, thus, never part of the bourgeoisie. Instead, the American bourgeoisie consisted of merchants, manufacturers, and bankers, while professionals such as lawyers and white-collar managers remained on its margins. Nearly all bourgeois Americans were located in cities, not in the countryside, and the vast majority lived in the major urban centers of the day. Because this group did not include small shopkeepers or artisans, schoolteachers or clerks, it was not a "middle class." Because no nobility ever arose in the United States and because among the bourgeoisie can be counted thousands of merchants, manufacturers, and bankers, the social group we are focusing on in this volume was more than a narrow "plutocracy," a "ruling class" or an "aristocracy."[4]

A shared position within the economic structure did not, however, by necessity lead to an articulation of shared identities, a sense of distinction, or a capacity for collective action. In fact, competition in the marketplace constantly put individual bourgeois men and women at odds with one another: they struggled over markets, and they often had quite divergent interests. Some favored tariffs on particular goods, and others opposed them. Some benefitted from new railways, and others suffered because of them. Visions of political economy often diverged. Their shared structural position indeed drove capital-rich Americans just as much apart as it might have consolidated them into a class.

An avenue for consolidation emerged in the realm of culture, and this volume investigates how, in the course of the nineteenth century, bourgeois New Yorkers, Chicagoans, Philadelphians, and others overcame conflicts and divisions by forging common preferences and habits, manners and ideas, networks and institutions. Creating a common class culture, thus, was not just an expression of the power of the American bourgeoisie, but one of its preconditions. The creation of cultural capital, acquired in educational and social institutions, sharpened a sense of distinction, which could then serve as a basis for the forging of social networks.[5] Cultural activities, family ties, and institutions could further strengthen these networks and, at times, function as the basis for collective mobilizations in labor conflicts or politics. This class culture, moreover, could be universalized and, thus, serve as a model to other aspiring social groups. Bourgeois Americans attempted to set the cultural standards for the nation at large, although in that project, they often met with resistance and competition from middle-class and lower-class citizens.[6]

A common class culture achieved a shared sense of purpose and a connection among fellow economic elites, despite divergent sources of capital, potential internal economic competition, and ethnic and religious diversity. Equally important, a common class culture also served as a measure of distinction, which could further separate the bourgeoisie from other economic groups, such as manual laborers, skilled artisans, middle-class shop owners, and white-collar managers. Consolidation and distinction, of course, were never completely fixed states of bourgeois being. Formulating a sense of themselves as a distinct social group with shared identities, while simultaneously setting themselves apart from other citizens, was an extended and continually negotiated process.

In this book, we approach the emergence of an American bourgeoisie as an active process of class formation, not as an automatic or pre-determined result of peoples' places within the social structure.[7] Our emphasis is on culture as a process of negotiation and contestation, a matter of consolidation as well as conflict, where adaptability and resourcefulness proved crucial.

The process of bourgeois class formation ranged across activities, ideas, and institutions. Indeed, a striking feature of the bourgeoisie in the United States was the diversity of its cultural involvement. Food consumption, leisure pursuits, and home design and decoration, for example, offered opportunities for shaping distinctive and exclusive patterns of behavior and social habits. Social clubs and networks worked to institutionalize bourgeois values and interests, further expanding the economic and social reach of America's bourgeois men and women. In stretching out across a cultural spectrum—favored foodstuffs, musical tastes, holiday itineraries, and urban activities—a bourgeois sensibility asserted its presence and, even more important, inserted itself into daily life.

A significant source of the American bourgeoisie's strength derived from its diverse "portfolio of practices." The extent of that diversity is suggested by the kinds of categories that emerge in looking at bourgeois cultural expressions. Specifically, we can talk about three major categories: first, the manners and habits in terms of self-presentation among the bourgeoisie; second, the institutions and networks the bourgeoisie established and maintained; and, third, the more public face of bourgeois life, particularly in terms of philanthropic work and the arts, activities specifically meant to reach much broader and socially less exclusive audiences.

These cultural practices were closely related to one another, mutually facilitating their emergence. Shared manners and habits, such as courtship practices or forms of speech, could serve as the basis for the construction of social networks. Social networks, in turn, often strengthened by family ties, formed the basis for the construction of social institutions, which, in turn, could organize and reorganize public space and embed bourgeois culture into the larger American society, so that by the end of the nineteenth century, the American bourgeoisie exercised its cultural authority across diverse realms.

Especially in comparison to the bourgeoisie across Europe, the nineteenth-century bourgeoisie in the United States exhibited an adaptability and a readiness to creatively invent itself, a circumstance no doubt stimulated by the absence of a formal, historically entrenched aristocracy. Less encumbered by tradition or strict and longstanding social conventions and codes of behavior, the bourgeoisie in America had the freedom to pick and choose its cultural ground, albeit one primed by a particular reading of the cultural practices of ruling classes at other times and in other countries.

This collection of essays focuses on cities in the northern United States because it was here that the American bourgeoisie was most significant and powerful. In the nineteenth century, certainly, bourgeois activity in the United States was most prominent on an urban stage: It was in cities that most merchant, manufacturers, and bankers lived, and where they built the densest, most powerful, and longest-lasting shared identities and institutions. While there was a bourgeoisie in southern cities as well, and the wealth of southern agriculture was important to constituting the wealth of the northern bourgeoisie, the models of bourgeois culture were largely of northern origin.[8]

These essays demonstrate that, within these northern cities, a shared economic status, rather than national origin, ethnicity, or race, proved the decisive factor in shaping manners, habits, networks, and institutions. This argument goes against much of the scholarship on the cultural history of cities, which has tended to emphasize the importance of national origin, ethnicity, and race. While these issues certainly structured public life and politics, our findings suggest that when it came to the formation of bourgeois culture, what mattered most was ownership of capital. Americans of diverse ethnic, national, and religious backgrounds found common ground in the construction of a set of shared manners and habits—a class culture that almost always excluded their co-ethnic, co-religious compatriots.[9] When it came to the construction of institutions, ethnic and religious distinctions sometimes mattered, but only insofar as they led to the emergence of parallel bourgeois institutions—social clubs, for example, that limited membership to Protestant or Jewish bourgeois Americans.

The cultural power of the bourgeoisie changed significantly in the twentieth century. While this development is outside the scope of the book, a few features are noteworthy. Bourgeois manners and habits became increasingly generalized, as members of other social groups sought to embrace them as well. Markers of distinction that had developed a coherence and consistency among nineteenth-century bourgeois Americans were undercut by the panoply of new styles and the conscious rejection of uniformity by many capital-rich Americans by the late twentieth century. The public sphere also became less and less a place to perform class distinction, as the political mobilization of large numbers of working- and lower-middle-class Americans challenged the political power of the bourgeoisie. One stronghold remained, however: the bourgeoisie's control of institutions—the social clubs, art museums, and universities that continued to be pillars of bourgeois influence into the twenty-first century.

As a scholarly subject, nineteenth-century bourgeois Americans have traditionally appeared as background characters. While the social history of the 1970s and 1980s has provided us with rich new insights into the history of subaltern groups—from workers to slaves to women—merchants, bankers, and manufacturers have largely escaped the attention of historians, who have worked to give voice and agency to the disenfranchised. Discussion of the bourgeoisie in much of that scholarship occurred as a foil—an undifferentiated group of people who in one way or another were responsible for the exploitation and repression of those below them. Scholarly interest in economic elites, with few exceptions, has been limited to scholars of business. These historians have analyzed the United States bourgeoisie in two distinct ways: The more sociological accounts, indebted to the work of the twentieth century's leading business historian Alfred D. Chandler Jr., feature business elites principally as people who take on predetermined positions in larger institutions. Other accounts have detailed the heroic histories of entrepreneurs and how such capitalists nearly single-handedly changed the fortunes of firms, industries, and regions. The work of such scholars is not a history of the bourgeoisie as a class.

Only in the last decade has the history of the American bourgeoisie in the nineteenth century been the subject of academic scrutiny: Jeff Hadyu recently compared the networks, identities, and collective action of the Cincinnati and San Francisco bourgeoisie; Jonathan Daniel Wells addressed the subject of the bourgeoisie of the antebellum South; Sven Beckert chronicled the history of the bourgeoisie of New York; Thomas Adam wrote about bourgeois philanthropy; and Steve Fraser published a collection of essays about the history of economic elites in the United States.[10] While disagreeing on some matters, these authors all agree that an identifiable group that could be labeled bourgeoisie emerged in the nineteenth-century United States. This emerging interest certainly was the result of historians during the 1990s and 2000s living through an age of dramatically sharpening social inequality, what some have termed a "second Gilded Age."[11]

This book is indebted to this literature, but it draws its particular strengths from two other sources. For one, its focus on culture is indebted to the extensive writings on nineteenth-century culture by historians, sociologists, art historians, scholars of literature and music, and others, during the past two decades. This literature contains fascinating insights into such matters as leisure and consumption, architecture and interior design, and social clubs and museums. Without these studies, this volume could not have been assembled, and, indeed, many of the authors represented here have contributed in important ways to the literature on nineteenth-century United States culture. But by isolating their discussions of particular aspects of bourgeois culture from the larger question of the emergence, consolidation, and self-definition of the bourgeoisie as a social class, they fail to address what is perhaps most significant about the cultural worlds they describe—namely its utmost importance to the process of the formation of the bourgeoisie as a class.

For this reason, we draw on a different, vibrant literature that can serve as an example for the analytical and interpretative possibilities of the study of bourgeois culture: the rich literature on the European bourgeoisie. Ever since the 1950s, historians, such as Ernest Labrousse in France, have studied the history of the European bourgeoisie in its primary aspects—politics, economic structure, ideas, and culture. In Europe, the social history revolution of the 1970s and 1980s, in contrast to its effects on the United States, motivated an outpouring of works on the French, English, Italian, German, and Dutch bourgeoisies, among others. Struggling with the issue of what held together these economically heterogeneous and competing social groups, with their diverse political interests, historians increasingly focused on the social glue provided by the construction of a shared culture. This scholarship was propelled especially by the work of Jürgen Kocka in Germany, Boudien de Vries in the Netherlands, Adeline Daumard in France, and Leonore Davidoff and Catherine Hall in England. These historians concluded that the building of this shared culture helped the bourgeoisie as a class to emerge and mobilize collectively. They realized that shared manners and habits, institutions, and the domination and definition of high culture are at the very core of understanding the history of the bourgeoisie.[12]

Combining the insights of this European literature with the rich scholarship on American culture and the social history of American business-people, we present a novel view of the formation of bourgeois culture in the United States. This volume transcends the tradition of community-focused studies to look at a wide variety of places and social practices across the United States. The American bourgeoisie—its merchants, bankers, industrialists, and their families—ascended because they combined their ownership of capital and access to political power with an ability to forge shared cultural identities and networks, and the one can not be understood without the other.

To structure our investigation of nineteenth-century bourgeois culture in the United States, this collection of essays focuses on three distinct but related areas: bourgeois self-presentation, the institutional and organizational reproduction of the bourgeoisie, and bourgeois practices in the public sphere. These particular perspectives on bourgeois life give us insight into how bourgeois women and men related to one another and confirmed a sense of cohesion, and the ways these men and women interacted with the surrounding society to cast a common cultural vocabulary. Although this volume avoids a strict chronological organization in favor of exploring these salient themes, many of the essays, by themselves and collectively, track change over time.

We begin with the issue of self-presentation, specifically manners and tastes that shaped bourgeois life—from aesthetic preferences to leisure habits. Anne

Mendelson's opening essay exemplifies the dominant theme of consolidation and distinction as a class strategy through an examination of retail food-buying over the course of the nineteenth century and the increasing use of foodstuffs as tokens of exclusivity and as markers of class. Maureen Montgomery's analysis of bourgeois travel habits in Europe and Alide Cagidemetrio's discussion about the compatibility of democracy and privilege through her careful reading of works by Henry James provide two examples of the bourgeoisie's search for distinction. The domestic environment is the focus of the final two essays of the section; Anne Verplanck addresses elite Philadelphians' persistent interest in an outmoded portrait form, while Katherine Grier analyzes interior design as an extension of personality and character, a meticulously crafted performance of identity, probing how consumption patterns were strategically linked to individual moral agency.

The second section deals with the maintenance and perpetuation of bourgeois networks and identities. The authors focus specifically on the institutions and networks that established a sense of tradition and continuity and allowed the bourgeoisie to replicate its values and interests over successive generations. Sven Beckert surveys the organizational efforts of bourgeois New Yorkers throughout the nineteenth century, emphasizing the significant changes taking place in the second half of the century, when bourgeois institutions became more insular and more concerned with maintaining distinctions from other social group. Ethan Robey's essay on the American Mechanics' Institute Fairs of the mid-nineteenth century details a specific aspect of this story demonstrating how discrete segments of elite New Yorkers, specifically merchants and industrialists, came together by re-envisioning elite production and notions of productive craftsmanship. Francesca Morgan finds another unifying institution in the genealogical societies, which proliferated over the nineteenth century. In their preoccupation with blood ties and social stature, these societies emphasized an invented "racial" solidarity over divisions related to occupation, sources of capital, politics, or sectionalism. Mary Rockwell argues for the institution of marriage and the activities of women as critical agents in the process of class formation, following young women in the city of Buffalo through the ritual of "coming-out" in society and onto the "marriage market." Finally, Peter Dobkin Hall focuses on the higher-education institutions that emerged in the second half of the century as a powerful instrument not only for producing a homogenous governing class but also for ensuring its national reach.

The final section of the book emphasizes avenues of self-conscious public distinction, the kinds of activities and behaviors in which bourgeois Americans engaged that worked to differentiate them from other social groups. More often than not, such activities brought them squarely into the public arena, particularly through the arts and the notion of cultural philanthropy. The essays here illuminate the struggles that ensued in the bourgeoisie's bid to assert a position of leadership. Julia Rosenbaum opens the section with a focus on specific pieces of public sculpture to examine bourgeois attempts to shape public space and set the terms of social decorum and behavior. Complicating this story of the classification and sacralization of the arts by economic elites, Paul DiMaggio explores the history of Chicago's nineteenth-century cultural institutions and asks why they turned out so differently from those of New York and Boston. Michael Broyles turns to music to consider the process of institutionalization as an arena of distinction for the bourgeoisie, highlighting both its ethnic and gender dynamics. Broyles's essay takes a bird's-eye view as he compares bourgeois responses to music and musical performance among major American cities. Alan Wallach extends this discussion with a essay on the bourgeoisie's investment in art institutions: A phenomenon culminating in the second half of the nineteenth century, those institutions represented an effective seizure of the reins of cultural power. Some of the more specific fault lines of bourgeois control are explored in the concluding essay by John Ott, who looks at the case of art patronage in San Francisco and the face-off between industrial workers and management. Together, the three sections present an ensemble of activities, discourses, and aesthetic preferences that shaped American culture, and speak to who and what we are today.

The essays in this volume serve as a departure point for how future scholars might continue their explorations of the history of the United States bourgeoisie. They represent a claim by historians, art historians, sociologists, and literary scholars that studying the bourgeoisie both as a structural social category and as a process enables us to understand the dynamic history of that class, in particular, and American society, in general, in new and intriguing ways. Indeed, it is a multi-disciplinary view that allows fresh insights into core questions of class formation throughout United States history. The authors here do not just study the cultural history of the bourgeoisie, they also claim that this cultural history is important to understanding what distinctive gathering of forces constituted the bourgeoisie in the first place.

Notes

1. *Twelfth Census of the United States* (1900), Census Report, vol. 1, part 1, LXXXII.
2. Stephen Skowronek, *Building a New American State, The Expansion of National Administrative Capacities, 1870–1920* (New York: Cambridge University Press, 1982); Sanford Jacoby, "American Exceptionalism Revisited: The Importance of Management" in Sanford Jacoby, ed., *Masters to Managers: Historical and Comparative Perspectives on American Employers* (New York: Columbia University Press, 1991), 182.
3. See, for example, references to "bourgeois" and "bourgeoisie" in the *New York Times* from 1851 to 1900, such as February 24, 1855, 4; June 7, 1858, 4; March 18, 1877, 4; September 3, 1893, 3; December 25, 1898, 17.
4. See Sven Beckert, "Propertied of a Different Kind: Bourgeoisie and Lower-Middle Class in the Nineteenth-Century United States," in Burt Bledstein and Robert Johnston, eds., *Middling Sorts: Essays in the History of the American Middle Class* (London: Routledge, 2001), 285–295. Ronald Story, *The Forging of an Aristocracy: Harvard & The Boston Upper Class, 1800–1870* (Middletown: Wesleyan University Press, 1980); Gabriel Almond "Plutocracy and Politics in New York City" (Ph.D. dissertation: University of Chicago, 1938). For the use of the term "bourgeoisie" similar to our uses in this volume, see T. Jackson Lears, *No Place of Grace: Anti-modernism and the Transformation of American Culture, 1800–1920* (New York: Pantheon Books, 1981), especially xvi. See also David Scobey, "Anatomy of the Promenade, The Politics of Bourgeois Sociability in Nineteenth-Century New York" *Social History* 17 (May 1992), 203–227.
5. Pierre Bourdieu's seminal work *Distinction: A Social Critique of the Judgement of Taste* (originally published in 1979) explored these basic dynamics. See also Andrew Hemingway and William Vaughan, eds., *Art in Bourgeois Society, 1790–1850* (Cambridge, U.K.: Cambridge University Press, 1998).
6. Here we disagree with Louis Hartz, *The Liberal Tradition in America: An Interpretation of American Political Thought Since the Revolution* (New York: Harcourt Brace, 1955).
7. See for the general idea Ira Katznelson, "Working-Class Formation: Constructing Cases and Comparisons," in Ira Katznelson and Aristide R. Zolberg, eds., *Working-Class Formation: Nineteenth Century Patterns in Western Europe and the United States* (Princeton, NJ: Princeton University Press, 1986), 3–41. Jürgen Kocka suggests a class formation approach as the most fruitful approach to the study of the bourgeoisie. See Kocka, ed., *Bürger and Bürgerlichkeit im 19. Jahrhundert* (Göttingen: Vandenhoeck & Ruprecht, 1987), 41.
8. Jonathan Daniel Wells, *The Origins of the Southern Middle Class, 1800–1861* (Chapel Hill: University of North Carolina Press, 2004), 5–16.
9. See Geoffrey Blodgett, "Yankee Leadership in a Divided City, 1860–1910," *Journal of Urban History* 8:4 (August 1982), 371–396, and Oscar Handlin, *Boston's Immigrants, 1790–1880: A Study in Acculturation* (Cambridge, MA: Belknap Press of Harvard University Press, 1959).

10. Wells, *The Origins of the Southern Middle Class*; Sven Beckert, *The Monied Metropolis: New York City and the Consolidation of the American Bourgeoisie, 1850–1896* (Cambridge, UK: Cambridge University Press, 2001); Thomas Adam, *Buying Respectability: Philanthropy and Urban Society in Transnational Perspective, 1840s to 1930s* (Bloomington: Indiana University Press, 2009); Steve Fraser and Gary Gerstle, eds., *Ruling America: A History of Wealth and Power in a Democracy* (Cambridge, MA: Harvard University Press, 2005).
11. Michael McHugh, *The Second Gilded Age: The Great Reaction in the United States, 1973–2001* (Lanham, MD: University Press of America, 2006).
12. See, among many others, Ernest Labrousse, "*Voies Nouvelles Vers une Histoire de la Bourgeoisie Occidentale aux XVIIIeme et XIXeme Siecles*," in *Relazioni del X. Congresso Internazionale di Scienze Storiche*, 4, Storia Moderna (Firenze: G.C. Sansoni, 1955); Kocka, ed., *Buerger und Buergerlichkeit im 19. Jahrhundert*; Hans-Juergen Puhle, ed., *Buerger in der Gesellschaft der Neuzeit: Wirtschaft, Politik, Kultur* (Goettingen: Vandenhoeck & Ruprecht, 1991); Hartmut Zwahr, *Proletariat und Bourgeoisie in Deutschland: Studien zur Klassendialektik* (Koeln: Pahl-Rugenstein-Verlag, 1980); David Blackbourn and Geoff Eley, *The Peculiarities of German History: Bourgeois Society and Politics in Nineteenth-Century Germany* (New York: Oxford University Press, 1984); Blackbourn, ed., *The German Bourgeoisie: Essays on the Social History of the German Middle Class from the Late Eighteenth to the Early Twentieth Century* (New York: Routledge, 1991), especially David Blackbourn's introduction; Thomas Mergel, *Zwischen Klasse und Konfession: Katholisches Bürgertum im Rheinland, 1794–1914* (Göttingen: Vandenhoeck & Ruprecht, 1994); Ralf Roth, *Stadt und Bürgertum in Frankfurt am Main: Ein besonderer Weg von der ständischen zur modernen Bürgergesellschaft, 1760–1914* (München: R. Oldenbourg, 1996); Dolores L. Augustine, *Patricians and Parvenus: Wealth and High Society in Wilhelmine Germany* (Oxford and Providence: Berg, 1994); Ernst Bruckmüller et al., eds., *Bürgertum in der Habsburgmonarchie*, vol.1 (Wien: Böhlau Verlag, 1992); Adeline Daumard, *Les Bourgeois et la Bourgeoisie en France depuis 1815* (Paris: Aubier, 1987); Theodore Zeitlin, *France, 1845–1945: Ambition & Love* (Oxford: Oxford University Press, 1973); Michael B. Miller, *The Bon Marche: Bourgeois Culture and the Department Store, 1869–1920* (Princeton, NJ: Princeton University Press, 1981); Bonnie G. Smith, *Ladies of The Leisure Class: The Bourgeoisie of Northern France in the Nineteenth Century* (Princeton, NJ: Princeton University Press, 1981); Richard Holt, "Social History and Bourgeois Culture in Nineteenth-Century France," in *Comparative Studies in Society and History* 27 (October 1985), 713–726; David Garrioch, *The Formation of the Parisian Bourgeoisie, 1690–1830* (Cambridge, MA: Harvard University Press, 1996); W. D. Rubinstein, "Wealth, Elites and the Class Structure of Modern Britain," in *Past and Present* 76 (August 1977), 99–126; Leonore Davidoff and Catherine Hall, *Family Fortunes: Men and Women of the English Middle Class, 1780–1850* (London: Hutchinson, 1987); Peter Earle, *The Making of the English Middle Class, Business, Society and Family Life in London, 1660–1730* (London: Methuen, 1989); R. J. Morris, *Class, Sect, and Party: The Making of the British Middle Class: Leeds, 1820–1850* (Manchester: Manchester University Press, 1990); G. R. Seale, *Entrepreneurial Politics in Mid-Victorian Britain* (Oxford: Oxford University Press, 1993); Philip Hills, "Division and Cohesion in the Nineteenth-Century Middle Class, The Case of Ipswich" (Ph.D. Dissertation, University of Essex, 1988); Charles A. Jones, *International Business in the Nineteenth Century: The Rise and Fall of a Cosmopolitan Bourgeoisie* (Brighton: Wheatsheaf Books, 1987); Richard H. Trainor, *Black Country Élites: The Exercise of Authority in an Industrialized Area, 1830–1900* (Oxford: Clarendon Press, 1993); Eleanor Gordon and Richard Trainor, "Employers and Policymaking: Scotland and Northern Ireland, c. 1880–1939," in S. J. Connolly, R. A. Houston and R. J. Morris, eds., *Conflict, Identity and Economic Development: Ireland and Scotland, 1600–1939* (Preston: Carnegie Publishing, 1995), 254–267; Marco Meriggi, "Italienisches und deutsches Buergertum im Vergleich," in Kocka, ed., *Buergertum im 19. Jahrhundert*, 141–159; Francesco Volpe, *La Borghesia di Provincia Nell'Eta Borbonica* (Napoli: Edizioni Scientifiche Italiane, 1991); Daniela Luigia Caglioti, "Voluntary Societies and Urban Elites in Nineteenth-Century Naples," (unpublished paper, presented at the Fourth International Conference on Urban History, Venice, 1998); Boudien de Vries, *Electoraat en Elite: Sociale Structuur en Sociale Mobiliteit in Amsterdam, 1850–1895* (Amsterdam : Bataafsche Leeuw, 1986); Albert Tanner, *Arbeitsame Patrioten, wohlanständige Damen: Bürgertum und Bürgerlichkeit in der Schweiz, 1830–1914* (Zurich: Orell Füssli, 1995); Gunilla Budde, *Blütezeit des Bürgertums* (Darmstadt: WBG, Wissenschaftliche Buchgesellschaft, 2009), surveys the most recent literature.

Part I

Habits and Manners

1
Goodbye to the Marketplace: Food and Exclusivity in Nineteenth-Century New York

Anne Mendelson

In 1800, few Americans could have entertained certain kinds of aspirational fantasies linked to "epicureanism," a word that scarcely existed. No one dreamed of demonstrating membership in a wealthy and powerful elite by dining with sublime unconcern for prosaic criteria such as seasonal ripeness or peak flavor. A hundred years later, however, such notions vividly appealed to the imagination of the consuming public across a wide demographic spectrum. This paper examines one crucial factor behind the change: a revolution in the mechanisms of retail food distribution that has received little attention, even from social historians familiar with other aspects of nineteenth-century class division. In all American cities, the greatest single contributor to differentiated expression of social standing through food was the relentless decline of the public markets as centers for the sale of perishable foods throughout the century and their replacement by an array of other retail sources.

City consumers who earlier would have bought local produce directly from farmers were eventually outnumbered by those whose food arrived in neighborhood shops through a series of distribution processes. At all social levels, from the plutocracy to the laboring classes, concrete knowledge of anything bought to put in one's stomach was replaced by notions of quality that would become increasingly arbitrary, subjective, and easily manipulated. Our most plentiful evidence on transitions in the food trade and in food as lifestyle statement comes from New York and, to some extent, Boston, though the process of change eventually reached every American town and metropolis.

The Markets and the Grocers

From antiquity until well into the eighteenth century, the public markets were the only urban venue for the retail sale of perishable foods like butchers' meat, poultry, fresh fish, and spring or summer vegetables and fruit. No rapid transport existed to make possible a wholesale trade in such articles the year round. Of necessity, they were supplied only by local farmers in season, almost always in one-on-one transactions. The facilities at which they changed hands were not fixed-premise shops but various kinds of open or enclosed spaces owned by the municipality, where each vendor leased a stall, booth, or patch of ground. Few articles sold at market could come from farther than a couple of dozen miles away, especially in summer.[1]

The nonperishable food trade operated in another sphere. Its most prestigious segment was Far Eastern spices and other tropical luxuries such as sugar, which in medieval France and England had been the province of wholesale importers called "grossers" or "grocers" (i.e., dealers "in gross," or in bulk).[2] The original meaning of the word had disappeared by the eighteenth century, when English and North American grocers branched into retail selling. Eventually, many gave up their overseas connections and simply bought from the importers.

North American and especially New York urban grocers split into two major types late in the eighteenth century. The traditionalists dealt in "West India goods," meaning a class of luxury articles that embraced spices, tea, coffee, ingredients for drinking chocolate, bottled wines and liquors, almonds, dried fruits, perhaps some fresh citrus fruits, and above all sugar. In addition, most carried a few nonfood items such as tobacco, toiletries, china, and some yard goods. Gradually, they also began stocking household necessities, including kindling, brooms, candles, and cellar vegetables. Toward the end of the century, a grubbier order of grocers appeared who were in effect slum publicans selling liquor by the glass (traditional groceries sold only bottled liquors), along with a dilapidated stock of other household items.

The fortunes of the city markets received remarkable documentation from the nineteenth-century New York market butcher, amateur historian, and sometime superintendent of markets Thomas F. De Voe (1811–1892), author of a history of the New York markets and a guide to their offerings—based on his indefatigable diggings into City Council records and newspapers at the New-York Historical Society, as well as unpublished researches into other cities' public markets. Almost from the start, New York markets tended to be inadequately built, confusingly administered, subject to frequent relocation when rising land values overtook their surroundings, and endlessly profitable to City Hall boodlers.[3]

The markets of the early Federal era nonetheless possessed one signal quality never to be matched by the private businesses that eventually replaced them: They were among the most intrinsically democratic of American institutions. In 1870, an account of post-Civil War markets in a report by the U.S. Commissioner of Agriculture nostalgically recalled old-style city markets as the place "where the merchant or other citizen, basket on arm, could meet the farmer face to face."[4] Everyone understood them as theaters of at least temporary equality for all classes, an image unforgettably captured in Theophilus Eaton's 1813 collection of verse sketches titled *Review of New-York:*

> The place where no distinctions are,
> All sects and colours mingle there,
> Long folks and short, black folks and gray,
> With common bawds, and folks that pray,
> Rich folks and poor, both old and young,
> And good, and bad, and weak and strong,
> The wise and simple, red and white,
> With those that play, and those that fight,
> The high, the low, the proud, the meek,
> And all one common object seek,
> For lady, belle, and buck and lass,
> Here mingle in one common mass,
> Contending all which shall be first,

To buy the cheapest, best or worst;
In fact, their object is to get
Such things as they can 'ford to eat—
Some beef, some pork, some lamb or veal,
And those who cannot buy, must steal—
Nothing more clear, I'll tell you why,
All kinds of folks must *eat* or *die*.[5]

The food was displayed for everyone's inspection at the stalls or spaces leased to individual vendors, and in Knickerbocker New York, the customers shoving through the crowd might be black slaves sent by an owner or, not infrequently, the owner in person. It was common practice for either the master or the mistress of affluent households to do the actual marketing. The only consistent class divide was that the best stuff in peak condition generally went to members of the merchant and professional classes, who got there first. De Voe, writing in 1866, relates that a couple of generations back "the thrifty 'old New Yorker' "— male—commonly took his way to market at daybreak so as "to select the *cuts* of meat wanted from the best animals; to meet the farmer's choice productions, either poultry, vegetables, or fruit, and *catch* the lively, jumping fish, which, ten minutes before, were swimming in the fish-cars [submerged containers admitting a flow of seawater]." The next arrival would be "'the good housewife,' who would not trust anybody but herself to select a fine young turkey, or a pair of chickens or ducks." She consigned her purchases to a basket "being carried by a stout servant." Such times, De Voe, lamented, were gone: "We now find many heads of families who never visit the public markets."[6]

De Voe, an inveterate market cheerleader, did not care to tease out the causes of this falling-off, or ponder the implications to come. But the common marketplace as he knew and loved it had many built-in limitations. It was incompatible with kinds of change that would eventually break down distinctions between perishable and nonperishable or seasonal and nonseasonal items, setting people thousands of miles away to growing both delicacies and necessities once supplied to urban tables only by nearby farmers during a few months or weeks of the year. It could not make a show of exclusively catering to particular clienteles. Nor could it come to the streets they lived on, mean or grand. Consequently, the public markets were destined to be less and less frequented by the developing bourgeoisie of late-nineteenth-century New York, whose preferences were increasingly being served (and shaped) by new distribution mechanisms and more sophisticated selling strategies.

The Market Butchers as Bellwethers of Change

In the New York City markets, which numbered about a dozen throughout most of the century, the case of the market butchers may serve as a prophetic illustration of the process that would eventually eliminate the public market from city life. Artisan butchering, a skilled and necessary profession, stood at the top of the market hierarchy and was in a sense the backbone of the institution. It was also a major public nuisance. Meat, of course, had to get into the city on four legs. The butchers slaughtered it, with much attendant filth and smell, at their own slaughterhouses, which were located as close as possible to the markets where they held stalls. (De Voe, who was a pillar of the Jefferson Market at Sixth and Greenwich Avenues, had his slaughterhouse in a large field at Sixth Avenue and Nineteenth Street.) But starting in the 1820s, the handling of fresh meat began to be revolutionized by large-scale commercial ice harvesting and new developments in transportation—steamboats, canals, railroads, clippers, oceangoing steamships—that gradually divorced the sites of slaughter and final dressing from the place of retail sale.[7]

As early as 1830, American market butchers were encountering competition from the proprietors of fixed-premise neighborhood "meat shops." Bypassing the graft-ridden process of competing for market stall leases auctioned by the municipality, these small retail outfits bought partly dressed meat wholesale at market and sold it, cut to order, at a certain markup. The New York market butchers, with De Voe in the forefront, launched a bitter campaign for the exclusive right to dress and sell fresh meat, but in 1843 the meat shops carried the day, with a city ordinance once and for all affirming their legitimacy. The market butchers fought a progressively dwindling rear-guard action before gradually moving into a new role as wholesalers.[8]

In truth, time-consuming trips to jostle for fresh meat at market with "all kinds of folks" were becoming distasteful to the wealthy, while both neighborhood residents and the Board of Health saw the sanitary advantages of meat shops well-removed from slaughterhouses. The city's steady expansion northward meant increased anti-slaughterhouse pressures (De Voe closed his around 1870) and increased distances between the population and the markets. The picture changed further after the late 1860s, when the city managed to banish Manhattan slaughtering operations to a few locations north of Forty-Second Street, relegating much of the work to modern, partly mechanized abattoirs across the river in what is now Hudson County, New Jersey.[9] This freed the remaining market butchers from the demanding tasks of slaughter. Now they could handle larger volumes of meat, buying already dressed carcasses, or often sides or quarters, along with any special items they cared to order. The neighborhood retail butcher shops (the term "meat shop" soon vanished) could order from the market men in various ways matching the needs or whims of their own customers, either by using large dressed pieces (sides or quarters) to produce many kinds of lesser cuts or by asking to be directly supplied with specific pieces or cuts—in affluent enclaves, perhaps hindquarters (rather than forequarters), sirloins for steaks and roasts, or specialties like sweetbreads that formerly had been limited by the number of animals one old-style butcher might have slaughtered in the preceding few days.

The new situation allowed neighborhood retailers to handily supply the wants of different demographic sectors clustered around certain street addresses. But it did not permit the individual relationships with local farmers that had enabled the old artisan butchers to understand meat literally on the hoof and to offer something for every pocketbook. It also meant that more and more consumers had never seen a dressed carcass or quarter, and had no idea of quality aside from the prestige of certain cuts.

Neighborhood butcher shops had already displaced the all-things-to-all-buyers market butchers in the retail meat trade before the 1880s, when beef slaughtered and dressed in Chicago began reaching northeastern cities in huge volume and at notably reduced prices, thanks to large-scale midwestern and western cattle ranching, in tandem with refrigerated rail cars. With this expanded supply, patterns of meat consumption shifted. Cured pork, historically the cheapest and most plentiful American meat, acquired an even more plebeian aura as fresh beef became more affordable. To present a main course featuring sirloin, tenderloin, or filet was now an option not only for the wealthy but also for the almost-wealthy or the well-off middle class.[10] Indeed, late in the century, some culinary advisers began decrying American consumers' devotion to steaks, chops, and big roasting joints as vulgar and monotonous. A one-time luxury had been diffused partway down the income scale, a pattern to be endlessly repeated with other sorts of food.

The very rich quickly searched out other signs of superior taste and means. An early manifestation of "something new in our public markets" attracted De Voe's curiosity in 1861: a stall where two French vendors were offering not only all conceivable pork products but also "boned turkeys, capons, larded bird-game, *filet de boeuf*, &c., many of which are cooked ready 'for parties, breakfasts, dinners, or suppers, cold or warm.' " Not far away were the stalls of "L. Bonnard & Co., displaying numerous canisters, containing 'Alimentary Preserves'—such as beef, mutton, poultry, game, fish, &c., besides vegetables, truffles, fruits, and the celebrated *pates de foie gras*, or large *geese-livers*."[11] That canned meats and vegetables or party dishes cooked to order could ever be anything but extravagances for the wealthy was not yet obvious.

The Produce Supply Transformed

In the case of meat, the main disincentive to old-style market dealing was the incompatibility of city life with cattle clumping along streets and blood draining into gutters. Locally grown fresh fruits and vegetables were another case. Their nemesis would be a combination of urban sprawl and expanded overseas/overland transportation that paved the way for major shifts in retailing demographics.

The early nineteenth-century markets had offered the same array of fresh produce to rich and poor. The finest articles went to prosperous householders simply because they got to market first and chose with discrimination. The poorest and humblest planned on coming late enough to snap up battered or mildly spoiled leavings, usually at knocked-down prices.

In English and European markets, likewise, the best produce had always gone to prizers of quality who beat others to the punch. The only way to bypass the markets as a source of vegetables was to have one's own garden, and to duplicate the diversity of a large market's offerings required kitchen gardens and hothouses maintained on a baronial (or higher) scale. By the report of James Fenimore Cooper, writing in 1828 in the fictional persona of a traveling Frenchman, the American equivalent of the landed gentry also enjoyed "a far better quality [of produce from their own gardens] than in the markets."[12] Their Knickerbocker New York, counterparts got the most out of the markets by taking marketing seriously and recognizing excellence when they saw it. On May 30, 1821, the one-time merchant and banker John Pintard, who in his sixties was still often doing the family marketing first thing in the morning, related to a daughter in New Orleans:

> This morn[in]g [I s]aw green peas in market from Virga the first at 2/6 half peck. Cheap enough bu[t th]ey cd have no flavour. The diff[eren]ce of a single day is perceptible. Ve[g]etables can only be tasted in perfection, gathered the same day. I can get asparagus, occasionally, cut the same morn[in]g by paying extra, 3d to 6d a bunch. Some very fine at one shilling I purchased this morn[in]g.[13]

Such judgments bespoke a lifelong acquaintance with vegetables during peak local season not as an epicure's hobby but as the practical concern of city people who knew where and how something had been grown, usually by purchasing it from the grower. The same was true of orchard fruit, an ancient symbol of privilege and exclusivity that until the 1820s or '30s almost never reached the markets out of local season. Pintard's 1821 reference to Virginia peas makes it clear that growers and shippers elsewhere were already seeking profit in supplying a greatly valued spring delicacy a little ahead of the New York season. Within a few decades, the outlines of both seasonality and quality would begin to be blurred for city purchasers. So would the notion of the marketplace as the locus of retail sales between basket-carrying merchant and nearby farmer.

The lion's share of the market business was conducted at Fulton Market, on the East River waterfront, and Washington Market, within reach of the Hudson River docks. By 1850, Fulton Market on a summer morning could strike an *Evening Mirror* reporter as a cross-section of the world's foods and peoples:

> . . . there lay glittering and smoking in the hot sun, on the dirty side-walk, large square lumps of ice, which looked as though they might just have fallen from a Swiss glacier, they were so hard, so cold, and so green. . . . Close by, sitting under a piece of canvas supported by four bean poles, sat a pock-marked daughter of Erin, with a small pyramid of Messina oranges; a heap of pine-apples from the Bahamas, and bunches of ripe bananas from Cuba. Strange fruits for a region of ice. But not far off was a woolly head from Africa, selling Alpine strawberries in little Long Island baskets; near him was a Dutchman, with a heap of Virginia water-melons, and a Yankee selling green corn from New Jersey. There was a Scandinavian offering for sale mince pies from Connecticut. A red-headed Scotchman was selling Java coffee at "only waun sant a mug." A Turk was offering fig paste from Smyrna, and a little child in female attire was dealing out ice-cream in wine glasses. There were Valparaiso pumpkins, manna apples [probably mamey sapote] from Cuba, peaches from Delaware; lobsters from the coast of Maine; milk from Goshen; chickens from Bucks County, Pennsylvania; hens from Cochin China; potatoes from Bermuda; peas, beans, and squashes, from Long Island; whitefish from Lake Michigan; there was beef that had been fattened on the banks of the Ohio; hams smoked in Westphalia; sausages stuffed in Bologna; mutton from Vermont; and cheese from the region of the St. Lawrence.[14]

The market, as this observer realized, had become a promiscuous jumble of local or general East Coast produce and international delicacies. It would have been almost unrecognizable to John Pintard, not only in the scope of what it sold but also in its advancing independence of seasonality. Both trends would only accelerate. In 1867, a writer for *Harper's Monthly* was nearly at a loss to describe the stunning volume of apples, peaches, pears, and grapes, together with "a prodigious quantity of watermelons" and "piles of berries of all descriptions," entering Washington Market.[15]

For a time, having season-challenging imported produce on the table marked a consumer as belonging to a social stratum that could command rarities as a lifestyle statement. Bermuda peas could not possibly have tasted fresh-picked or Bermuda peaches summer-ripe. The point, however, clearly wasn't taste, but displaying the means to buy nonlocal or out-of-season specialties at premium prices.

By the time of the *Harper's* article, the Washington and Fulton Markets were international nexuses, transacting at least as much wholesale as retail business. The reporter estimated that Washington Market alone "provides food for about two millions of persons every day," with about half of this immediately departing again in massive rail or water shipments to the rest of the country, or the world.[16] This prodigious increase in volume meant recurrent collisions with the nineteenth-century urban real-estate juggernaut. The ungainly facilities—an obstacle to traffic in almost any neighborhood where they were situated—kept city-owned ground from being developed for more lucrative purposes. Meanwhile, produce grown hundreds or thousands of miles away competed with local carrots or tomatoes in the city markets—and this at a time when new factories and mushrooming suburban towns were pricing farmers out of their land in the nearby rural areas that, as De Voe noted, had until recently "furnished the city with a plentiful and cheap supply of vegetables."[17]

The Market System Breaks Down

Retail meat shops, as we have seen, had been siphoning customers from the markets since at least the 1830s. The traditional grocers' shops were poised to do likewise well before the Civil War. Some of them tentatively started branching into sales of fresh produce and other perishable foods, becoming steady wholesale market purchasers receiving a regular stream of seasonal and less seasonal fruits and vegetables. Unlike the markets, they did not have to minister to the world at large from predetermined sites. Grocers' shops could be set up in individual neighborhoods as they came into being, while the markets were blocked from relocating as the city marched northward. No true public market was ever built north of Fourteenth Street, though for a time some wholesale depots, abattoirs, and limited retail street-selling zones (these last called "markets" for want of a better term) were allowed to occupy a few sites well away from most residential development. The new grocers' shops, however, could fit smoothly into developing patterns of neighborhood segregation. As the Manhattan bourgeoisie became concentrated in particular uptown enclaves far from the markets, nearby retail shops came to match the affluent character of their surroundings.

The markets continued to become more and more inconvenient for both patrons and the remaining local farmers, who could scarcely squeeze through congested streets to overflowing market facilities where the system of municipally allotted spaces apparently had broken down into a free-for-all. With luck, farmers could find a selling space during the small hours of market day and a wholesale buyer for an entire cartload before morning; otherwise, they hung around as long as they had to in order to unload their perishable stock to budget-minded retail customers playing their own waiting game in hopes of bargain-basement prices.[18] Over time, the huge volume of business transacted at Washington and Fulton tilted steadily in the direction of wholesaling.

The loss of retail business at the markets is repeatedly remarked upon by city observers from about 1850 on. Edward K. Spann's *The New Metropolis* quotes a newspaper summation of the falling off: "It has become so fashionable to have a meat-shop on almost every corner and fruits and vegetables in almost every grocery, and fish and oysters well nigh swimming through the streets that our large markets are to some extent foresaken."[19] In 1872, the urban panoramist James D. McCabe claimed, "Two-thirds of the people of the city, to save time and trouble, deal with the 'corner groceries,' and 'provision stores,' and never see the markets."[20] This may have underestimated the loss. The 1870 Commissioner of Agriculture's report on the nation's market systems stated of Faneuil Hall in Boston: "Not over 2,000 of 50,000 families go there to market." The same source examined the New York situation with an eye to serious class inequities. It observed that people obliged to think of both quality and economy had to waste an hour getting to and from markets "wholly inadequate" to their needs, where they either overpaid "at a fashionable stall where meats are good" or joined "the million"— officially, New York's population was about 943,000—in buying inferior stuff at some "third-rate stand." The story was very different for the fortunate 20,000 of the upper crust, who

> . . . live in five-story brownstones, and spend from $5 to $10 daily in the purchase of perishable food and as much more for pantry articles.[This indicates weekly totals of $70 to $140.] For such, nearness to a market-house [i.e., retail purchasing venue; note the altered use of "market"] is a prime necessity; hence the steady increase in the number and neatness of outfit of grocers' and butchers' establishments on or near fashionable streets. The proprietors of these go to Washington, West Washington, and Fulton, as wholesale houses, and take the cream of all that comes, the tenderloins, the fat chops, the finest chickens, and fattest turkeys, paying well and expecting their customers to pay better.[21]

The New Food Scene: Names and Images

Leaving the markets to lesser folk, moneyed city dwellers sought other retail-purchase options while turning to romantic dreams of elegance embodied in the very act of buying food—or having it bought for them by servants. The age of gastronomic swank that dawned in the last decades of the century offered to the wealthy a plethora of novel or newly vaunted delicacies, sold out of prestigious new private establishments and extolled by a growing cadre of writers.

Two persistent phenomena may be noted here. One was a diffusion process that kept turning pricy rarities for the few into ever more affordable commonplaces for a broader or even mass clientele. The other reduced opportunity for even (or perhaps especially) the most gilded consumers to see and judge apples, cauliflowers, or chickens at the point of production. Firsthand acquaintance with what you bought was on the wane, leaving more and more room for manipulation of images.

Among America's first modern commercial image purveyors were the retailers, manufacturers, and advisers who supplied upper-class food-shopping wants. The infant art of shaping consumer perceptions was was being consciously practiced in New York as early as 1873 at a new breed of elite retail groceries, exemplified by James Duffy's shop on Beaver Street. We can grasp some of what was happening by comparing a description of the Duffy offerings in a short-lived publication called *The Table* with the stock of a classic West India goods shop, Silas Peirce in Boston, half a century earlier. A printed card from Peirce, tentatively dated 1822 in a company history, prosaically presents a roster of articles—some still recognizable as grocery staples—that certainly were not within everyone's range but that were not being calculatedly touted as the stuff of glossy fashion:

> Teas, Sugar, Coffee, Spices, Figs, Raisins, Currants, Grapes, Prunes, Nuts, Oils, Wines, Spirits, Cordials, Capers, Fish Sauces, Preserves, Spanish Cigars, Dun Fish [a particularly fine form of salt cod], Mustard, Cayenne, Chocolate, Shells [the husks of roasted cacao beans], Bird Seed, Oranges, Lemons, &c.&c. With a great variety of other Luxuries, Delicacies, and Necessaries.[22]

Allowing for the difference between stock list and (apparently planted) journalistic puff piece, Duffy seems to have consciously planned his shop with a view to romancing the buyer:

> There was an artistic effect displayed in the arrangement of the cases of wine—a building up of the various kinds of cheese, native and imported, in a way that

> implied more than ordinary appreciation, in the arranger and builder thereof, of the good things in this life. There were sundry bottles, too, filled with amber colored olive oil, jars of pickles and chow-chow, cans of sardines, and blue, bamboo-covered jars of preserved ginger. Boxes of cigars, suggestive of Cuba, cans of French peas, and champignons, and English mustard, and gray stone jugs implying that something good to drink could be put in them, met our sight.[23]

In this account, premises and contents form an atmospheric stage setting for goods that anyone would have recognized as luxuries, from olive oil and Canton ginger to sardines, which at this date came only from France. At a store like this, the pickles and chowchow were most likely an imported English brand; French canned peas were an expensive new item, prized for the brilliant green imparted by a solution of copper sulfate.

Grocers, now beginning to recognize themselves as a professional cohort, were acquiring more sophisticated ideas about the business of selling—more precisely, about building customer loyalty and name recognition. One of their early weapons in this department was home delivery service, an amenity that the marketmen could rarely supply. A company history of S. S. Pierce in Boston (unrelated to the Peirce firm) claims that "the Autocrat"—Oliver Wendell Holmes—once told a salesman who had sought to woo him to a rival firm: "I have been brought up on Pierce's groceries and wouldn't dare to change."[24] Delivery wagons bearing the company name and sometimes pulled by matched teams of horses undoubtedly helped to consolidate this kind of customer allegiance over several generations. The historian Samuel Eliot Morison would later recollect that even though his maternal grandfather kept up the old-fashioned tradition of a Saturday morning market visit to Faneuil Hall for the major perishables ("meat, poultry, eggs and fish") throughout Morison's childhood in the 1890s, his grandmother and the cook collaborated on daily grocery orders for everything else, which "'the man from Pierce's' " would jot down "in a notebook, for delivery later in the day."[25] By 1911, the company stable numbered 273 horses, probably drawing more than a hundred wagons, which must have made Pierce one of the most visible names on the city streets.[26]

A novel and elegant addition to shop décor during this period was the display of goods in cans or glass containers. We must remember that the first canning attempts were in no way cheap or labor-free. By the time of the Civil War, a few canned foods like tomatoes were widely available at affordable prices, but almost every new item required some period of costly experimental technology (not infrequently accompanied by outbreaks of food poisoning). The price of canned peas, for instance, was kept high for decades by the cost of manually picking pods from vines and shelling the peas. Salmon, which had first been canned in California in 1862, could not evade high production costs until a Seattle inventor introduced a trimming and cleaning machine called the "Iron Chink" (i.e., Chinaman) in 1903.[27] For a time, buying canned goods as they appeared in select shops could be thought to certify the buyer's privileged status—like buying new peas in April half a century earlier, though canning did not just push back the limits of seasonality but miraculously abolished them. Advances in canning also opened up promising vistas for manufacturers and wholesale distributors. At a time when the general importance of brand names was expanding together with the technology of packaging food for retail sale, food in bottles, jars, or cans soon proved to be a glorious labeling opportunity, a guarantee that a proprietary name could be memorably visible at the very point of kitchen use.

Advertisements and price quotations in grocers' professional journals, as well as women's "service" magazines and many cookbooks, demonstrate the growing importance attached to name recognition of food products. In the early and mid-1880s, grocers consulting wholesale price lists in *Merchants' Review*, the organ of the New York importer-distributor Austin Nichols & Co., would have seen weekly mentions of Libby and Armour canned meats, Nestle's and Dr. Gerber's baby food, Durkee's salad dressing, Doxsee canned littleneck clams and clam chowder, Crosse & Blackwell pickles and bottled sauces, and chocolate or cocoa from English and French firms like Fry, Menier, and Maillard. Austin Nichols itself used the lofty appellations "Monarch" and "Royal" as brand names for assorted items ranging from flavor extracts to condensed milk, a transparent appeal to the developing American fascination with title and rank.[28]

A Multiplicity of Choices

Grocery "shopping"—formerly quite a separate activity from "marketing," which originally had involved going to markets, not shops—now meant depending on the grocer or clerk for guidance through a maze of familiar or unfamiliar articles. Brand names provided further signposts. Since about 1870, even flour and sugar had taken on bewildering new complexities, reaching retail shops in a range of less or more refined forms that were hard to make sense of without someone to explain why "granulated sugar" was superior to the grade called "yellow C" or Pillsbury's prestigious roller-patent-process hard-wheat Minnesota flour cost more than something else. In addition, a swelling tide of entirely new "fancy pantry" items kept being introduced to the grocery-buying public: "evaporated" or "compressed" vegetables, more and more prepared bottled condiments, gelatin, packaged imported or domestic "macaroni" (the name for most sorts of pasta) and vermicelli, domestic sardines in tomato or mustard sauce.

Perishable and semiperishable foods—still generally entering the nation's food supply through the great Manhattan markets, but now most often going to wholesale customers—kept pace with their nonperishable counterparts. We can form an idea of the expanded offerings from G. T. Ferris's penetrating 1890 *Harper's Weekly* article "How a Great City Is Fed" and the mentions of produce in another fleeting attempt at a magazine of gastronomy, Thomas J. Murrey's weekly *The Cook* (launched in 1885). Every issue of *The Cook* devoted space to the newest market prices (presumably gathered from Washington and Fulton Markets) for several hundred items, most of them perishable. The lists show out-of-season fruits and vegetables appearing in great plenty, now from commercial hothouses as well as distant warm-weather regions.[29]

Ferris, surveying the Washington and Fulton Market scenes, accurately pointed to refrigerated transport and "cold storage" (meaning ice-cooled refrigeration and freezing, as well as mechanical freezing by compressed ammonia) as the most crucial factor for change in the modern supply of foods for both the masses and the privileged few. "The limitations of season," he noted, "have ceased to be any bar to the demands of appetite. The development of cold-storage warehouses has banished in large measure the divisions of summer and winter, and the epicure can feast on pecan-fed turkey and canvas-back ducks on the Fourth of July with as much relish as he can at Christmas."[30]

One of the most extraordinary signs of the new order was increased access to game, which now provided employment to distant bush-beaters: "Shooting for the market is a business now for thousands of hunters, some of whom do not sleep under a roof for months, except when they bring the trophies of the gun to a shipping depot. These men are scattered throughout the West to the Rocky Mountains, and brave every kind of hardship and danger to supply the urbane epicure with the choicest *plats* of the dinner or supper party."[31]

To an extent, Western game was replacing depleted Eastern supplies, but at steep prices and with a heightened perception of exclusivity reinforced by the imposition of federal or state hunting limits on some species. Among the delicacies mentioned in contemporary sources as reaching the New York markets were various wild ducks (the prized canvasback and redhead, along with the less elegant teal, mallards, and widgeon), pheasant, several kinds of grouse, plover, snowbirds, wild turkey, wild swan, bear, venison, pronghorn antelope (when venison was off limits), and hare.[32]

This deluge of options was as stupendous as the corresponding tide of nonperishable foods. By the turn of the century, affluent customers only infrequently visited the markets, but perishable and nonperishable rarities both imported and domestic now poured into grocery shops or other specialized retail venues catering to wealthy households, and often graced elegant restaurant menus. The situation was not unlike that of the period between 1970 and 2000, when upwardly mobile city shoppers scarcely could keep pace with the names of the latest "in" foods. High-end grocers consequently found the role of educator profitable, as did food writers.

The cutting-edge cookbooks and other food-oriented publications of the 1880s and 1890s addressed people with more gastronomic ambition than kitchen sense. Between 1884 and 1894, several former Delmonico's employees who weighed in as cookbook authors all contrived to treat the best seasons for market items in a manner calculated to put putative buyers at ease with the *absence* of seasonality.[33] Already, the very rich could erase some of the distance between June and December at the wave of a checkbook, and the same goal had now become intermittently attainable for a larger spectrum of the eating public. One of the ex-Delmonicans, Alessandro Filippini, adroitly managed to work salmon into all twelve of his monthly fish-buying guides, and—though he admitted that hothouse asparagus wasn't much good—cheerfully included asparagus in menus for every month of the year.[34] If the menus were to be taken at face value (which is not certain), he expected people wealthy enough to dine on his dishes also to have the means for buying canned or hothouse spring vegetables between June and February. It seems fair to say that buying certain delicacies out of season—inasmuch as "season" still existed—indicated a combination of privilege and insensitivity to quality.

Beyond Shop or Market: Endgame Bastions of Status

At century's end, the moneyed classes had seen many twists and turns in the mechanisms that supplied their food wants, with the old egalitarianism of the public markets being replaced by class-defined differentiation in food buying. Many kinds of people could now make some fashion statement by buying food from certain kinds of purveyors and tricking it out with painstaking cleverness. The very rich or cliquish, nevertheless, had a few exclusive strings to their bow.

One remaining emblem of privilege was eating kinds of game and seafood that were becoming scarce to the point of extinction, especially diamondback terrapin, canvasback duck, and the outrageously overfished lobster. Available supplies of all three were eagerly snapped up by elite retailers, restaurant purveyors, and private chefs to the rich. These last were another new element in affairs of gastronomic status.

Earlier in the century, the prosperous citizens who had proudly done their own basket-on-arm marketing had gone home to hand over their prizes to the cook, an invariably female household servant (though an important one). After about 1840, family cooks were most often either black or Irish, the latter stereotyped as the coarse and slovenly "Bridgets" and "Noras" who could produce nothing fit for decent folk without vigilant supervision. The enlarged kitchen staffs of the late-century bourgeoisie usually assumed the responsibility of actual food purchasing, either in person or by telephone. By 1900, the master or mistress of a prominent household who went either "marketing" or "shopping" was a throwback.

The private chefs who cooked for New York plutocrats from about the 1880s and 1890s operated on another plane. Of course, they, too, were hired servants, but the word "servant" scarcely seemed applicable to people rumored to out-earn (and, according to some wits, do more for society than) college presidents or congressmen. An 1889 *Harper's* article on the French community in New York mentions typical wages of perhaps $100 to $300 a month; in 1906, a *New York Times* reporter cited annual salaries of $1,800 to $8,000.[35] (Faye Dudden, in *Serving Women,* points out that $2.50 a week—about $130 *a year*—was the servant's wage offered to the heroine of an 1894 novel.)[36] In the households of the Havemeyers, Goulds, Astors, and Vanderbilts, such acquisitions justified their price by being *professionals,* a status from which women were almost by definition excluded. The product of rigorous apprenticeships, Old World chefs reputedly possessed consummate mastery of ingredients as well as the generalship to direct a staff of kitchen subordinates—or more than one staff, if their employers kept several residences. Chefs with French ideas of detail assumed responsibility for the marketing and shopping, tasks to which some cachet might still accrue when a Frenchman did them.

In the words of the *Times* headline, such employees were "gastronomic artists." No one used such terms about female Irish cooks, though the cognoscenti allowed that female black cooks sometimes had innate instincts approaching culinary artistry. At bottom, what chefs' "artistry" meant to the *fin-de-siècle* grandees who hired them was the organizational ability to pull off French-swathed menus too complex for anyone else to have prepared at home.

A general American notion of French supremacy in the culinary arts was not new, and the language of hotel and restaurant menus had been liberally Frenchified since at least 1840. But until the Gilded Age, forthrightly English-descended cooking had dominated the home scene. Writers addressing American women had most often told them that what their French counter-parts really had to teach them was not a profusion of *à las* on the table but commonsensical buying practices at market or butcher shop, followed by thrifty, neat-handed treatment of food at home.[37] From the late 1880s on, however, the menus of lengthy, elaborate chefs' dinners, complete with "Franglish" names, increasingly became the model for anyone wishing to entertain in style. Chefless households imported professional crews for the evening or held the dinner at a hotel or restaurant.

The sort of food served by Edith Wharton's parents—the recollections she set down in *A Backward Glance* most likely date from the 1870s—belonged squarely to a pre-chef school of fine American cooking. It was prepared by "our two famous negro cooks, Mary Johnson and Susan Minneman," and seems to have had not a smidgen of Frenchness:

> Who will ever taste anything again in the whole range of gastronomy to equal [Johnson and Minneman's] corned beef, their boiled turkeys with stewed celery and oyster sauce, their fried chickens, boiled red-heads, corn fritters, stewed tomatoes, rice griddle cakes, strawberry short-cake and vanilla ices?[38]

The entry that Samuel Morison found in his grandmother Eliot's household notebook giving the bill of fare for an 1888 dinner in honor of distinguished visitors similarly shows a foundation of Anglo-American tastes although with some quasi-Gallic updatings grafted on:

Oysters
Brown Soup
Smelts, sauce tartare
Sweetbreads in cups
Chops broiled, macédoine
Chicken zephyre with peas
Ducks, celery & lettuce
Water ice
Sauterne, Sherry, Champagne, Burgundy[39]

(The "macédoine" on this menu probably was a composed presentation made from a medley of finely diced vegetables; the "chicken zephyre" a creamy quenelle-like chicken mixture served in either pastry cases or small molds. The very old-fashioned "brown soup" was a beef broth simmered for hours to the richness and depth of a consommé.)

Already at this date, more advanced menus were reversing the emphasis, with a wilderness of foreign names relieved by few recognizable American touches. "Macédoine" and "zephyre" would have baffled some American cooks and diners, but most of the dinner menus in Filippini's *The Table* from 1889 would have been semi-unintelligible to nearly everyone (and remain so today). Here is part of a fairly typical example:

Small Blue Point Oysters
Purée à la Gentilhomme
Sheep's-Head* à la Créole
Celery Olives
Tenderloin of Beef à la Hussard
Sorrel au Gras
Chicken à la Ranhofer
Cardons à la Moëlle[40]

*Not the head of a sheep, but the well-known Atlantic and Gulf Coast fish

There is more in this vein, with few rays of light piercing the general opacity. Unlike Grandmother Eliot's dinner, for which the family most likely had to hire an extra servant or two for the evening, Filippini's schemes for entertaining were simply beyond the powers of anyone without *haut* restaurant training and a brigade of skilled underlings. People wishing to execute (i.e., have their cooks execute) even the portion of the menu given here would have needed to have on hand cooked puréed lentils, game quenelles, *duxelles,* smoked beef tongue, veal forcemeat quenelles, tomato sauce, *sauce espagnole,* and 18 slices of beef marrow. Even straightforward-sounding items like celery or bluepoint oysters turn out to require painstaking preparation; the olives would have been painstakingly whittled into thin spiral ribbons before serving.

A few years later, M. E. W. Sherwood's *The Art of Entertaining* (1893) blandly sketches the bill of fare for what she calls "a splendid dinner"—a marathon in something like 10 or 11 courses, many containing several options at once. Among the recommended dishes are "*Crème d'Asperges*," "*Filet de Boeuf*, with Truffles and Mushrooms," "*Timbale de Macaroni*," "Roman Punch," "Quail with Water-Cresses," "Cabinet Pudding," and "*Crème glacée aux tutti frutti*." Having paused to condescend to anyone ignorant of French, Mrs. Sherwood then explains to her readers that "this dinner will be a failure" if tackled "in a private home" without a *cordon bleu* chef and the wherewithal for perfect service: "It is better to order such a dinner from Delmonico's or Sherry's or from the best man you can command. Do not attempt and fail."[41]

A series of catch-up games had brought successive tokens of bourgeois privilege and exclusive "discovery" within reach of the affluent (and sometimes less affluent) middle class. By the late 1880s, the youthful magazine *Good Housekeeping* was quoting market prices on such items as California rainbow trout and Cuban pineapples, and giving subscribers the inside dope on a stunning new "morceau" called the "alligator pear" (avocado).[42] Meanwhile, the last decades of the century found New York retail sellers and purchasers at many social levels increasingly ignorant of and unconcerned with whether (as one journalist put it) asparagus grew on bushes.[43] People of higher and lesser standing were in their several ways equally fixated on the romance of meals as lifestyle statement and unequipped to know their onions as sold at the public markets.

Neither John Pintard nor Thomas De Voe's "thrifty 'old New Yorker'" would have recognized the remnants of the one-time market scene in 1904, when a USDA statistician named George K. Holmes wrote an article for the *Department of Agriculture Yearbook* relating the impositions practiced on a food-buying public that deserved them. All aspects of food production and marketing, he noted with unconcealed disgust, were "becoming questions of art and psychology." If citified ignoramuses were ready to pay top prices for "pretty red apples stuffed with cotton," why not pander to their folly? One might as well cash in on the fact that a consumer's decisions could be effectually programmed through "the seller's subtle knowledge of his fancies, which need not be and often are not either sensible or reasonable, but, on the other hand, often verge upon the notional, and seem superfluous to an unsophisticated farmer."[44] The rest of the twentieth century would prove Holmes a prophet.

Notes

1. The evolution of European markets is treated by Fernand Braudel in *The Wheels of Commerce*, translated by Siân Reynolds (volume 2 of *Civilization and Capitalism, 15th–18th Century*, New York: Harper & Row, 1982). For information on early American markets and grocers' shops, see Helen Tangires, *Public Markets and Civic Culture in Nineteenth-Century America* (Baltimore and London: Johns Hopkins University Press, 2003), 3–68; James M. Mayo, *The American Grocery Store: The Business Evolution of an Architectural Space* (Westport, CT: Greenwood Press, 1993), 1–41 and 43–51; and Thomas David Beal, *Selling Gotham: The Retail Trade in New York City from the Public Markets to Alexander T. Stewart's Marble Palace* (PhD. dissertation, State University of New York at Stony Brook, 1998), 108–154, 169–217, and 371–430.
2. Artemas Ward, *The Encyclopedia of Food* (New York: Peter Smith, 1923), 240–241; C. Anne Wilson, *Food and Drink in Britain from the Stone Age to Recent Times* (New York: Barnes and Noble, 1974), 282–283.
3. Thomas F. De Voe's *The Market Book* (New York; self-published, 1862) provides case-by-case narratives of the individual markets' checkered fortunes from colonial times to the eve of the Civil War. See also Thomas F. De Voe, *Report upon the Present Condition of the Public*

Markets of the City and County of New York (New York: Evening Post Steam Presses, 1873) and Edward K. Spann, *The New Metropolis: New York City, 1840–1857* (New York: Columbia University Press, 1981), 124–128.

4. "The Market Systems of the Country, Their Uses and Abuses," in United States Department of Agriculture, *Report of the Commissioner of Agriculture in the Year 1870* (Washington, DC: Government Printing Office, 1871), 244.
5. Theophilus Eaton, *Review of New-York; or, Rambles through the City: Original Poems Moral, Religious, Sarcastic, and Descriptive* (New York: John Low, 1813), 29–31.
6. Thomas F. De Voe, *The Market Assistant* (New York: Hurd and Houghton, 1867), 211.
7. See Richard Osborn Cummings, *The American and His Food* (Chicago: University of Chicago Press, 1941, rept. New York: Arno Press, 1970), 36–39; Daniel Boorstin, *The Americans: The Democratic Experience* (New York; Vintage Books, 1974), 327–329.
8. The triumphs and travails of the embattled butchers are a running theme in De Voe's *The Market Book*.
9. Edward Winslow Martin (James D. McCabe), *Secrets of the Great City* (Philadelphia and Chicago: Jones Bros., 1868), 494–495; "How New York Is Fed," *Scribner's Monthly*, October 1877, 734–738.
10. Richard J. Hooker, *Food and Drink in America: A History* (Indianapolis and New York: Bobbs-Merrill, 1981), 112–113, 217–218, 221–222.
11. De Voe, *The Market Book*, 557.
12. James Fenimore Cooper, *Notions of the Americans: Picked up by a Travelling Bachelor*, edited by Gary Williams (Albany: State University of New York Press, 1991), 125.
13. John Pintard, *Letters of John Pintard to His Daughter Eliza Noel Pintard Davidson*, 1816–1833 (New York: New-York Historical Society Collections, 1937–1940), vol. 2, 46.
14. Quoted in *The Literary World: A Journal of Science, Literature, and Art*, August 10, 1850, 115–116.
15. "The Markets of New York," *Harper's Monthly*, July 1867, 233–234.
16. "The Markets of New York," 231.
17. De Voe, *The Market Assistant*, 321.
18. Marc Linder and Lawrence S. Zacharias, *Of Cabbages and Kings County: Agriculture and the Formation of Modern Brooklyn* (Iowa City: University of Iowa Press, 1999), 53; "A Municipal Mouth at Daybreak," *Appleton's Journal*, February 18, 1871, 192–194.
19. Spann, *The New Metropolis*, 127. Unfortunately the attribution of this passage (p. 460, n. 32) is garbled, and I have not been able to establish the date and source.
20. James D. McCabe, *Lights and Shadows of New York Life: Or, The Sights and Sensations of the Great City* (Philadelphia: National Publishing Company, 1872; rept. New York; Farrar, Straus & Giroux, 1970), 489.
21. "The Market Systems of the Country," 244–245.
22. John Bouvé Clapp, *A Century of Service, 1815–1915* (Boston: Silas Peirce, 1915), 24.
23. "A Good Place to Drop Into," *The Table: A Monthly Publication Devoted to the Refinements of the Table*, undated 1873, 189–190.
24. S. S. Pierce, *Annals of a Corner Grocery: 80th Birthday of S.S. Pierce Co. 1831–1911* (Boston: S.S. Pierce, 1911), unpaginated.
25. Samuel Eliot Morison, *One Boy's Boston, 1887–1901* (Boston: Houghton Mifflin, 1962), 39–40.
26. *Annals of a Corner Grocery*.
27. A. W. Bitting, *Appertizing: Or, The Art of Canning: Its History and Development* (San Francisco: California Trade Association, 1937), 551, 810.
28. *Merchant's Review*, February 16, 1883, 253.
29. See, for instance, the quotations for seasonal and out-of-season items in *The Cook: A Weekly Handbook of Culinary Art for All Housekeepers*, March 30, 1885, 2 and 7.
30. G. T. Ferris, "How a Great City Is Fed," *Harper's Weekly*, March 22, 1890, 228.
31. "How a Great City Is Fed," 232.
32. See *The Cook*, March 30, 1885, 2; Mrs. F.A. Benson, "Seasonable Table Supplies," *Good Housekeeping*, March 20, 1886, 304; and the game chapter in Alessandro Filippini, *The Table: How to Buy Food, How to Cook It, and How to Serve It* (New York: Charles L. Webster, 1889), 276–287.
33. The works in question were Filippini's *The Table*, Felix J.Deliee's *The Franco-American Cookbook* (New York: G. P. Putnam's Sons, 1884; the title is unrelated to the later brand name) and Charles J. Ranhofer's *The Epicurean* (New York: R. Ranhofer, 1893).

34. Filippini, *The Table,* 15; see also the menu section, 25–150.
35. George J. Manson, "The French" (part of series "The Foreign Element in New York City"), *Harper's Weekly,* January 26, 1906, 80; "Gastronomic Artists in the Kitchens of the Rich," *New York Times Sunday Magazine,* January 14, 1906, 7.
36. See Faye E. Dudden, *Serving Women: Household Service in Nineteenth-Century America* (Middletown, CT: Wesleyan University Press, 1983), 99–100.
37. See, for instance, Catharine E. Beecher and Harriet Beecher Stowe, *The American Woman's Home* (New York: J. B. Ford, 1869; rept. Hartford, CT: Harriet Beecher Stowe Center, 1975), 178–180, 190.
38. Edith Wharton, *A Backward Glance* (New York: Charles Scribner's Sons, 1962), 59.
39. Morison, *One Boy's Boston,* 49.
40. Filippini, *The Table,* 117.
41. M. E. W. Sherwood, *The Art of Entertaining* (New York: Dodd, Mead and Company, 1893), 97–98.
42. *Good Housekeeping,* November 26, 1887, iv; and March 20, 1886, 304.
43. "The Multitude at Market," *New York Times,* October 5, 1884, 5:3.
44. George K. Holmes, "Consumers' Fancies," In *United States Department of Agriculture Yearbook for 1904* (Washington, DC: Government Printing Office, 1905), 417, 424, 433.

2

"Natural Distinction": The American Bourgeois Search for Distinctive Signs in Europe

Maureen E. Montgomery

In her 1907 novel *The Shuttle,* Frances Hodgson Burnett describes transatlantic crossings for leisure, before they had become an established feature of American bourgeois life by the last third of the nineteenth century. "Steamers," she writes, "crossed and recrossed the Atlantic" with considerable discomfort to their small number of cabin-class passengers, who "did not lightly run over to London, or Paris, or Berlin," but rather "gravely went to 'Europe.'" In those days, Burnett suggests, American travelers thought of their European trip as something accomplished only once in a lifetime, and infers that much was gained in the way of social and cultural capital by visiting "authentic" sites of high culture and society:

> People who could speak with any degree of familiarity of Hyde Park, the Champs Élysées, the Pincio, had gained a certain dignity. The ability to touch with an intimate bearing upon such localities was a *raison de plus* for being asked out to tea or to dinner. To possess photographs and relics was to be of interest, to have seen European celebrities even at a distance, to have wandered about the outside of poets' gardens and philosophers' houses was to be entitled to respect.[1]

Burnett infers here that mid-nineteenth-century travelers acquired social distinction by breaking with the bonds of everyday experience and undertaking a major overseas adventure. To have walked or ridden in a carriage in the famous parks and boulevards of European capitals, to have seen famous people in person, and to have visited the homes of noted writers conferred a cultural superiority over those who could only experience other worlds vicariously through looking at photographs or souvenirs.[2]

After the Civil War, American bourgeois undertook leisure travel to Europe perhaps four or five times within a lifetime, beginning with a tour for educational purposes during late adolescence, followed by a wedding tour, and then subsequent trips to open up and maintain European social connections and extend one's knowledge of European culture and society. Some families undertook extended visits to the European continent when their finances became a little stretched during times of high inflation, or for health reasons. By the 1870s, visiting Europe had become an integral part of a broader pattern of American bourgeois consumption, alongside of, *inter alia,* the decoration of houses, residential segregation, food, dress, education, religion, social activities, and leisure. With reference to both Americans and Europeans, James Duncan and Derek Gregory assert that travel to foreign places in the nineteenth century was "construed as a quintessentially bourgeois experience."[3] Americans joined the throngs of European bourgeois travelers in greater numbers after the Civil War, as the safety, comfort, and speed of transatlantic transportation improved and the number of shipping lines increased. Their European counterparts had begun to take advantage of improvements in travel after the end of the Napoleonic Wars. The development of railways and the growth in various businesses ranging from hotels and restaurants to guidebooks catered to the needs of leisure travelers and helped to determine the routes they took and the sites they visited.[4] As Rudy Koshar has argued, the Murray guidebooks, which were available from the late 1830s onward, catered to "English professionals, intellectuals, industrialists and entrepreneurs" who wished to use their time efficiently, and, therefore, provided information on "what ought to be seen." Americans were directed by the popular Murray and Baedeker guidebooks to "statues and monuments, historical buildings such as Gothic cathedrals and castles, and ruins" as well as sites of natural beauty.[5] As such, they were participating in an already established leisure practice that, for the English at least, had its roots in the grand tour.[6]

Traveling to Europe was an act of acculturation. As Richard Brodhead has argued with respect to the second half of the nineteenth century and the development of an American translocal social elite, the European tour was a distinctive leisure practice that contributed to self-definition. It went hand in hand with their promotion of high culture.[7] Traveling around European cities, in particular, Americans sought an "'authentic' cultural experience,"[8] one that brought them into contact with the art and architecture of Europe from ancient Rome to the present and enabled them to formulate aesthetic judgments and then talk or write about their experience with authority. Visiting Europe in and of itself signified the value that American bourgeois placed on Europe and the originary relationship the Continent had with the United States. It was part of their heritage as European Americans, and what they chose to see and visit often reflected that sense of connection. Ralph Waldo Emerson pronounced: "All educated Americans, first or last, go to Europe; perhaps because it is their mental home, as the invalid habits of this country might suggest."[9] With less circumspection than Emerson, Grant Allen, who was born in Canada, briefly lived in New England, and spent most of his adult life in England, exhorted with brio young American men to spend a year in Europe as "an indispensable part" of their "liberal education." It would teach them more than three years at Yale or Princeton, he claimed. If they wanted to know about the origins of the arts of building, painting, and sculpture, then they must "look them up in the churches and the galleries of early Europe." Furthermore,

> If you want to know the origin of American institutions, American law, American thought, and American language, you must go to England; you must go farther still to France, Italy, Hellas, and the Orient.[10]

If traveling was an act of acculturation, it was also an act of self-identification as a member of a national and one or more ethnic groups. In 1860, Emerson was already appreciative of the fact that Americans went to Europe "to be Americanized."[11] It was a process that involved tracing one's roots (racial, political, cultural) and identifying the different directions in which U.S. society had developed. American travelogues reveal balancing strategies of identification and difference, particularly with regard to English or Anglo-Saxon culture.[12] On the one hand, there are to be found strong statements of affinity with England, but there are equally strong statements about the superiority of the United States. Waving the Stars and Stripes while in Europe was deeply frowned upon, and it was a conventional device in travelogues of the period to assure American readers that any admiration for European life and culture must not be read as an act of betrayal of American values. On the other hand, if traveling to Europe constituted a process of Americanization, how was "American" defined, and who was being Americanized?[13] We need to be mindful of the domestic context in the United States, with the increase in European immigration after the Civil War and, in particular, the rapid rise in the number of immigrants from southern and eastern Europe at the end of the nineteenth century. Anglo-American Protestant hegemony was deemed to be under threat by the impact of this flow of people.[14] Returning American travelers could not fail, after all, to be aware of the occupants of steerage. Westbound steamers were a graphic illustration of the class and ethnic stratification of U.S. society. A remarkable act of compartmentalization was achieved in the way in which Anglo-Saxon bourgeois were highly selective in designating certain aspects of European society and culture as desirable. A fascination with Italian Renaissance art did not extend to a fascination with contemporary Italians. This is amply demonstrated in their travel writings and, while this powerfully demonstrates how class-bound their judgments were, it also shows how these were deeply inflected by contemporary discourses on scientific racism.

The symbolic value that American seaboard elites both north and south of the Mason-Dixon Line gave to European travel encouraged to the newly wealthy to venture forth from the main ports of New York, Boston, and Philadelphia in order to acquire the social distinction associated with touring Europe.[15] A correspondent for the *New York Times* described them as going abroad "not from any spontaneous inclination, [but] only because so many others have gone; because it is held to be desirable; because it seems to add to their consequence."[16] After the Civil War, older members of the northern bourgeoisie, whose wealth was inherited or whose major economic activities were focused on trade, banking, insurance, and real estate, found their ranks swollen by those who were making their fortunes in mining, railroads, manufacturing, and corporate finance. In seeking to add social distinction to financial wealth, those new to wealth exploited established forms of cultural capital, from funding museums and institutions of art and music to displaying their taste for opera, fine clothes, and food, architecturally designed residences filled with old masters and antique furniture, as well as travel to places of historic and cultural interest and socially exclusive resorts. The oppositions between what Pierre Bourdieu calls "the economically richest" and "the culturally richest," then, were played out within the American bourgeoisie both at home and abroad.[17]

The grievances of "the culturally richest" with regard to the behavior and actions of the nouveaux riches were amply articulated in contemporary writings, such as novels, travel writings, and etiquette manuals. These kinds of text participated in the construction of a bourgeois civilized identity for the benefit of both an American and European readership. It is possible to read such texts as examples of what Norbert Elias has characterized as "ceaseless attempts of human groups . . . to preserve . . . a higher position than potential competitors," which involved "continual attempts to emphasize in deeds as well as words the merits of one's own group and the demerits of another."[18] These writings performed the cultural work of class formation and definition, particularly with regard to their representation of appropriate behavior. There are two main threads in the critique of the actions of the "economically richest" who traveled in Europe. One is the affront to the attempt by the established to build up a sense of tradition, to its insistence on the multigenerational accretion of social distinction and cultural knowledge. The other is injury to national pride born of a defensiveness about the newness of the American republic. In consolidating a bourgeois identity through developing protocols that governed interaction with Europeans of different classes, "the culturally richest" had been at pains to assert a distinctively American style of conduct befitting a democratic republic, and to seek acceptance in European society on their own terms.

The class project of "the culturally richest" was also a national one. Preserving their higher position at home involved not only distancing themselves from compatriots who had not yet fully assimilated into the bourgeoisie, but also denouncing their vulgarity and their fawning over aristocrats. It was difficult, however, to police the social boundaries in Europe, where they were not in control of social encounters—especially when Europeans seemed woefully ignorant about American society and unable to differentiate between those considered the "better sort" and those whose claim to social distinction was at best tentative. Mary Sherwood, whose Scotch-Irish great-grandfather had emigrated to the colonies and fought in the Revolutionary War, recalled being amused, but also offended, by the ignorance of the English about the United States, despite the fact that "two steamers a week ran between Liverpool and New York." This was in 1869, when she made her first visit with her lawyer-husband. "And the worst of it is," she wrote, "they do not come to know much in the social way about the United States."[19]

This essay argues that, while European travel was part of a broader pattern of bourgeois consumption in the last third of the nineteenth century, it signified more than a class identity; it also contributed to a sense of national identity that American bourgeois imagined to be synonymous with their class and ethnic group. The increase in fortunes from industrial capitalism and the growing ethnic diversity of the U.S. population prompted the established bourgeoisie to emphasize their ancestral history and its intertwining with the formation of the American Republic. Touring around Europe, visiting sites that commemorated events and contributors to Western civilization—as historicized and taught as part of a gentleman's education—served to enhance Anglo-Americans' sense of heritage, as well as their beliefs in how they had built on that heritage. Central to my argument is a discussion of the behavior of the American abroad, because what was deemed appropriate behavior when interacting with Europeans and responding to European culture became a site of heated contestation. National and class pride appeared to be at stake, and the resources of etiquette advisors, travel writers and novelists were brought to bear on the issue.

Transatlantic Crossings

After 1865, leisure travel was greatly facilitated by the technological improvements in transatlantic ocean steamers and the increase in the number of shipping lines. The old packets usually had only 20 staterooms, and these were comparatively small and cramped. Passengers were lucky if they were able to undertake the voyage in three weeks. The vicissitudes of the weather were reduced by the development of the "ocean greyhounds," which knocked a week off the fastest voyage by a packet. While oceangoing travel became faster and safer with advancements in mechanical engineering and improvements made in the appointments of first-class cabins, many travelers' accounts pass quickly over the details of their ocean voyage. Mal de mer in midocean soon banished the initial enthusiasm of embarking on the 3,000-mile trip. As Ella Thompson, who traveled to Europe in the early 1870s with six other women, recorded in her travelogue:

> The motion of a screw-steamer is like riding a gigantic camel that has the heart disease, and you do not miss a single throb. . . . One must be very young and

> very joyful, or very old and very weary, to really squeeze any juice of delight out of that greenest of lemons, a steamer passage across the Atlantic. . . . At the best, it is a sort of intermediate state between death and life . . . and the last day, when the steamer plods by the Irish coast, is like the resurrection.[20]

The comfort of passengers was, nevertheless, greatly increased with the provision of larger, well-ventilated cabins, lounges for socializing, and deck seating.[21] The White Star Line, launched in 1870, was best known for its improvements in this regard. Before numbers grew too large, the *New York Times,* among other newspapers, printed the cabin-class passenger list, contributing to the social significance of undertaking a trip to Europe. By the same token, it also printed the names of travelers who registered with banks in London, Paris, and Geneva, from which they picked up their mail.

In 1882 the *New York Times* carried a column from *Galignani's Messenger*[22] remarking on the "wonderful increase in the number of American travelers to Europe," predicting that the numbers would reach the hundreds of thousands in a few years. The surge in first class passenger traffic was noted in 1881, with 22,245 traveling to Europe for the season, compared to 19,496 the previous year. It was anticipated that the figure for 1883 would exceed 30,000, especially as the number of lines had risen from 13 in 1881 to 21 in 1883, and with most reporting that they were fully booked. The economic significance of this outflow of American dollars was registered: *Galignani's Messenger* calculated that this would amount to $90 million, allowing for $3,000 in spending money for each passenger. This figure was based on information from bankers who said they had been issuing letters of credit varying between $1,000 and $5,000.[23]

"The Delicious Purposes of Travel"

There were diverse reasons for American bourgeois traveling to Europe for visits that ranged from a season to a year or more. There were those who lived on inherited income and sought financial relief at times of high inflation by living more cheaply on the European continent.[24] Others sought to benefit their health, while some went for educational purposes. Maintaining old family ties, participating in social seasons, and wedding tours also provided reasons for crossing the Atlantic. For many American sojourners, life and travel in Europe became an extension of communal behavior at home, and enabled them to extend and consolidate networks of kin, friends, and acquaintances on both sides of the Atlantic. For others, European travel was undertaken for the simple enjoyment of visiting places that they had read about in histories and novels. Mary Sherwood described the trip she took with her husband in 1869 as one being undertaken "for the delicious purposes of travel." "We wished," she later wrote, "to realize the reading of a lifetime; to see the Tower and Westminster Abbey and Eastcheap; to hear Bow Bells; to see the Queen; to look at Madame Tussaud's waxworks." This did not preclude, however, enjoying the London Season—her first of five. After calling on John Lothrop Motley at the U.S. Legation and presenting their letters, the Sherwoods were "launched on a sea of dinners and fetes, balls and social functions."[25] Furthermore, travel provided opportunities for Americans to display their cultivation and to delineate their distinctive tastes and lifestyle, both while abroad and on their return home. Shopping and sightseeing were practices that entailed a range of choices for people of different classes and class fractions to utilize in asserting social difference. The luxury trade represented by the shops of the rue de la Paix in Paris or Regent and Bond Streets in London, where clothes were ordered and fitted, enabled bourgeois Americans to distinguish themselves from those who purchased designer derivatives or ready-made items at home or abroad.

Among the early cohorts of American travelers after the end of the Civil War was novelist Constance Cary Harrison of Virginia, who traveled to Paris with her mother on the *Arago* for private training in "languages and 'voice culture."' Mrs. Harrison noted how many other Southerners had likewise "flocked" to Paris "to get a glimpse of the gaiety of life after the long grim strain of their four years of bitter and disastrous warfare." After spending the winter and spring in Paris, Constance and Mrs. Cary traveled to Switzerland and then spent the autumn in England, where, upon arriving, her mother, the daughter of the 9th Lord Fairfax of Cameron, exclaimed, "Thank God, I have at last set foot upon the soil of home!" As Constance commented in her memoirs many years later: "The blood of her tory [*sic*] ancestors had evidently not been chilled in her veins by the lapse of a century of republicanism, or, perhaps, as she could no longer claim Virginia, she would have naught else but England!" Mother and daughter returned home in October on the *Western Metropolis,* "a poor old side-wheel steamer" belonging to the Guion Line that "rolled and plunged over mighty billows" for 16 days.[26]

Taking daughters to Europe to finish their education transcended any sectional differences between the north and south. Anna Pruyn, daughter of Judge Amasa J. Parker, a Democratic leader in New York, similarly undertook a yearlong trip to Europe with a view to "completing" her elder daughter's education. Anna had been married to lawyer, John Van Shaick Lansing Pruyn, who had been a director of the Mohawk and Hudson Railroad, a state senator in 1861–63, and a Democratic member of the House of Representatives in 1863–65 and 1867–69.[27] In 1872, on an extended trip to Europe with her husband, Anna had been presented at the Court of Queen Victoria. The couple had sailed on the *Bothnia,* a screw-ship nicknamed the "Jumping Jaws," and came back on the *Scythia.* Bad weather delayed their arrival for a week, during which time Mrs. Pruyn had to be lashed to her berth.[28] Anna showed an understandable predilection for booking passage on the most up-to-date steamers. In 1879, two years after her husband died, she took her daughters on Cunard's *Gallia,* then making its second trip across the Atlantic, and in 1885 they sailed on another new Cunard liner, the *Etruria.* Even so, the *Etruria* was still prone to steep rolling, with trunks and furniture sliding from side to side in their cabin, and Huybertie, her younger daughter, made special mention in her diary of the "horrible" food and the "bugs and rats."[29] Meanwhile, Anna noted in her diary that there were 420 passengers in first class.[30] The Pruyns spent a year abroad, based first in Paris, where Harriet was placed in a small private school run by a Protestant pastor and his wife, and where she received private tutoring in singing, the violin, and horseback riding.

Much of the Pruyns' Parisian life centered around shopping, especially at the dressmakers, and visiting American friends such as the architect Richard Morris Hunt, going to the theater and opera, and making tours of historic buildings, churches, textile factories, and artists' studios. Paris provided the opportunity for expanding the cultural knowledge of her daughters, with a packed itinerary that included taking in the Paris Opera and the Comédie Française, as well as the tourist sites of Notre Dame, the Conciergerie, Sainte-Chapelle, the Palais de Justice, the Louvre, Vincennes, Sèvre, Gobelin's palace, Napoleon's Tomb, Saint-Denis, Versailles, Saint-Sulpice, and Saint-Germain-des-Prés. All of these places were standard fare for the tourist in Paris. A knowledge of art, history, architecture, music, and theater undoubtedly prepared her daughters for their future role as hostesses in elite circles.

While in Paris, Mrs. Pruyn ordered court dresses for herself and Harriet at the famous Parisian couturiers, Worth's. Harriet noted in her diary for April 1886 how "the great man himself" tended to them, and seemed more like a doctor than a couturier in the way that Anna asked him what he "advised" for her.[31] After a trip around the Italian lakes, the Pruyn women picked up their gowns and went directly across the Channel to London in early May. They rented both Lady Rayleigh's townhouse at 90 Onslow Gardens and her carriage, and from this advantageous base, threw themselves into the social whirl of a London Season, making social calls, dining, and attending receptions and society sporting events such as the Henley Regatta and the Goodwood Races. Anna mixed in the innermost circles of London society, but not in the fast set that surrounded the Prince of Wales.[32] In contrast to their life in Paris, which had centered on the acquisition of culture and high-end consumer goods, their time in London focused on socializing and strengthening close ties with members of the aristocracy. The climax of the trip was Harriet's presentation at Court, arranged through the office of the U.S. Minister to the Court of Saint James.[33] In August, they toured the Scottish Highlands and the Lakes District, returning to London via Oxford a month before the departure home. Like many Americans before them, they made a pilgrimage to the home and grave of Sir Walter Scott. It was here that Harriet complained of the crowds of tourists, English, Scottish, and American. She clearly did not put herself in that category, noting in her diary:

> Every hotel is full & travelling is often very difficult. The romance & quiet of today were spoiled many times by the common acting of many of them. They all push & crowd for room & anyone with manners is generally left out—to do for himself as best he can.[34]

While the Pruyns visited many sites that were on the beaten track of tourists and took trains and ferries and steamers, they always went first class and stayed in the best available accommodations.

Democratic Identities and Anglo-Saxon Affinities

For long-established members of America's bourgeois elite, like the Pruyns, European travel constituted a way of asserting their equality with their counterparts in France and England, as well as adding cachet to their position of privilege in the United States. They constructed an identity for themselves as democratic republicans who derided any slavish imitation or adoration of European aristocratic customs, while still showing respect for Europe's traditions. One of the more enthusiastic statements of affinity can be found in Mrs. E. A. Forbes's *First Impressions of Europe* (1865), in which she greatly admires England for its tenacity to hold onto its "conservatism" and "ancient laws and customs" while "fostering institutions of learning and religion at home, and planting them beside their flag abroad; spreading the white wings of their commerce upon every sea, and laying the strong grasp of their power upon every land." Congruent with the discourse of Anglo-Saxonism, she points to the connection between the soil where the "acorn of civil and religious liberty was planted . . . by no less than a divine hand" and its transplantation to North America. Belaboring her metaphor of natural ties, she traces "the principles of our political life, the nourishment of our intellectual power, and the spirit of our religion from this root." It is for this reason, she writes, that Americans "must feel bound to this great Saxon heart of civilization by a thousand ties of sympathy and association, such as belong to no other land. Her history is our history; her literature is our literature."[35] Others were less enthusiastic, though they felt closer to England than other European countries. Self-confessed Anglophile Adelaide Hall, a clubwoman of Chicago and president of a large art club, acknowledged America's debt to the Old World, and undertook her six-month trip in the 1890s in order "to estimate justly the mature civilization of Europe," in the belief that "the knowledge thus gained is one of the chief elements of culture." In England she took delight in the countryside, the architecture, and the manners of the people, but this did not detract one iota from her staunch identification as an American.[36] Charles Carroll Fulton, publisher of the *Baltimore American,* abhorred "the worship of blood and the toadyism to the scions of aristocracy," while Mary Cadwalader Jones struck a measured tone at the end of the nineteenth century: "Although we have become different in some ways from the English, we are many of us descended directly from them and have a common inheritance in their past."[37] These attempts at collective self-definition seen here may well reflect, in part, the shifting balance of economic power between Britain and the United States.

The wavering ambivalence about the Anglo-American relationship is evident in American etiquette manuals of the second half of the nineteenth century. Some authors justified their advice on the grounds that it was important to describe an American, as distinct from an English, code of manners.[38] Others framed decorum in terms of an essential feature of any civilized country.[39] As a civilized people, Anglo-Americans affiliated themselves racially with the English. Their worldview was shaped by an increasingly rigid set of ideas about racial characteristics and growing pessimism about the ability of alleged inferior races to achieve civilized status. Authorities on decorum frequently used the terms "civilized," "barbaric," and "savage" to emphasize differences in the knowledge of manners, and, as such, these terms were racially coded. Another coded way of referring to class and racial differences was to divide the social world into those who were "respectable" and those who were "disagreeable."[40]

"Disagreeable" encounters between white bourgeois Americans and the local populace in Europe became more pronounced the farther south they traveled. Italy was by far the most popular of all southern European destinations. In the tradition of the grand tour, thousands of American visitors were drawn to the natural beauty of its northern lake region and to the ancient and Renaissance treasures of Venice, Florence, Rome, Milan, and Naples. It was in Italy that travel accounts make frequent mention of obstructions to the pleasures of sightseeing. Baedeker, in his 1899 *Handbook* for northern Italy, warned that "there are few countries where the patience is more severely taxed than in some parts of Italy."[41] His comments were borne out by the responses of the following American women travelers. Lucy Culler, whose parents had emigrated from England to the United States when she was a young child, referred to the Neapolitans as "indolent, slovenly, squalid, hungry, naked, dirty human beings," and described being beset by beggars in both Naples and Venice.[42] Kate Reynolds had a similar reaction to the tenements along the Naples waterfront, which she found to be "the dirtiest and most odiferous imagined," with people living outdoors and conducting their toilet in the street. She recorded in her travel diary how her hotel in Palermo, Sicily, was a veritable "oasis in a desert of poverty and filth," where the "streets were filled with crowds of dirty, unhealthy looking peasants."[43] Stark spatial contrasts are also a feature of the travel account of Mary Reed Edwards, daughter of a former newspaper businessman. In 1903, when she sailed to Italy to join her husband, a military attaché at the U.S. Embassy in Rome, there were 2,053 returning Italian passengers in the steerage of Cunard's *Carpathia.* While she dined on "roast partridge, raw oysters, [and] six salted almonds," the

Italian men, segregated from the women, danced at night to a concertina. Nevertheless, Edwards described them as "a disgustingly dirty lot, and happy in their filth." Landing at Naples, she predictably found the city "dirty and tawdry," and made her way quickly to Rome. After a month of struggling with Italian house servants, she wrote to her mother: "They are dirty, dishonest and shiftless; and so far as I have discovered, their only virtues are cheerfulness and love of country." Embarking at Naples for her return voyage to the United States, Edwards, in her passing shot, condemned the Neapolitans as "the scum of the earth."[44]

These American women's characterization of the poorer classes in Italy, especially in Naples and Sicily, as dirty and indolent can be seen as a rhetorical ploy to set them apart as a separate race and class. Metaphors of dirt carry symbolical significance, designating impoverished Italians as a threat to the health of the American body politic, not merely to these three white women located temporarily in close proximity to them. Reynolds's experience was framed by the context of the mass migration of Italians to America at the turn of the century and probably by debates about immigration restriction, as well as by her four-year residence in Rome. Mrs. Culler and Kate Edwards were tourists reiterating the common complaint about beggars around popular sites in Italy.[45] Nevertheless, all three women registered the contamination of their space and, in doing so, transformed the local inhabitants into intruders. Their encounters mirrored bourgeois discourses at home about the undesirability of working-class Italian immigrants, who made up the largest single national group entering the United States in the decades around 1900.

Unlike social reformer Jacob Riis, these American women did not find the "conditions of destitution and disorder . . . , set in the frame-work of Mediterranean exuberance, . . . the delight of the artist."[46] Instead, they compartmentalized their aesthetic enjoyment of Italian art, history, and music from their daily encounters with the local people. They located their cultural enrichment in the artistic achievements of Italy's past and implicitly denied any connection between those achievements and the Italian masses. As such, an appreciation of high culture is designated as a transnational class project. Meanwhile, they cast themselves and their country as superior to contemporary Italians and Italy, taking pride in America's modernity and progress.[47] While their racialization of Europe's poor is more noticeable in their comments as they ventured farther south, their qualified responses to Italian society and culture are representative of a large number of American bourgeois travelers' attitudes toward countries in Europe. Travel simultaneously reinforced existing prejudices, affirmed American superiority, and strengthened American bourgeois identity as predominantly Anglo-Saxon.

The Contest over Taste and Social Place

Travel to Europe became, in Mary Suzanne Schriber's words, "an instrument of social leverage in a ferociously competitive economy in which, paradoxically, the class mobility associated with a rhetorically classless, middle-class society [made] Americans sharply conscious of class and anxious to scale the ladder of class status."[48] The response of the established to the social competition of new wealth was to try and impose tighter controls on entry into high society. Mary Sherwood extolled the virtues of social exclusiveness as a way of discriminating between the refined and those who were vulgar and pretentious.[49] Some newcomers managed to circumvent the rigidity of social rituals and marshaled their financial resources to assert their claims through conspicuous consumption and attention-seeking strategies that guaranteed newspaper publicity and firmly imprinted themselves in the public's imagination both at home and abroad. The success of those who gained entry into European high society deeply offended those who had spent years building up their social contacts or who had consciously not sought to make themselves conspicuous. The process of acculturation, social or personal, required time and was not something that could be bought.

What made the situation particularly egregious for people like the Pruyns and Mary Sherwood or Henry James and Edith Wharton was that Europeans seemed incapable of differentiating between the various fractions of the American bourgeoisie, regarding the behavior of the newly enriched as typically American. This is encapsulated by James in his 1883 story "The Siege of London," in which Mrs. Dolphin, an American expatriate established in London society, complains when a multiple divorcée from the American West is taken up:

> English society has become scandalously easy. I never saw anything like the people that are taken up. . . . What I see is a fine race—one of the oldest and most honourable in England, people with every tradition of good conduct and high principle—and a dreadful, disreputable, vulgar little woman, who hasn't an idea of what such things are, trying to force her way into it.[50]

In her disdain for this "vulgar little woman," Mrs. Dolphin refuses to be identified with Nancy Headway in any way, and later attempts to prevent the latter's marriage to an English baronet. She prides herself on her "rarity" among American women who have married British husbands.[51] But rarity was not a value that any American expatriate could maintain after 1880. By the 1890s, the ranks of American peeresses had swelled, along with the numbers of women who had married the younger sons of peers, baronets, and members of the landed gentry. The stakes had been considerably raised, with marriage into the European aristocracy now constituting the ultimate sign of distinction—and with hundreds of bourgeois Americans seeking their chances in European marriage markets. The resentment against parvenus merely became more strident.[52]

The class and cultural dramas of transatlantic high society proved fertile ground for the creative imagination of both popular writers and those who wrote for a highbrow readership. Wharton, a celebrated member of old New York, relished the license that fiction afforded her to satirize wealthy parvenus who flaunted themselves in Europe. She articulated the intense class tensions in her native city, and paid particular attention to the international context of both these tensions and those that arose out of encounters between New Yorkers and aristocratic Europeans. As a deep admirer of French culture and a frequent visitor to France herself, she watched with fascination and contempt as her compatriots jumped onto steamers, eager to spend their newly acquired wealth on whatever amusements they could procure in Europe and giving "all their time & strength to forcing their way into a society not particularly anxious to receive them."[53] She was personally irritated and professionally intrigued by the clash of national cultures and manners, which became the stock-in-trade of her transatlantic fiction.[54]

The affront to taste and tradition committed by an uncultured class fraction of the economically rich is given greater edge by Wharton when she moves the field of struggle from old New York to Paris.[55] The tawdry side of transatlantic marriages is exposed in her 1909 short story *"Les metteurs en scène,"* in which Blanche Lambart, an educated American with good social connections but little money, collaborates with Jean Le Fanois, a Parisian aristocrat who pays off his gambling debts by introducing nouveau riche Americans to French aristocrats. Together, they arrange marriages for their clients. The manipulation involved in arranging marriages between parties of different nationalities and classes reveals that the acquisition of distinction is anything but natural: it takes work and effort. When Blanche meets Le Fanois, the Frenchman has grown tired of the "childish" circle of Americans who live an idle life of luxury. He has found that they lead "a completely empty existence, devoid of fixed occupations and stable relationships" but somehow manage to disguise "its yawning emptiness under the appearances of frantic activity!" Wharton uses the character of the French aristocrat to deliver a stinging rebuke of her compatriots' idea of absorbing European culture:

> Cruises on yachts, automobile trips, sumptuous dinners in fashionable restaurants, afternoons of elegant strolling at Bagatelle or Saint-James, trips to the race track and to art exhibits, evenings at those small theaters designed for tourists in the know: all of these expensive and monotonous diversions followed in succession time and time again without exhausting a need to be busy inherited from enterprising and tenacious ancestors, who had directed the same furious activity toward amassing fortunes that their descendants devoted to squandering them.[56]

Here, Wharton makes a point of showing that the process by which the nouveaux riches believed they were acquiring culture and displaying good taste was "unnatural" and shallow, concurring with the complaints of people she herself knew. In effect, through her writings she functioned as a spokesperson for the older, New York bourgeois elite of Anglo-Saxon and Dutch heritage. She specialized in articulating differences of class, race, and national cultures in order to preserve such differences—to insist on respect for them. In her novels and short stories dealing with high society, she focused on the point of contact between new and old money. In doing so, she defined the boundaries, pointed to the violations and transgressions, and excoriated the chauvinism and parochialism of her compatriots. Her autobiography, her travel writings, and her fiction all testify to her cultural competence and her privileged upbringing. Family background and wealth alone gave her social position and the informed gaze through which to decipher the machinations of newcomers seeking entrée and of the established elite trying to keep them out, but her ambition was not simply to be a society novelist. She sought to define herself as an aesthete, a writer of serious fiction, a *belle lettriste*. She transformed her social knowledge into cultural capital and constructed her own salon of a few select, like-minded friends who could engage in what she called "general conversation," the kind that represented the intellectual vigor of French salons at their height.[57] This was part of her own struggle "for the exclusive appropriation of the distinctive signs which make 'natural distinction.' "[58] As such, this made Wharton an active participant in the "symbolic struggles" going on around her in New York and Paris.

Wharton insisted that she suffered every time she returned to the United States after a sojourn in Europe. The tastes that she had acquired since she was a little girl, when her parents used to take her on extended trips to France, Italy, and Spain, could not be gratified in a country so lacking in beauty and tradition.[59] As she told her friend Sara Norton:

> I must avoid the subject of America. . . . I despair of the Republic! Such dreariness, such whining sallow women, such utter absence of the amenities, such crass food, crass manners, crass landscape!![60]

Her words echo those of Henry James in a letter to his mother more than 30 years earlier, though James used the word "vulgar" rather than "crass" to describe Americans abroad.[61] It was not just the lack of culture Americans displayed at home that distressed both James and Wharton but also their lack of culture when traveling in Europe, and their inability to appreciate what they saw or to appreciate European customs and traditions.[62] What grated on Wharton's sensibilities (as well as on James's) was the way in which the "new class of world-compellers" failed to see how European traditions and manners were based on centuries of cultural accretion—of deliberate choice—and were not things to be appropriated unreflectingly as commodities with price tags attached.[63] James Buzard defines "appropriation" as "any action (physical, financial, imaginary) which converts the 'culture' encountered through travel into exchangeable items, tokens of cultural accomplishment that are legal tender in the sign-market of personal acculturation at home."[64] He builds his argument regarding James's attitudes toward American tourists around a distinction between the kind of cultural appropriation that James favored—the thoughtful selection of aspects of European culture that appreciated what they represented within their original context—and the thoughtless appropriation of cultural commodities for show at home. While James posited that Americans had "an excellent preparation for culture" and "exquisite qualities as a race," Wharton did not believe that Americans, while "eager and richly endowed," were "naturally endowed with taste," nor did they pay much attention to being cultivated. In her eyes, Americans took "short-cuts to knowledge" and purchased their "taste in tabloids" wherever possible.[65]

Wharton's cynicism about the newly enriched American bourgeois is represented with devastating force in her 1913 novel *The Custom of the Country,* when her heroine, Undine Spragg, sweeps aside the traditions of a French aristocratic family (into which she has married) and runs roughshod over its pride of possessions accumulated over many generations by having a dealer price their Boucher tapestries. Her third husband, Count Raymond de Chelles, goes into a tirade at the thought of her trying to sell them:

> "And you're all alike," he exclaimed, "every one of you. You come among us from a country we don't know, and can't imagine, a country you care for so little that before you've been a day in ours you've forgotten the very house you were born in—if it wasn't torn down before you knew it! You come among us speaking our language and not knowing what we mean; wanting the things we want, and not knowing why we want them; aping our weaknesses, exaggerating our follies, ignoring or ridiculing all we care about—you come from hotels as big as towns, and from towns as flimsy as paper, where the streets haven't had time to be named, and the buildings are demolished before they're dry, and the people are as proud of changing as we are of holding to what we have—and we're fools enough to imagine that because you copy our ways and pick up our slang you understand anything about the things that make life decent and honourable for us!"[66]

Once more, it is through the French aristocratic male voice that Wharton delivers the damning indictment of American nouveau riche pretensions.

Authors of etiquette manuals in the late nineteenth century were at pains to educate the real-world counterparts to Undine Spragg. Alongside novels of manners, these books were agents in the class project to cultivate bourgeois bodies and preserve the body politic in a democratic republic founded on the virtue, among others, of self-control.[67] The role of the American woman was clearly prescribed in the hundreds of manuals that appeared in the second half of the nineteenth century, a role that was delineated not only in terms of the American household, family, and society but also in terms of how the American woman represented the nation abroad. The American bourgeois female embodied the nation as white and civilized. Europeans harbored crude stereotypes that had to be countered. Lady Randolph Churchill, a New Yorker by birth and one of the social pioneers who married into the British peerage, recalled how, in England, "the American woman was looked upon as a strange and abnormal creature, with habits and manners something between a Red Indian and a Gaiety Girl."[68] Mary Sherwood, whose *Manners and Social Usages* went through several editions between 1884 and 1918, was particularly mindful of European criticisms of American society: "Men and women educated in the creeds of the Old World, with the good blood of a long ancestry of quiet ladies and gentlemen, find modern American society, particularly in New York and at Newport, fast, furious, and vulgar." She asserted that Americans needed to consider the "faults and inelegancies" that foreigners pointed out, especially those identified by English writers and critics—namely, "our bumptiousness, our spreadeagleism, and our too great familiarity and lack of dignity"—if they desired self-improvement and wanted to avoid being "held up as savages."[69] As evident in Mrs. Sherwood's and other authors' comments, there was a deep-rooted desire for Americans to be seen as "civilized." At a time of intense debate over the "racial fitness" of new immigrants and colonial subjects to be incorporated into the body politic, the possibility of being equated with "savages" by Europeans carried the damning implication in the mind of the white Anglo-Saxon bourgeoisie that the United States had not sufficiently "progressed along the path of civilization."[70] A civilized body was a body that was highly controlled, governed by reason, and showed evidence of taste, refinement, and good breeding.[71]

In providing guidance to Americans in how to behave abroad, etiquette authorities advised people to tone down their nationalism and not draw attention to themselves. Moving inconspicuously through public space was a basic rule of decorum in any case, especially for women, but it is also possible to see how the application of this rule with regard to participating in foreign societies was consistent with the fundamental notion of etiquette as keeping social machinery well oiled and protecting the "well-bred" from "the coarse and disagreeable." Rudeness and loudspokenness, according to Annie White, were repulsive, whereas "modesty, gentle speech and ease of manners" made social intercourse easy.[72] To encourage their compatriots to exercise self-restraint abroad and, thus, be seen as respectable, etiquette authors instructed them in the differences in European national customs, and advised them to read up in advance on the countries they intended to visit. Emily Post asserted that it was necessary to have some knowledge about foreign customs "if we would be thought a cultivated and charming people instead of an uncivilized and objectionable one."[73] Among Florence Hall's dos and don'ts, she chastised those who assumed airs of superiority over their fellow travelers, made unfavorable comparisons between their own country and the one they were visiting, and treated the "natives of a foreign country in a condescending or supercilious manner." The flaunting of American superiority was obviously a well-known problem, and Hall, in particular, advised: "keep the American eagle very quiet when . . . travelling in foreign countries."[74] Mary Cadwalader Jones, Wharton's sister-in-law, was adamant on this point, too, asserting that, "unless travellers are willing to leave national prejudices behind them, and ready to see whatever is characteristic and excellent in a foreign country, without finding fault because it is unfamiliar, they had better remain at home." There was nothing worse than "the man who growls because he cannot get buckwheat cakes, or the woman who fusses when she has to do without iced-water."[75]

Conclusion: European Travel and American Bourgeois Identity

Bourgeois formation throughout the nineteenth century was always in process, along with the rise of industrialization and corporate capitalism, urbanization, and migration. As a class, the bourgeoisie were never completely unified, but this did not prevent efforts to construct codes of behavior and establish—or invent, for that matter—traditions. These efforts, alongside representations of bourgeois life in books and art, signify an act of collective self-identification and an expression of what they valued. Prescriptive literature, novels, and travelogues may only provide a partial representation of the variety of everyday experience of travel and life abroad, but their descriptions and prescriptions of behavior abroad speak to the "dialectics of social classification," as John Kasson has so forcefully argued in his work, and "illuminate [the] boundaries" between acceptable and unacceptable behavior for the bourgeoisie.[76] What this essay has attempted to do is to seek out the points of emphasis that cut across the written evidence, and to focus on aspects that speak to bourgeois definition. With regard to the latter, I chose to highlight a period when those who regarded themselves as established bourgeois expressed alarm at what they called an invasion of outsiders who sought inclusion within their ranks. It was the sheer number of new fortunes that overwhelmed the established and created an identity crisis that prompted iterations about social boundaries and appropriate behavior. The competition for social acceptance, as we have seen, was played out in Europe, in countries where the finer points of distinction between American bourgeois tended to be lost on the European aristocracy, who homogenized Americans. The grievances of the established included not only despair about the ignorance of European aristocrats but also resentment over the scale of expenditure, extravagance, and, most egregiously, the commodification of culture in lieu of years of accretion of cultural knowledge by the nouveaux riches. National pride entered into the debate, with the established expressing concern about how "Americans"—meaning the country's "best" representatives and those of Anglo-American heritage—were characterized by Europeans. American bourgeois not only sought distinctive signs in Europe that they could exchange for social and cultural capital at home but also to define themselves as distinctive people from a republican society.

Notes

1. Frances Hodgson Burnett, *The Shuttle* (London: Heinemann, 1907), 51, 2.
2. I am drawing here upon Dean MacCannell's argument in *The Tourist: A New Theory of the Leisure Class* (1976; repr., Berkeley: University of California Press, 1999).
3. James Duncan and Derek Gregory, eds., *Writes of Passage: Reading Travel Writing* (London: Routledge, 1999), 5.
4. William W. Stowe, *Going Abroad: European Travel in Nineteenth-Century American Literature* (Princeton, NJ: Princeton University Press, 1994), 17. In addition, Americans read travel writings by both Americans and the English in preparation for their journeys, which influenced their selection of places to visit.
5. Rudy Koshar, "'What Ought to be Seen': Tourists' Guidebooks and National Identities in Modern Germany and Europe," *Journal of Contemporary History* 33, no. 3 (1998): 323–27.
6. James Buzard, "The Grand Tour and After (1660–1840)," in *The Cambridge Companion to Travel Writing,* ed. Peter Hulme and Tim Young (Cambridge: Cambridge University Press, 2002), 37–52.
7. Richard H. Brodhead, *Cultures of Letters: Scenes of Reading and Writing in Nineteenth-Century America* (Chicago: Chicago University Press, 1993), 123–26. *See also* Stowe, *Going Abroad,* 5–6.
8. James Buzard, *The Beaten Track: European Tourism, Literature, and the Ways to "Culture" 1800–1918* (New York: Oxford University Press, 1993), 6–7.

9. Ralph Waldo Emerson, *The Conduct of Life* (Boston: Ticknor & Fields, 1860), 125.
10. Grant Allen, *The European Tour* (New York: Dodd, Mead, 1899), 11.
11. Emerson, *Conduct of Life,* 127.
12. These balancing strategies are also apparent in etiquette manuals whose authors claimed, for example, that American rules of decorum were not simply "handed down to us from the courts of Europe" but adapted from the best "in all codes . . . and adapted to the needs of a republican government" (*Our Manners at Home and Abroad: A Complete Manual on the Manners, Customs, and Social Forms of the Best American Society* [Harrisburg: Pennsylvania Publishing Company, 1883], 23). *See also* Mrs. Abby Buchanan Longstreet, *Social Etiquette of New York* (New York: Appleton, 1878), 5; and *A Woman of Fashion: Etiquette for Americans* (Chicago and New York: Herbert S Stone, 1898), 5.
13. One might also ask how this related to the Americanization of European immigrants.
14. Eric Kaufmann provides a comprehensive overview of how American national identity was based on "non-conformist Protestantism and pre-Norman, Anglo-Saxon genealogy" in "Ethnic or Civic Nation? Theorizing the American Case," *Canadian Review of Studies in Nationalism* 27 (2000): 133–54.
15. As far as can be ascertained from available data, the majority of Americans traveling to and from Europe used these ports in the nineteenth century. See Brandon Dupont, Alka Gandhi, and Thomas J. Weiss, "The American Invasion of Europe: The Long Term Rise in Overseas Travel, 1820–2000" (Working Paper No. 13977, National Bureau of Economic Research, May 2008), 12.

    Daniel Kilbride provides a comprehensive overview of Southern planters who traveled to Europe "in the English genteel tradition of the Grand Tour" before the Civil War, and their responses to Europe. One of his main arguments is that Southerners expressed themselves in national rather than sectional terms, and that, in mingling with "other privileged Americans" while in Europe, they "became more aware of the class-based qualities that transcended regional affiliations." See Daniel Kilbride, "Travel, Ritual, and National Identity: Planters on the European Tour, 1820–1860," *Journal of Southern History* 69, no. 3 (2003): 549–84, esp. 550, 554, and 583.
16. *New York Times,* "Two Kinds of Travelers," May 5, 1879, 4.
17. Pierre Bourdieu, *Distinction: A Social Critique of the Judgement of Taste,* trans. Richard Nice (Cambridge, MA: Harvard University Press, 1984), 219.
18. Norbert Elias and John L. Scotson, *The Established and the Outsiders,* vol. 4 of *The Collected Works of Norbert Elias,* ed. Cas Wouters (Dublin: University College Dublin Press, 2008), 222.
19. Mary Elizabeth Wilson Sherwood, *An Epistle to Posterity: Being Rambling Recollections of Many Years of My Life* (New York and London: Harper & Bros., 1899), 145.
20. Ella W. Thompson, *Beaten Paths; Or, A Woman's Vacation* (Boston: Lee & Shepard, 1874), 11–13.
21. *New York Daily Times,* "The Days of the Old Packet," December, 13, 1891, 17.
22. *Galignani's Messenger* was an English-language daily newspaper published in Paris between 1814 and 1884.
23. *New York Times,* July 24, 1882, 6. The same newspaper reported that 1907 was a banner year for Americans traveling abroad. Elisha Flagg, general agent of the American Express Company in London, is quoted as estimating that 150,000 Americans had visited Europe that year, with expenditures ranging from $500 per person ("students, teachers, and wives and daughters of small businessmen") to the tens of thousands for "very wealthy" individuals. Flagg thought $100 million a conservative estimate of the total that Americans spent abroad (*New York Times,* September 1, 1907, C1).
24. Edith Wharton, *A Backward Glance,* in *Novellas and Other Writings* (1934; repr., New York: The Library of America, 1990), 817.
25. Sherwood, *Epistle to Posterity,* 132–56. The Sherwoods traveled from Liverpool to London via Chester and Shrewsbury. During June they visited Westminster Abbey, the National Gallery, Westminster Hall (to hear Gladstone and Disraeli speak), Hampton Court, Windsor Castle, Richmond, the Crystal Palace, and Covent Garden. They attended balls at Marlborough House and Lambeth Palace, among "other great houses." They had letters of introduction from Bishop Potter of New York to Dean Stanley, and to the bishops of London, Chester, and Rochester.
26. Constance Cary Harrison, 1867 diary, Burton N. Harrison Family Papers, Manuscript Division, Library of Congress, Washington, DC. Parts of the diary were published later in

her life in *Recollections Grave and Gay* (New York: Charles Scribner's, 1912), 254–72. On her return from Europe, Constance married Burton Harrison, a lawyer and former private secretary to Jefferson Davis, in November 1867 and settled in New York City.

27. See Huybertie Pruyn Hamlin, *An Albany Girlhood,* ed. Alice Kenney (Albany, NY: Washington Park Press, 1990), 334.
28. Huybertie Pruyn Hamlin, "Trips to Europe," AF121, Box 22, Folder 10, Huybertie Pruyn Hamlin Papers, McKinney Library, Albany (NY) Institute of History and Art.
29. Hamlin, *An Albany Girlhood,* 129.
30. Anna Pruyn, 1885–86 diary, Anna Park Pruyn Papers, McKinney Library, Albany (NY) Institute of History and Art.
31. Harriet L. Pruyn, 1886 diary, vol. 2, AN 162, Harriet L. Pruyn Rice Papers, McKinney Library, Albany (NY) Institute of History and Art.
32. Anna's diary contains long lists of people with whom she visited and dined. She was particularly intimate with Lady Camperdown, Sir Lyon Playfair and his American wife, the U.S. Minister to the Court of St. James and his wife, Lord and Lady Abercromby, and Lord and Lady Rosse.
33. Both Harriet and Huybertie came away from their experience at the British court with a certain disenchantment with the process and behavior of the royals. The Drawing Room did not strike Harriet as regal, and she had the impression that the Queen, who looked tired, was looking forward to the end of the time-consuming ritual (Pruyn, 1886 diary, vol. 2, entry for May 5, Harriet L. Pruyn Rice Papers). Huybertie refused to curtsey to the dukes of Cambridge and Connaught, who had their backs turned to her; she was castigated by an Englishwoman who accused Huybertie of thinking that, as an American, she was a member of "the most favored race on earth," and said she should be forced to go back in and make her bows (Huybertie Pruyn, "The Coming Out Years and through Our Wedding Trip 1891–1898," Huybertie Pruyn Hamlin Papers).
34. Pruyn, 1886 diary, vol. 2, entry for Agusut 12, Harriet L. Pruyn Rice Papers.
35. Mrs. E. A. Forbes,*A Woman's First Impressions of Europe: Being wayside sketches made during a short tour in the year 1863* (New York: Derby & Millers, 1865), 338–39.
36. Mrs. Adelaide S. Hall, *Two Women Abroad: What they saw and how they lived while travelling among the semi-civilized people of Morocco, the peasants of Italy and France, as well as the educated classes of Spain, Greece, and other countries* (Chicago and Philadelphia: Monarch Book, 1897), ix,455, and 482.
37. Charles Carroll Fulton, *Europe Viewed through American Spectacles* (Philadelphia: J. B. Lippincott, 1874), 274. This publication was a compilation of Fulton's travel articles and was offered to intending travelers as more "valuable" than a guidebook. While England lacked attractions for Fulton, he was nevertheless relieved to return there after his travails across the Continent, because "Old England . . . notwithstanding all its drawbacks . . . is the only land in Europe, except Switzerland, where there is any real semblance of 'liberty, fraternity, and equality' " (quoted in Mary Cadwalader Jones, *European Travel for Women: Notes and Suggestions* [New York: Macmillan, 1900], 17).
38. See, for example, *A Woman of Fashion: Etiquette for Americans* (Chicago and New York: Herbert S Stone, 1898), 5, 9–10; *The Bazaar Book of Decorum* (New York: Harper & Bros., 1871), 12; Mrs. H. O. Ward, *Sensible Etiquette of The Best Society, Customs, Manners, Morals, and Home Culture* (Philadelphia: Porter & Coates, 1878), xii, 357; Mrs. Burton Kingsland, *The Book of Good Manners: Etiquette for All Occasions* (New York: Doubleday, Page, 1906), 6; Longstreet, *Social Etiquette,* 12; *Our Manners at Home and Abroad,* 23; and Florence Marion Howe, *Social Customs* (Boston: Estes & Lauriat, 1887), 13, 18.
39. See, for example, Walter R. Houghton et al., *American Etiquette and Rules of Politeness* (Indianapolis: A. E. Davis, 1882), 13; John A. Ruth, *Decorum: A Practical Treatise on Etiquette and Dress of the Best American Society* (Chicago: Chas. L. Snyder, 1881), 12; Abby Longstreet, *Good Form: Manners Good and Bad, at Home and in Society* (New York: Frederick A Stokes, 1890), 14; John H. Young, *Our Deportment on the Manners, Conduct, and Dress of the Most Refined American Society* (Detroit: F. B. Dickerson, 1879), 13.
40. See, *inter alia*, Ruth Frankenberg, *The Social Construction of Whiteness: White Women, Race Matters* (Minneapolis: University of Minnesota Press, 1993), 1.
41. Karl Baedeker, *Italy: Handbook for Travellers. First Part: Northern Italy,* 11th ed. (Leipsic: Karl Baedeker/London: Dulau, 1899), v.

42. Lucy Yeend Culler, *Europe through a Woman's Eye* (Philadelphia: Lutheran Publication Society, 1883), 47–48, 87, 98; Fulton, *Europe Viewed through American Spectacles*, 192.
43. Kate Reynolds, 1902–03 diary, Daniel Lamont Papers, Manuscript Division, Library of Congress, Washington, DC. Reynolds accompanied Daniel Lamont and his family on a tour of Europe and Egypt. Lamont had been private secretary to Grover Cleveland (1885–89) and, later, secretary of war (1893–97), and was the vice president of the North Pacific Railway Company. *See also* Jones, *European Travel*, 231.
44. Mary Reed to Mrs. Alexander Reed, December 2, 1903, December 11, 1903, and January 19, 1904, vol. 1; July 25, 1905, and May 17, 1906, vol. 3, Mary Reed Edwards Papers, Manuscript Division, Library of Congress, Washington, DC.
45. *See also* Fulton, *Europe Viewed through American Spectacles*, 192; and Daniel F. Beatty, *"Beatty's Tour in Europe," in "Foreign Lands," or "Europe as I Saw It"* (Washington, NJ: Daniel F. Beatty, Publisher, 1880), 35–40.
46. Jacob Riis, *How the Other Half Lives: Studies among the Tenements of New York* (1890; repr., New York: Hill & Wang, 1957), 37.
47. The Rome correspondent for the *New York Times* wrote critically of the extremes of wealth and poverty and shamelessness of a patrician class "mingling its blood with upstart rich," with no concern about "the scandal of squalid mendacity thrust in the face of foreign visitors from countries in which labor is exalted to the rank of the noblest civic virtues" (March 17, 1874, 2).
48. Mary Suzanne Shriber, *Writing Home: American Women Abroad, 1830–1920* (Charlottesville: University of Virginia Press, 1997), 20.
49. Sherwood, *Epistle to Posterity*, 365–71.
50. Henry James, "The Siege of London," in *The Complete Tales of Henry James*, vol. 5, ed. Leon Edel (1883; London: Rupert Hart-Davis, 1963), 5:13–111.
51. Mrs. Dolphin, we are told, "was usually not taken for an American, but she made a point of being one, because she flattered herself that she was of a type which, in that nationality, borrowed distinction from its rarity" (James, "Siege of London," 96).
52. The *Chicago Record Herald* reported that American women in London society "resent being classified with some other Americans who come over and try to push themselves into the inner circles" (September 10, 1905, clipping in Whitelaw Reid Papers, Manuscript Division, Library of Congress, Washington, DC). Wharton confirmed this sentiment in her autobiography, with her comment that those Americans "who forced their way into good society in Europe were said to be those who were shut out from it at home" (*A Backward Glance*, 831). For a detailed analysis of transatlantic marriages between American women and members of the British peerage, see Maureen E. Montgomery, *"Gilded Prostitution": Status, Money, and Transatlantic Marriages, 1870–1914* (London: Routledge, 1989).
53. Edith Wharton to Margaret Terry Chanler, March 8, 1903, in *The Letters of Edith Wharton*, ed. R. W. B. Lewis and Nancy Lewis (New York: Collier Books, 1988), 78.
54. In one of Wharton's earliest novels, *The House of Mirth* (1905), the field of struggle is located primarily in New York and she presents Society as a series of concentric circles with social climbers intent on breaking into the innermost circle through strategies of display and marital alliances. Her 1913 novel *The Custom of the Country* picks up the theme, but the action takes place in more public venues of sociability, both in New York City and in Paris.
55. Bourdieu, *Distinction*, 244.
56. Edith Wharton, "Les metteurs en scène," in *The Collected Short Stories of Edith Wharton*, ed. R. W. B. Lewis (New York: Charles Scribner's, 1968), 2:558.
57. Wharton, *Backward Glance*, 895–908, 987–93, 1004–15.
58. Bourdieu, *Distinction*, 250. *See also* Maureen E. Montgomery, *Displaying Women: The Spectacles of Leisure in Edith Wharton's Old New York* (New York: Routledge, 1998), 164–65.
59. Edith Wharton to Sara Norton, June 5, 1903, *Letters of Edith Wharton*, 84. Sara Norton was the daughter of Harvard professor Charles Eliot Norton, and a frequent correspondent of Wharton's. Charles Norton had spent a considerable amount of time in Europe in between his early career in the East India trade and his eventual career at Harvard, to the extent that he felt at home in Britain. His letters to home in the mid-nineteenth century make repeated references to the devastating impact of American materialism on Europe. See *Letters of Charles Eliot Norton* (Boston: Houghton Mifflin, 1913), 1:137, 372, 384, 399; 2:66.
60. Edith Wharton to Sara Norton, August 19, 1904, *Letters of Edith Wharton*, 93.

61. Henry James to Mrs. Henry James Sr., October 13, 1869, in *Henry James' Letters,* ed. Leon Edel, vol. 1 (Cambridge, MA: Belknap Press, 1975), 152.
62. Wharton wrote to Sara Norton when the latter was visiting London: "I like it *all*—institutions, mannerisms, conservatisms, everything but the women's clothes, & having to go to church every Sunday" (June 5, 1903, *Letters of Edith Wharton,* 84).
63. Edith Wharton, *The Custom of the Country* (1913; New York: The Library of America, 1985), 802–3.
64. Buzard, *Beaten Track,* 225.
65. Henry James to T. S. Perry, 1867, quoted in Buzard, *Beaten Track,* 224; Edith Wharton, *French Ways and Their Meaning* (1919; Lee, MA: Berkshire House Publishers, 1997), 53–55.
66. Wharton, *Custom of the Country*, 982. Compare this passage with the one in James's "Siege of London," cited earlier.
67. I am drawing on the arguments of Ann Laura Stoler in *Race and the Education of Desire: Foucault's History of Sexuality and the Colonial Order of Things* (Durham, NC: Duke University Press, 1995), Chapter 4; and John F. Kasson, *Rudeness and Civility: Manners in Nineteenth-Century Urban America* (New York: Hill & Wang, 1997), Chapter 2. Kasson points out that, "under the pressures of an emergent industrial capitalist society," the bourgeois order "redefined gentility in its own image" (34).
68. Mrs. George Cornwallis-West, *The Reminiscences of Lady Randolph Churchill* (London: Edward Arnold, 1908), 47.
69. Mrs. John Sherwood, *Manners and Social Usages* (New York: Harper & Bros., 1884), 4–5.
70. See Matthew Jacobson, *Whiteness of a Different Color: European Immigrants and the Alchemy of Race* (Cambridge, MA: Harvard University Press, 1998), for a discussion of the suitability of new immigrants for citizenship. The most graphic illustration of the sliding scale from white Anglo-Saxon civilization through to the "savagery" of African peoples was laid out along the midway at the 1893 World's Columbian Exposition.
71. Kasson, *Rudeness and Civility,* 195.
72. Annie White, *Polite Society at Home and Abroad* (Chicago, Philadelphia, and Stockton: Monarch Book, 1891), 12–13.
73. Emily Post, *Etiquette in Society, in Business, in Politics, and at Home* (New York and London: Funk & Wagnalls, 1923), 593.
74. Florence Marion Howe Hall, *The Correct Thing in Good Society* (Boston: Estes & Lauriat, 1888), 177, 184–85.
75. Jones, *European Travel for Women,* 1.
76. Kasson, *Rudeness and Civility,* 4.

3

Henry James and the American Evolution of the Snob

Alide Cagidemetrio

Are All Bourgeois Snobs?

Are all bourgeois snobs? Maybe not, but one etymology suggests that their children are, for, in the seventeenth century, "s.nob" was the shorthand version of *sine nobilitate,* a qualification attached to the sons of wealthy bourgeois families by registrars when prestigious English public schools admitted them. The bourgeois as snob first appears in literature at about the same time, with Molière's *Bourgeois gentilhomme* (1670), a comedy in which a would-be gentleman embodies the conflict between *être* and *paraître*—being and appearing. Molière's comic character combines obscure origin with achieved economic status, matched with ridiculed aspirations to knowledge, taste, and social propriety. His figure positions the bourgeois as the individual inbetween people and aristocracy. As the aristocratic Marivaux put it:

> Le bourgeois à Paris, madame, est un animal mixte, qui tient du grand seigneur et du peuple. Quand il y a de la noblesse dans ses manières, il est presque toujours singe: quand il y a de la petitesse, il est naturel; ainsi il est noble par imitation, et peuple par caractère.[1]

Aristocrat by imitation and man of the people by character—the bourgeois, in Marivaux's definition, is characterized by class hybridity and the desire to be like the aristocrat and unlike the people.

There is clearly some overlap between "snob" and "bourgeois" when the focus is on social behavior, and not on class only. The bourgeois-as-snob can be seen as the character who denies belonging to a particular class—neither a member of the aristocracy nor of the people—and is engaged in negotiating a culturally relevant identity. The snob's negotiation thus implies denial and imitation: the denial of one's class in the snob's imitation of aristocracy may be read as the desire to acquire a lifestyle that suggests superiority to, and distance from, the lower classes. It may be read as an exemplary case of bourgeois ambition, a passion that figures prominently in the nineteenth-century imagination, and indeed from Molière's seventeenth-century comedy to nineteenth-century fiction, from Honoré de Balzac to Henry James, the figure of the snob has evolved, at a pace matching that of the bourgeoisie coming to power. Starting in the late 1870s, the bourgeoisie felt the need to define its class limits from within. While aristocracy was easy to define—by birth, estate, income, or royal ennoblement—it was difficult to differentiate status within a class whose most distinctive characteristic, social mobility, threatened to mean limitless inclusion. The invention of a bourgeois lifestyle, Eric Hobsbawm maintains, was a response to this uncertainty about one's status.[2] The new cultural practices, the social behavior, and the institutions generated—the response to such uncertainty—did indeed provide a model for the newcomers to prosperity, which eventually extended its appeal, beyond ideologies, to the universality of the middle classes. The crisis, in other words, was real, but the bourgeois struck back, investing, among other things, in culture or the distinction of "cultural nobility."[3]

The character of the snob in nineteenth-century literature suggests how deeply felt the need for the negotiation of a viable bourgeois identity was—all the more so in a democratic environment such as the United States,[4] where the denial of the existence of a bourgeoisie may enforce the intra- and interclass claim for the distinction of snobbishness, giving rise to the notion that snobbishness is characteristic of a democratic, universal classlessness, thus fashioning a paradoxical American triumph of bourgeois identity, of its dreams and its power. Transplanted onto American soil, the *sine nobilitate* of the European bourgeoisie could be culturally fashioned as the working ideal for distinction in American democracy. Deprecatingly, yet prominently, this working ideal has been labeled as the quest for status, from Thorstein Veblen to sociologists like C. Wright Mills and Vance Packard. Paul Fussell further qualifies such quest as a search for the distinctive signs of class differences within an imagined classless society.[5] These "visible and audible signs" are made democratically conspicuous by consumption and the exhibition of a desired hierarchy, and by a type of imitation that is supposed to show evidence of being, or aspiring to be, "the real thing." Whatever "the real thing" is, it is related to matters of aesthetic, cultural, and social import which haunt writers such as James, Howells, Wharton, or Fitzgerald. In their writings, a new type of snob appears, the American who aspires simultaneously to elitism and egalitarianism, and whose quest for an "art of life" dwells on the practices of snobbery, or on the work done in the effort to match wealth with cultural distinction. James, especially, turned to a representation of society and "manners."

In a 1904 article—with the significant title "Why Is American Literature Bourgeois?"—Gertrude Atherton registers the phenomenon as a betrayal of American originality and "genius," as the symptom of an antidemocratic strain that is enfeebling the nation's culture. Atherton gives voice to a commonplace in American literary history: that there should not be a literature of the bourgeoisie in a country without it. James's fiction, and that of his fellow "Bostonians," is Atherton's main target, for he and they are guilty of insisting on "the mild distractions of 'society'" and on the imitation of "the bourgeois spirit of Europe."[6] Still, the Californian Atherton reacts to a distinctive change in her country's culture: in the last 30 years of the nineteenth century, incorporated and metropolitan America faced new issues of identity, socialization, and morality that entered the national imagination, often masked as a confrontation with Europe and its classes. Deprived of an aristocracy, of the European bourgeois advantage to ennoblement by royalty, yet engaged in acquiring distinction through culture, the American in literature emerges as a problematic presence in an imaginary international social scene.

To unravel the tradition of snobbery in American literature, this essay focuses on the work of the master, Henry James, touching upon the question of manners and on that of "Europe" as a cultural discourse, which involves the creation of a new model for American identity. The invention of a need for an imagined confrontation with European aristocracy, and with the past of Western civilization, suggests both the aspiration to bridge class differences by imitation and the desire to possess class status, either by claiming cultural nobility or by claiming possession of valuable people or objects. Within this discourse, the American is fashioned as a bourgeois elitist whose superior form of snobbishness is founded on moral grounds and can thus be offered as a model. The type James introduced, however, faces the characteristic ambiguity of his condition, as neither a member of the aristocracy nor one of the people, suspended between the denial of and the desire for class distinctions.

James himself was emblematic of the American snob as elitist bourgeois. As a third-generation descendant of an Irish immigrant who had made his fortune in upstate New York, Henry the writer, had he been born European, would have sociologically fit into the development of bourgeois roles from the first to the third generation, from the craftsman or merchant to member of an intellectual class, with social function and recognizable market value. Being an American, Henry, his Irish origins notwithstanding, belonged to the cultural enclave of Waspdom, to the Eastern tradition of gentility, and, like many of his circle, from Thomas Sergeant Perry to Henry Adams, he believed in the supremacy of a "world of the educated," as opposed to the world of crass moneymaking. He was proud of his place in "society," and incensed by the ostentatiousness and lack of manners of the American plutocrats. He suffered from an indistinct awe in crowds of people, however, and embraced European society—and English upper-class society in particular—both as a subject for study and as an exemplary arena for testing American notions of Europe and the peculiarities of the American type.

Unlike many of his characters, James was not enormously wealthy, nor did he court or marry a European aristocrat; still, he admired old aristocratic values, deplored their disappearance, and cherished the art of living as much as of the art of the novel. His formulation of the latter, in the 1884 essay "The Art of Fiction," was: "It is Art that makes life." Accordingly, one's achievement was to be measured in the ability to select, exercise reticence, and analyze the interactions between the self and social acts, and he distinctively projected the American character as a figure of inbetweenness, lured by Old-World complexities yet taking center stage in them: for James, the condition of snobbery was at the core of a social drama and of an intricate quest for self-definition.

In 1903 Henry Adams wrote to Henry James congratulating him upon his recently published biography of a Bostonian confrere, William Wetmore Story, and gloomily summarizing their common experiences of a lifetime:

> Type bourgeois-bostonien! A type quite as good as another, but more uniform. . . . God knows that we knew our want of knowledge! The self-distrust became introspection—nervous self-consciousness—irritable dislike of America, and antipathy to Boston. *Auch ich war in Arcadien geboren*! (Schiller 1786, Resignation).
>
> So you have written not Story's life, but your own and mine. . . . You strip us, gently and kindly like a surgeon, and I feel your knife in my ribs.

To which James replied:

> The truth is that *any* retraced story of bourgeois lives (lives other than the great lives of "action"—*et encore*!) throws a chill upon the scene, the time, the subject, the small mapped-out facts.[7]

Their lives, as Adams and James imagined them, did not call for epics, appropriated in their lifetime by tycoons' biographies and journalistic accounts of business geniuses; as members of the intellectual elite, both James and Adams retained the wish for an ideal American Arcadia, alongside the consideration that retracing the story of bourgeois lives, as James wrote to Henry Adams, "throws a chill upon the scene, the time, the subject, the small mapped-out facts." To that very "chill" James devoted his work, following in footsteps of Balzac, who had declared, in his "avant-propos" to the *Comédie humaine* (1842), his intention to write a "history of manners"—that is, a type of history "forgotten by many historians." As Erich Auerbach has pointed out, Balzac conceptualized "the novel of manners as philosophical history," and "his people and atmospheres, contemporary as they may be, are always represented as phenomena sprung from historical events and sources."[8] Like Balzac, James saw the profession of the novelist as that of the "historian of contemporary manners," and, drawing a comparison between the work of the historian and that of the novelist, he found that they shared the perspective of "the ultimate steps of a movement," of the "final manifestations of conduct." It was the novelist's task to tackle with "the fixedness and sacredness" of "social custom and reputation," all the more so when change produced its effects: "The manners, the ideas, the tone of the moment, may always be seized by a genuine observer, even if the moment lasts but three months."[9] In the hybrid nature of the novel—between chronicle and imagination—a generation's sense of history finds expression, and the *histoire des moers* may offer a deeper truth than that offered by contemporary chronicles.[10]

Manners and Morals

"Snob" as a word acquired a wider currency in English following the publication of William M. Thackeray's *Book of Snobs* (1848), a satirical investigation of types and behaviors marking the pretensions to gentility of the bourgeois. For the English writer, the monied bourgeois irrupting on the genteel world revealed the falsity of an order founded on the imagined identity between nobility as a moral category and the gentleman as its social type:

> What is it to be a gentleman? Is it to be honest, to be gentle, to be generous, to be brave, to be wise, and, possessing all these qualities, to exercise them in the most graceful outward manner? Ought a gentleman to be a loyal son, a true husband, and honest father? Ought his life to be decent—his bills to be paid—his tastes to be high and elegant—his aims in life lofty and noble? In a word, ought not the Biography of a First Gentleman in Europe to be of such a nature that it might be read in Young Ladies' Schools with advantage, and studied with profit in the Seminaries of Young Gentlemen?[11]

Thackeray's satirical mode lashed out at the apparent gap between morality and manners in the snobbish gentleman, at a time when the cultural production of codes of conduct, of manuals on how to become a gentleman or a lady, made of appearances a supreme fetish for cultural distinction.[12] To imagine what James called the "art of life," connecting form with ethics became a serious concern of the nineteenth-century novel of manners.

In the classic essay "Morals, Manners, and the Novel" (1947), Lionel Trilling famously denied the existence of an interest in manners in American fiction, for was not American society mannerless and lacking social complexity—a belief expressed by Crèvecoeur, Cooper, Hawthorne, and James. Trilling explains this national peculiarity:

> It would seem that Americans have a kind of resistance to looking closely at society. They appear to believe that to touch accurately on the matter of class, to take full note of snobbery, is somehow to demean themselves. It is as if we felt that one cannot touch pitch without being defiled—which, of course, may possibly

> be the case. Americans will not deny that we have classes and snobbery, but they seem to hold it to be indelicate to take precise cognizance of these phenomena.[13]

Since in Trilling's view the modern realistic novel "is born in response to snobbery," the fact that Americans do not "take full note of it" poses a serious limitation to their "moral" imagination, or to the expression of the "problem of knowledge." Trilling, a passionate reader of Proust and James, among others, and shaped by his early encounter with Matthew Arnold, gave to snobbery a meaning that partakes of the late-nineteenth-century interest in culture, as both a field of social science and of morals. Coupling manners and morality, he focuses on the divergence between appearance and reality brought about by "money as a social element" and the ensuing unease of "the shifting and conflict of social classes." "The characteristic work of the novel," he writes,

> is to record the illusion that snobbery generates and to try penetrate to the truth which, as the novel assumes, lies hidden beneath all the false appearances. Money, snobbery, the ideal of status, these become in themselves the objects of fantasy, the support of the fantasies of love, freedom, charm, power.[14]

At the origin of the modern bourgeois novel of manners, Trilling, significantly, sets Miguel de Cervantes and his *Don Quijote,* the knight who could no longer be such. Don Quijote comes to represent the crisis that makes bourgeois realism an agent of morality in the process of civilization. He is not the character of comedy but the representative of a historically new human condition, caught in the gap between behaving and being: as an imitator of Amadis de Gaul, Quijote is the most poignant figure of the snob. Since for Trilling snobbery is "pride of status without pride in function," novels both denounce it and dwell on it, striving to make of it the characteristic, moral energy that shapes modern fantasies of "love, freedom, charm and power."

If Trilling is right and snobbery is the condition the modern novel captures and responds to, American fiction from the late nineteenth century onward does indeed offer a relevant contribution to its tradition.[15] "Americans succeed wonderfully with novels of 'manners,'" wrote L. B. Walford in 1894,[16] and one may wonder whether Trilling's dismissal of this American contribution, with the possible exception of James, has something to do with unresolved issues that seem to hover over his essay; that is, how can classless, democratic Americans be seen as examples of social "snobbery" on a national scale? Can one be both inwardly "authentic" and socially "snobbish"? How can a culture morally devoted to authenticity seriously identify itself with snobbery, dependent as it is on hybridism and illusion? Snobbery, as Judith Shklar wrote, is "one of the ordinary vices of democratic society" that may resonate dramatically when "the power fantasies" of a "post-commercial aristocracy" give people "false" notions of class based on status and of race based on "gene pools." In a culture of democracy and authenticity, the corrective of social mobility does not erase the possibility of the haunting dystopia of falsity and inequality. It appears that it is through snobbery, however, that the modern novel of manners can respond to cultural and social instability, and reinstate class in a culture of classlessness, dramatizing its aspirations, fears, and self-deceptions.

The American Claimant

The classlessness of American society may generate a special anxiety of belonging to a class; the *sine nobilitate* of the snob may literally become the energy by which the meaning of class is asserted. The fictional foundling who in the end turns out to be legitimate the son of aristocrats becomes in America the son whose ancestry is divided between America and England: This archetypal figure of an American returning to the land of origin and claiming the name, title, and estate of English ancestors was invented by Nathaniel Hawthorne as early as 1858, in a novel he ultimately left unfinished and whose many versions have been collected under the title *The American Claimant*. As it was planned, the story centers on a young American of means and a political future who goes to England to retrace his origin and claim his position there. The projected ending was to bring the young man back to America, wedded to a "new Eve," after he had renounced the title and estates granted to him. The novel fragments record unresolved contradictions: "Where was America and the Republic in which he hoped for such great things," the young protagonist is made to ask in horror while under the impression of living, uncannily, in the Middle Ages.[17] His returning to Olde England from a nation proud of being young—a nation looking toward the future—inherently denies that American democracy and European feudalism had been separated by immigration and revolution. Hawthorne shows that the claimant's quest is as dangerous as it is inevitable, being that of "an American rambling about in quest of his country."[18] It is not surprising that in the age of Anglo-Saxonism the American claim to an English aristocratic lineage would become a popular motif, as demonstrated by the immensely successful reduction of it to both a children's story, in Frances Hodgson Burnett's *Little Lord Fauntleroy* (1886), and farce, in Mark Twain's *The American Claimant* (1892).

James, too, had revisited the "American claimant" type in the short story "A Passionate Pilgrim" (1871), whose protagonist, Clement Searle, is on his way to claim an English title and estate, not for any material advantage but for "the beauty of it." Searle is called a "snob," one whose passionate wish to undo the original act of migration is almost allegorically balanced by the similarly passionate wish of an Englishman to go to America. The Oxford-educated "gentleman commoner," Mr. Rawson, is an example of a decadent bourgeois, and as such he is "the victim of some fatal depreciation in the market value of pure gentility." For this prospective, new immigrant America is the fabled "land of chances," while for Clement Searle, England is the country of his "visions" of "pure gentility": "Sitting here, in this old park, in this old land, I feel—I feel that I hover on the misty verge of what might have been!" he says. "I should have been born here and not there; here my vulgar idleness would have been—don't laugh now!—would have been elegant leisure."[19] Searle is too weak to uphold his claims and, like a Jamesian Don Quijote, wishes to revive an imaginary past in the present—a time before America was even "invented," as Mark Twain's Hank Morgan puts it in *A Connecticut Yankee in King Arthur's Court* (1889). Musing on his early tale in 1908, James identifies his American claimant with the author's own youthful self, infected with a "nostalgic poison" in his American exile from Europe:

> [T]he future presented to him but as a single intense question: was he to spend it in brooding exile, or might he somehow come into his "own"?—as I liked betimes to put it for a romantic analogy with the state of dispossessed princes and wandering heirs.[20]

Searle has indeed the constitution of a romantic dreamer, as he is "the last of" the American claimants in the Hawthorne tradition, he dies at the end of the story, since, by his own admission, he "was too great a fool to be even a snob."[21]

Discarding the claim to an aristocratic birthright, James finds the claim's interest in the quest not for literal ancestry but for the inheritance of "civilization." Underplaying the contradiction between feudalism and democracy, the Jamesian novel invents

Europe as the figure of the "visitable past," surviving not only in art and architecture but also in manners and their formation. As Cooper had imagined the space of the frontier as a place where races could meet, fight, and work out differences, so James imagined the European world as a sort of "neutral ground," a no-man's-land where select Americans and Europeans could work out what appears to be a "clash of civilizations" or reenact the old, pre-Revolutionary European class war between bourgeois and aristocrat. If *Don Quijote,* Trilling's archetypal modern novel, anchors the "illusion" of his hero's outdated quest for the noble ideal of chivalry to the exemplary book of Amadis de Gaul, then James links his American characters to a figure of "Europe" that is a product of American expectations—the palimpsest of old forms of society, the land of ancient nobility. In James's fictional world, European washerwomen are as absent as European magnates, industrialists, bankers, and public functionaries. This absence of a confrontation of the working and making of class may score a point for Trilling's thesis: there can't be a modern novel without "the shifting and conflict of social classes." Yet, the fact that James ignores the economically active and politically powerful modern European bourgeoisie entrenches his "Europe" within the boundaries of an ahistorical, paradigmatic confrontation between old and new orders, the test tube for cultural values, in which "Americanness" is the locus both of conflict and of a desired outcome.

The Evolution of the American Snob

If one were to draw a line between the novels written in America before 1870 and those written later, it would have to be along the line of wealth. How to live with and how to dispose of one's wealth, how to learn the "art of life" at the level required by one's wealth, how to acquire "culture"—these are the main concerns of the American "bourgeois" fiction of the period:

> Upon the uses of money, upon what one might do with a life into which one had succeeded in injecting the golden stream, he had up to his thirty-fifth year very scantily reflected. Life had been for him an open game, and he had played for high stakes. He had won at last and carried off his winnings; and now what was he to do with them? He was a man to whom, sooner or later, the question was sure to present itself, and the answer to it belongs to our story.[22]

This is from Henry James's *The American.* By 1877, when the novel was published, a new, indigenous type of plot was developing in which the main protagonist is a rich, successful American of obscure origin whose second quest in life, after having lived the (democratic) Horatio Alger formula and risen from rags to riches, is to become a gentleman of leisure, possibly provided with a mate representing the desired, yet so far denied, world of aristocratic, gentlemanly manners.[23]

Manners respond to the historical moment when tradition and change meet, or collide, and form a "social capital" of culture—as James wrote in *The Golden Bowl* (1904)—that is projected as a marker of class. Exposure to European manners, marriage, or outright purchase is the answer to the perceived need to incorporate culture into financial capital, in the fictional as in the real world. The Jamesian character may or may not succeed in a matrimonial alliance with the aristocracy, or even fail to purchase the right thing; exposure to the "question of manners," however, is stylized as the inevitable ground for his or her ideal *Bildung.*[24]

James's notion of manners is not disjointed from the moral crusade that ran through the late-nineteenth-century debate between idealism and materialism, within which his lifelong friend and elitist Bostonian Thomas Sergeant Perry wrote an interesting little treatise, *The Evolution of the Snob* (1887), to uphold the figure of the snob as the potential incarnation of an American provided with cultural and moral distinction. Though Perry lashed out at current snobbish behavior, he also considered snobbery a potential good practice for elitist, morally sound Americans, as beneficial in the crusade for the renovation of ethics. Snobbery, he reasoned, is a historical phenomenon originating in the aftermath of the egalitarian impulse of the French Revolution and matched by the appearance in literature of a taste for ghosts. They are the revenants of an old order, dismissed in the name of equality and liberty but surviving as the signs of the historical degradation of an ancient nobility of character in need of being revived. In associating the snob with a ghost claiming lost values, Perry lashed out at those contemporary snobs who were as yet unable to shoulder the task of vindication, at a time when the "living question" was the "settlement of the various claims to wealth." Rich Americans were on their way to becoming "the masters of the world," and, regrettably, fell short of their ideal obligations. In Perry's view, "le monde s'Americanise" and a quest for value had become the new priority, since the restoration of the "admiration for the dignity of life" was badly needed in a society engaged mostly in "the practical worship of the material side of wordly success."[25] Thus, Perry contributed to a shift in the meaning of snobbery. Though the initial ridicule of claiming distinction by imitation was reinforced, there was also a new and different mission for the snob, that of matching wealth with a notion of culture that included the superiority of morals, the acquisition of "manners" in their noblest sense.[26]

Idealistic crusaders insisted on finding nobility of manners not in America's past but in Europe's. In the wake of the extraordinary revision of taste and aspirations initiated by John Ruskin, the ideal bourgeois type was imagined as a man of the early Renaissance or the late Middle Ages, achieving "nobility," or that upper tier of social life belonging to the higher spirits. Another influential Bostonian, Ralph Adams Cram, invited his American readers to build a new life "on the wide ruins of a mistaken civilization," thus reforming the preceding three centuries.[27] This is what the protagonist of James's *The American* (1877), tellingly named Newman, wishes to do in 1868 Paris—two decades after the revolution of 1848 and three years before the Paris Commune—when he combines his wish to "better" himself by marrying an aristocratic young lady with the desire to reform her doomed, donjuanesque brother, Valentin: "Come over to America with us," Newman says, "and I will put you in the way of doing some business. You have a very good head, if you will only use it."[28] Yet, decadent aristocrat that he is, Valentin will not become a sound businessman; he perishes instead, in an outmoded duel. Unable to reform European aristocrats, Newman in the end finds himself morally superior to the old French aristocracy, and, in the confrontation with its class pretensions and misdemeanors, proves to be true to his own claim: "But I say I am noble. I don't exactly know what you mean by it," he tells a spiteful Monsieur de Bellegarde, "but it's a fine word and a fine idea; I put in a claim to it."[29]

In his Europe, James repeatedly tested and questioned a national type as both the opponent of contemporary aristocracy and the heir to an aristocratic ideal. The claim to a past of virtuous nobility is fashioned by Newman in language strongly reminiscent of Puritan typology shaping the immigrant's image of America: "I seemed to feel a new man inside my old skin, and I longed for a new world,"[30] he says of his decision to leave for Europe. Moving back, inverting the course of immigration, is to be born again in an "unknown" old world, or in a new "Promised Land" where the rift between past and present, the historical and cultural gap that separates

America from Europe, is bridged by the successful claim of a classless American with a symbolic *bon sauvage* ancestry in the American West. In the past, European aristocracy was distinguished by virtuous nobility; now, Newman's discovery of his own original nobility of character qualifies him as the only true gentleman of manners. Thus, young James, anticipating Perry's *The Evolution of the Snob*, turns the ridicule of snobbish imitation—Newman in Paris "had often admired the copy more than the original"—into the agent for the realization of the American's superiority. The answer to his story, promised at the beginning of the novel, is that he is no longer interested in business, and if the "uses" of his money are still vague, he is happy to be rich and has a fancy to carry out his life as a "religion" of unexceptionable social behaviors: he had seen too much of the "mistaken civilization" of French aristocracy not to come to the rescue of civilization itself.

Dramatic Asymmetries

In often excessively decorated drawing rooms, or in new public institutions—the park or the museum—James's American characters are exposed to "manners," both as cultural behavior and, more important, as a creative ground for knowledge and self-knowledge. Drawing rooms and public places are turned into intimate spaces where privileged consciences are provided with the leisure of contemplation and the detection of possibly "real" meanings whose nature becomes increasingly problematic. The characters to whom these consciences belong are also of a special set: no toiling folks of any kind, but rather representatives of old and new money, culturally adequate or inadequate members of the upper echelons of American society. Observing American and European manners in Paris in 1878, James had mused upon the American imitation of Europe, recognizing in his compatriots a cultural dependence that belittled their own native traditions. Imitation as a ridiculed snobbish practice rests on the asymmetry of manners between one group and another; for James, however, the asymmetry in manners between Americans and Europeans is at the core of the dramatic energy of American snobbery which shaped *The Portrait of a Lady* (1881), a novel opening with "the ceremony known as afternoon tea" in a time-honored English country residence, echoing similar scenes in Jane Austen's foundational novels of manners. Two American-abroad types are later introduced to represent the perfection of American imitation of European manners : Madame Merle and Gilbert Osmond—at least, this is the opinion of the sensitive and educated young American Isabel Archer. She embodies the culture of her country: a reader of German philosophers and Ralph Waldo Emerson, and a self-reliant, curious figure of Columbia, "dressed in stars and stripes" and proud of her country: "I like the great country, vast and fresh," she says. A representative figure of American democratic "originality," Isabel arrives in Europe on a self-centered plan of exploration and acquisition of knowledge. Unlike Christopher Newman, this young woman does not desire to marry into the aristocracy; on the contrary, she rejects the best of suitors, the very essence of old British aristocracy, Lord Warburton. The plot obviously thwarts readers' expectations of an established "American snob" mythos, and it does so with a purpose: Isabel is a character doomed to find out the perturbing nature of American imitation of Europe.

James dwells at length on Isabel's culturally determined vision. Looking at Madame Merle for the first time, Isabel thinks: "She is a Frenchwoman." Or, on second thought, she might be German, yet to Isabel, "her distinction" was "inconsistent with such birth." In any case, she is sure that Madame Merle is a great lady, someone with "cultivated natural talents." When it turns out that Merle grew up near Brooklyn's Navy Yard, Isabel is surprised that "an American should so strongly resemble a foreign woman," yet her surprise only deepens her admiration, and she elects the older woman as her model. As an appointed mediator of European cultural ways, Merle successfully concocts a marriage plot for Isabel after the girl inherits a hefty portion of her uncle's banking fortune. Gilbert Osmond is the chosen one: though he is an American of obscure origin, he appears to Isabel as "the first gentleman in Europe"—a definition lifted from Thackeray's *Book of Snobs*. Being a gentleman and an American makes him a precious "rarity" for Isabel, and she even wonders whether his being "gloriously provincial" might not be "the last refinement of higher culture." Against the advice of longtime expatriates such as her cousin and her aunt, or of her American radical friend Henrietta, Isabel marries Osmond. But with her marriage she comes to realize that her own, and her country's, attraction to Osmond's type of snobbery, founded only on "performative aspects of identity,"[31] may be fatal. She recognizes that she mistook a successful production of effects for the "real thing." Dazzled by Osmond's "art of living," she had not seen that his own seeming-perfection was "a thing of forms, a conscious calculated attitude." Isabel had harbored the notion of an aristocratic life as "simply the union of great knowledge and great liberty; the knowledge would give one a sense of duty, and the liberty a sense of enjoyment."[32] Osmond's imitation is that of a cultural "predator," a snob who is left with "nothing to restrain or direct his conduct—no work, no family, no country, no obligation."[33]

What Osmond does not have makes Isabel's difference. Her transformation into "a lady" rests on discarding imitation as a thing of effects, and on recognizing in imitation the value of a process: the aspiration to the "art of life." This type of recognition is crucial in distinguishing between the inferior snob and the ideal American elitist. "Recognition" is a process as vital in James's novels as the rebuilding of a productive order was in Daniel Defoe's *Robinson Crusoe* (1719), a foundational bourgeois novel. Isabel's productive vigil is not initiated by an actual shipwreck but by its equivalent in terms of manners. Returning home from a ride in the Campagna, she sees through the door to the drawing room an apparent transgression in the exquisite social practices of Merle and Osmond: she, a lady, is standing; he, a gentleman and the host, is seated. There is only one cultural explanation in the Victorian world: it is the sign of an illicit intimacy so far unsuspected by Isabel, but familiar to the reader—who knows that the two had been lovers and were the parents of Pansy, conveniently presented as Osmond's orphaned daughter. Isabel's "horror" in taking in what she sees marks the beginning of her looking at herself as a "character"—that is, as an American girl whose identity is made of dominant cultural aspirations that prove to be "asymmetrical" once tested within the complex "web of relations" of actual society. By extending the plot function of "recognition"[34] into a process of "knowing again"—or, rather, knowing anew—James fashions for Isabel a "conscience," or a narrative space where asymmetries are questioned and cultural truths are sifted by a pragmatic intelligence bent on identifying a position for one's self. The position achieved is that of a "conscience," yet it is a disconcerted one. On the one hand, there is the discovery that American cultural socialization is working in idealized Europe; on the other, that it is asymmetrical and contradictory, definable neither in terms of class nor in terms of origin, economically driven and culturally dependent, devoted to the new and seeking the old and patriotic, yet dreaming a world elsewhere.

Providing the snob with a conscience means to recognize and defamiliarize "manners" as "the state of that which is cultivated," while at the same time showing the process of "cultivating."[35] There is no end to the process, no resolution. The Jamesian novel is a novel of ambiguity and suspended endings. It adds, however, to the literary tradition an anatomy of the ways culture works in shaping modern characters. The Jamesian "conscience" is a serious "response to snobbery," so much so that it may appear as mining the notion of social snobbishness itself, to make it a possible figure of a moral drama of culture.

The Grandiosity of the Collector

At the very center of this drama, James imagines the figure of the collector as the character who actively turns to "things" to confer nobility to wealth. Collecting, however, may not be the social activity that matches the "good" snob's aspiration to realize the art of life: in *The Portrait of a Lady,* the morbid aesthete, Osmond, is surrounded by the exquisite objects he has passionately acquired; in *The Princess Casamassima* (1886), Christina Light, the poor Euro-American who marries into Italian nobility, theatrically arranges her collection in her drawing room, as does Madame Merle. Each of them shows that their passion for objects is not matched by a passion for knowledge, for the authentic pursuit of "the union of great knowledge and great liberty." Such pursuit, invoked by Isabel in*The Portrait of a Lady,* has indeed been the moving principle for turning wealth into nobility since the early Renaissance, when "spending money on art became itself an outward sign of particular virtues," and nobility was more a matter of ethical "forms of behaviour" rather than of "noble birth, in a society in which, with new money flowing, traditional feudal models were becoming eroded."[36] Collecting may be read as a renewed claim to nobility, suggesting that the collector may prove to be the authentic American claimant, exchanging a claim to aristocracy of birth with that to a full possession of the value of art. A successful claim would prove not only that money can be turned into cultural capital but also that art itself is revalued as (American) culture through the action of money.

In Americanized nineteenth-century Europe, however, the imitation of the claim to nobility of the Renaissance bourgeois may also turn into a shallow quest for the outward signs of status or result in an immoral passion for acquisition, as happens in James's play on collecting, *The Outcry,* which he turned into a novel in 1911. The title refers to the outcry generated in England by the ruthless acquisitions of a rude American millionaire, Breckenridge Bender—probably modeled upon J. P. Morgan.[37] Bender writes huge checks and disregards manners and formalities, and his oxymoronic "voracious integrity" matches his excessive personal ambition and mystifies the value of art. Bent on exchanging money with art, he wants not merely a beautiful picture but "an ideally expensive thing." He does not measure the aesthetic value of an object but rather acquires the evidence of the cultural distinction bestowed by the categories of "art" and the "past." In Bender's case, the appreciation of objects is socially motivated and does not entail a subjective process of recognition, of knowing anew, the real challenge for the collector in the Jamesian world. Bender, as well as Osmond, and even Adam Verver in *The Golden Bowl* are not given an active conscience reflecting their appreciation of art; no analytical detailing of their impressions matches their declaredly passionate pursuits. Such absences signal a gap between object and subject, or the absence of an "articulation of self through the medium of things," which James's kindred spirit Georg Simmel, in his *Philosophy of Money* (1900), saw as the core of the impending "tragedy of culture" of the modern age. Thus, in *The Golden Bowl* the disjunction of self and things is represented through the metaphor of collecting, things and human beings alike. Collecting may be read as both the embodiment of a desire, of an ideal aspiration, and a damning practice obliterating the self and turning art and man into objects of acquisition. In one of the narrator's rare interventions in *The Golden Bowl*, Verver's collecting is thus commented upon:

> Nothing perhaps might affect us as queerer, had we time to look into it, than this application of the same measure of value to such different pieces of property as old Persian carpets, say, and new human acquisitions; all the more indeed that the amiable man was not without an inkling, on his own side, that he was, as a taster of life, economically constructed.[38]

Verver's ideal plan is to house his collection in the "Museum of Museums," to be erected in the symbolic American City beyond the Mississippi, where, for "thirsty millions, the higher, the highest, knowledge would shine out to bless the land." Since a "great collection," as Kenneth Clark wrote, "is never the result of a pure motive, not even pure snobbery,"[39] Verver's noble or snobbish motive is likewise impure: his buying power matches and exceeds his desire to possess. No obstacle is encountered in the process of accumulation, and his "impunity of appropriation" goes unchecked. As Simmel wrote (and James would probably have agreed with him), "Objects are not difficult to acquire because they are valuable, but we call those objects valuable that resist our desire to possess them. Since the desire encounters resistance and frustration, the objects gain a significance that would never be attributed to them by an unchecked will."[40]

The tragic note of Verver's collecting rests on his "unchecked will," his exposure to excess, leading to a grandiose fantasy of power. With the body and the appearance of a petit bourgeois, he harbors an ambition that transcends the reality of his relations to people and things alike. In his case, snobbishness almost reaches the hypertrophy of all its evolutionary categories in a megalomania nourished by the highest models, since he believes himself equal to the great patrons and collectors of the Renaissance, "equal, somehow, with the great seers, the invokers and encouragers of beauty—and he didn't after all perhaps dangle so far below the great producers and creators."[41] In an almost Hollywood-like image of the rise of a new empire in the contemplation of the ruins of the old, a transcendental "affinity of Genius, or at least of Taste, with something in himself" is suddenly revealed to him contemplating Rome, the eternal city, and the grandiosity of the revelation leads him to identify with Homer, Keats, and Cortez, inducing some bewilderment and incredulity on the reader's part, and the suspicion of a certain authorial irony on Verver's oversized pretensions.

In the only extended internal focalization allowed him, Verver's museum plan and its relation to himself, his life and deeds, are told in a language of languages, a summa of the state of Western culture. In the language of the Bible, mundane enterprises are transfigured: the "years of darkness" of moneymaking are followed by "the years of light" of collecting, the museum is likened to an American "house on a rock," whose social and cultural mission is to "release from the bondage of ugliness" his countrymen. Religious culture shapes both personal experience and the project of the "supreme idea": "he had wrought in devious ways but he had reached the place," through "good faith," "patience and piety"—these last echoes from *Pilgrim's Progress*, marking the exemplary progression of the individual in pursuit of "perfection." While the site of "the religion he wished to propagate" is imagined as a compact "Greek temple," standing for "civilisation condensed, concrete, consummate," the actions needed to realize it are linked to mundane deeds, such as war ("polishing and piling up his arms"), calculations, gambling, and the creation of "interests." Both ideal and material semantic fields, however, are deemed organic to nature: the "soil propitious for the flower of the supreme idea," the "warm rich earth" from which the "first sharp tender shoot" struggles "into day." Verver's religion of art and his mission to educate are voiced in the emphatically democratic language of the time (the "thirsty millions"). While Barnum-like advertising language is excluded—"comic matter in large lettering, diurnally 'set up,' printed, published, folded and delivered"—care is taken to dazzle everyone with a great opening "show," aiming at the "rite" effect, or the effect of making sacred the secular, for the museum's "opening exercises."[42]

Cultural imperialism might be the snob's ultimate, grandiose dream; Adam Verver's collecting, however, both draws him into and excludes him from a flawed society, from a "web of relations" of his own making. The plot of the novel starts with an acquisition that is indeed "supreme": Verver acquires for his daughter, Maggie, a husband, a genuine *morceau de musée,* "a rarity, an object of beauty, an object of price," an authentic if impoverished Roman Prince, Amerigo, issuing from a family of ancient nobility to which is dedicated "one of the ampler shrines of the supreme exhibitory temple [the British Museum], an alcove of shelves charged with the gold-and-brown, gold-and-ivory, of old Italian bindings."[43] As a precious item in Verver's collection, the Prince, by a perverse turn of human emotions, stages a sort of rebellion of perfect "things" against their possessors, and menaces the order of the collection by the disorder of passion, committing adultery with Charlotte Stant, the recently acquired wife of Verver and the instrument both for enhancing the collector's "supreme idea" as a patron of the arts and for balancing with his own marriage the symmetry required by his daughter's. The order of the double marriage is disrupted, and reflects on the dialectal tension of the collector's enterprise, on its precarious equilibrium, "between the poles of order and disorder."[44]

The golden bowl symbolizes the dramatic clash between the aspiration to the perfect beauty of art and the difficulty of matching it with the fragile art of living. In the object with the appearance of a "perfect crystal" that Charlotte wishes to give to the bride-to-be, James might have suggested a similarity to a famous mid-fifteenth-century Venetian cup, "The Triumph of Hymen," in the collections of the British Museum, a gilded and ornate example of the triumphal iconography of virtue suited to the magnificent public displays of Renaissance weddings.[45] Only Amerigo, authentic as he is, recognizes the cup as flawed, preventing Charlotte from buying it; it is, however, later acquired by Maggie as a gift for her father's birthday. As a critical presence in Maggie's household: "The golden bowl put on, under consideration, a sturdy, a conscious perversity; as a 'document,' somehow, it was ugly, though it might have a decorative grace." The ugliness is not intrinsic to the bowl but to its spatial and symbolic connection to the function of collecting and its subjective outcome, Maggie's marriage. As a *trouvaille,* sold in a dingy shop by an ambiguous trader, it documents the reference to a higher form of past art and social order (the Renaissance cup), and though it retains some "decorative grace," it is metaphorically humanized by a "conscious perversity," embodying the ugliness of the process that turns every thing, and every human being, into a collectible. If the objectification of the Prince and of Charlotte is the work of Verver's "unchecked will," the bowl itself perversely embodies both his aspiration to nobility, though in a lesser form, and his tragic disjunction from the reality of relations.

His daughter, to whose consciousness James resorts to compose the drama in an ambiguous "happy ending," will shatter the fatal cup, and, the bowl in fragments, Verver's collecting comes to an end. His collection is packed in a multitude of crates, and he and his adulterous wife leave Europe for American City. All-understanding Maggie, waiting in her richly decorated drawing-room for the "august emergence" of her father and his wife, a "royal couple" on their last visit, unexpectedly and emphatically says to the Prince: "We are distinctly *bourgeois*!" The oddity of Princess Maggie's self-definition fades if bourgeois and snob are considered synonyms: the *sine nobilitate* of the old bourgeoisie may in the end become a value in itself, the goal of a moral quest, provided that the exchange of roles between aristocrat and bourgeois successfully proves the latter superior in the practice of virtuous nobility of character, or of conscience. Still, the American snob enhances, in the figure of the collector, the drama of the culture of modernity. As Walter Benjamin argued, collecting carries with it the obsession of possessing history—an impossible mission, as evidenced by the fragmentary nature of the objects collected. The fractured bowl in James's novel may suggest that such fragmentation is in tension with Verver's megalomania; his titanism is not different from the American romantic hero, Melville's Ahab, his goal being not to sound the metaphysical ocean waters but to possess the whole of Western civilization. As a "document" of his endeavor, the foundation of the Museum of Museums proves both the grandiosity and the "perversity" of the aspiration.

The end-of-century rise of the middle classes and the social massification of culture are both resisted and supported by the Jamesian elitist; in his Euro-America, however, the snob acquires for himself the high task of claiming an "art of life" that is both philanthropically oriented and aristocratically distant from the masses. It would be reductive to consider James's representation of this national type as unproblematic. His American snobs may have become both socially and culturally prominent, and as individuals they may aspire to match their "pride of status" with a "pride of function," either through the seriousness of their consciousness's work or through civilizing reform such as Verver's museum; their personal destiny, however, remains ambiguous: the original sin of imitation or the obsession with possessing linger on, as they do for Maggie, who apparently is the bourgeois winner in the competition with the Italian prince, and seem to possess him completely at the end, yet she cannot look her husband in the eyes "for pity and dread of them." This last sentence of *The Golden Bowl* echoes another at the beginning of the novel, when she said to her husband-to-be, "You are at any rate part of his collection . . . one of the things that can only be got over here."[46] It would also be reductive to consider James's representation of the American as a full-fledged imperial subject. Nonetheless, his type enters the domain of Western fiction as a novelty, neither the man of the wilderness (the transcendental nature man) nor the all-encompassing democratic Whitmanian self but rather a distinctively turn-of-the century character, showing that the new man, the American, replays the historical making of the European bourgeoisie, or of a bourgeois social identity shaped in between the aristocracy and the people.

It was perhaps the intrinsic hybridism of snobbery that appealed to James, who, as a young man had written to his friend Perry:

> We young Americans are (without cant) men of the future. . . . We are American born—*il faut en prendre son parti*. I look upon it as a great blessing. . . . We are ahead of the European races in the fact that . . . we can deal freely with civilizations not our own, can pick and choose and assimilate and in short (aesthetically etc.) claim our property wherever we find it.[47]

At this early stage, James thought young Americans like himself could possibly become the "heirs of all ages," appropriating an appellation common in the discourse of social evolutionism. The claim to become the heir of all ages can easily be suspected of falsity, of an excess of confidence and self-importance, were it not—as he wrote in 1907 in the Preface to *The Wings of the Dove*—for the "supremely touching value" of such condition in a culture nourished by transcendental idealism and the belief in democratic social mobility. James's American faces the dramatic, modern destiny of a peculiar brand of snobbishness, embodying the suspension of the meaning of class, yet desiring to shape it anew, forging the identity of a non-aristocratic elitist and of a democrat alienated from the masses.

This is for James a "perilous part to play out"; it provides the ground for the moral drama of his American, whose distinction, however, happens to become identified with the cultural project of turning class hybridism into a universalizing example. James's "snob" fosters a notion of the ideal bourgeois as a subject always in the making, both the heir to European class distinctions and the proponent of a classless ideology. This character's universalizing social function rests on the strength of an energy generated by the desire of imitation. Such desire has been evolving into different forms of snobbery, high and low, or into different forms of bourgeois living, epitomized, by the omnipresent, interclass desire for status and its display. If we are all snobs, then we are all bourgeois.

Notes

1. Pierre Carlet de Chamberlain de Marivaux, "Lettres sur les habitants de Paris," in *Journaux et oevres diverses* (Paris: Garnier, 1969), 14. ["The bourgeois in Paris, madame, is a mixed animal, partaking of the gentleman and of the people. When he has noble manners he is almost always a monkey: when he is low, he is natural; therefore he is noble by imitation, and people by character." My translation.]
2. See Eric Hobsbawm, *The Age of Empire:1875–1914* (New York: Pantheon Books, 1987).
3. Pierre Bourdieu, *Distinction: A Social Critique of the Judgement of Taste* (Cambridge, MA: Harvard University Press, 1984), 2. Bourdieu's discussion of the cultural capital to be acquired in order to achieve signs of distinction may be read in the context of this essay as the practice of the bourgeois self-fashioning himself or herself as a snob. Such practice finally sustains the desire for "status" of the middle class, or is instrumental in "democratizing desire," in the cultural transition of the late nineteenth century toward a more universal claim to "equality of desire," as William Leach suggests in *Land of Desire* (New York: Vintage Books, 1994), 6.
4. For Joseph Epstein, American snobbery is a nineteenth-century invention, flourishing in a democratic environment because of its characteristic culture of social mobility and classlessness; see *Snobbery, the American Version* (Boston: Houghton Mifflin, 2002).
5. See Thorstein Veblen, *The Theory of the Leisure Class*, with an introduction by C. Wright Mills (New Brunswick, NJ: Transaction Publishers, 1992); Vance Packard, *The Status Seekers* (New York: D. McKay, 1959); and Paul Fussell, *Class: A Guide to the American Status System* (New York: Summit Books, 1983).
6. Gertrude Atherton, "Why Is American Literature Bourgeois?" *North American Review* 175 (May 1904): 770–81.
7. George Monteiro, ed., *The Correspondence of Henry James and Henry Adams* (Baton Rouge: Louisiana State University Press, 1992), 60, 62. Adams quotes the first line of Friederich Schiller's poem, "Resignation" [even I was in Arcadia born], suggesting that he shares the German poet's sentiment of exclusion from life's earlier hopes.
8. Erich Auerbach, *Mimesis: The Representation of Reality in Western Literature* (Princeton, NJ: Princeton University Press, 1968), 477, 480.
9. *Literary Criticism: Essays on Literature; American Writers and English Writers* (New York: The Library of America, 1984), 1155.
10. Within the never-ending debate on literature and history, see Carlo Ginzburg, *Il filo e le tracce: Vero, falso, finto* (Milan: Feltrinelli, 2006); and Gary Samuel Morson, ed., *Literature and History: Theoretical Problems and Russian Case Studies* (Stanford: Stanford University Press, 1986).

11. William M. Thackeray, *The Book of Snobs* (Boston: Ester & Lauriat, 1891), 186.
12. In the United States, gentility was a major preoccupation for the "new urban upper class composed of both established families and those of new wealth, eager to acquire cultural capital and to set themselves off as a quasi aristocracy from those below" (John Kasson, *Rudeness and Civility: Manners in Nineteenth Century Urban America* [New York: Hill & Wang, 1990], 36).
13. Lionel Trilling, *The Moral Obligation to Be Intelligent: Selected Essays*, ed. Leon Wieseltier (New York: Farrar, Straus, Giroux, 2000), 112.
14. Ibid., 109–10.
15. For the importance of manners in American fiction, see Susan Goodman, *Civil Wars: American Novelists and Manner, 1880–1940* (Baltimore: Johns Hopkins University Press, 2003). Debating Trilling's essay, Goodman writes: "It should be self-evident that any perceived lack of manners has only served to feed interest in the topic. The drama or the *donnée* of the American novel of manners lay in *not* knowing one's place" (10).
16. L. B. Walford, "The Novel of Manners," in *On the Art of Writing Fiction* (London: Wells Gardner, Darton, 1894), 31.
17. Nathaniel Hawthorne, *The American Claimant Manuscripts* (Columbus: Ohio State University Press, 1977), 12:309.
18. Ibid., 221.
19. Henry James, "A Passionate Pilgrim," in *A Passionate Pilgrim and Other Tales* (Boston: Houghton Mifflin, 1903), 35.
20. Henry James, preface to *New York Edition,* 13:xix.
21. James, "Passionate Pilgrim," 28.
22. Henry James, *The American* (1877; New York: Norton, 1978), 32
23. For the growing turn-of-the century debate on the meaning of gentility in America, see David Castronovo, *The American Gentleman: Social Prestige and the Modern Literary Mind* (New York: Continuum, 1991).
24. For Alex Zwerdling, James's international fictions should be seen as "ethnographic" novels describing European and American manners for the education of a new Euro-American readership; see *Improvised Europeans: American Literary Expatriates and the Siege of London* (New York: Basic Books, 1998).
25. Thomas Sergeant Perry, *The Evolution of the Snob* (Boston: Ticknor, 1887), 184.
26. The semantic transition in the meaning of snobbery from "an object of imitative disdain into a paragon of arrogant distinction" is for Sean Latham the pervasive trait of modernist aesthetics; see *"Am I a Snob?" Modernism and the Novel* (Ithaca, NY: Cornell University Press, 2003), 13.
27. Ralph Adams Cram, *The Gothic Quest* (New York: The Baker and Taylor Company, 1907), 30.
28. James, *The American,* 199.
29. Ibid., 105
30. Ibid., 35.
31. See Latham, *Am I a Snob?* 19.
32. Henry James, *The Portrait of a Lady* (1881; New York Edition, 1908), 2:198.
33. Shklar, *Ordinary Vices,* 114.
34. "In James's fiction, manners work by inference, construction and divination to advance the plot. His best scenes of recognition emerge from point of manners" (Goodman, *Civil Wars,* 52).
35. Bourdieu, *Distinction,* 11.
36. Luke Syson and Dora Thornton, *Objects of Virtue: Art in Renaissance Italy* (Los Angeles: The J. Paul Getty Museum, 2001), 23.
37. See Jean Strouse, *Morgan, American Financer* (New York: Random House, 1999), 652–55.
38. Henry James, *The Golden Bowl* (1904; New York Edition, 1909), 1:196.
39. Kenneth Clark, Introduction to *Great Private Collections*, ed. Douglas Cooper (New York: Macmillan, 1963), 17.
40. Georg Simmel, *The Philosophy of Money* (London: Routledge, 1978), 67.
41. James, *Golden Bowl,* 1:141.
42. Ibid., 1:145–46.
43. Ibid., 2:147.

44. See Walter Benjamin, "Unpacking My Library," in *Illuminations* (New York: Schocken Books, 1969), 59–67.
45. Syson and Thornton, *Objects of Virtue,* 66.
46. James, *Golden Bowl,* 1:12.
47. Henry James to Thomas Sergeant Perry, in *The Letters of Henry James,* ed. Leon Edel (Cambridge, MA: Harvard University Press, 1984), 1:77.

4

Patina and Persistence: Miniature Patronage and Production in Antebellum Philadelphia

Anne Verplanck

In nineteenth-century America, men and women commissioned portraits to foster family memory and, occasionally, for institutional or political purposes. These images reminded the viewer of a particular individual and often captured the sitter at a specific point in his or her life cycle or career. Portrait consumption was part of Americans' growing desire to acquire things, as well as a step in crafting an individual's identity. In antebellum Philadelphia, many bourgeois chose portrait miniatures (watercolor images on ivory), a form that had largely waned in popularity. In previous decades, miniature portrait consumption had primarily been the purview of those with inherited wealth and position. Established bourgeois Philadelphians continued to choose miniatures, a mode of representation that symbolized their taste, sense of feeling, tradition, and refinement. Through the acts of commissioning, exchanging, and viewing miniatures, an art form with historical associations, new sectors of the bourgeois population helped stake their claims within the city's social and cultural spheres.

The growth in popularity of miniatures, which swelled between 1790 and 1810 in cities along the eastern seaboard, followed a similar demand abroad. Trends toward close familial relationships, privatization, and intimacy may have contributed to the desire for personal, intimate portrait forms that expressed both feeling and taste.[1] Yet miniatures were only one of several types of portraits available to Philadelphians in the nineteenth century. Between 1820 and 1860, numerous painters of portraits in oil, including Thomas Sully, John Neagle, Bass Otis, Henry Inman, and Jacob Eichholtz, flourished in the city and its environs. In 1839, Philadelphians quickly took up daguerreotypes and the medium had crucial effects on painted forms of portraiture, just as painting affected photographic images.[2] Scholarship on portrait miniatures and daguerreotypes acknowledges the juncture of these two modes, noting their similar size and, for a time, housings.[3] However, the extent to which miniatures persisted in the presence of the daguerreotype—and the reasons why—invite elucidation. By examining the demand for and use of miniatures well after their peak, we can begin to see how different sectors of Philadelphia's bourgeois population chose to represent themselves to those closest to them and, through this analysis, better understand the modes of group delineation and cohesion in antebellum America.

For Philadelphia, the period from 1820 to 1860 was a time when many individuals of established wealth looked backward to what they perceived to have been better times, when economic and political power was more firmly in their hands.[4] Philadelphians went to great lengths to commemorate the colonial past, marking Lafayette's

Figure 4.1 John Henry Brown, *Edward Coles*. Watercolor on ivory, 1852. Courtesy Winterthur Museum, Gift of Marie Robbins Barlow, Mary Robbins Lemon, and Edward J. Robbins in memory of Oliver W. Robbins, 2001.43.1

visit with much fanfare and founding the Historical Society of Pennsylvania in 1824; and encouraging the city's purchase of colonial and early national portraits from Peale's Museum in 1854. From the 1840s to the 1860s, Philadelphians—particularly bourgeois Philadelphians—deeply inscribed their fascination with the past into the written record, the photographic record, and the cultural landscape.[5] Their interest in the past extended to choices in self-representation. Many of the city's bourgeoisie chose to be portrayed in a medium that connected them to Philadelphia's broadly construed mythic past (fig. 4.1).[6]

Why did people continue to spend large amounts of money on miniature likenesses, when they could obtain a less expensive, more precise rendering from a daguerreotype?[7] Who were the sitters who preferred miniatures to daguerreotypes? Did longevity of wealth or residence in Philadelphia affect patronage? Why was it important to these sitters to be portrayed in miniatures? The miniature persisted as a portrait form in part because it allowed both established and new sectors of Philadelphia's non-Quaker upper class to demonstrate their taste for patinaed goods within their immediate social and kinship groups and for future generations.[8]

Antebellum Philadelphians' production and consumption of portrait miniatures was closely linked to the traditional uses of these images and to the additional meanings that could be assigned to them. Often as expensive as small oil portraits, miniatures were generally painted in watercolors on ivory, a more precious and costly material than paper, canvas, or board.[9] Patrons chose how they wanted their miniatures presented: in bracelets, brass or gold lockets, wooden frames, or leather cases (fig. 4.2).

Historically, most miniatures were made to be worn next to the body; their placement, as well as their form and materials, suggests the physical and emotional closeness among the sitter, the wearer, and the viewer.

Miniatures allowed the giver and the recipient to express feeling and to partake in luxury with those who shared such cultural preferences, for patrons of miniatures chose to spend a large amount of money on a form of portraiture that only a small, select audience would see.[10] To receive a miniature from its subject through a ritual of gift or exchange endowed the item with a private meaning that was heightened if the miniature also enclosed such a personal token as an inscription, initials, or a lock of hair. The long European lineage of the form, with its connections to royalty and, later, the gentry, further imbued miniatures and their users with centuries-old associations of wealth, taste, and power.

The nature of Philadelphians' demand for miniatures did not solely lie in artists' ability to provide costly possessions or patrons' desire to improve their status through the display of such goods. Nor did individuals' desire to mark relationships or rites of passage fully account for the patronage of miniatures.[11] The visual appeal—indeed, the recognizability—of individual artist's work contributed to bourgeois Philadelphians' demand for miniatures.[12] By choosing a private art form, miniature patrons could represent themselves to their immediate kinship and social groups. These viewers would recognize and fully grasp the meaning of these images, as well as the significance of being allowed to see such luxurious, private objects.

Fundamental differences between miniatures and daguerreotypes affected Philadelphians' choices and uses of these media: miniatures were more expensive, highly colored, and available in a different venue: the artist's studio. A midsize (about 4¼-by-3½ inches) daguerreotype, with the largest amount of hand coloring, cost from $3 to $6 in 1855.[13] At the same time, most of the miniatures by John Henry Brown (1818–1891) ranged in price from $100 to $250, with price largely depending upon size (fig. 4.1). A miniature's cost, whether compared to a daguerreotype or to a less expensive miniature, may have increased its desirability.[14] Even though bourgeois non-Quaker Philadelphians were intrigued by the invention of the daguerreotype—and indeed, some had these portraits taken—photographic images did not fully meet their needs for portrayal during the 1840s and 1850s.

A broad group of the bourgeoisie chose to be represented and remembered in the same way. Mercantile fortunes, past and present, predominated among Philadelphians who sat for miniatures; only a few families who derived their wealth from industrial pursuits were interested in this art form. Lawyers, physicians, and university and military officials are well represented among sitters, as are local, state, and national political figures. In addition to area residents, Philadelphia artists drew

Figure 4.2 Benjamin Trott, *Benjamin Chew Wilcocks.* Watercolor on ivory, ca. 1800–10. Courtesy Winterthur Museum, 1955.92

patrons from other locales, particularly more southern ones. These patrons of miniatures chose a historical mode of representation that allowed both they and future generations to tie themselves to a sitter and, by extension, to his or her past in a similar way.

Anthropologist Grant McCracken connects patina with old, inherited goods that can signify long-standing status, noting that in Elizabethan households "newness was the mark of commonness while the patina of use was a sign and guarantee of standing."[15] McCracken's analysis can be extended to include goods with aged *associations*. In many respects, antebellum miniatures looked like those from the eighteenth and early nineteenth century (fig. 4.2); the sitter, patron, and viewer could easily associate themselves with earlier men and women who commissioned, sat for, and viewed miniatures. The high cost and time commitment further added to miniatures' preciousness; they were intended to survive and to be treasured for future generations, creating or extending the history of a family line.[16] Through the longevity of the form and its associations with taste, refinement, and sensibility, miniatures, even when new, had the patina of age.

The reasons why there was a sustained demand for the miniature form in Philadelphia and why, despite its aura of beauty and its associations with wealth and lineage, the miniature was superseded by the photograph in the 1860s are connected to several artists' ability to meet and shape patrons' changing demands. John Henry Brown's well-documented production and patronage between 1839 and the 1860s demonstrates new and established bourgeois taste for patinaed goods. The range of his patronage, his own remarks about the changing demand for his work over time, and reviewers' comments provide evidence of his ability to meet and shape bourgeois needs.[17] Whether painted directly from daguerreotypes or not, the miniatures by Brown and other artists incorporated many attributes of the new medium. For hundreds of patrons, several artists produced miniatures that simultaneously looked forward and backward, partially adopting new technologies while retaining established modes of marking relationships.

Production and Patronage of Miniatures, 1839–64

Why did miniatures endure in an important center for daguerreotypy, and how did the two media affect each other? In Philadelphia, there is limited evidence of miniaturists becoming daguerreotypists. Instead, other individuals opened daguerreian galleries, where location, price, and quality determined their clientele.[18] John Henry Brown sent sitters to several of the higher-end galleries for the daguerreotypes (positive images on silvered copper supports) and, later, ambrotypes (negative images on glass supports, available after 1854), from which he worked. Beginning in the 1860s, he produced his own opalotypes (albumen photographic images on opaque white glass) and other photographic images (fig. 4.4).[19]

Brown's remarks, as well as the newspaper clippings that he included in his combined account book and diary, make it clear that he was keenly aware of photographic practices and participated in the ongoing dialogue about the merits of "art" versus those of photographic media. Occasionally—as when he noted, "I had daguerreotypes taken of the children, I cannot afford the time to paint them and therefore must content myself, like other poor people, with daguerres"—Brown drew a distinction between the class of miniature patrons and that of daguerreotype sitters.[20] Philadelphia's bourgeoisie were interested in daguerreotypes, although, with the exception of Quakers, they did not widely embrace these images. Quakers were drawn to daguerreotypes after 1839 for many of the same reasons that had attracted them to silhouettes earlier in the century: they perceived these images as accurate ones that required relatively little intervention on the part of the artist.[21]

Daguerreotypes were a black-and-white form, with gradations of gray, that could have color added for a price. In Philadelphia, this coloration generally consisted of sparingly applied pale pink, translucent washes on sitters' cheeks, which presented markedly different visual qualities from the bright, varied colors of miniatures. After noting the advantages of daguerreotypes as "studies and as aids to the memory"—with the result that "better artists have found their work in greater demand, as they have been able to impart to them higher excellence"—a reviewer described one of Brown's miniatures: "It was painted entirely from a daguerreotype, and from recollection, yet the truth of representation is startling, and infinitely superior to any daguerreotype, as, indeed, good painting always is and must be. The hand of an artist is guided by his mind—by his thought and feeling—and if this be true, they communicate to his work the character, the real meaning of the original, with far more force than can be obtained by mere mechanical accuracy."[22] Many perceived miniatures as artistic, while daguerreotypes were viewed as mechanical. Thus, the artist's role in creating a miniature, the medium, the price, and the materials used all made it a more distinctive commodity for bourgeois consumption. Antebellum miniatures had all the virtues of older ones, including a smooth, expensive, ivory surface. Miniatures took more time, necessitated appointments, required more negotiation between the sitter and the artist, and more likely came with a peer's recommendation.

Miniatures produced after the advent of the daguerreotype often bear a more precise rendering of features and details than those produced before 1839; the later works also differed in terms of format and the use of color. A greater accuracy in proportions and less stylization further contributed to an old form with a different look. Whether Brown painted sitters partly or entirely from life, his miniatures incorporated, to varying degrees, daguerreotypic attributes, and this contributed to the appeal of his work.[23] By taking a traditional form and modifying it, he allowed his patrons to make reference to the past using a contemporary format.

The Demand for Antebellum Miniatures

During the 1840s and '50s there was a strong demand for Brown's miniatures.[24] He generally completed from 20 to 30 miniatures per year, primarily of Philadelphians.[25] By the mid-1840s, Brown regularly painted sitters in part or in full from daguerreotypes; he also employed daguerreotypes to paint miniatures of deceased men and women. The demand for his work makes it clear that he was fulfilling a need for his patrons.

Through political connections, exhibitions at the Pennsylvania Academy of the Fine Arts and the Artists Fund Society, and extensive kinship networks of sitters, Brown attracted a broader range of patrons than previous miniaturists in Philadelphia.[26] A cross-section of Philadelphia's bourgeoisie and the upper end of the middle-income population went to Brown.[27] The balance between patrons of new and established wealth, and the types of likenesses they preferred, did not change over time. Like the sitters for earlier miniatures by artists such as Benjamin Trott (ca. 1770–1843) and Anna Claypoole Peale (1791–1878), many of Brown's patrons had ties to those who had social, economic, and political power in eighteenth-century Philadelphia.[28] The history of the bourgeoisie and their past consumption of miniatures affected the demand for and use of the form in antebellum Philadelphia.

In Philadelphia, the years immediately surrounding the American Revolution were marked by the rise of many non-Quakers whose political and economic interests and, sometimes, military participation, were intertwined; Quaker political hegemony declined during the period.[29] Revolutionary officers such as Arthur St. Clair and Anthony Butler often received commissions because of political or economic status. Through their participation in the Continental Congresses, the Revolution, or the early federal government, men such as Nathaniel Greene, George Clymer, and Robert Morris established or expanded their wealth. For these and other members of the city's non-Quaker bourgeoisie, the late eighteenth century was a period of relative cohesion on myriad economic and political issues, such as a strong central government, that affected their wealth.[30]

One of the ways these individuals memorialized themselves and their roles in the founding of the nation was through miniature portrait commissions. Men like St. Clair, Greene, and Butler went to the same artist, Charles Willson Peale (1741–1827), who portrayed by them in a similar manner and frequently in their military uniforms (well past the end of the American Revolution). The commissioning, exchanging, and viewing of images that embodied the roles of these men in the public and private worlds of the Revolutionary era reinforced their place in the nation's history. In addition to Revolutionary War participation, networks of kinship, business, and friendship connect Peale's sitters. Miniatures and the attendant behavior of gift, exchange, hiding, and revealing reinforced individual's positions with respect to one another, within their family, and in association with a select group who made comparable choices or recognized the significance of such choices. For Peale's sitters, his miniatures served as indicators of shared circumstances and ideals.[31]

Philadelphia's bourgeois communities further evolved with the arrival of the federal government in 1790. The two central portions of the upper strata of the population—newcomers with government associations and established local families—moved in independent but overlapping economic, political, and social spheres. Divided over such political issues as the French Revolution and the power of America's federal government, many nonetheless had in common a social sphere. Those affiliated with the national government dominated Philadelphia's social world, and wealth—new or established—became the central criterion for social inclusion at the highest levels. During this period, Republicans and Federalists chose similar possessions, whether furnishings or portraits.[32]

In the late eighteenth and early nineteenth centuries, the city's upper class was not a unified group but rather made up of many subunits that combined, broke apart, and recombined in response to a range of interconnected economic, social, political, and religious conditions. Historian Thomas Doerflinger has characterized Philadelphia's bourgeoisie during this period as being composed of intersecting circles of the independently wealthy, merchants, and those who derived their income from rents and loans.[33] After 1800, Philadelphia was no longer the seat of either the state or the federal government. Despite such exceptions as Nicholas Biddle, the descendants of the families who had once grasped the social, political, and economic reins in Philadelphia largely were left with only social power.[34] Cultural, benevolent, and voluntary associations such as the Pennsylvania Academy of the Fine Arts, the Library Company of Philadelphia, and the Pennsylvania Hospital became a significant focus for the upper strata during the early decades of the nineteenth century.[35] Some men and women sought to maintain their hegemony and authority through these extragovernmental means.

Members of the city's established mercantile bourgeois emphasized their (perceived) distinction through their small-scale portrait choices. In the early 1800s, numerous members of the city's established mercantile bourgeois, including Nicholas Biddle, Benjamin Chew Wilcocks, and Thomas White, had their miniatures painted by Benjamin Trott (fig. 4.2). Extended networks of business, kinship, and friendship characterize Trott's patronage even more strongly than that of Charles Willson Peale. Patronage by distinct groups also suggests that the possession and recognition of images of those of comparable position led to another use—that of binding like people together—and contributed the demand for these portraits. At a time of political and economic displacement, members of Philadelphia's established mercantile bourgeois wanted to be portrayed in a manner that could leave little doubt as to their shared high social status. The unusual degree of similarity among Trott's miniatures appears to be related to the desire of a discrete sector of Philadelphia's bourgeois to draw together between the late 1790s and 1820.[36]

By the antebellum years, there was a long tradition of bourgeois involvement in—even retreat to—cultural spheres. Bourgeois behavior during the 1840s and '50s is inflected by industrial development, including a growing antagonism between the industrial and commercial bourgeoisie in Philadelphia. Daniel Greenstein argues that "the balance of political power in the city was soon tipped in favor of an emerging industrialist class when industrialists entered into alliances with a new breed of professional party politicians who were able to win electoral support in the different working-class communities throughout the city."[37] Rapid political and economic transformation had a significant effect on social and cultural life. Historian Elizabeth Geffen has observed that "many of the new industrial and financial leaders and successful speculators in real estate were admitted to the upper social stratum in the 1840s and '50s," but notes that their reception was often mixed.[38] What permitted the social inclusion of some but not others? A statement in an 1846 compilation of wealthy Philadelphia citizens may provide part of the answer: "In England, and in some parts of this country, all the rich men are aristocrats; not so, however, in Philadelphia; most of our wealthy citizens are plain men, and although they pride themselves for having made their own money, live in a plain way, and do not spend their entire income."[39] In a city that had largely shed its Quaker beliefs and practices, but not its image, living "in a plain way" was perhaps a key to social and cultural acceptance.[40]

During the changes that accompanied the city's evolution from a commercial to an industrial center, some Philadelphians also used certain cultural products to foster or reinforce social relationships. Longevity of wealth—or former wealth—was all that remained for some bourgeois; it, and the acquisition and use of certain cultural products associated with wealth and taste, became a form of distinction. For those who had acquired their fortunes during the eighteenth century, such private, traditional activities as exchanging and viewing miniatures by specific artists within very circumscribed kinship and social circles further reinforced the differences among themselves: those of more recent wealth and those without wealth. For those of newer wealth, patronage of an art form with aristocratic ties had the capacity to bolster self- and family identity.

A broadening group of patrons sought a traditional art form that had decades-long associations with wealth, refinement, and taste in Philadelphia, and carried centuries-old connotations of lineage and authority. In the 1840s and '50s, Brown's patrons included extended networks of members of the Biddle, Hopkinson, and Willing families, as well as many other established bourgeois families whose wealth was primarily obtained from mercantile pursuits.[41] Patrons of newer mercantile wealth, such as the Kitchen, Bailey, and Bohlen families, commissioned images of multiple family members over many years.[42] Although the fortunes of most antebellum sitters were derived from mercantile activities, some were founded on manufacturing wealth.[43] Lawyers and military figures were among Brown's patrons from the professional classes.[44] Despite the range of sources and longevity of wealth among sitters, neither patterns of patronage nor the prices charged for his work were related to longevity of residence or wealth. At a moment when the age of wealth had become an important marker of distinction, so, too, had the choice of a miniature as a portrait form.[45]

Brown painted politicians and statesmen, including Abraham Lincoln, James Buchanan, and Henry Muhlenberg, as well as Philadelphia's mayor, Alexander Henry.[46] Over the course of his long career, he produced eleven miniatures and opalotypes of members of the family of former Illinois Governor Edward Coles (Winterthur Museum), who resided in Philadelphia (figs. 4.1, 4.3 , 4.4). Brown was not the only artist who produced miniatures of Philadelphia politicians: Robert Taylor Conrad (1818–58, New-York Historical Society, ca. 1845–50), who was elected mayor in 1854, was painted by James Passmore Smith (1803–88).[47] Attorney Jonas Altamont Phillips (1806–62) had his miniature painted by Hugh Bridport (1794–1870).[48] Other representatives of the city's growing professional ranks include Dr. and Mrs. Paul, painted by Brown in 1854.[49] Miniatures appealed to a broadening group of Philadelphians who had the wealth as well as the desire to commission this private, expensive form of portrait.

Kinship ties clearly link many patrons, suggesting that satisfied sitters recommended Brown and his miniatures had a particular appeal for varied segments of Philadelphia's bourgeois population. In addition to the Willing, Hopkinson, and Biddle families noted above, several other extended families patronized Brown. He created miniatures and opalotypes of Philadelphia Mayor Ellis Lewis and three members of his family (Atwater Kent Museum, Historical Society of Pennsylvania Collection; hereafter, Atwater Kent Museum, HSP Collection). These associations among sitters reveal that Brown relied on a time-honored method of receiving commissions: the "strong and particular recommendations" that Benjamin Trott had remarked upon near the end of his career in 1839.[50] The sitter's choice artist and the *medium* of the miniature were both important. A reviewer noted in 1858, "Many families of this city possess works of his, which, independent of artistic excellence, are, in the eyes of affection, of priceless value. We have been led to allude to them chiefly for the purpose of art, in that department which, if not the highest, is most intimately connected with our sympathies and feelings."[51] Going to the same artist and commissioning a similar portrait, one that embodied modern and historic allusions to sentiment and feelings (especially, as we shall see, those related to mourning), helped those of new and established wealth, of mercantile and industrial fortunes, separate themselves from an emerging middle class.

The process and setting for creating a miniature made it a more rarified, costly, and time-consuming experience than having a daguerreotype taken. After visiting Brown, one needed to enter one of the better daguerreian galleries and then return to the artist's studio for sittings. Brown often spent 11 to 13 days painting the miniature, with and without the sitter present.[52] A few sitters, not entirely satisfied with their miniatures, returned to have them modified.[53] Thus, while having a miniature painted often involved going to a daguerreian gallery, having a miniature painted was a distinctive experience and produced a markedly different result.[54] Creating a miniature involved artistry, mimesis, and—as the reworking of some of Brown's miniatures shows—an element of control by the sitter. Regardless of its photographic qualities, it was handmade.

Many antebellum Philadelphians enhanced their choice of a conservative art form by having their miniatures housed in traditional settings that contributed to their appearance as distinctive, patinaed forms. A significant number of Philadelphia miniatures are oval and not appreciably larger than their counterparts from the 1820s. The lockets of some of Brown's miniatures from the 1840s, such as *Ellis Lewis,* adhere to the earlier custom of providing a space on the verso to hold a lock of hair.[55] Other sitters had their oval portraits housed in rectangular cases or open frames (figs. 4.1, 4.3). Some of the miniatures Brown created in the 1840s were intended to be worn on bracelets, a practice that was largely discontinued after the 1780s.[56] Moreover, Brown's remark that he "had the occasion to go to my case maker to order work,"[57] indicates that there may have been a custom element to the housing of some of his work. Whether their own ancestors were portrayed in miniatures with similar settings or not, Brown's—and other artists'—patrons referred to these earlier traditions through their commissions.

Brown's miniatures have both shared and separate characteristics with the aesthetic attributes of earlier miniatures. A comparison of the degree of finish, the amount and rendering of detail, the use of contrast among elements, the sitter's pose, and the position of the sitter in relation to the picture plane in his extant portraits reveals that Brown's work did not simply embody more daguerreotypic attributes over time but varied according to sitters' desires. Former Illinois Governor and Philadelphia resident Edward Coles (fig. 4.1) is shown in a stiff half-length pose that presents his face at a three-quarter angle to the viewer—elements related to photographic portraiture.[58] His pose and the prominent lines on his face suggest a strong influence of daguerreotypic aesthetics that may have been the product of time, the sitter's preferences, and, perhaps, the circumstance of the miniature being produced from a daguerreotype. Yet many qualities could be achieved only with paint. Coles's face is richly colored, and the many gradations of black in his vest emphasize the play of light on its folds.

The artist's miniatures of women from the 1840s and '50s also show diversity in their modes of depiction. Brown painted Sally Roberts Coles twice, in 1853 and 1855 (fig. 4.3); these and other miniatures demonstrate that there was a range of aesthetics and conventions desired by sitters and produced by Brown, rather than a simple trajectory of increasing frontality and exactness over time.[59] Coles's portrait of 1853 is highly colored: the rich texture of her black dress is in sharp contrast to her multicolored shawl, and her white collar sets her face apart from the green background. Her facial features in both portraits are delineated with seeming precision, as are the facial features in Brown's other portraits of women.[60]

Brown's images from this period show a wide range of flesh tones, individuated facial features, and hair rendered with precision and a high degree of finish. His *Sally Coles* of 1855 (fig. 4.3) is also presented in a three-quarter pose, with a nearly frontal head. Proportion in this and other works became more accurate over time, likely reflecting the influence of photographic images. One rarely sees examples of exaggerated, elongated necks such as in the earlier portrait of Benjamin Chew Wilcocks (fig. 4.2); the sloping of shoulders in Brown's miniatures also shows a true range of poses rather than the stylized examples from decades before. The details of Coles's clothing, down to the pleats and tucks in her dress, are carefully rendered. If one measures daguerreotypic attributes in portraits in terms of the subject's relative position on the picture plane, degree of frontality, and precision of features of the face and clothing, Coles's portrait, the latest in date of the miniatures discussed, incorporates no more daguerreotypic qualities than do earlier miniatures by Brown.[61]

In an instance in which Brown probably painted exclusively from a daguerreotype, the portrait of Mrs. John Willis Ellis (1846; Smithsonian American Art Museum), his work embodies more daguerreotypic conventions.[62] The image suggests that Brown's miniatures that were taken directly and solely from daguerreotypes incorporate the latter medium's qualities to a greater degree than do his portraits painted from life or partially from a daguerreotype. Although the need to streamline the production of miniatures and his decision to portray deceased sitters partially explain why Brown employed daguerreotypes, aesthetic choices also dictated his use of photographic images. Brown noted in 1861 that he "went to see Mrs. Waln, an old lady, whose picture I was engaged to paint, but could not see her. Disappointment follows disappointment. As she is not able to leave her House, to have a Daguerre taken I must lose this picture."[63] His remark reveals that, either for his purposes or to meet the

Figure 4.3 John Henry Brown, *Mrs. Edward Coles Sr. (Sally Logan Roberts)*. Watercolor on ivory, 1855. Courtesy Winterthur Museum, Gift of Marie Robbins Barlow, Mary Robbins Lemon, and Edward J. Robbins in memory of Oliver W. Robbins, 2001.43.2

patron's desires, it was necessary by this time that he work from a daguerreotype. Brown's oeuvre from this period demonstrates that the incorporation of daguerreotypic attributes in miniatures, along with what might be called a normalization of daguerreotypes that put them more in line with other types of portraits, made people accustomed to photographic representation.[64]

Daguerreotypes enabled Brown to create miniatures that were perceived as accurate. A newspaper critic remarked upon Brown's realism: "His backgrounds are so delicately delineated as without any depreciation of their truthfulness, to bring the minutest lineaments of the bright expressive continents, fully into view, with all the charms of a glowing complexion . . . The hands, also, are beautifully and naturally drawn, exhibiting a roundness and fairness of the tapering fingers, and the delicate curves of the transparent nails, in a manner calculated to excite the highest admiration."[65] Extant images and contemporary comments make it clear that the pose, delineation of clothing and facial features, and background contributed to an image that had attributes of both painted and daguerreotypic portraits.[66] Brown had the ability to paint miniatures in a range of styles that variably included daguerreotypic attributes. This diversity of photographic qualities suggests a wide range of tastes among Philadelphia's bourgeoisie and an environment that permitted the exercise of individual patrons' wishes. Established and new bourgeois, as well as politicians, went to the same artist and did not distinguish themselves from one another through their choice of casing, daguerreotypic attributes (if any), or the size and cost of their portraits.

The bourgeoisie's knowledge of artistry and desire to view objects that they saw as vessels for sentiment and taste are acknowledged through their commissioning of miniatures and confirmed through contemporary writings. One of Brown's clippings, titled "The Attraction of Art," reads:

> The uneducated mind may be moved by classic forms of beauty but the emotion excited has little intensity and less permanence. He, on the other hand, whose taste has been cultivated and whose mind, refined by education, strives to realize the ideal of the old masters of human sympathy, is at once attracted to the classic picture or statue. It has, moreover, for him, a personal attraction. He lives over the golden days of his youth, when yet unhackneyed to the world, he dwelt in the sunny regions of imagination and poetry. The toil with which he labored through the wearisome preliminaries to scholarship is rewarded tenfold by the wealth of intellectual pleasure which is ever after open to him; and which is most appreciated when the imperishable legacies of genius to mankind are presented to his examination. To see is, with him, to possess.[67]

Acquisition of a distinct type of art by a particular artist was one way of codifying a specific taste. Brown depicted his patrons, from a wide range of Philadelphia's bourgeoisie, in ways that permitted them to distinguish themselves from those whose sole portraits were daguerreotypes. Philadelphia's bourgeoisie inhabited this corner of the artistic arena together, regardless of the source or longevity of their wealth, commissioning like portraits done in like ways. Patrons referred to the historical nature of miniature portraiture and patronage through their choices and, by extension, the taste, wealth, and power that they associated with earlier Philadelphians.

Mourning Portraiture

Although the demand for miniatures was due to the physical and aesthetic qualities and the traditional, often romantic, associations of the medium, changing mourning customs also account for the sustained interest in miniatures.[68] Brown's patronage, especially after 1848, heavily depended upon posthumous portraiture. His practice of painting miniatures of deceased men and women from daguerreotypes increased over time: from three of 25 in 1856 to at least 16 of 21 in 1859.[69] The demand for posthumous portraits in all media grew over time, reflecting and codifying an evolving fascination with, and sentimentality about, death.[70] Even though the visual memory of a sitter after his or her death took on increasing importance in the 1840s and '50s, the means of portrayal is significant as well. Posthumous daguerreian portraiture thrived nationally as well as in Philadelphia, but a broad cross-section of the bourgeoisie continued to gravitate toward Brown for miniatures. Miniatures allowed the viewer to relate the deceased person to the past and to connect him or her to a longer lineage of colonial and early national sitters

Sidney George Fisher (1808–1881), a Philadelphian from an established bourgeois family, describes viewing Brown's miniatures of his brother and sister-in-law under different circumstances. In 1855 he remarked that he "saw Sarah Ann [Fisher] who showed me an admirable miniature just finished of Henry [Fisher]. The likeness is perfect, & it is beautifully painted."[71] Fisher's stronger reaction to Brown's miniature of his then-deceased sister-in-law in 1858 may have been more of a response to her memory than to Brown's work: "Some days ago Henry [Fisher] brought me a miniature of Sarah Ann [Fisher], painted by Brown, and just finished. It was painted entirely from a daguerreotype which was aided by his recollections, as he had seen her whilst he painted the miniatures of Henry and Jim. The likeness is so admirable that it quite overcame me. It seemed like a resurrection."[72] Brown clearly captured her likeness in a manner that strongly appealed to Fisher; the latter was less enthusiastic about the daguerreotypes taken of family members.[73] Having miniatures painted from daguerreotypes of deceased relatives conformed to the broader practice of mourning, but it did so in a highly specialized, personal, and costly way. Brown's miniatures, with their depth of color and, often, sumptuous housings, created a different aura around the deceased than did a daguerreotype.

The proportion of documented portraits of female sitters by John Henry Brown rose over time and coincided with the rise in the number of deceased men and women who were depicted. This increase suggests that women's images may have been used as objects for emotion and sentiment generally and, later, for expressing those feelings related to mourning. The predominance of female sitters also suggests that miniatures, rather than serving as tokens of male power and possession as they had in federal Philadelphia, were sites of female—and perhaps male through female—sentiments about death in antebellum Philadelphia.[74] Miniatures served as a vehicle for those of new and established wealth to express feeling and to remember their loved ones in a format that could be as private or public as they chose. Brown's miniatures incorporated both traditional and modern elements, and these seemingly contradictory attributes apparently had great appeal for bourgeois portrait sitters.

Bourgeois Nationalization

Brown's patrons came from established as well as new sectors of Philadelphia's bourgeoisie, apparently satisfying the needs of both groups. His patronage from residents of other cities, particularly those with active miniaturists, suggests that his works also met bourgeois needs elsewhere.[75] His extensive use of daguerreotypes to produce miniatures and the daguerreotypic qualities of his paintings reveal that these attributes of his work were integral elements in the demand for it. They allowed patrons to express sentiment, including about death, in a private, refined way that met contemporary aesthetic criteria.

Many of Brown's sitters who resided outside of the Philadelphia came from surrounding communities; others came from North Carolina, Missouri, and Kentucky, where it was more difficult to find a miniaturist. But his sitters also lived in cities where miniaturists are known to have had established practices, such as Charleston, South Carolina, and New York. This broad geographic demand for Brown's miniatures suggests that his work met the needs of an increasingly mobile bourgeoisie. The regional styles evident in most late eighteenth- and early-nineteenth-century miniatures largely disappear in the antebellum period.[76] Photography, too, played a role in creating more national (and international) standards of portrait consumption.

Brown was unable to maintain his level of patronage past the early 1860s, however. In 1860 he wrote that he "had less work engaged now, than I ever had since I commenced business."[77] A year later, Brown attributed patrons' unwillingness to spend money on miniatures to the impending war; he recorded his growing anxiety about obtaining commissions, having fewer actual commissions and seeing a reduction in income between 1861 and 1863.[78] Brown's subsequent business decisions reveal that he was aware of a growing preference for photographic images and, therefore, kept a close watch on the decline in the demand for his miniatures. By 1860, faster, cheaper, and easily duplicable photographic images on paper were increasingly available.

A Period of Decline for Miniatures

Brown cited the war as a reason for falling demand for his miniatures, but this does not fully explain his lack of commissions after 1865. Despite its aura of historicity and elegance, the painted miniature could not continue to compete with more modern techniques. Daguerreotypes and other photographic images had been available for 25 years. People had also begun to see differently, with changed expectations about what constituted a good likeness. A critic wrote in the context of viewing Brown's miniatures at the beginning of the revival of miniature painting in 1876, "Photography for a time pretty effectually put a stop to the business of ivory miniature painters."[79] Although Brown's difficulty in obtaining commissions in the early 1860s confirms this statement, the demand for his opalotypes among former miniature patrons complicates the picture.

During the 1860s and 1870s, some Philadelphians chose a photographic medium that had many of the qualities of miniatures. Brown and others produced opalotypes, or albumen photographic images on opaque white glass.[80] In 1864 Brown stated that he stopped painting miniatures, found financial backers for a photographic business, and embarked upon a partnership known as Wenderoth, Taylor, and Brown.[81] In the years that followed, Brown also advertised his ability to paint miniatures. However, his 1876 remark that "after a lapse of 12 years, I have returned to miniature painting on ivory," suggests that he had little success in obtaining commissions between 1864 and 1876.[82]

Brown created opalotypes of Edward Coles (fig. 4.4) and other members of the Coles family, his earlier patrons, probably between 1864 and 1868.[83] The Coles portraits, as is the case with other opalotypes by Brown, are heavily tinted, with pale washes of many colors; they are more intensely colored than daguerreotypes or paper photographs, but they lack the richness of coloring of the artist's earlier miniatures (figs. 4.1, 4.3). Like many of his miniatures from the late 1850s and early 1860s, Brown's opalotypes are housed in deep velvet-lined cases that may have enhanced their aura of preciousness. Brown's work in these intervening years had the support of several of his earlier patrons, suggesting that opalotypes may have fulfilled some of the demand for miniatures during the 1860s and 1870s.[84] Despite the lack of variety or depth of color in Brown's opalotypes relative to his miniatures, they nonetheless may have satisfied some bourgeois Philadelphians.[85] Their visual similarity to miniatures, their novelty, and their lower price influenced demand for them, probably in varying degrees for different patrons.[86] However, they were unique and far more expensive than paper photographs, which were frequently done in multiples

Figure 4.4 John Henry Brown, *Edward Coles*. Photographic emulsion on milk glass, ca. 1864–68. Courtesy Winterthur Museum, Gift of Marie Robbins Barlow, Mary Robbins Lemon, and Edward J. Robbins in memory of Oliver W. Robbins, 2001.43.5

and easily circulated. The hand-painted aspects (and, thus, the singularity) of opalotypes, their sumptuous housings, and their connection to earlier art forms made them intrinsically and extrinsically more precious.

In contrast to the 1840s and '50s, when miniatures were made to appear more like daguerreotypes, a photographic medium was brought closer to the aesthetics of miniatures. In the opalotypes Brown produced in the 1860s and '70s, he attempted to duplicate some of the qualities of miniatures at a lower price.[87] Yet he made a clear distinction between sitters for miniatures and those who had their portraits done in a photographic medium by only recording the names of the former. Opalotype commissions sustained Brown and his family between 1864 and 1876, a period when miniatures could not. Brown's production of miniatures would not revive (and the production of other forms begin) until after 1876, and it would fulfill a different set of needs.[88]

Conclusion

Artists produced substantial numbers of miniatures of Philadelphians after 1839, when the daguerreotype became widely available, suggesting that miniatures fulfilled specific needs for patrons. Miniatures appealed to a broadening group of patrons, shifting from those of established wealth and position in the early nineteenth century to those of new and established status in the 1820s through the early 1860s. Choosing a painted miniature, particularly over a daguerreotype, was one way that some of Philadelphia's antebellum bourgeois could associate themselves and future generations with long-established wealth and distinguished ancestors. Grant McCracken, referring to Tudor portraiture, notes that "most conspicuous among the furnishings [that were capable of patina] was the family portraiture, tangible proof of a noble lineage and an exact measure of the number of generations it had claimed high standing."[89] The large investment, precious (or precious-looking) materials involved, and historical associations meant that miniatures, even when new, had patina.

The laments of Sidney George Fisher make it clear that for some, ancestry was paramount and was reflected in inherited, rather than purchased, goods. He remarked in 1838 and 1841 upon attending parties where there was "plenty of old family plate & china" and "many paintings and furniture, relics of former luxury."[90] He contrasted this patinaed display with the "gaudy show, crowded glitter and loaded tables of certain vulgar people here, who by mere force of money have got into a society to which they are not entitled by birth, education, or manners" (March 4, 1839).[91] Although Fisher and other members of established bourgeois Philadelphia families placed a premium upon old goods, they also purchased new ones. In antebellum Philadelphia, the miniature was a good that was not aged but rather, through its tradition and use, had associations with fine, inherited, and inheritable goods. Whether new or established bourgeois, members of the professional classes, or politicians, commissioning (and, sometimes, exchanging) a miniature included one in a sphere of cultural knowledge. A miniature connected the sitter to a long line, whether real or desired, and met the standards of tasteful display that Fisher and other critics deemed appropriate. Miniatures also enabled bourgeoisie to communicate such widespread contemporary feelings as sentimentality and mourning in a setting that was only as public as the possessor of a miniature chose to make it.

Miniatures were susceptible to and capable of incorporating influences from technical innovations, without losing the social value they derived from their fundamentally conservative nature. The cost, time needed for sittings, and materials made the medium intrinsically more precious than the daguerreotype and perhaps a weightier repository of sentiments and values. The traditions associated with miniatures allowed the medium to help carry such messages. At a time when, and in a place where, wealth was not the only indicator of social position, Philadelphians granted particular meanings, not necessarily consciously, to some possessions. Antebellum miniatures produced in Philadelphia exhibit varied elements of new technologies and new ways of seeing, yet a miniature could, through the use of color, historical associations, and a particular size and shape, make the sitter look like those in earlier miniatures. Although many of the reasons behind the need for miniatures had changed with time, commissioning, exchanging, and viewing miniatures continued to allow bourgeois Philadelphians, regardless of ancestry or longevity of wealth, to take part in luxury consumption in a private setting with others who shared such cultural preferences.

Notes

I thank Sven Beckert and Julia Rosenbaum for their insightful comments on this essay. For their comments on earlier drafts, I would like to thank Carol Aiken, Mark Bockrath, Robin Bolton-Smith, Margaretta Lovell, the late Lillian Miller, Mary Panzer, Alan Wallach, and Kirsten Swinth. The panelists and audience of the 1997 American Studies Association Annual Meeting and the participants in the conference on bourgeois culture held at Harvard University in 2003 also provided valuable suggestions.

1. See Lawrence Stone, *The Family, Sex and Marriage in England, 1500–1800* (New York: Harper and Row, 1977), 20, 270–74, 283–87, 320–21; and Margaretta Lovell, "Reading Eighteenth-Century American Family Portraits: Social Images and Self-Images," *Winterthur Portfolio* 22 (Winter 1987): 243–64.
2. Many scholars have noted the influence of daguerreotypy and photography on oil portraiture. See Van Deren Coke, *The Painter and the Photograph: From Delacroix to Warhol* (Albuquerque: University of New Mexico Press, 1972), 25, 83, 85; Monroe H. Fabian, *Mr. Sully, Portrait Painter: The Words of Thomas Sully (1783–1872)* (Washington, DC: National Portrait Gallery, 1983), 119; and Robert Torchia, *John Neagle: Philadelphia Portrait Painter* (Philadelphia: Historical Society of Pennsylvania, 1989), 70–71.
3. Dale T. Johnson, *American Portrait Miniatures in the Manney Collection* (New York: Metropolian Museum of Art, 1990), 24–25; Marion Rinhart and Floyd Rinhart, *American Miniature Case Art* (South Brunswick, NJ and New York: A. S. Barnes, 1969), 17.
4. Edwin Wolf, "The Origins of Philadelphia's Self-Depreciation, 1820–1920," *Pennsylvania Magazine of History and Biography* 104 (January 1980): 58–73; Frederic Cople Jaher, *The Urban Establishment: The Upper Strata in Boston, New York City, Charleston, Chicago, and Los Angeles* (Urbana: University of Illinois Press, 1982), 68–69.
5. Charlene Mires, *Independence Hall in American Memory* (Philadelphia: University of Pennsylvania Press, 2003), 67–69, 101–06. Gary Nash, *First City: Philadelphia and the Forging of American Memory* (Philadelphia: University of Pennsylvania Press, 2002), 214–22. I thank Mary Panzer for her insights on the role of Philadelphia's photographic community in constructing perceptions of the past. See also Kenneth Finkel, ed., *Legacy in Light* (Philadelphia: Philadelphia Museum of Art, 1990), 24.
6. In a few places, notably Philadelphia, New York, and Charleston, the miniature endured in significant strength despite the presence of the daguerreotype. The revival of miniatures that began about 1876 and continued during the first half of the twentieth century is beyond the scope of this essay.
7. I use the term daguerreotype (a positive image on a silvered copper support) but also include ambrotypes (negative images on glass supports, available after 1854) in this discussion; both were produced as singular, cased images. Although much work remains to be done on the relationships between photography and portrait painting of all scales, a review of published portraits from major cultural centers suggests that standards of artistic representation became more consistent and less regional during the antebellum and, to a greater degree, the postbellum period. Philadelphians commissioned miniatures in abundance in comparison to most of their counterparts in other cities. These conclusions are based on Catalog of American Portraits, National Portrait Gallery, surveys for Baltimore, Boston, New York, Newport, R.I., rural areas of New England, and Charleston. Other sources include Caroline Sloat, ed., *Meet Your Neighbors: New England Portraits, Painters, and Society, 1790–1850* (Sturbridge, MA: Old Sturbridge Village, 1992); Charles C. Sellers, *Portraits and Miniatures by Charles Willson Peale* (Philadelphia: American Philosophical Society, 1953); Martha R. Severens, *The Miniature Portrait Collection of the Carolina Art Association* (Charleston: Carolina Art Association, 1984); Ruel Pardee Tolman, *The Life and Works of Edward Greene Malbone, 1777–1807* (New York: New-York Historical Society, 1958);

Mona L. Dearborn, *Anson Dickinson: The Celebrated Miniature Painter, 1779–1852* (Hartford: Connecticut Historical Society, 1983); Johnson, *American Portrait Miniatures in the Manney Collection*; Museum of Fine Arts, *New England Miniatures, 1750 to 1850* (Boston: Museum of Fine Arts, 1957); Maryland Historical Society, *Portraits Painted before 1900 in the Collection of the Maryland Historical Society* (Baltimore: Maryland Historical Society, 1946); and New-York Historical Society, *Catalogue of American Portraits in the New-York Historical Society* (New Haven, CT: Yale University Press, 1974).

8. Relatively few miniatures or paintings of Philadelphia-area Quakers are known, for they perceived silhouettes and daguerreotypes as more direct images that met their largely unwritten strictures about plainness. Other than Quakers, there was a diversity of religious affiliation among sitters for miniatures in the antebellum period. See Anne Verplanck, "Facing Philadelphia: The Social Functions of Silhouettes, Miniatures, and Daguerreotypes, 1760–1860" (Ph.D. diss., College of William and Mary, 1996), 26, 66–117, 148–49.
9. On prices, see Verplanck, "Facing Philadelphia," 32.
10. On emotional responses, see Anita Brookner, *Greuze: The Rise and Fall of an Eighteenth-Century Phenomenon* (Greenwich, CT: New York Graphic Society, 1970), 1–50; and Colin Campbell, *The Romantic Ethic and the Spirit of Modern Consumerism* (London: Basil Blackwell, 1987), 173–79.
11. On mutable meanings of objects, see Nancy Bercaw, "Solid Objects/Mutable Meanings: Fancywork and the Construction of Bourgeois Culture, 1840–1880," *Winterthur Portfolio* 26, no. 4 (Winter 1991): 231–48; and George Kubler, *The Shape of Time: Remarks on the History of Things* (New Haven, CT: Yale University Press, 1967), esp. 24–30.
12. On the creation of social identity via comparison, see Polly Weissner, "Style and Changing Relations between the Individual and Society," in *The Meaning of Things: Material Culture and Symbolic Expression*, ed. Ian Hodder (London: Unwin Hyman, 1989), 56–59.
13. James McLees, *Elements of Photography* (Philadelphia: James McLees, 1855), 18.
14. John Henry Brown, account book and diary, March 31, 1843, and 1855, Rosenbach Museum and Library (hereafter cited as Brown account book). The manuscript account book and diary covers the period from 1839 to 1890. The relative price of Brown's miniatures appears to have depended upon their size rather than whether they were taken from a daguerreotype; see entries for Mrs. Vanderkemp (1847), John Butler (1848), and Mrs. Edward M. Hopkins (1849, 1850).
15. Grant McCracken, *Culture and Consumption: New Approaches to the Symbolic Character of Consumer Goods and Activities* (Bloomington and Indianapolis: Indiana University Press, 1990), 13–14, 32–43.
16. On the descent of miniatures within the Coles and Lewis families, see accession file 2001.43, Winterthur Museum; and Nicholas B. Wainwright, *Portraits and Miniatures at the Historical Society of Pennsylvania* (Philadelphia: Historical Society of Pennsylvania, 1974), 151–52.
17. Brown was not the only artist who produced miniatures in antebellum Philadelphia. Anna Claypoole Peale, Hugh Bridport, Henry Inman, and George L. Saunders provide comparative and corroborating data on patronage, form, and function. Although no documentation of these artists' use of daguerreotypes has been found, their work, particularly that of Saunders, bears photographic qualities that suggest their engagement with or use of these images; see Anne Sue Hirshorn, "Legacy of Ivory: Anna Claypoole Peale's Portrait Miniatures," *Bulletin of the Detroit Institute of Arts* 64, no. 4 (1989): 16–27. On Philadelphia miniaturists' patronage, see Verplanck, "Facing Philadelphia," 126–50.
18. Daguerreotypist Frederick de Bourg Richards, a landscape painter, is an exception; see William and Marie Brey, *Philadelphia Photographers, 1840–1900* (Cherry Hill, NJ: Willowdale Press, 1992), n.p. For a rating of galleries, see "Cuique Suum," "The Photographic Galleries of America. Number Two – Philadelphia," *The Photographic and Fine Art Journal* 9, no. 4 (April, 1856): 124–26.
19. Brown account book, October 16, 1850 (M. P. Simons); extant daguerreotype by McLees and miniature by Brown of Thomas H. Powers, Esq. (?) (Rosenbach Library and Museum). An article in the *Philadelphia Inquirer,* February 20, 1849, compares daguerreotypes taken by M. A. Root with Brown's corresponding miniatures (Brown account book).
20. Given Brown's success, his description of his family as "poor people" may be an exaggeration. His remark does not encompass those who chose daguerreotypes for reasons other than cost, including Quakers (Brown account book, July 10, 1852).

21. Contrary to practices among miniature-portrait sitters, a given social group or class did not flock to a single daguerreotypist. Local scientific interest made Philadelphia a site for early experimentation with daguerreotypes. See Verplanck, "Facing Philadelphia," 4–5, 196–203.
22. Clipping from *North American Gazette,* October 2, 1858 (Brown account book).
23. The daguerreotypes and ambrotypes Brown used to create miniatures appear to have been perceived as a means to an end. Only the daguerreotype used to create the miniature of Thomas H. Powers, Esq. (?) and the ambrotypes used to make Abraham Lincoln's miniature survive. On the Lincoln commission, see Verplanck, "Facing Philadelphia," 146–47.
24. Brown account book, January 1852. His entries of December 28–31, 1850, note that he had an 18-month backlog of commissions and was declining work. His prices increased over time. Before 1846, he earned between $15 and $22 for a portrait; between 1846 and 1850, he recorded from $20 to $218 per image, with his price range rising each year. After 1850, Brown charged up to $500, though few cost more than $250.
25. He noted in 1848 that, "I have been obliged to refuse a great deal of work lately on account of being already too full" (Brown account book, January 2–4, 1848). The percentage of Philadelphia sitters ranged from 44 percent in 1846 (the first year he was based in Philadelphia) to 86 percent in 1856; in most years he painted from 72 to 80 percent Philadelphians. His patronage by Philadelphians varied dramatically from year to year and does not show a linear increase over time.
26. Brown exhibited at the Pennsylvania Academy of the Fine Arts in 1843 and, regularly, at the Artists' Fund Society between 1844 and 1864. See Brown account book, March 3 and April 26–28, 1844; and Anna Wells Rutledge, *Cumulative Record of the Pennsylvania Academy of the Fine Arts, 1807–1870* (Philadelphia: American Philosophical Society, 1955), 38–39.
27. Sitters' ancestry and sources of wealth are derived from the following sources: John A. Garrity and Mark C. Carnes, eds., *American National Biography* (New York: Oxford University Press, 1999); Henry Simpson, *The Lives of Eminent Philadelphians Now Deceased* (Philadelphia: William Brotherhead, 1859); A Merchant of Philadelphia, *Memoirs and Auto-Biography of Some of the Wealthy Citizens of Philadelphia* (Philadelphia: The Booksellers, 1846); Charles Robeson, ed., *The Biographical Dictionary of Pennsylvania* (Philadelphia: Galaxy, 1874); Stephen Winslow, *Biographies of Successful Merchants* (Philadelphia: James K. Simon, 1864); Philadelphia City Directory, 1847, 1853, 1856; and A Member of the Philadelphia Bar, *Wealth and Biography of the Wealthy Citizens of Philadelphia* (Philadelphia: B. Ziegler, 1845). Brown's faith (Lutheran) appears to have had little effect on his patronage.
28. On the Peales, see Verplanck, "Facing Philadelphia," 44–55, 126–41. On Trott, see Anne Verplanck, "Benjamin Trott: Miniature Painter" (M.A. thesis, College of William and Mary, 1990), esp. 58–79.
29. Doerflinger, *Vigorous Spirit,* 188–96.
30. Stephen Brobeck, "Changes in the Composition and Structure of Philadelphia's Bourgeois Groups, 1756–1790" (Ph.D. diss., University of Pennsylvania, 1972), 162; Robert Gough, "Towards a Theory of Class and Social Conflict: A Social History of Wealthy Philadelphians, 1775–1800" (Ph.D. diss., University of Pennsylvania, 1977), 151, 163, 165, 635.
31. Verplanck, "Facing Philadelphia," 44–51.
32. Amy Henderson, "Furnishing the Republican Court: Building and Decorating Philadelphia Homes, 1790–1800," (Ph.D. diss., University of Delaware, 2008), 70, 266–68, 363–70; Ethel Rasmusson, "Democratic Environment—Aristocratic Aspirations," *Pennsylvania Magazine of History and Biography* 90 (April 1966): 155–82; Beatrice Garvan, *Federal Philadelphia* (Philadelphia: Philadelphia Museum of Art, 1987), 22–26.
33. Doerflinger's model, like the studies of Gough and Blumin, assumes economic status as the primary determinant of position. Neither Gough nor Doerflinger considers *past* status—particularly economic or political status—as a characteristic of the bourgeoisie. See Thomas Doerflinger, *A Vigorous Spirit of Enterprise: Merchants and Development in Revolutionary America* (Chapel Hill: University of North Carolina Press, 1987), 15–16, 44–45; Stuart Blumin, *The Emergence of the Middle Class: Social Experience in the American City, 1760–1900* (Cambridge [U.K.]: Cambridge University Press, 1989), 44, 51; Gough, "Towards a Theory of Class," 99, 189, 462, 625, 635; and E. Digby Baltzell, *Philadelphia Gentlemen: The Making of a National Upper Class* (Glencoe, IL: Free Press, 1958), 60, 83, 276–79. For a discussion of the use of these and related terms, see Sven Beckert, *The Monied Metropolis: New York and*

the Consolidation of the American Bourgeoise, 1850–1896 (Cambridge: Cambridge University Press, 2001), 6–7.

Although there have been several studies of social, benevolent, and cultural organizations in Philadelphia during this period, none correlates involvement in these groups with withdrawal from economic and political realms. See Lee Schreiber, "The Philadelphia Bourgeois in the Development of the Pennsylvania Academy of the Fine Arts" (Ph.D. diss., Temple University, 1977), 3, 318–23; and Margaret Haviland, "In the World, but Not of the World: The Humanitarian Activities of Philadelphia Quakers, 1790–1820" (Ph.D. diss., University of Pennsylvania, 1992), viii, 161.

34. J. William Frost, *The Quaker Family in Colonial America: A Portrait* (New York: St. Martin's Press, 1973), 159–60, 218–19; Robert W. Doherty, *The Hicksite Separation: A Sociological Analysis of Religious Schism in Early Nineteenth-Century America* (New Brunswick, NJ: Rutgers University Press, 1967), 65; Daniel Greenstein, "Urban Politics and the Urban Process: Two Case Studies of Philadelphia" (Ph.D. diss., Oxford University, 1987), 26–36, 418; Andrew Shankman, *Crucible of American Democracy: The Struggle to Fuse Egalitarian and Capitalism in Jeffersonian Pennsylvania* (Lawrence: University Press of Kansas, 2004), 204.
35. Lillian B. Miller, *Patrons and Patriotism: The Encouragement of the Fine Arts in the United States, 1790–1860* (Chicago: University of Chicago Press, 1966), vii–ix, 8, 15; Schreiber, "Philadelphia Bourgeois," 3, 318–23.
36. Verplanck, "Facing Philadelphia," 36, 46.
37. Greenstein, "Urban Politics," 27.
38. Elizabeth Geffen, "Industrial Development and Social Crisis, 1841–1854," in *Philadelphia: A 300-Year History,* ed. Russell Weigley (New York: W. W. Norton, 1982), 330.
39. A Merchant of Philadelphia, preface to *Memoirs,* n.p.
40. Anne Verplanck, "Introduction to Quakers and Modernity," in *Quaker Aesthetics: Reflections on a Quaker Ethic in American Design and Consumption,* ed. Emma J. Lapsansky and Anne Verplanck (Philadelphia: University of Pennsylvania Press, 2003), 237–45.
41. In 1847 Brown painted Mrs. Meta Biddle, Thomas Biddle, and Mrs. Ann Biddle; in 1848, Mr. Biddle; in 1856, J. Williams Biddle; and in 1859, Miss Rebecca Biddle. In 1849 he painted Joseph Hopkinson; in 1850, Mrs. Judge Hopkinson; in 1855, Oliver Hopkinson; and in 1857, Mrs. Oliver Hopkinson. Brown painted Mrs. Willing and Mary Swift ("granddaughter of Mrs. Willing") in 1849, and Master Willing Lewis in 1850. See Brown account book, 1847–1860. On these individuals' eighteenth-century ancestors, see Dumas Malone, ed., *Dictionary of American Biography* (New York: Charles Scribner's Sons, 1961), 2: 728–36, 11: 190–93; 23: 530–32.
42. The firm of Bailey and Kitchen, "Importers and extensive jewelers and silversmiths," displayed one of Brown's miniatures in their window in 1846 (perhaps "Miss Kitchen, wife of Kitchen of the firm Bailey & Co.," which Brown recorded in his account book that year); it was noted in the *Pennsylvanian* (Philadelphia), June 12, 1846 (clipping, Brown account book). In 1846 and 1847 he painted Mrs. Kitchen, and in 1848, Mrs. Bailey; in 1854 he completed a miniature of the late Joseph T. Bailey from a daguerreotype. Although Brown does not mention the source of the case work for his miniatures, it is possible that it was supplied by Bailey and Kitchen.

    In 1849 Brown painted Mrs. John Bohlen and the late Henry Bohlen; the following year, he painted Mrs. Bohlen again, "from a Daguerre" after her death, as well as Miss Catherine Bohlen (Brown account book, 1849, 1850); John Bohlen made his fortune "in the Holland trade." See Robeson, *The Biographical Dictionary of Pennsylvania,* 57–58; and A Merchant of Philadelphia, *Memoirs,* 6, 9). Catherine Bohlen is discussed in Robin Jaffee Frank, *Love and Loss: American Portrait and Mourning Miniatures* (New Haven, CT: Yale University Press, 2000), 293–300.
43. Brown account book, 1849–55; A Merchant of Philadelphia, *Memoirs,* 39. Brown painted four portraits of members of the Joseph Lovering family between 1849 and 1855. Lovering ran sugar refineries. Several of Brown's Lancaster-area patrons, such as G. Dawson Coleman, amassed their wealth from iron furnaces. See Robeson, *The Biographical Dictionary of Pennsylvania,* 159–160.
44. He painted lawyers such as Peter McCall, Charles Janeway Stille, and Joseph Swift, along with members of their families; military figures included Lieutenant Handy and several other naval officers, as well as the wives of Captain Alden, Lieutenant Trenchard, and Lieutenant Rush (Brown account book, 1844–60).

45. Joseph Sill, diary, October 25, 1841, June 1, 1846, and June 10, 1853, microfilm, Archives of American Art. On Sill, an amateur artist, see Elizabeth M. Geffen, "Joseph Sill and His Diary," *Pennsylvania Magazine of History and Biography* 94 (July 1970): 275–330. Sill describes his belief that those of established position controlled facets of cultural arenas in antebellum Philadelphia.
46. These commissions spanned from 1844 to 1860 (Brown account book).
47. Conrad also was a writer and served as a judge; see New York Historical Society, *Catalogue of Portraits,* 1:161–62.
48. The miniature, formerly in the Pennsylvania Academy of the Fine Arts, is unlocated.
49. Brown account book, 1854; Burton J. Bledstein, *The Culture of Professionalization: The Middle Class and the Development of Higher Education in America* (New York: W. W. Norton, 1978), esp. 80–128.
50. Benjamin Trott to A. Wolcott, January 2, 1839, Dreer Collection, HSP Collection. See also Sill diary, November 29, 1840; January 6, 1842; May 18, 1843.
51. Clipping from *North American Gazette,* October 2, 1858 (Brown account book).
52. Mrs. Coles, 1853; Mrs. Hopkinson, 1857; Mrs. Meigs, 1857; Miss Fisher, 1861 (Brown account book).
53. Brown noted on August 23, 1844, that he "retouched the drapery of a miniature of Miss Emmett, which I painted two years ago" (Brown account book; see also entry for March 26, 1853).
54. Shirley T. Wajda, "'Social Currency': A Domestic History of the Portrait Photograph in the United States, 1839–1889" (Ph.D. diss., University of Pennsylvania, 1992), 334–492; Alan Trachtenberg, *Reading American Photographs: From Mathew Brady to Walker Evans* (New York: Hill and Wang, 1989), 29.
55. Oval miniatures gave way to rectangular ones over time and, after 1840, ivory could be cut from the circumference of a tusk (in a spiral), allowing larger miniatures; see Johnson, *American Portrait Miniatures,* 24. Oval miniatures by Brown include *Ellis Lewis* (1845), *Martha Stocker Lewis* (1847), and *Juliet Lewis Campbell* (1845; all,Atwater Kent Museum, HSP Collection), as well as his own portrait and his daughter Ada's (both, Metropolitan Museum of Art). James Smith's oval locket housing *Robert Taylor Conrad* (ca. 1845–50; New-York Historical Society) also has a space for hair on the verso. The limited number of miniatures by these artist make drawing conclusions about preferences for lockets versus cases problematic.
56. Brown account book, July 2, 1844; March 22–24, 1847; October 18, 1848; December 26, 1850.
57. Brown account book, January 25, 1849.
58. Brown's self-portrait (ca. 1846; Metropolitan Museum of Art) presents his face almost frontally; his body, however, is slightly turned. The blue-and-white background suggests sky, a technique often found in earlier miniatures. Brown's self-portrait has many features in common with *Ellis Lewis* (1845; Atwater Kent Museum, HSP Collection). There is no notation visible on either Brown's or Lewis's miniature, or any reference in the account book about the images being produced from daguerreotypes.
59. Although the account book makes no note of the miniature being taken from a daguerreotype, Brown wrote in his diary: "Met Mrs. Coles at a Daguerreotype room for the purpose of getting her daguerre" (Brown account book, March 9, 1853). For comparison, see Brown's miniature of Mrs. John Jordan Jr., which probably was done at least in part from life in 1848 (Smithsonian American Art Museum). It presents the sitter's head in a nearly frontal manner, but turned slightly to the side. Her pose more closely resembles the ones in Anna Claypoole Peale's miniatures, such as *Anna Smith Larcombe* (ca. 1818; Metropolitan Museum of Art) and *Elizabeth Brick* (1830–40; Pennsylvania Academy of the Fine Arts) than the fully frontal poses of many daguerreotypes or miniatures clearly derived from daguerreotypes. *Mrs. John Jordan Jr.* exhibits gradations of color, the colors are relatively strong, and the details of her clothing are precisely rendered. Her portrait fades, like a daguerreotype, toward the edges of the picture.
60. See *Frances Butler* (1856) and *Martha Lewis* (1847); both, Atwater Kent Museum, HSP Collection.
61. See, for example, *Mrs. John Jordan Jr.* (note 59, above).
62. He notes on the backing of the miniature and in his account book (1846) that it was copied from a daguerreotype ("dec'd"). See also the Smithsonian American Art Museum object file.

63. Brown account book, March 10, 1861.
64. This meshing and interchange of aesthetics and attributes of painted and daguerreotypic works is repeatedly discussed in the daguerreian literature. See, for example, "The True Artist," *The Daguerreian Journal* 2, no. 8 (September 1851): 216; and "The Artist," *The Crayon* 1, no. 11 (March 14, 1855): 170. Williams argues that daguerreotypy also was naturalized through general literature, such as *The House of Seven Gables,* as well as daguerreian literature; both helped mediate portrait conventions. See Susan S. Williams, "The Confounding Image: The Figure of the Portrait in Nineteenth-Century American Fiction" (Ph.D. diss., Yale University, 1991), 25, 27.
65. *Lady's Dollar Newspaper,* March 4, 1849 (Brown account book).
66. The Sill diary provides corroborating data on the reception of miniatures and daguerreotypes; see entries for October 25 and November 22, 1841; May 23, 1843; September 3, 1844; February 2, 1845; March 18, 1846; December 5, 1846; and December 9, 1847.
67. *North American and U.S. Gazette,* October 2, 1858 (Brown account book).
68. The portraits he painted of Mr. and Mrs. George Lewis were "painted for each other, without the knowledge of either, as Christmas presents" (Brown account book, 1849).
69. The totals include both Philadelphians and non-Philadelphians; two additional images in 1859 are simply labeled "from a Daguerre." See Brown account book, 1846, 1859.
70. Martha V. Pike and Janice Gray Armstrong, *A Time to Mourn: Expressions of Grief in Nineteenth-Century America* (Stony Brook, NY: The Museums at Stony Brook, 1980), 17, 23–26, 71–87; Randolph J. Ploog, "The Account Books of Isaac Augustus Wetherby: Portrait Painter/Photographer," *History of Photography* 14, no. 1 (January-March 1990): 77–85.
71. Sidney George Fisher, *A Philadelphia Perspective: The Diary of Sidney George Fisher Covering the Years 1834–1871,* ed. Nicholas B. Wainwright (Philadelphia: Historical Society of Pennsylvania, 1967), 252). The miniature cost $200; whether or not it was taken from a daguerreotype is unknown (Brown account book, 1855).
72. Fisher, *Philadelphia Perspective,* 308; Brown account book, 1858, 1859.
73. Fisher, *Philadelphia Perspective,* 336.
74. Anne Verplanck, "The Social Meanings of Portrait Miniatures in Philadelphia, 1760–1820," in *American Material Culture: The Shape of the Field,* ed. Ann Smart Martin and J. Ritchie Garrison (Winterthur, DE: Winterthur Museum, 1997), 195–223. There are no discernable patterns in the changes over time between the percentage of deceased women and men painted by Brown.
75. Few patrons came from New York, a city with an established community of artists and long-standing interest in miniatures; the work of John McDougall (1810/11–1894) provides strong visual evidence of the use of photographic images. Among Charleston artists, both Charles Fraser and Henry Bounetheau are known to have employed daguerreotypes. I thank Carol Aiken, Carrie Rebora Barratt, Angela Mack, and Elle Shushan for their insights on antebellum miniaturists.
76. Fourteen to 56 percent of his sitters came from outside Philadelphia. See Brown account book;; and Martha Severens and Charles Wyrick Jr., eds., *Charles Fraser of Charleston: Essays on the Man, His Art, and His Times* (Charleston: Carolina Art Association and Gibbes Art Gallery, 1983), 123–25.
77. Brown account book, July 25, 1860.
78. Brown account book, February 25–27, 1861. On Brown's anxiety, even during his relative prosperity, see the entries for March 28–30, 1860; April 5, 1861; July 8/9, 1861; August 17, 1861; February 6, 1862; April 1, 1862; January 7, 1863; and June 30, 1864. Between 1855 and 1859 he painted from eighteen to twenty-one miniatures per year, while between 1860 and 1864 he painted seventeen to nineteen per year. Brown's annual income also declined: in 1859 he earned $3,930; in 1860, $3,698.85; in 1861, $2,170; in 1862 $2,662.50; and in 1863, $3,598.
79. The article, from an unknown source, is glued in Brown's account book. The article also discusses Brown's miniatures exhibited at Memorial Hall at the Centennial that year, for which he received a medal; see Brown account book, May 11, 1876.
80. The firm of Suddards and Fennemore, listed in Philadelphia directories between 1870 and 1879, also produced ivorytypes (two of Elizabeth J. Lea, The Library Company of Philadelphia). The ivorytype, a photographic image on imitation ivory or glass with ivory-colored paper backing, is, like the opalotype, an unusual process that may not be correctly identified in collections.

81. Brown's entry into the firm required a commitment of $8,000; he borrowed funds from "Dr. Washington Atlee," "Mr. Norton" (or Morton), "Judge Lewis" (probably his patron, Ellis Lewis), and "Mr. Shaffner" (Brown account book, 1864). On Wenderoth, Taylor, and Brown, see "F. A. Wenderoth," in Robert Sobieszek, *Masterpieces of Photography: From the George Eastman House Collections* (New York: Abbeville Press, 1985); and Mary Panzer, "Merchant Capital: Advertising Photography before the Age of Mechanical Reproduction," in *Occasional Papers 4, Ideas about Images: Essays on Film and Photography,* ed. William S. Johnson, (Rochester, NY: George Eastman House, 1990). Several months before joining Wenderoth and Taylor, Brown noted, "All day at an opal glass photograph of Mr. Howard Peale dec'd for [prominent photographer] Mr. Gutekunst, the first of the kind I ever painted" (Brown account book, July 26, 1864).
82. A notice, printed between about 1871 and 1875, suggests that Brown employed both painting and photographic techniques to create portraits: "Taylor & Brown / 912 & 914 Chestnut St., Philadelphia / Invite attention to their / various DESCRIPTIONS OF PORTRAITURE, / Photographs of all sizes, plain and / finished with India Ink. / Painted photographs, all sizes. / 'Crayons.' 'Illuminates.' / AQUATINTS, / IVORYTYPES AND OPALOTYPES, ON PORCELAIN, / MINIATURES BY J. HENRY BROWN / of the firm. / wm. curtis taylor. / j. henry brown" (1033, Box 2, William Gibbons Rhoads Papers, Rhoads Collection, Haverford College). Taylor and Brown appear in the Philadelphia city directories at 914 Chestnut Street between 1873 and 1875; see Brey, *Philadelphia Photographers*, n.p.
83. Brown noted that he started taking opalotypes in 1864; Edward Coles died in 1868. Mrs. Coles's clothing suggests the portrait was made in the 1860s, and the similar structural characteristics of the two miniatures indicate that they were executed at about the same time; see conservation report, file 2001.43, Registrar's Office, Winterthur Museum.
84. Examples include *Woman of the Fisher (?) family* (1858) and *Fisher (?) family children* (ca. 1858; both, Atwater Kent Museum, HSP Collection), and six members of the Coles family (Winterthur Museum). The latter include *Sally Coles* (1879; signed J. Henry Brown); *Edward Coles Sr.* (bearing a Wenderoth, Taylor, and Brown label on the frame and the notation "Copy/$85"); *Edward Coles Jr.* (1868); and *Virginia Coles* (ca. 1871–74). The only known price, $85, is less than that for Brown's miniatures in the 1850s; it may reflect the relative cost and demand for opalotypes.
85. His foray into photographic media appears to have been remunerative, for between 1865 and 1870 he netted from $4,334.65 (in 1868) to $7,254.77 (1866) annually. Yet the large sum Brown borrowed from backers resulted in profits that he perceived as small. See Brown account book.
86. Maxine Berg, "New Commodities, Luxuries, and Their Consumers in Eighteenth-Century England," in *Consumers and Luxury: Consumer Culture in Europe 1650–1850,* ed. Maxine Berg and Helen Clifford (Manchester: Manchester University Press, 1999), 77, 81–82.
87. An opalotype of Ellis Lewis (Atwater Kent Museum, HSP Collection) bears the note "Painted by J. Henry Brown miniaturist while with McLees & Co. Photographers, Phila. between 1865 & 1870" (Wainwright, *Portraits and Miniatures,* 151). Whether this information is incorrect or whether Brown worked for McLees and Wenderoth, Taylor, and Brown at the same time is uncertain; he makes no note of working for McLees in his account book.
88. The firm of Taylor and Brown was dissolved in February 1876 (Wenderoth was removed from the partnership in 1871). Brown participated in the revival of miniatures as a portrait form, taking a case of ivory miniatures to the Centennial Exhibition in May 1876, and in June of that year recorded that he was painting miniatures again; he continued painting miniatures until 1890. See Brown account book, February 8, 1876; March 8, 1876; June 12, 1876; July 1876; and September 1876. An opalotype of Mrs. Edward Coles Sr. dated 1879 (Winterthur Museum) documents his continued production of that form.
89. McCracken, *Culture and Consumption*, 13.
90. Fisher, *Philadelphia Perspective,* iii–iv, 67, 121. Fisher's declining fortune, or his perception thereof, may account for his remarks. See also Malone, *Dictionary of American Biography,* 6:410–11.
91. Fisher, *Philadelphia Perspective*, 76.

5

The "Blending and Confusion" of Expensiveness and Beauty: Bourgeois Interiors

Katherine C. Grier

> Any valuable object, in order to appeal to our sense of beauty, must conform to the requirements of beauty and expensiveness both. . . . This blending and confusion of the elements of expensiveness and beauty is, perhaps, best exemplified in articles of dress and household furniture.
>
> —Thorsten Veblen, *The Theory of the Leisure Class* (1899)

> The greater American residence is a mixture of the most modern mechanical improvements with the most time-worn decorative relics.
>
> —Harry W. Desmond and Herbert Croly, *Stately Homes in America: From Colonial Times to the Present Day* (1903)

Between the antebellum era, when American capitalists began to build the empires that transformed individual personal wealth, and the early 1900s, when the fully developed bourgeoisie experienced its greatest success as an extended group of self-confident tastemakers until the late twentieth century, the living spaces that well-to-do Americans created or commissioned evolved into extraordinarily complex sites. In cities, suburbs, resorts, and new country estates, the owners of what journalists Harry W. Desmond and Herbert Croly called the "greater American residence"—industrialists, bankers, real estate speculators, and wealthy professionals and businesspeople—commissioned houses that were exercises in high material rhetoric, from their grounds and architectural facades to their technologically advanced domestic systems and their elaborate interiors—the principal subject of this essay.[1] Not only did these living spaces manifest the sheer size of their owners' new fortunes, but their decorative programs also made ingenious claims for the owners' self-proclaimed identities as the vanguard of the new age of industrial wealth, and, as patrons, a new American Medici. The multiple rhetorical purposes to which these entrance halls, drawing rooms, dining rooms, art galleries, and music rooms were put partly explains the "blending and confusion" of "expensiveness and beauty" that Thorstein Veblen noted as characteristic of both dress and furniture in the arena of competitive consumption.

Even as the planning of bourgeois interiors was increasingly carried out by a growing cohort of professional interior decorating firms rather than by the owners themselves, the results expressed a common set of cultural principles and beliefs. These consisted of an aesthetics of refinement that viewed differentiation, material proliferation, and a high degree of physical detail and finish as pleasurable manifestations of civilized progress; a belief that the ability to tap into the historical associations attached to styles was one of the pleasurable outcomes of individual cultivation and a statement about American power vis-à-vis the Old World; and a set of gender conventions that divided styles, objects, and rooms into material adjuncts to the performance of manliness and femininity. The bourgeois interior was serious business to both creator and owner, but it must also be regarded as a form of play with representations, based on a sophisticated, metonymic use of space, objects, and decor.

The Rise of the "Greater American Residence"

In the eighteenth century, prosperous Americans—typically merchants and great landowners—built large houses and furnished them in ways that demonstrated their material success, their gentility, and their place in a new, national elite of merchants and large-scale landowners.[2] During the first half of the nineteenth century, however, a new cohort of Americans with money to spend began to invest in increasingly theatrical and expensive decor, exploring in turn the neoclassical styles of England and France, and the curvaceous shapes and elaborate representations of natural forms employed in a reinterpretation of eighteenth-century rococo.[3] By the middle of the century, however, new industrial wealth changed the greater American residence in important ways. Self-made men desired houses that were different from the dwellings of the older American elite, houses capable of making new social claims in material form, including a statement about the unprecedented nature of their own climbs to the economic, social, and cultural heights.

Take, for example, Armsmear. In 1855 Samuel Colt (1814–1862), inventor and founder of the Colt Patent Fire-Arms Manufacturing Company, and his wife, Elizabeth Hart Colt (1826–1905), broke ground in Hartford, Connecticut, for the first house of their own, which they named "Armsmear" (the mansion that "arms" built on the "mere," or lowlands, of the city). The house was actually part of a larger exercise in architecture and town planning, as Colt also built a model community for his workers and a modern, highly productive armory.[4] (The transitional nature of this enterprise is also revealed by the proximity of Armsmear to these sites. As the greater American residence evolved, it was increasingly located far from the sources of the wealth that made it possible.) A local architect, Octavius Jordan, seems to have provided concept drawings but not a full set of plans for the two dozen rooms contained in three stories of brownstone in the Italianate style, embellished by a five-story tower and an iron-framed conservatory with a large glass dome. Colt and his contractor also seem to have been intimately involved in the evolving structure as building progressed. Armsmear was in a constant state of construction and remodeling even after the family moved in, and the process continued for some years after Colt's untimely death at 47 in 1862. Along with its novel use of building materials, like structural iron, the Colts' mansion featured striking innovations in domestic technology, especially in the hundreds of gaslights powered by the plant that also lit the Colt armory. Such technological innovation in domestic systems, with the superior comfort they brought, soon became a trademark of the greater American residence.

No one guiding talent shaped Armsmear's interiors, however, even though Sam and Elizabeth Colt purchased the most important furnishings through the New York office of a French decorating firm, Ringuet-LePrince and Marcotte. The business provided furniture, draperies, and carpets in several French styles, including the popular rococo revival and an interpretation of Louis XVI neoclassicism. The couple had visited the firm's Paris office during their bridal tour of Europe and made selections for the interiors there. However, Colt himself provided chair covers purchased while traveling in Russia and other rarities to embellish the rooms. Despite the substantial contribution of Ringuet-LePrince and Marcotte to the look of Armsmear's rooms, the house was an autobiographical shrine full of souvenirs, featuring such unique, if perhaps *nouveau riche*, touches as scores of translucent "lithophane" porcelain panels inserted into the window frames. Armsmear reflected the success of its owners well, but it is notable that its spaces changed as the uses of bourgeois houses evolved. In the 1870s and 1880s, Colt's widow undertook a major redecoration that made the interiors of Armsmear more like the rooms created by the next generation of big money, as the house became an important site in the social life of Gilded Age Hartford, a setting for large receptions and musicales.

The story of Armsmear anticipates the elephantine, elaborately decorated houses that appeared just one generation later. Mid-century possessors of large new fortunes like the Colts understood the use of elegant houses as a way of claiming and consolidating social capital. They also recognized the utility of professional expertise in interior design. The serious work of creating rhetorically effective rooms required competent creative advice, either directly from the great international fashion center of Paris or through intermediaries with direct access to stylish French goods. Further, public interest in Armsmear foreshadowed the way in which the greater American residence became a focus of publicity and apparent public interest later in the century, thanks partly to the rise of national periodical literature.

A generation later, the greater American residence began to demonstrate its mature form, ballooning in size and ambition. As architecture, it encompassed more space, and its facades tended to be more cohesive in both massing and ornament than those of Armsmear, reflecting the greater status and authority, as well as the better training, of American architects. For our purposes, the interiors of this second generation of houses also represented something new: the full ascendance of the professional interior decorator who worked from European (mostly French or English) models and created complex, unified interior schemes.

Here Leland and Jane Lathrop Stanford's Nob Hill mansion, completed in 1877 and destroyed by fire during the San Francisco earthquake of 1906, offers a case study.[5] Stanford, a migrant to California in 1852, became a prosperous merchant, then governor of California in 1862 and 1863. His political ties almost certainly enhanced his investment opportunities in the plans for a transcontinental railroad, and he soon became president of the Central Pacific Railroad. The road's directors relocated its headquarters from Sacramento to San Francisco in 1873, setting off a building boom that made Nob Hill the "hill of palaces." Diana Strazdes's perceptive study of the surviving photos and archives associated with the Stanford house points out that Nob Hill's palaces were part of a national trend among the new American economic elite, who now regarded this kind of display almost as a public good. The houses were "intended for the public gaze and enjoyed as much celebrity status as their occupants. They were the sites of lavish receptions, banquets, and balls; their music rooms, libraries, and art galleries offered desirable emblems of art and culture."[6] Begun in 1875, the Stanford house had 50 rooms, totaling 41,000 square feet. Apart from the service staff, it housed only three people—Stanford, his wife, and their only child, Leland Jr.—and seems never to have been the family's favored residence.

But creating a comfortable setting for family life was not the point here. The Stanford mansion was "a quasi-public structure that relied on design elements appropriate to seats of aristocratic power," its purpose made manifest through a "carefully contrived iconographic program" that alluded to the Stanfords' wealth and cultural standing by recycling the kinds of decor previously found in "royal palaces."[7]

Stanford hired local architects S. C. Bugbee and Son to design his mansion, but its three-story masonry-and-stucco exterior, embellished with columns on its porches and portico and heavy pediment "eyebrows" over each window, was not all that much different than its new neighbors. Rather, the house was noted for its interior spaces. It was both technologically marvelous (the house had seven water closets and running water in its 19 bedrooms) and "artfully designed to a degree never before seen in California."[8] The rooms were arrayed in a profusion of historical-revival styles by Pottier & Stymus Manufacturing Company of New York. The firm had recently evolved from furniture manufacturing to interior decoration; whether this development reflected the ambitions of the firm's owners or a response to requests from clients is unknown. The Stanford commission raised the bar for decor on both coasts, however. It required the coordination of legions of skilled craftspeople, from decorative plasterers to drapery cutters.

At the time Pottier & Stymus was completing the Stanford mansion, the firm also received attention at the United States Centennial Exposition and in the nascent interior-design press for both the luxury of its furnishings and its approach to decor, which involved complete control of all details in the service of a "unified" or "harmonious" effect.[9] The enormous interior spaces of the Stanford house included examples of the firm's most luxurious historically inspired decorations, including a Pompeian drawing room, a Turkish dining room, a French neoclassical music room, an East Indian reception room, a Flemish billiards room, a family parlor in the "French Renaissance" style, and bedrooms reflecting eighteenth-century Louis design. One dinner guest recalled that the house "looked as if the old palaces of Europe had been ransacked of their art and other treasures to embellish the home of an American gentleman."[10] This phraseology soon became the formulaic description applied to the greater American residence throughout the Gilded Age; it was more than a throwaway line, as tons of salvaged architectural features, tapestries, carpets, art objects, and furniture were shipped to America for reinstallation, and appropriation, by wealthy owners over the next four decades. Fortunately, the Stanfords hired Eadweard Muybridge to photograph this masterwork, and images survive in the archives of Stanford University.

Like Armsmear, the Stanford mansion also contained idiosyncratic elements, particularly within its impressive two-story rotunda. There, a complex program of allegorical murals and decorations, juxtaposed to the adjoining rooms, represented the benefits that technology, particularly the railroad, brought to America and the triumph of America over the Old World. This astonishing decorative rhetoric was actually presented to the public in the first coverage of the house by local journalists; in 1876 one reported that the mansion was "as purely a high work of art as a great historical picture."[11]

The use of domestic architecture and interior design to claim the cultural legacy of the Old World was one manifestation of what has been called the American Renaissance (1876–1917), in which a community of increasingly numerous and prosperous "establishment" artists—painters, sculptors, architects, designers, and others—set itself the task of articulating in material form the new role of the United States in the world.[12] They chose the Renaissance as the controlling metaphor for their own work, representing their "special connection with the grand traditions of history" as well as their sense of being part of a unique moment in American society and culture.[13] The metaphor became a common trope in other popular forms of American expression too, although it was not uncontested; not everyone concurred that William H. Vanderbilt or J. P. Morgan were great and worthy cultural figures, although they certainly were financial giants.

By the 1880s, American Renaissance interiors as ebulliently didactic as the Stanford mansion tended to be found in truly public buildings—libraries, museums, and the like—not houses. By then, the rhetorical program of the greater American residence had become more systematized, and its decorative formulas spread throughout the United States.[14] It consisted of series of quasi-public rooms—entrance halls, reception rooms, paired parlors or drawing rooms, dining rooms, music rooms, even ballrooms—that carefully categorized social life, each decorated in a different historical style, with French, English, Italian, German, "Oriental," or even ancient antecedents. While the Stanfords had relied on the vision of one firm, in grand houses the assignment for each room was sometimes parceled out to a different interior design firm, which made every space a tour de force of what its principals' signature effects. Some rooms, particularly drawing rooms or parlors and lady's boudoirs, were almost always in some form of French taste. The decor of each room was planned from floor to ceiling, and the luxurious architectural details and finishes were echoed in furniture carved from expensive woods and ornamented with gilded bronze and marquetry, and in upholstery, including elaborate carpets, window and door curtains, tapestries, and furniture coverings. Each space was ornamented by paintings and groupings of other objects of art that mixed antiques with modern things. (The proportion of antiques to period objects varied depending on the deep pockets and ambitions of the owners, along with their inclinations to travel and collect souvenirs.)

The characteristics of bourgeois taste by the 1880s are evidence in *Artistic Houses*, a remarkable two-volume compendium published by D. Appleton & Company of New York in 1883 and 1884. Subtitled "Being a Series of Interior Views of a Number of the Most Beautiful and Celebrated Homes in the United States with a Description of the Art Treasures Contained Therein," *Artistic Houses* was not intended as a popular treatise on design; only 500 copies were printed, using the finest photographic reproduction techniques of the day.[15] It was sold by subscription, and the identities of the subscribers are unknown. Its influence on interior design is also unclear, but it does reflect the activities of a coterie of decorative-art workers and their East Coast patrons, and interpretations of these sorts of rooms subsequently appeared from coast to coast.

The photos in *Artistic Houses* reveal the ongoing American love affair with the aristocratic interiors of old Europe, although the styles of eighteenth- and early-nineteenth-century France so beloved of the Colts and the Stanfords had now been partially supplanted by English styles, including the quasi-medieval and orientalist "aesthetic" taste and more literal interpretations of grand medieval and Renaissance rooms. The deliberately public, and often decisively nondomestic, character of some of these rooms is striking, although some hours of the owners' days may have taken place in some of them. (My sense is that most of the ordinary activities of daily life took place in breakfast rooms, private sitting rooms, and other spaces that were rarely photographed.) In the most ambitious cases, the rooms of the greater American residence depicted in *Artistic Houses* are domestic museums of conservative European painting and sculpture, as well as collections of expensive decorative objects. The blurring of public and private in grand decor was reflected not only in the uses to which these grand rooms were put but also in the way they were discussed in the text, as if their simple presence were a great public good. When they covered such houses, newspapers and magazines of the day also used the same approving tone.[16] In 1888, for example, the *New York Times* published an appreciation of the house built by

J. J. Van Alen, who had married a member of the Astor family and served as United States ambassador to Italy under Grover Cleveland. This "True Elizabethan House" was praised as a model for "all the cottage world" (i.e., the families who intended to build their own summer houses in the seaside resort) because of its stylistic accuracy, due in part to the "old English doors, stairways, wainscoting, trimmings, tapestries, and furniture imported by Mr. Van Alen for this place. . . . The special features are the broad, old-style baronial hall; the small, dark-colored oak-trimmed dining room; the fine ballroom on the north, and the Adams room, furnished in careful imitation of the old masters of decoration."[17]

At least some of the homogeneity of bourgeois interiors across the country can be traced to the professionalization of interior design, including the rise of a design press and the appearance of the interior decoration firm. In its modern sense, the term "interior decorator" was in use by the 1870s. As the case of Pottier & Stymus suggests, interior decorating firms rose from several places in the furnishings trades: the makers of expensive, custom or semicustom furniture, the new department stores, and upholsterers, whose expertise in the procurement and use of furnishing textiles probably put them closer to the modern decorator than any other single trade. While the careers and products some of the most famous interior decorators have been studied in detail—Louis Comfort Tiffany and his colleagues in the short-lived firm of Associated Artists are perhaps the most familiar of these—more research needs to be done on these men, and a few women, who became the tastemakers and purveyors of elegant objects in large and small provincial cities all over the country, and whose work received notice in periodicals like *The Decorator and Furnisher, The Art Amateur,* advertising-driven women's monthlies such as *Ladies' Home Journal* and early "lifestyle" magazines like *Country Life* that proliferated at the end of the century. Given the absence of formal training in most places, becoming a local professional tastemaker seems to have been a process of apprenticeship and self-education, with developments in New York standing in for Paris and London. In fact, one aim of the elites who established the art museums that appeared in larger cities during these decades was educating the taste of designers and craftspeople—the very people who would subsequently be servicing the building campaigns of the newly wealthy.[18]

The decorative conventions that shaped expensive interiors all over the United States also represent the national consolidation of American economic elites. The popular press clearly identified the dwellings of the wealthy as the embodiment of their expanding public roles as cultural and economic forces in industrial America, and the analogies journalists chose are revealing. While some houses were "merely the inobtrusive homes of wealthy gentlemen," others were now "the dwellings of merchant princes, comparable, not in artistic originality and propriety, but in general atmosphere and style, to the palaces of Florentine and Venetian nobility," said the authors of *Stately Homes in America* (1903). Their houses "show something of the same pleasure in rich and 'stunning' furniture and fabrics, something of the same love of strong and compelling effects, something of the same willingness to advertise their wealth and power."[19] Even as preferences for particular styles or finishes shifted, or as new decorating talents emerged, in general terms the conventions of bourgeois decor remained remarkably intact into the twentieth century. Nob Hill, New York and its suburbs, the seaside resort of Newport, and Chicago offered the most famous clusters of grand houses, but examples could also be found wherever American enterprise created sizable new personal fortunes.

The Vanderbilts seem to have been particularly interested in, and adept at, pursuing house-building campaigns at the highest level. Not only did the Vanderbilts effectively colonize a large stretch of Fifth Avenue in midtown Manhattan, but they also continued their building campaigns in other places as well, constructing 25 large houses between 1878 and 1930. Cornelius Sr.'s sole heir, William Henry, and his eight children patronized America's first Beaux Arts architect, William Morris Hunt, and other society architects of the day for dwellings in New York, Newport, and along the Hudson River. In their first building campaign, William Henry and his sons Cornelius II and William Kissam constructed merchants' palaces on Fifth Avenue in New York. Completed in the early 1880s, the houses dominated the streetscape from Fifty-first to Fifty-eighth Street.[20] As the first neared completion in 1881, the *New York Times* gushed: "A few Princes and Emperors of the Old World may have more pretentious palaces, but it has been reserved for an American sovereign to eclipse them in the construction of an edifice which, while it contains all that can be desired in architecture and art, is also replete with everything that contributes to the comfort of a real home."[21] As with the Leland Stanford house, the interiors, rather than the architecture, captured much of the contemporary attention paid to these urban mansions. William Henry's house—really a double house, with a wing that housed several of his daughters and their families—was the largest, and it was the only one of the three illustrated in *Artistic Houses,* which also provided detailed descriptions of its "beautified and delectable" rooms.[22] However, the rooms in the dwellings of all three men were the products of important decorating firms based in New York.[23] William Henry Vanderbilt hired the design firm Herter Brothers to create the settings for his large collection of paintings and effectively gave them a blank check; he celebrated the completion of the house with a reception for 2,000; and he underwrote production of *Mr. Vanderbilt's House and Collection,* a four-volume catalogue of the premises' contents, in 1883 and 1884. William Kissam Vanderbilt's house was subsequently documented in a book published in 1925, while Cornelius II's was never photographed. At the time, the Cornelius Vanderbilt II house was regarded in the art press as the most significant because of the people he hired to create "aesthetic" rooms: Louis Comfort Tiffany and Associated Artists, along with John La Farge and Augustus Saint-Gaudens.[24]

Proliferation and Refinement: Decoding Bourgeois Decor and Tracing Its Influence

By the late nineteenth century, the greater American residence was a fixture in the collective imagination of a national audience, which had been primed to find cultural meanings in decor by a debate about taste that extended back to the colonial era. In the first half of the nineteenth century, this discourse of domestic environmentalism had posited an opposition between dwelling and rooms that embodied republican "comfort" and those shaped by aristocratic "fashion." It found a crucial setting for the creation of a virtuous citizenry in the former, which gave household furnishing practices real moral weight.[25] By the late nineteenth century, however, the argument opposing comfort and fashion had faded somewhat, or had in any event become less centered on the dwelling as a literal embodiment of republican virtue. What remained was the idea that houses were representations of more than the private tastes of their owners, although the *New York Times,* quoted above, still made a point of domesticating the expression of great wealth by praising William Henry Vanderbilt's Manhattan dwelling as a "real home."

In general, the transmission of style ideas for interior decor was decisively a top-down phenomenon, although modest households did considerable adaptation to suit their own circumstances. This was even the case when style leaders occasionally produced adaptations of vernacular interior decor. For example, in the 1880s and 1890s, elite men's smoking rooms occasionally took the form of mountain cabins decorated with hides, taxidermic mounts, and the working gear of hunters or trappers—which were then introduced to middle-class consumers for their own third-hand adaptations.

Still, bourgeois and middle-class interiors shared qualities that were more fundamental than the decorative skin provided by quotations of historical styles. As representations of the full flowering of bourgeois interior decor, the photographs in *Artistic Houses*—and in the many subsequent magazine articles and advice books on fashionable interior decoration—exhibit a level of decorative detail that is both fascinating and mind numbing, and which must have exerted a powerful effect when experienced in three dimensions and full color. The rooms represented the ability to command, and pay for, an extraordinary amount of specialized labor, and some were among the most extreme examples of the aesthetics of their time.

Elite domestic interiors, along with rooms such as hotel parlors created by the new cohort of professional decorators, also provided fantasy models and inspiration for more modestly prosperous amateurs. And much of what was made available to middle-class customers through the design and production processes of the architectural millwork, furnishings, and fancy-goods trades (the "accessories" shops of their time) reflected, however faintly, the stylistic qualities of expensive examples in historical revival styles.[26] One of the marvels of the production systems that made furniture, machine-woven lace and other furnishing fabrics, silver-plated vessels, and other decorative items was their flexibility and sensitivity to fashion, as factory owners figured out how to combine machinery, less expensive materials, and a limited amount of hand finishing to making versions of high-style objects.[27] The fact that some authors of elite decorating advice excoriated the results of this manufacturing ingenuity should be read as a testimonial to its success.

Comparisons between images of these and other elite rooms and those of more modest interiors reveal the proliferation of decorative possessions much further down the economic ladder, especially by the 1890s, and striking similarities in the modes of display. The symmetry that characterized rooms of the eighteenth and early nineteenth centuries and the tidy, open space characteristic of the arrangement of those rooms when unoccupied had both disappeared. The interior architecture of bourgeois and aspiring middle-class interiors was blurred by textiles covering windows, floors, and tabletops. Papers and other coverings with large vivid patterns made walls seem less solid. Interior space was increasingly fragmented by constellations of carved and upholstered furniture that forced occupants to negotiate along carefully plotted interior pathways. In many of the rooms, small items collected in drifts on tabletops; they crept up the walls in elaborate arrangements; they were presented for inspection on étagères, ornate pieces of furniture intended for nothing more than the display of other objects.

Was this simply a matter of accumulation, a sort of collective pack-rat response to the new possibilities of material abundance? Written clues as to the motives that shaped complexity in decor are actually abundant. People wrote and read about both bourgeois and middle-class rooms, and about interior decor, in many genres of commercial texts. Accepting the limitation that these are normative literature, texts including "household art" books, daily newspapers and trade papers, mail-order catalogs, popular periodicals, and even magazine fiction offer a vocabulary of appreciation and interpretations that can be compared to the rooms themselves (or at least to their image traces, since most are long gone). When these texts are compared to one another, and to other genres of advice, such as etiquette literature, their vocabulary is revealed as a semantic taxonomy that cut across many categories of experience.[28] Take, for example, the popular preference for elaborate, highly finished objects, from carved chairs to silver teapots. Beautiful manners and beautiful objects were both highly "polished" (one figuratively, the other literally). Well-bred people were "refined"; so were beautifully detailed, perfect objects. This taxonomy, which I have written about elsewhere, developed into a fully realized aesthetics of refinement.[29]

In all but the most expensive, ambitious cases, or when rooms pronounced self-consciously advanced tastes, bourgeois interiors and more modest aspiring rooms were shaped by the same set of cultural principles, articulated through a core set of material and visual conventions. The heart of this aesthetics of refinement was a preference for complexity, which was associated with the advance of civilization. Successful rooms were intended to reveal themselves slowly, with each vignette encompassing a level of detail equivalent to what the eye could perceive when taking in the room as a whole. The ability to attend to detail and to appreciate highly ornamental, beautifully finished artifacts was now implied by the act of ownership, which in turn suggested the cultivation of the room's owners. Some of this detail operated at the level of sensibility, as carpets, draperies, and other luxurious textiles reshaped the sensory experiences of touch and sound; but much of it was devoted to a newly self-conscious pleasure in the sense of sight. Some details, particularly objects of art and nature such as print folios or Wardian cases (the first terrarium), operated as metonyms for entire realms of cultural experience that their owners apparently possessed, which introduces the second facet of the aesthetic: a love of play with cultural association.

Recent writing has suggested that middle-class displays of Japanese fans, Chinese ceramics, water pipes and brass trays from the Levant, and other exotica purchased from fancy-goods shops be taken seriously as a manifestation of globalization, and a way in which women could participate in discourses of international relations.[30] The great American houses set the tone for this form of cultural play. In an age when even the wealthy had access to a smaller array of amusements, and where much of social life took place in private houses, people actually talked about their prized possessions as part of sociality. This conversation took two forms. The first consisted of personal stories associated with the acquisition of the object. While this account could be genealogical, in the modern era of acquisition it was often about the occasion of travel leading to contact with the artifact, the circumstances of receiving a gift, or, in the case of competitive collectors, the kind of "fish story" that still gives them pleasure today. Descriptions of rooms published in journals like *The Decorator and Furnisher* often took pains to discuss the rare origins of objects on display, and the text of *Artistic Houses* is full of this kind of storytelling, for example, discussing the main hall of Marshall Field's house in Chicago, the text notes that, "Every article of furniture here is medieval, and has its history—from the San Marco seat, which grim old Savonarola may have used, to the stiff but handsomely-carved settee, which once was an ornament in some baronial hall about the time of the Mayflower's first voyage."[31] The second kind of conversation about possessions was less personal but more culturally loaded. It had to do with codes of cultural associations that refined individuals were expected to know and to tap into as part of the performance of cultivation. A midcentury etiquette manual offers this interpretation of what was actually the eighteenth-century theory of associations:

> Our tastes and distastes proceed, for the most part, from the power that objects have to recall other ideas to the mind. And persons of superior cultivation have not only established for themselves a higher standard of grace or excellence, to which they can refer, but they have attained a quicker perception of the relation of things to each other.[32]

Apart from whatever personal, idiosyncratic meanings household furnishings bore, people believed that they also carried with them objective sets of conventional associations with which an educated person was familiar. Like-minded people meeting in the social space of private dwelling were expected to talk about these meanings. In this sense, the aesthetics of refinement was democratic: possessions did not themselves have to be expensive; however, they had to be usable as prompts for the game of associations.

The associate codes of the aesthetic of refinement also made use of historical styles, particularly the varied manifestations of eighteenth- and early-nineteenth-century French furnishing tastes. The authors of the catalogue for the groundbreaking exhibition *The American Renaissance 1876–1917* point out that American interest in historical styles grew more "scientific" as the century passed. Scientific eclecticism, "the selection and usage of styles, motifs, and details drawn from a variety of sources," was based on new scholarly knowledge of past design that was contemporaneous with the creation of the modern academic disciplines and the establishment of cultural institutions, including museums.[33]

While the interest in appropriating historical styles was always romantic, it was also strategic, especially in the last quarter of the nineteenth century. Over time, historical styles became a key part of a commonly understood set of material conventions suggesting the appropriately hierarchical character of social life, a pervasive belief that could be—and perhaps had to be—presented indirectly through things in a country where political rhetoric continued to emphasize equality. As we have seen, for the capitalists who purchased large European architectural fragments, art, and decorative objects from both Europe and Asia to furnish their new houses, appropriating historical styles also demonstrated the rise of American economic power and American freedom to, as a young Henry James put it, "deal freely with forms of civilization not only our own . . . pick and choose and assimilate and in short (aesthetically and culturally) claim our property wherever we find it."[34] Historicism in decor was available as a form of cultural play for both economic elites and consumers of more modest means. While ordinary people who purchased Renaissance Revival parlor suites were not claiming to be just like America's merchant princes or French aristocrats, their purchases did claim a small role in the advancement of civilization for their owners.

The third part of the aesthetic of refinement was the highly specific, highly stylized gendering of rooms and their contents, where spaces, styles, forms, colors, ornamental motifs, and artifacts were also coded as either masculine or feminine. This was often seen in the juxtaposition of feminine "French" drawing rooms, parlors, or even ballrooms with masculine dining rooms and libraries that contained loosely interpreted "Renaissance" furnishings. This fully developed coding of light colors versus dark, curvaceous shapes versus rectilinear, and associated iconography still needs a full historical accounting, although some elements, such as the continuing use of the iconography of the hunt for dining rooms, have received scholarly attention.[35] The broader cultural discourse of civilization's progress that underlay the quest for material refinement also encouraged highly gendered interior decor, since the most civilized nations also displayed the greatest differentiation between men and women.[36] The stylistic gender coding of most public rooms was only highlighted by the presence of one style, the Turkish mode, which was always viewed as exotic and a little raffish because, in Western eyes, its gender attributes were ambiguous.

However, the gendering of rooms also took another form, and it is here that we can begin to see some significant rhetorical differences between bourgeois decor, which I have already described as not being particularly "domestic," and the decorative efforts contained in more modestly prosperous middle-class households. This was partly a matter of scale; few of the rooms illustrated in *Artistic Houses* would be described as cozy. But there is more to this distinction than sheer scale and expenditure.

One of the most potent cultural principles associated with the emergence of the antebellum middle class was what historians have labeled "domesticity." Acknowledging that reality was considerably more complex than the discourse suggested, domesticity created parallel realms of cultural authority for men and women, claiming the household for the latter. By the 1840s, a distinctive written and material rhetoric of middle-class comfort, already mentioned in the context of inscribing the house as the embodiment of cultural ideals, was an important element of the discourse of domesticity. This rhetoric warned homemakers to avoid the temptation of creating rooms that not only wasted family resources but also could actually damage family happiness.

What made this argument so potent was its linkage between decor and maternal care; rooms had begun to stand in for women's, particularly mothers', bodies. Historian Beverly Gordon pointed out in a 1996 essay that the "historical conception, treatment, and decoration of the body and the house" were not just "closely interrelated," but that there was also a "deep structural or conceptual equation among house, clothing, body, and the woman who was held to be responsible for them in the industrial age."[37] Harriet Beecher Stowe was the most famous proponent of this formula, which appeared in domestic advice guides, popular periodicals, and fiction. In her 1876 novel *We and Our Neighbors,* she argued that the home was, for her newly wed heroine, a "new world of power," where her "self" would begin to "melt away into something higher" as she adorned the rooms that were the "new impersonation of herself," the "expansion of her own being."[38] In middle-class rooms, the handwork that women used to create refined décor was, in this view, a kind of self-adornment, and the bricolage of ordinary parlors and dining rooms was a dialogue between the aesthetic of refinement and the quest for a specifically middle-class comfort. The high-style bourgeois interiors that inspired the look of much of this handwork, however, were themselves embellished through the appropriated labor of others, including the anonymous women who had to sew for a living. The quasi-public qualities and the decorative agendas of the greater American residence also were sampled, admired, and paraphrased in cheaper goods but could not be fully appropriated for more modest interiors. Still, the fact that modestly prosperous people also made photographic portraits of their own unoccupied rooms, a practice popular among the bourgeoisie as seen in the publication of *Artistic Houses,* suggests their own beliefs that rooms were more than demonstrations of the ability to spend, but representations of, and claims for, social and cultural selves.

Even the convention-laden formulas that shaped bourgeois interiors evolved as the twentieth century opened. The elaborate decorative programs employed by the "new Medici" grew simpler; the aesthetics of refinement faded and were replaced by decor that still employed historical revivals, but with less visual and rhetorical bombast. For example, some made America's own past, with its relatively simple material culture, the focus of expenditure and ambition. While watering holes for the wealthy were still the sites of clusters of palaces, and newly fashionable locations, such as the Florida coasts, still saw major new building campaigns by the wealthy, the public imagination was now drawn to a different sort of theatrical decor, found in the homes of a new sort of elite—movie stars or media moguls like William Randolph Hearst, whose "castle," La Cuestra Encantada, constructed over an extended period between the 1920s and late 1940s, was a fantasy for entertaining in the " Mediterranean Revival" style. What Hearst shared with the Vanderbilts and other builders of great houses in previous generations, however, was his delight in grabbing up material fragments of the diminished European aristocracy.

While most of the palaces of America's merchant princes are gone, either demolished or adapted to other uses, some are still private residences, even remaining in the hands of descendents, and scores survive as historic house museums. Newport, Rhode Island, contains the largest surviving public collection, where it is possible to see first hand several generations of building (and remodeling) activity. However, regional examples can be visited throughout the United States, including the Henry Clay Frick House in Pittsburgh, Villa Louis in Prairie du Chein, Wisconsin, and the Moody Mansion in Galveston, Texas. None of these can surpass the surviving mansions of the Vanderbilts, however. George W. Vanderbilt's Biltmore is still in family hands, but it is now a multimillion-dollar tourist attraction and resort as well as a museum, and five other mansions are protected by stewards that include the National Park Service. Visits to the abandoned palaces of America's bourgeoisie offer insight into the expansive imaginations and egos, as well as the expanded means, of the first generations with great wealth in this county. However, the aesthetics of the complex bourgeois interiors of the Gilded Age now look to most visitors like little more than clutter, and the rooms' material rhetoric is regarded as posturing, no longer resonant to Americans whose primary aesthetics for decor are based on sentiment and bodily comfort.

Notes

1. Sven Beckert, *The Monied Metropolis: New York City and the Consolidation of the American Bourgeoisie, 1850–1896* (Cambridge [UK] and New York: Cambridge University Press, 2001), 7. One wonders about the effect of this particular assignment on Progressive journalist and reformer Herbert Croly.
2. Richard L. Bushman, *The Refinement of America: Persons, Houses, Cities* (New York: Knopf, 1992); T. H. Breen, "'Baubles of Britain': The American Consumer Revolutions of the Eighteenth Century," *Past & Present* 119, no. 1 (May 1988): 73–104.
3. For examples of this trend, see the discussion of one elite Boston family's lifestyle in Eleanor Pearson DeLorme, "The Swan Commissions," *Winterthur Portfolio* 14, no. 4 (Winter 1979): 361–95; and Katherine C. Grier, *Culture and Comfort: Parlor Making and Middle-Class Identity, 1850–1930* (Washington, DC: Smithsonian Institution Press, 1997), Chapter 2: "The Comfortable Theater: Parlor Making in the Middle-Class Victorian Household, 1850–1910)," 64–77.
4. For a well-illustrated history of Colt house, see William Hosley, *Colt: The Making of an American Legend* (Amherst, MA: University of Massachusetts Press, 1996) especially pages 138–165.
5. For this account of the Stanford mansion, I rely on a superb essay by Diana Strazdes, "The Millionaire's Palace: Leland Stanford's Commission for Pottier & Stymus in San Francisco," *Winterthur Portfolio* 36, no. 4 (2001): 213–43.
6. Ibid., 214.
7. Ibid., 215.
8. Ibid., 214.
9. David A. Hanks, "Pottier & Stymus Mfg. Co.: Artistic Furniture and Decorations," *Art & Antiques* 7, no. 5 (1982): 84–91.
10. James J. Ayers, *Gold and Sunshine: Reminiscences of Early California* (Boston: R. G. Badger, 1922), 281; quoted in Strazdes, "Millionaire's Palace," 226.
11. "An Art Treasure: The Decoration of the Stanford Mansion," *San Francisco Chronicle,* 1876; quoted in Strazdes, "Millionaire's Palace," 236.
12. Brooklyn Museum, *The American Renaissance, 1876–1917* (New York: Brooklyn Museum, 1979). This is the informative and beautifully illustrated catalogue of the exhibition of the same title.

13. Ibid., 12.
14. For examples of the national spread of complex interior decor, see William Seale, *The Tasteful Interlude: American Interiors through the Camera's Eye, 1860–1917* (New York: Praeger, 1975); and Cynthia A. Brandimarte, *Inside Texas: Culture, Identity, and Houses, 1878–1920* (Fort Worth: Texas Christian University Press, 1991), esp. Chapter 7, "Art Good Enough for Texas: Refinement," 143–65, and Chapter 13, "Deep in the Heart of Anywhere: Architects and Decorators," 337–95. For examples that feature both elite houses and middle-class apartments in the Gilded Age, see Joseph Byron, *Photographs of New York Interiors at the Turn of the Century: From the Byron Collection of the Museum of the City of New York,* text by Clay Lancaster (New York: Dover Publications, 1976).
15. *Artistic Houses* was reprinted in a single volume in 1971 by Benjamin Blom of New York. The plates from the text, along with a detailed and perceptive essay on the publication history of the book and extended new photograph captions, are available in Arnold Lewis, James Turner, and Steven McQuillin, *The Opulent Interiors of the Gilded Age: All 203 Photographs from "Artistic Houses"* (New York: Dover Publications, 1987).
16. Ibid., 21, 23. Diana Strazdes points out that "Stanford, 'the railroad king,' was able, through his mansion, to take on the role of munificent agent of the public's prosperity. His showpiece residence exemplified the blending and confusing of personal, corporate, and community profit typical of the rapidly growing cities of the American West" (Strazdes, "Millionaire's Palace," 216).
17. "A True Elizabethan House: J. J. Van Alen's Newport House Is Opened with a Grand Ball," *New York Times,* August 24, 1888, 3.
18. Neil Harris, *Cultural Excursions: Marketing Appetites and Cultural Tastes in Modern America* (Chicago: University of Chicago Press, 1990), Chapter 3: "Museums, Merchandising, and Popular Taste: The Struggle for Influence," esp. 57. For an exemplary study of one of these early interior decorators, Tiffany protégé Candace Wheeler, see Amelia Peck and Carol Irish, *Candace Wheeler: The Art and Enterprise of American Design, 1870–1900* (New Haven, CT: Yale University Press, 2001).
19. Harry W. Desmond and Herbert Croly, *Stately Homes in America: From Colonial Times to the Present Day* (New York: D. Appleton, 1903), 12, 15, 22.
20. "The New Vanderbilt Mansions: Plans for the Four Elegant Dwellings to be Erected on Fifth-Avenue," *New York Times,* December 9, 1879, 8. For an example of the social life that was conducted in the public spaces of the houses, see "Mr. Vanderbilt's Musicale," *New York Times,* February 22, 1884, 5.
21. "The Vanderbilt Palaces: An Interior View of the Great Houses on Fifth-Avenue," *New York Times,* August 25, 1881, 3.
22. *Artistic Houses* (1883; repr. New York: Benjamin Blom, 1971), vol. 1,125.
23. For a chronological listing of these buildings, see http://www.vanderbiltmuseum.org.
24. The largest Vanderbilt project was Biltmore, the life work of youngest son George W. Vanderbilt. This 250-room French Renaissance mansion and its 8,000-acre country estate in Asheville, North Carolina, was described in 1895 as "the most valuable as well as the most extensive private property in America" ("Biltmore Thrown Open: George W. Vanderbilt Entertains at His Country Estate," *New York Times,* December 26, 1895, 2).
25. Grier, *Culture and Comfort,* Chapter 3: "'Orthodox as the Hymn Book': The Rhetoric of Parlor Furnishing, 1850–1910," 89–116.
26. There were a couple of exceptions to this trend. The first was the rise in the 1870s of "Eastlake"-style furniture, which, although it bore the name of an English design reformer, was not much like the designs he showed in his influential book *Hints on Household Taste in Furniture, Upholstery, and Other Details* (1st American ed., Boston: J. R. Osgood, 1872). What made Eastlake furniture so successful was its relative ease of production; its rectilinearity was suitable for woodworking machinery, and its ornament was easy to paraphrase with power tools, wood appliqués, and paint. The second exception appeared in the early twentieth century, when the distinctive Arts and Crafts style, intended for use in simplified family dwellings, was adopted with enthusiasm by middle-class customers.
27. For an overview of producer strategies for "styled" consumer goods, see Phillip Scranton, *Endless Novelty: Specialty Production and American Industrialization, 1865–1925* (Princeton, NJ: Princeton University Press, 1997.
28. Grier, *Culture and Comfort,* Chapter 5: "The Quest for Refinement: Reconstructing the Aesthetics of Upholstery, 1850–1910," 143–75.

29. Ibid.
30. See, for example, Kristin Hoganson, "Cosmopolitan Domesticity: Importing the American Dream, 1865–1920," *American Historical Review* 107 (2002): 55–83.
31. *Artistic Houses*, vol. 2, 44.
32. Emily Thornwell, *The Ladies' Guide to Perfect Gentility, in Manners, Dress, and Conversation . . .* (New York: Derby and Jackson and Cincinnati: H. W. Derby, 1856).
33. Brooklyn Museum, *American Renaissance*, 35.
34. Ibid., 37.
35. Kenneth L. Ames, "Death in the Dining Room," in Ames, *Death in the Dining Room and Other Tales of Victorian Culture* (Philadelphia: Temple University Press, 1992), 44–96.
36. Gail Bederman, *Manliness and Civilization: A Cultural History of Gender and Race in the United States, 1880–1917* (Chicago: University of Chicago Press, 1995), 26–30.
37. Beverly Gordon, "Woman's Domestic Body: The Conceptual Conflation of Women and Interiors in the Industrial Age," in "Gendered Spaces and Aesthetics," ed. Katherine C. Grier, special issue, *Winterthur Portfolio* 31, no. 4 (Winter 1996): 301.
38. Harriet Beecher Stowe, *We and Our Neighbors* (New York: J. B. Ford, 1875), 142–43.

Part II

Networks and Institutions

6
Bourgeois Institution Builders: New York in the Nineteenth Century

Sven Beckert

When in 1831 a Frenchman, a count, took upon himself the burden of crossing the Atlantic to inquire into the inner workings of the strange new society that was taking shape on the North American continent, he stumbled across a vast universe of voluntary associations.[1] "I confess I had no previous notion," he admitted to his readers, that Americans "of all ages, all conditions, and all dispositions constantly form associations . . . of a thousand . . . kinds, religious, moral, serious, futile, general or restricted, enormous or diminutive." Indeed, he asserted, in "no country in the world has the principle of association been more successfully used or applied to a greater multitude of objects than in America."[2] While the objects of such associations might often be trivial, he said, the result of this busy organizing was highly significant, since it formed nothing less than the foundation of "the most democratic country on the face of the earth."[3] A vibrant civil society begot modern democracy. For this reason, the count concluded, "Nothing in my opinion is more deserving of our attention than the intellectual and moral associations of America."[4]

This Frenchman on the search for the underpinnings of democracy was Alexis de Tocqueville. A brilliant political theorist and a most sensitive observer of society, he set the terms of debate on voluntary associations for the next 180 years and located them squarely at the center of the analysis of "modern" society. Indeed, so compelling were his arguments that in the 1990s state builders in countries that had recently turned democratic still attempted to follow his prescriptive observations, wishing for a flowering civil society to stabilize their fragile regimes.

Tocqueville's sense of urgency in understanding the character and place of voluntary associations has carried over to historians trying to make sense of the nineteenth century. Consequently, his questions will also animate this essay, though with more modest goals. In the following pages, I will look at the associations of only one city—New York. I will only focus on associations dominated by a relatively small group of citizens—the bourgeoisie (here defined as people who own capital, do not work for wages, do not work manually, and do hire others to work for them in exchange for wages).[5] And I will refrain from speculations about the relationship between civil society and democracy.

In doing so, I hope to make sense of the history of bourgeois associations in nineteenth-century New York. My discussion will be informed by questions that allow us to compare the "associational experience" of bourgeois New Yorkers with that of economic elites elsewhere and to make some general arguments about the place of associations in the process of bourgeois class formation. The argument I am going to make is twofold. First, I will maintain that associations were central to a sense of cohesion and unity for a group of New Yorkers who were engaged in very different kinds of economic undertakings. Associations helped to foster shared identities and, at times, allowed for these identities to translate into collective action. Social, economic, and political might, in short, unfolded jointly. And, second, I will argue that the specific forms of associations changed in the course of the second half of the nineteenth century in three ways: (1) They became more inclusive by admitting bourgeois New Yorkers of diverse economic sectors into their ranks. (2) They became more socially homogenous by limiting access to the city's economic elite. (3) They became increasingly successful in capturing the public sphere. As a result, by late in the century, New York civil society had divided along class lines to a degree unknown at the time of Tocqueville's visit 50 years earlier.

Bourgeois New Yorkers—the city's merchants, manufacturers, and bankers—created numerous associations: social clubs, missionary societies, employers' associations, ad hoc political committees, musical societies, ethnic organizations, and religious congregations, to name just a few. It was not unusual for individual merchants, industrialists, bankers, and professionals to belong to half a dozen of these organizations simultaneously, which might include one or several social clubs, the Chamber of Commerce, a benevolent association, an ethnic organization, or the board of directors of a museum. Indeed, a representative sample of bourgeois New Yorkers for 1891 suggests that, on average, they belonged to more than five social clubs each.[6] The scope of these organizations varied widely: Some, such as social clubs, focused on bourgeois sociability; others, such as the New York Historical Society, concentrated on cultural enlightenment for its members; while numerous employers' associations fought trade unions and strikes; and a few associations even focused on joint political mobilization to affect the abolition of slavery, higher tariffs, or the disenfranchisement of New York's workers in municipal elections.[7] So vast was the associational universe that one contemporary observed it to be "so large and complex a system that to determine its component parts, its many intersecting circles and relations, would require the time and the skill, almost, of an astronomer who would map out the heavens."[8] Indeed, by late in the century, few cities in the Western world sported such an intricate web of bourgeois associations as did New York.

In order to understand this complicated and varied associational universe, we need to take a bird's-eye view. This can be done most successfully by contrasting and comparing two points in time: the 1850s and the 1880s. During these thirty years, important and dramatic shifts occurred that throw a light on the character and function of bourgeois associations in New York City.

In the 1850s, as Tocqueville had observed earlier, there was an overwhelming number of voluntary associations in New York City, formed for every conceivable purpose. These associations were created by and served the needs of different social groups, including recent immigrants, skilled workers, shopkeepers, and the city's industrialists and merchants. While New Yorkers with access to resources were able to build the most stable associations, gathering for a given purpose, constituting an organization, and deliberating about its goals were not pursuits unique to the members of the city's economic elite.

However, while many burgeois New Yorkers built associations, single organizations usually organized specific segments of the city's economic elite. By the 1850s, the city's mercantile elite especially had created a number of institutions that were unusually stable and powerful. The most important of these, uniting mercantile interests at large, was the Chamber of Commerce, devoted to supporting the economic and political interests of the city's traders. Beyond the Chamber of Commerce, subsets of merchants and bankers organized into heritage societies: Traders from Connecticut and Massachusetts, for example, founded the New England Society of New York in 1805, and in 1835 their colleagues of "old New York" ancestry united in the St. Nicholas Society, whose activities focused on celebrating a shared place of birth.[9] Above this landscape of organizations towered the social clubs, though they were a relatively new phenomenon and still few in number. The oldest, the Union Club, was formed in 1836 by "gentlemen of social distinction."[10] The club allowed its members to enjoy a parlor, a library, a reception room, a billiard room, and a dining room with "carved black walnut paneling, and . . . beautiful paintings of game over the chimney pieces."[11] Three similar social clubs of importance existed in the 1850s: the New York Club, which was most like the Union Club; the small New York Yacht Club, founded in 1844 and dedicated to the "cultivation of naval sciences," pleasure outings, and boat races; and the Century Club, founded in 1847 to bring together writers and artists with their wealthy benefactors.[12] Admittance to these four exclusive clubs was selective: ancestry and identification as a "gentleman" (a term in the 1850s applied mostly to merchants, bankers, and professionals) being the decisive factors.

These associations, though socially homogenous in their membership, systematically excluded an important segment of the city's economic elite—the manufacturers. Though in 1850 about 20 percent of all well-to-do New York taxpayers were manufacturers, they accounted for only 2 percent of the members of the New York Club, 3 percent of the members of the Union Club, and a meager 2 percent of the members of the Chamber of Commerce. The city's mercantile elite decisively dominated these associations.[13] They looked down upon manufacturers, who had often risen to wealth through the ranks of artisanal workshops. Lawyer George T. Strong, for example, derided the city's wealthiest manufacturer, Peter Cooper, as a "self-made millionaire glue boiler."[14]

Indeed, as the structure of club membership suggests, there was a sharp divide between the institutions created by merchants and bankers on the one side and those created by the city's manufacturers on the other. Until the 1820s, industrialists—instead of becoming part of the merchants' social universe—had built shared associations with skilled workers, the interests of their specific craft providing the impetus for organization. By the 1850s, however, they had also opted for organizations of a socially more homogeneous character. Yet despite having accumulated considerable amounts of capital, they did not enter the exclusive associations created by the city's merchants earlier in the century. Excluded from the social universe of the city's mercantile elite, they built their own associations, which were fundamentally different in character from those of the city's merchants.[15] The Mechanics' Institute was one such association. Founded in 1830, the institute offered lectures on "natural and mechanical philosophy," classes in mechanical drawings and mathematics, and "Meetings, Debates, and Discussions for the benefit of its members."[16] In typical fashion, the institute provided a forum for exchanging technical expertise and opportunities to train apprentices—two central concerns of industrialists.[17] Similarly, the American Institute, founded in 1829, organized industrialists for "the purpose of encouraging and promoting domestic industry in this State."[18] Representing those "citizens who enjoy that extraordinary genius for originality of thinking and invention so distinguishing this new world," they exhibited the products of America's manufacturers, provided training in engineering and mathematics, and discussed "philosophical subjects."[19] No merchant joined the Mechanics or American Institutes, further reaffirming the sharp divide between the industrial and mercantile world of voluntary associations.

While New Yorkers built numerous associations whose memberships were clearly limited to the city's economic elite, they still expressed their beliefs in the social cohesiveness of American society and reached out to other social groups. "[T]he more opulent citizens take great care not to stand aloof from the people," observed Tocqueville.[20] Wealthy congregations, for example, financed and paid for so-called mission chapels in the poorer areas of town to serve the spiritual needs of the poor. Moreover, both the city's mercantile elite as well as its rising manufacturers formed and financed numerous benevolent associations.[21] Some, such as the American Home Missionary Society, dispatched preachers, spread the Gospel, or advocated temperance; others, such as the Association for the Improvement of the Conditions of the Poor (AICP), distributed charity. Still others demanded the abolition of slavery.[22] The most important concern of these associations was the reform of the city's working class and poor, and many of the associations concentrated on building institutions to rescue the "worthy poor," for instance by building asylums for widowed women or orphans. Activists in these organizations were inspired by deeply held religious and political convictions, seeing themselves as moral guardians of society. This sense of stewardship translated into responsibility for the less fortunate, a firm belief that poverty was "an anomaly in our country, an exotic to our soil."[23] Bourgeois women, in particular, translated their role as guardians of the home into that of guardians of society, thereby achieving central roles in these associations.

While these socially exclusive organizations directed their vision toward all social classes, there remained during the 1850s a few associations dominated by the city's economic elite that still admitted working-class New Yorkers into their fold. Most important here were the ad hoc political movements that mobilized voters outside traditional party channels, such as the "City Reform League."[24] While dominated by upper-class citizens, they attracted a number of skilled workers to their ranks, testifying to the still somewhat permeable social boundary between the city's economic elite and other social groups.

As a result of the vibrancy of American civil society, as well as its particular class structure and political traditions, by the 1850s, New York's economic elite shared the public sphere with other social groups. They neither dominated the public sphere in opposition to other social groups nor did they succeed in claiming the social neutrality of the institutions that they built.[25] For many of New York's merchants, manufacturers, and bankers, the cityscape itself did not adequately reflect the economic importance of New York, lacking the grand boulevards or pastoral parks of some European cities. The overwhelming impression the city left on the minds of its upper-class citizens was one of incomprehensible chaos. As the *New York Herald* complained, the "swearing, drinking, silly boors" of the Bowery had "destroyed all enjoyment" of carriage drives along city streets.[26] The city was noisy, it stank, and it permanently threatened encounters with its most undesirable inhabitants—but there was little that New York's economic elite could do about such a deplorable state of affairs.

This environment of toil, exertion, and sweat was more than an aesthetic affront; it symbolized the unprecedented openness and democratic dynamism of the city's shared spaces. Indeed, here in New York City, as nowhere else in the mid-nineteenth century world, all social groups vied for the control of public space and public sphere. In the hurly-burly atmosphere of the city, the merchants, bankers, and industrialists were, often to their great displeasure, jostled and circumvented in the creation of the central institutions of the public sphere such as museums, orchestras, theaters, and opera houses. The commercialized origins of mid-century cultural institutions made them resistant to the financial control and the aesthetic vision of the city's mercantile elite. Museums, for example, which would later in the century become leading pillars of bourgeois self-definition, at mid-century remained socially inclusive institutions driven by profit. "Tasteful" art collections were to be found only in fashionable homes, such as the remarkable collections of George T. Strong, William Aspinwall, August Belmont, William B. Astor, and Cornelius Vanderbilt. The public display of such art, however, proved difficult; for example, the pioneering New York Gallery of Fine Arts closed its doors in 1854, "plagued by chronic debts."[27] Three years later, in 1857, the New York Historical Society opened a small art gallery whose somewhat defensive mission was "to prove to mankind that in art the present is not inferior to the past, or the New World to the Old World."[28] Despite these small efforts, New York would not see a major public fine arts institution until the late 1870s. And it was only in 1854 that the first substantial opera house—the Academy of Music—got off the ground, after earlier efforts to build such an institution had failed.[29] Even then, however, these institutions were small in comparison to those of Paris or London and even to those of the German, French, or British provinces.

Furthermore, other social groups successfully contested control over the public sphere. Most tellingly, in the 1850s, the New York Philharmonic Society performances—often to the consternation of their elite supporters—were faced with rebellious cross-class audiences who lacked the decorum and behavior that elite New Yorkers thought appropriate, an audience that refused to yield to the economic elite's conceptions of proper behavior. The New York Philharmonic Orchestra, which would later in the century turn itself into a leading bourgeois cultural institution, was in the 1850s a discordant cultural battlefield which New York's merchants struggled to make into a sanctified space for the enjoyment of "high culture" music.

The cross-class nature of cultural institutions and practices was evident, for example, in 1849 when riots broke out in front of the Astor Place Opera House. On the eve of a much-publicized performance, a brawl flared up between working-class supporters of popular Shakespearean actor Edwin Forrest and the police, who protected an audience supporting an elite actor of British heritage, William Charles Macready. In effect, the city's merchants, manufacturers, and bankers lacked the power and authority to impose their cultural vision. As a consequence, the Opera House faltered, and finally closed its doors in 1852.[30] An effort of New York's economic elite to create a class-defined public sphere faltered on the shoals of popular claims to broad cultural representation.

The vibrance of commercialized culture, a culture that attracted all social groups, further undermined emerging claims to the control of the public sphere by the economic elite. Most prominent here were the commercialized curiosity museums such as Scudder's or Barnum's, which exhibited "bearded ladies," "legless wonders," "live mud turtles," and "bed curtains belonging to Mary, Queen of Scots."[31] Barnum claimed to display 600,000 such curiosities by 1849.[32] These artifacts, along with themed exhibits on topics such as the "missing link" between men and apes—featuring "Mademoiselle Fanny" (an orangutan)—attracted an audience ranging from manual workers to millionaire manufacturer Peter Cooper.[33]

Hence, in the 1850s, associations of the city's economic elite were still very much related to the specific sector of the economy in which their members were engaged and deeply embedded in their sense of themselves as stewards of the community—a community, they believed, which did not know of any permanent class divisions. This combination of particularist identities and universalist claims, in turn, kept the public sphere socially diverse.

By the 1880s, however, things had changed fundamentally. For one, the city's economic elite was more thoroughly organized than ever before. There were increasing numbers of associations, as bourgeois New Yorkers made an unprecedented effort to organize along class lines, especially in the wake of the 1873 depression, which, according to one contemporary observer, separated "classes more than ever."[34] Bourgeois New Yorkers now increasingly saw themselves as a distinct social group, a reorientation most dramatically exemplified by their embrace of social Darwinism. New organizations, among them boarding schools, the Metropolitan Museum of Art, and the Museum of Natural History, as well as a large number of new social clubs, elaborated class identities and drew bourgeois New Yorkers closer to one another. This was exactly the kind of change that Tocqueville had anticipated and feared half a century earlier, when he had warned that "[t]he master and the workman have . . . no similarity, and their differences increase every day."[35]

The associational universe of the city's upper class became so vast that public markers of belonging to the "right" social circles became ever more important. In 1883, *The Season—An Annual Record of Society* was published for the first time, and served as a record for society's social occasions, including providing its readers ("those personally interested") with comprehensive lists of guests at these occasions.[36] In 1886, the *Social Register* began publishing an annual list of bourgeois New Yorkers considered among the socially elect, including their various club memberships.[37] Increasingly, class formation became a conscious "project."

In contrast to the 1850s, these numerous associations allowed access to all segments of the city's economic elite. During the 1880s, bourgeois identities were rooted to a lesser extent in the particular kind of capital the economic elite controlled. As a result, manufacturers became integrated into the social and cultural institutions of the city's merchants. By 1886, even the Chamber of Commerce had admitted a significant number of industrialists,[38] including Robert Hoe, the manufacturer of printing presses (joined in 1872), the ship builder John Roach (1881), railroad entrepreneurs Cornelius Vanderbilt (1881) and Chauncey Depew (1885), as well as iron manufacturers George W. Quintard (1865) and John M. Cornell (1881). In 1889, John D. Rockefeller joined, and in 1897 Charles H. Steinway followed suit. This integration spilled into all areas of bourgeois social life: The warden and vestrymen of St. George's Church had mostly been merchants (76 percent) during the 1850s, yet thirty years later their number had fallen to only 27 percent, the numbers enhanced by industrialists and bankers. Manufacturers also joined the most elite social clubs of the city, including the Union Club, the Union League Club, and the St. Nicholas Society. By the 1880s, brewers, appliance manufacturers, clothiers, hat makers, iron manufacturers, and oil refiners were walking their well-appointed halls. This would have been unimaginable three decades earlier.[39]

The integration of industrialists into the elite mercantile institutions did not occur without conflicts. One event in particular symbolized the end of the old mercantile families' rule over who was permitted *entrée* to the most exclusive social circles: the struggle over who would control the opera. The Academy of Music, which had provided an exclusive space for opera performances since 1854, had been a stronghold of the old commercial elite of the city: The Belmonts, Stuyvesants, Roosevelts, Rhinelanders and Astors monopolized its 18 private boxes.[40] When railroad tycoon William H. Vanderbilt, despite offering $30,000, was refused a box in the early 1880s, he, together with 70 others who also strove for social acceptance, built their own opera house instead. The Goulds, Vanderbilts, Morgans, Whitneys, Bakers, and Rockefellers all contributed $10,000 a person to incorporate the Metropolitan Opera House Company, which would eventually boast 122 private boxes.[41] In a major victory for the new industrialists and financiers, the Academy was unable to defeat the competition and had to close its doors in the spring of 1885, its owner stating that "I cannot fight Wall Street."[42] Though the *New York Times* had called the conflict a "social war of extermination," the old elites eventually also moved to the Metropolitan Opera, symbolically acknowledging the new power relations.[43] Now the newly wealthy Rockefellers and Vanderbilts rubbed shoulders with the city's older mercantile wealth.[44] As one historian remarked, "[M]utual interest drew the social elements together, and they ultimately fused in the rulership of the new house."[45]

This creation of a bourgeois world held together by a shared class culture, social networks, and institutions, however, did not preclude divisions nor the organized expression of competing identities. Indeed, because New York's economic elite continued to grow in numbers and change in composition during the two last decades of the nineteenth century, problems of social demarcation remained high on their agenda. Those who had inherited their capital and position continued to draw lines between themselves and those who had made their wealth in their own life times; all the while, these boundaries were undermined by marriages across these lines. As a result, boundaries were re-negotiated constantly, and achieving a balance between inclusiveness versus exclusiveness continued to be a struggle.

While class identities were becoming increasingly important to bourgeois New Yorkers, other identities persisted, especially those based on religion and heritage, ideas that, in turn, formed the basis of institutions. For a German immigrant such as William Steinway, attendance at the ethnic Liederkranz Society was important, while the Seligmans and Loebs participated in Jewish organizations such as the Harmonie Gesellschaft, the Beekmans and Depeysters celebrated with the St. Nicholas Society and the Morgans and Griswolds were fervent supporters of the New England Society.[46]

None of these identities and affiliations, however, contradicted class identities, not least because all of them were in the form of their activities classic examples of bourgeois socializing.[47] And, importantly, none of these identities or affiliations prevented frequent contact across lines of religion and nativity. Associations like the Philharmonic Society, the Hardware Club and the Republican Party counted among their members merchants and industrialists of native Protestant, Catholic, and Jewish background, born in New York City and New England, Germany and Ireland.[48] Among employers' associations, trade associations, elite Democratic Party circles, and elite Republican Party circles, none were divided on the basis of ethnicity, nor did bourgeois New Yorkers mobilize politically across class lines on the basis of shared ethnicity or religion.

In a further departure, the sense of discomfort and concern of the 1850s about the city's social tensions became more pronounced in the 1880s, when bourgeois associations lost a sense of stewardship and became more self-consciously class organizations, creating a bounded bourgeois world that distanced itself from other social groups, a departure partly expressed by the increasing embrace of elements of aristocratic culture by many bourgeois New Yorkers.[49] Fashion, for example, was orientated toward the tastes of European monarchs (truly wealthy New Yorkers had the same tailors as European rulers); Tiffany & Co. opened a heraldry department in the 1870s to design coats of arms; recreational hunting, one of the favorite pastimes of the European aristocracy, found its aficionados among upper-class New Yorkers; and elaborate country seats, sometimes of a size matching European castles, attracted the city's elite to the country.[50] Some bourgeois New Yorkers, especially those who had acquired their wealth recently, went so far in admiration of the aristocracy that they married their daughters to cash-poor or simply impoverished European aristocrats.[51]

The deal was straightforward: social honor in return for financial support. The trail of "dollar princesses" began in the 1870s, and by 1915 42 American-born princesses, 17 duchesses, 33 viscountesses, 33 marchionesses, 46 ladies (wives of knights or baronets), 64 baronesses, and 136 countesses lived in the United States and Europe.[52]

Existing social organizations that had once been motivated in their public activities by a universalist spirit, now metamorphosed into defensive class organizations.[53] Benevolent organizations, for example, which in the 1850s had seen their work as an effort to rescue society from evil influences, now increasingly saw their goal as the protection of their own class.[54] Charity, the New York Charity Organization Society argued, provided "insurance, terrestrial and celestial" for the property of the rich "at easy rates."[55] Having become more corporate, more professional and more scientific, these charity organizations "evinced a far more pessimistic and insulated perspective about human nature and the limits of reform" than they had two decades earlier.[56] Indeed, "[c]lass standing," writes historian Lori Ginzberg, "was now understood explicitly by the benevolent as something to protect."[57]

The mushrooming of employers' associations was also quite telling in this context, as were efforts to organize politically along class lines. In the late 1870s and early 1880s, employers' associations arose in most New York industries, and industry journals such as the *Oil and Paint Manufacturer* were untiring in their call for further efforts at organizing. This was the age of organization, and a prominent New York lawyer, John Bleecker Miller expressed the spirit of the age when he called for the association of "men with common material interests" in a "Business, Trade, Professional and Property-Owners Associations of the City of New York."[58] This was a stunning departure to earlier times: before 1873, most New York manufacturers had remained unorganized. By the 1880s, however, all important industries such as printing, metal, construction, furniture, and apparel featured an employers' association, as did the carriage makers, the chandelier manufacturers, and brewers, among them:[59] the United States Bottlers' Protective Association (including the Bottlers' Protective Association of New York and Vicinity), the Boss Piano Makers of New York, the Hat and Cap Manufacturer's Association of New York, the Manufacturing Furrier's Exchange of New York, the Iron League of New York, the Shoe Manufacturers of the United States, the Iron Founders' Association, the National Association of Stove Manufacturers, and the Real Estate Owners and Builders' Association.[60] In 1887, printers formed the United Typotethae of New York.[61] Hardware manufacturers and dealers organized the Hardware Club of New York "in the name of a common business interest," and by 1894 its 585 members even sported their own clubhouse.[62] These associations played an important role in containing trade unions and symbolized the transformation of bourgeois voluntary associations into self-conscious class organizations.

Other associations expressed an even greater sense of social distance, clouded in racialist assumptions. Perhaps the most self-conscious effort by bourgeois New Yorkers to set themselves apart was their search for genealogical legitimacy. Even if constructed out of whole cloth, heritage was important, providing a distinct line of ancestors that legitimized their powerful position and coincided with the group's social Darwinist beliefs. Societies such as the Sons of the American Revolution (1889) and the Daughters of the American Revolution (1890) emerged, creating imaginary communities of shared heritage.[63] The New York Genealogical Society, founded in 1869, exemplified the astonishing sense of separateness developed by a significant segment of New York's bourgeoisie by the last decades of the century. The object of the Society was "not the mere purpose of a hunt for ancestors to gratify personal or family pride." Instead, one member argued, the Society "is for the purpose, primarily, in my opinion, of forming a true and firm foundation on which those who are to come after us can establish the fact that they are the descendants of the original settlers and founders of civilized life upon this continent, not of the hordes of the foreigners." He claimed that those "original settlers and founders" "are primarily entitled to rule this country." Another of the society's activists asserted that "the descendants of well-mated husbands and wives . . . will be . . . morally and physically superior to those of the ill-mated feeble and indifferent."[64] Inequality, which traditionally had been explained in bourgeois political discourse as a result of individual exertion in the marketplace, now came to be seen increasingly in racial terms. The Society, in a further ironic twist, while founded by dedicated native-born Anglo-Saxons, counted among its members such illustrious immigrants as Andrew Carnegie (from Scotland), Jose Francis Di Navarro (from Spain/Cuba), and William R. Grace (from Ireland).[65]

This sense of separateness was also expressed in political associations that emerged in the 1870s and 1880s. This essay is not the place to review them in detail, except to note that these movements, uniting practically all segments of the city's economic elite, aimed to limit the political influence of workers in local politics, and, in 1877, mounted a class-wide mobilization to effect the disenfranchisement of workers in urban elections.[66]

Partly because of this greater class identity, by the 1880s, bourgeois New Yorkers had created a set of cultural institutions they clearly dominated and in which they set class-specific aesthetic standards. This was a departure from their more tentative and essentially ineffectual efforts of the 1850s. Most prominent among these institutions were the Metropolitan Museum of Art, the Metropolitan Opera, and the New York Philharmonic.[67] These institutions were financially dependent on bourgeois New Yorkers, derived their programmatic ideas from them, and principally catered to the city's economic elite.

These institutions served to define a particular set of artistic works as high culture. The Metropolitan Museum of Art, which opened its doors in 1880, displayed the works of ancient and more recent European painters and sculptors, classifying the works as legitimate forms of art. This was a great departure from the kinds of museums that had dominated the cultural landscape of mid-century New York, such as the commercialized show rooms of a Phineas T. Barnum with their eclectic collections and socially diverse audiences. Now, the definition and appropriation of a high culture served to distinguish the city's elite from the lower classes, as well as to exert cultural hegemony over lower-middle-class New Yorkers who strove to live up to the cultural standards of their betters.[68] Though the museum saw itself in an "educational" role, effectively it kept working-class New Yorkers out; until 1891, the museum remained closed on Sunday, the one day workers could have actually enjoyed its collection, and even then, the museum's administrators were not exactly welcoming to lower-class visitors. In 1897, for example, they turned away a plumber who came to view the exhibit, the director of the museum arguing that "[w]e do not want, nor will we, permit a person who has been digging in a filthy sewer or working among grease and oil to come in here and by offensive odors emitted from the dirt on their apparel, make the surroundings uncomfortable for others."[69]

The struggle to create a class-segregated public sphere, a prominent motif of the Metropolitan Museum's founding, was replicated by the New York Philharmonic Society. The Society, like the museum and the Metropolitan Opera, was largely an organization that institutionalized high culture, characterizing its audience in 1892 quite tellingly as "untouched by the freaks of fashion . . . of the majority of popular entertainments."[70]

This state of things, however, only had come about after decades of conflict. As early as the 1850s, the Society's purpose to give "public concerts of high-class instrumental music" had been difficult to achieve because "[t]he people of New York . . . did not [have] a refined appreciation of instrumental music." Instead, according to the Society, the "people" flocked to commercial entertainments with an enthusiasm that "was not the child of intelligent appreciation."[71] They were said to have a "rude taste," and "had to be cautioned not to stand on chairs, and rebuked for their habit of resting their boots on the cushioned rails of the theaters."[72]

The New York Philharmonic Society, "with its purposes diametrically opposed to those of the itinerant virtuoso, and with its resolute refusal to yield . . . to the demands of unformed taste," saw its own role as staking out a separate ground for high culture, and wresting control of the public sphere from the poorly behaved audiences that had been typical of concerts in earlier times, setting itself self-consciously apart from the "advertising-managers of the Barnum stamp."[73] Yet this was easier said than done: In the late 1850s, the Philharmonic Society itself still had to fight with an disorderly audience during its concerts; it was forced to insist in flyers "upon musical good manners. The inattention and heedless talking and disturbance of but a limited number of our audience are proving a serious annoyance."[74]

Only after the Civil War did things change and the Philharmonic Society evolve from an organizationally and financially fragile institution run by and for its musicians to an elite institution codifying high art as well as the good manners required for its enjoyment. Bourgeois New Yorkers now found concrete ways to define manners and to legislate codes of behavior. As a result, "[t]he audiences soon came to represent the choice spirits of the social world," and the atmosphere at concerts was, at last, "orderly" and "respectful."[75] During the 1867/68 season, a new president of the Society "invoked all the social and fashionable forces in behalf of the concerts, and soon made the Society's concerts the sensational features of the season." This strategy proved successful, as the income of the Society nearly tripled in four short years after 1866.[76]

By 1880, as we have seen, New York's bourgeois associations had metamorphosed in fundamental ways. Having emerged out of a vibrant and socially inclusive civil society, they increasingly became self-conscious class organizations. Civil society, in effect, had split along class lines. But why had this change occurred? Basically, it expressed the altered relationship of bourgeois New Yorkers to one another as well as to the rest of society during the 1870s and 1880s, as a self-aware and self-conscious bourgeoisie emerged. Since institution-building and class formation were tightly linked, the greater class awareness of bourgeois New Yorkers expressed itself in new kinds of associational patterns, while at the same time new associations furthered the formation of the bourgeoisie.

Four elements stand out in fostering greater class awareness: (1) Because industrial and finance capital increasingly dominated merchant capital, the relationship with labor became more important to a growing number of bourgeois New Yorkers. (2) Labor was ever more vocal and better organized, forcing bourgeois New Yorkers to come to terms with a society that was firmly divided along social lines. (3) The growing scale of capital controlled by all segments of the city's upper class increased the social distance between economic elites and workers, again furthering a more self-conscious bourgeoisie. And (4), the particular trajectory of economic development diminished the previously firm economic, social, and ideological divide between merchants and manufacturers, replacing identities based on the ownership of a particular kind of capital with identities based on the shared ownership of capital.

As one element in the emergence of greater class identities among bourgeois New Yorkers, associations played an important role. However, associations took only a specific and limited place in the process of class formation. There was much more to the constitution of the bourgeoisie then association building: access to resources made a crucial difference. While all New Yorkers were able to build voluntary associations, none of those associations were as stable and as powerful as those created by upper-class citizens, an important distinction, since they were the ones who eventually defined the public sphere along class specific lines. Consequently, living a bourgeois class culture and building associations in their specifically bourgeois incarnation demanded access to resources (time and money, most importantly), resources that only came with the ownership of capital. Capital and culture thus required one another, and neither of the two should be considered separate from the other.

The specific role of associations in the process of bourgeois class formation is not unique to New York City; it is arguably typical for the Western world at large. Still, New York's economic elite and its associations were in some fundamental ways different: In contrast to Europe, in New York, the history of associations from the early nineteenth century onward was linked to all social groups, not only the bourgeoisie. Moreover, bourgeois class identities emerged later in the United States than in Europe (with the possible exception of Switzerland and the Netherlands), since an American bourgeoisie did not face an aristocracy against which they might have defined themselves. If conflict begets class identity, it was only in the later decades of the nineteenth century that the confrontation with workers led bourgeois New Yorkers to a greater articulation of class.[77] Even more unique to the United States was the failure of bourgeois New Yorkers to wrest control of the cultural sphere from working-class citizens until later in the century. Finally, the particular patterns of associations reflect the relative weakness of the American state. On one side, this weakness encouraged the blossoming of associations early in the nineteenth century, since they filled spaces that the state occupied in Europe. On the other, the relative weakness of the state prevented the emergence of strong organizations that would have represented bourgeois interests vis-à-vis the state apparatus, something that did occur in Europe, where the state was more powerful and more autonomous.

As Alexis de Tocqueville saw so clearly, the nineteenth-century United States' civil society was in fundamental ways different from Western Europe. Simply put, it was a purer form of bourgeois society than any other.[78] However, as Tocqueville also noted, the United States experience was not beyond comparison. To the contrary, while its path to modernity might have been peculiar, the emerging bourgeois societies of many other countries had a lot in common with the American experience. It is at this intersection between difference and similarity that we can grasp the character and role of bourgeois associations in the nineteenth century.

Notes

1. Thank you to Thimo de Nijs, Julia Rosenbaum, and Boudien de Vries for their comments on an earlier draft of this essay. A version of this essay was first published in Graeme Morton, Boudien De Vries, and R. J. Morris, eds., *Civil Society, Associations And Urban Places: Class, Nation And Culture in Nineteenth-Century Europe* (Aldershot, Hampshire, England; Burlington, VT; Ashgate, 2006). It is reprinted here with permission from Ashgate.
2. Alexis de Tocqueville, *Democracy in America,* vol. 1, edited by Phillips Bradley (New York: Vintage Books, 1945), 198; Alexis de Tocqueville, *Democracy in America,* vol. 2, edited by Phillips Bradley (New York: Vintage Books, 1945), 114.
3. Tocqueville, *Democracy in America,* vol. 2, 115.
4. Ibid., 118.

5. For a discussion about defining the bourgeoisie, see Sven Beckert, "Propertied of a Different Kind: Bourgeoisie and Lower Middle Class in the Nineteenth-Century United States," in Burt Bledstein and Robert Johnston, eds., *Middling Sorts: Essays in the History of the American Middle Class* (London: Routledge, 2001), 285–295.
6. For the names, see "List of Young People Invited to Mrs. Havemeyer's Dance, February 2, 1891," Misc. Manuscripts, Mrs. Theo A. Havemeyer, 1891, NYHS. Three hundred and one guests were invited to the dance, of which 230 could be clearly identified. Of these 230, sixty-four were not listed in the *Social Register.* Thirty-eight others were listed in the *Social Register,* though without club affiliations. For 128 guests, club affiliations were found in the New York. For those people whose club affiliation could be identified, seventy-seven were members of the Union Club, sixty-nine of the Knickerbocker Club, sixty-two of the Country Club, seventeen of the Union League, and ten of the Century Club. For the club affiliations, see *Social Register New York* 6 (New York: Social Register Association, 1892).
7. Sven Beckert, "Democracy and Its Discontents: Contesting Suffrage Rights in Gilded Age New York," in *Past & Present* (February 2002): 114–155.
8. *The Season—An Annual Record of Society in New York, Brooklyn, and Vicinity, First Year, 1882–1883* (New York: White, Stokes, & Allen, 1883), 9.
9. Robert Greenhalgh Albion, *The Rise of New York Port, 1815–1860* (New York: Charles Scribner's Sons, 1939), 255; Edward F. DeLancey,*Memoir of James William Beekman: Prepared at the Request of the St. Nicholas Society of the City of New York* (New York: Published by the Society, 1877), 16.
10. Francis Gerry Fairfield, *The Clubs of New York* (New York: H. L. Hinton, 1873), 59. See also Reginald Townsend, *Mother of Clubs: Being the History of the First Hundred Years of the Union Club of the City of New York, 1836–1936* (New York: William Edwin Rudge, 1936). On Belmont, see David Black, *The King of Fifth Avenue: The Fortunes of August Belmont* (New York: Dial Press, 1981), 60.
11. Townsend, *Mother of Clubs*, 57.
12. See also Thomas Bender, *New York Intellect: A History of Intellectual Life in New York City, from 1750 to the Beginnings of Our Own Time* (Baltimore: Johns Hopkins University Press, 1987), 135.
13. *Annual Report of the Chamber of Commerce of the State of New York for the Year 1858* (New York: Wheeler and Williams, 1859), 340–350. The number of industrialists in the ranks of the Chamber of Commerce was negligible, totaling only six (2 percent). Three of the six were shipbuilders. These numbers are derived from an analysis of all members of the Chamber of Commerce in the year 1858. For the New York Club: Analysis of a sample of sixty-five members of the New York Club, 1862, of which forty-three could be located *in Trow's New York City Directory*, compiled by H. Wilson, vol. LXXV, for the year ending May 7, 1862 (New York: John F. Trow, 1862). For the names, see *Constitution of the New York Club, with a List of Members, May 1862* (New York: Charles O. Jones, Stationer and Printer, 1862). The numbers for the Union Club are derived from an analysis of the occupational background of 169 of its members.
14. Allan Nevins and Milton H. Thomas, eds., *Diary of George Templeton Strong*, vol. 3 (New York: Octagon Books, 1952), 52.
15. Alexander D. Bache, *Anniversary Address Before the American Institute, Of the City of New-York, at the Tabernacle, October 28th, 1856, During the Twenty-Eighth Annual Fair* (New York: Pudney & Russell, 1857), 32. Both institutions were clearly dominated by manufacturers, as demonstrated by an analysis of the officers of the Mechanics' Institute. For the names of members, see *Catalog of the Library of the Mechanics' Institute, of the City of New-York; Regulations of the Reading Room and Library; and Circular to the Public* (New York: A. Baptist, Jr., Printer, 1844).
16. *Catalogue of the Library of the Mechanics' Institute of the City of New York*, 63. For the composition of the leadership of the Mechanics' Institute, see James J. Mapes, *Inaugural Address Delivered Tuesday Evening, January 7, 1845, Before the Mechanic's Institute of the City of New York* (New York: Institute Rooms, 1845), 2, and *Catalogue of the Library of the Mechanics' Institute of the City of New York*, 64. Most of the institute's activists were in one way or another engaged in manufacturing, with the remainder working as professionals or in white-collar occupations. No merchants served in the leadership of the Institute.
17. Mapes, *Inaugural Address Delivered Tuesday Evening, January 7, 1845*, 9.

18. Oakey A. Hall, *Anniversary Address before the American Institute, at Palace Garden, October 29, 1859* (New York: n.p., 1859), 22. For the list of trustees and committee members of the American Institute, see *Transactions of the American Institute of the City of New-York for the Year 1855* (Albany: C. van Benthuysen, 1856).
19. *Transactions of the American Institute of the City of New-York for the Year 1855* (Albany: C. Van Benthuysen, 1856), 7; Hall, *Anniversary Address before the American Institute*, 29; *Transactions of the American Institute of the City of New-York for the Year 1856* (Albany: C. Van Benthuysen, 1857), 9.
20. Tocqueville, *Democracy in America*, vol. 2, 111.
21. Wilson, *Trow's New York City Directory for the Year Ending May 1, 1856*, Appendix, 44–47.
22. Clifford S. Griffin, *Their Brothers' Keepers: Moral Stewardship in the United States, 1800–1865* (Westport, CT: Greenwood Press, 1960), xi.
23. *The Ninth Annual Report of the New-York Association for Improving the Conditions of the Poor, For the Year 1852*, 16; *Eleventh Annual Report of the New York Association for the Improvement of the Conditions of the Poor, for the Year 1854* (New York: John F. Trow, 1854), 18.
24. Amy Bridges, "Another Look at Plutocracy in Antebellum New York City" in *Political Science Quarterly* 97 (1982), 64.
25. The category of "public sphere" comes from Jürgen Habermas. See Jürgen Habermas, *The Structural Transformation of the Public Sphere: An Inquiry into a Category of Bourgeois Society* (Cambridge, MA: M.I.T. Press, 19995), especially 31–43.
26. *New York Herald*, 15 July 1850, as quoted in Roy Rosenzweig and Elizabeth Blackmar, *The Park and the People: A History of Central Park* (Ithaca, NY: Cornell University Press, 1992), 28.
27. Douglas T. Miller, *Jacksonian Aristocracy: Class and Democracy in New York, 1830–1860* (New York: Oxford University Press, 1967), 162; Calvin Tomkins, *Merchants and Masterpieces: The Story of the Metropolitan Museum of Art* (New York: Henry Holt, 1989), 22, 27. The modest gallery had grown out of the private collection of wholesale grocery merchant Luman Reed's, which he had consolidated on the third floor of his home on Greenwich Street and made accessible one day a week.
28. New York Historical Society, *Proceedings at the Dedication of the Library* (New York: Printed for the Society, 1857), 6.
29. The theater, accommodating 4,600 spectators, opened with a performance of Bellini's *Norma*, but the real spectacle, according to historian John Warren Frick, Jr. was to be found in the private boxes that "provided their inhabitants [with an opportunity] for being seen." John Warren Frick, Jr., "The Rialto: A Study of Union Square, The Center of New York's First Theatre District, 1870–1900" (Ph.D. dissertation, New York University, 1983), 28, 29, 32, 37.
30. Peter George Buckley, "To the Opera House: Culture and Society in New York City, 1820–1860" (Ph.D. dissertation, SUNY Stony Brook, 1984), 9. For an excellent analysis, see Paul DiMaggio, "Cultural Entrepreneurship in Nineteenth-Century Boston: The Creation of an Organizational Base of High Culture in America," in *Media, Culture and Society* (982): 33–50.
31. Andrew Stulman Dennett, *Weird & Wonderful: The Dime Museum in America* (New York: New York University Press, 1997), 18, 26.
32. Dennett, *Weird & Wonderful*, 27.
33. Ibid., 30. Rossiter Raymond, *Peter Cooper* (Boston: Houghton, Mifflin, 1901), 69. For the general point, see also Mary P.Ryan, *Civic Wars : Democracy and Public Life in the American City during the Nineteenth Century* (Berkeley : University of California Press, 1997), 38.
34. Robert T. Davis, "Pauperism in the City of New York," *Journal of Social Science* 6 (1874): 74.
35. Tocqueville, *Democracy in America*, vol. 2, 169.
36. For a statement of purpose, see *The Season—An Annual Record of Society in New York, Brooklyn, and Vicinity, First Year, 1882–1883* (New York: White, Stokes, & Allen, 1883), 5.
37. Allen Churchill, *The Upper Crust: An Informal History of New York's Highest Society* (Englewood Cliffs: Prentice-Hall, 1970), 157; Social Register Association, *Social Register, New York, 1886–1900* (New York: Social Register Association, 1886–1900).
38. Forty-three percent of all industrialists who were members of the Chamber of Commerce in 1886 had joined after 1881. In contrast, only 32 percent of all merchants had joined during the same time period. For the members of the Chamber of Commerce, see Chamber of Commerce, *Annual Report* (1886).
39. See Henry Hall, ed., *America's Successful Men of Affairs: An Encyclopedia of Contemporaneous Biography*, vol. 2 (New York: *The New York Tribune*, 1895).

40. Jack W. Rudolph, "Launching the Met," in *American History Illustrated* 18 (1983): 21.
41. Frick, "The Rialto: A Study of Union Square, The Center of New York's First Theatre District, 1870–1900" (Ph.D. Dissertation, New York University, 1983), 57; Rudolph, *Launching the Met*, 21; Steinway also acquired a box. See *Steinway Diary*, entry of October 12, 1883, NYHS.
42. Lloyd R. Morris, *Incredible New York* (New York: Random House, 1951), 192.
43. Quoted in John Frederick Cone, *First Rival of the Metropolitan Opera* (New York: Columbia University Press, 1983), 21. See also note by J. Astor, October 11, 1886, Letterbook, 1884-1890, John Jacob Astor Papers, NYHS.
44. Apparently, it was the Astors who made the first overtures toward the Metropolitan Opera. After the opening of the Metropolitan Opera, the stockholders of the Academy of Music slowly withdrew their funds from the enterprise. See Cone, *First Rival of the Metropolitan Opera*, 87.
45. Cone, *First Rival of the Metropolitan Opera*, 185. Irving Kolodin, *The Metropolitan Opera, 1883–1966* (New York: Alfred A. Knopf, 1966). For the history of the Metropolitan Opera, see also Paul E. Eisler, *The Metropolitan Opera: The First Twenty-Five Years, 1883–1908* (Croton-On-Hudson: North River Press, 1984); Tompkins, *Merchants and Masterpieces*, 19.
46. *Eighty-First Anniversary Celebration of the New-England Society in the City of New York at Delmonico's, December 22,* 1886; One *Hundred Years, 1852–1952: The Harmonie Club* (New York: The Harmonie Club, 1952), 20.
47. The possibility for a positive relationship between ethnic and religious identities and working-class identities has long been established.
48. See *Hardware Club of New York, April, 1897* (New York: n.p., 1897), 31–94; *Proceedings at the First Annual Dinner of the Republican Club of the City of New York, held at Delmonico's, February 12, 1887* (New York: Mercantile Printing and Stationary Co., 1887), 73–79.
49. In a European context, it has been argued that the 'aristocratization' of the bourgeoisie was a sign of its weakness. See for example, Hans Ulrich Wehler, *Das Deutsche Kaiserreich, 1871-1918* (Göttingen, Vandenhoeck & Ruprecht, 1980), esp. 129–31; The United States, however, shows that the appropriation of cultural norms of another elite is first and foremost a sign of the strength and historical confidence of the bourgeoisie. See also Brandon,*The Dollar Princess*, 44.
50. Churchill, *The Upper Crust*, 196; Gail MacColl and Carol McD. Wallace, *To Marry an English Lord* (New York: Workman Publishing, 1989), 31. In 1871, the publisher of the *New York Herald*, James Gordon Bennett, Jr., together with General Phil Sheridan, Leonard Jerome, John G. Hecksher, Carrol Livingston, and J. Schuyler Crosby, ventured on one of these expeditions. Churchill, *The Upper Crust*, 167.
51. See on this subject also Montgomery, *"Gilded Prostitution,"* passim.
52. Ruth Brandon, *The Dollar Princesses: Sagas of Upward Nobility, 1870–1914* (New York: Knopf, distributed by Random House, 1980), 1.
53. Henry Bellows, *Historical Sketch of the Union League Club of New York: Its Origin, Organization, and Work, 1863–1879* (New York: Club House, 1879), 130.
54. Lori D. Ginzberg, *Women and the Work of Benevolence: Morality, Politics, and Class in the 19th-Century United States* (New Haven, CT: Yale University Press, 1990), 5, 198. For a similar argument see also Nicola Beisel, "Upper Class Formation and the Politics of Censorship in Boston, New York, and Philadelphia, 1872–1892" (Ph.D. dissertation, University of Michigan, 1990).
55. J. K. Paulding, "Democracy and Charity," in *The Charities Review* 4 (April, 1895): 287. Organizations such as the AICP or the Charity Organization Society, "evinced a far more pessimistic and insulated perspective about human nature and the limits of reform," than they had two decades earlier. Ginzberg, *Women and the Work of Benevolence*, 200. "Class standing," writes Lori Ginzberg, "was now understood explicitly by the benevolent as something to protect." The quote is from Ginzberg, *Women and the Work of Benevolence*, 198.
56. Ginzberg, *Women and the Work of Benevolence*, 200.
57. Ibid., 198.
58. John Bleecker Miller, *Trade, Professional, and Property-Owners' Organizations in Public Affairs* (New York: H. Cherouny, 1884), 5, 45. See also *Iron Age* (December 28, 1882), 14.
59. On the American Brewers' Association see *Scientific American* (June 19, 1880), 384.
60. *National Bottlers' Gazette* (March 1, 1886), 15; *Shoe and Leather Reporter* (November 23, 1886), 902; Bleecker Miller, *Trade, Professional, and Property-Owners' Organizations in Public Affairs*, 42.

61. Patricia Evelyn Malon, "The Growth of Manufacturing in Manhattan, 1860–1900: An Analysis of Factoral Changes and Urban Structure," (Ph.D. diss., Columbia University, 1981), 370.
62. *Iron Age* (September 15, 1892), 499. *New York Times* (June 1, 1894), 8; *Iron Age* (February 27, 1896), 551. The membership numbers are as of 1897. *Hardware Club of New York, April, 1897* (New York: n.p., 1897), 95.
63. M. J. Heale, *American Anti-Communism: Combating the Enemy Within 1830-1970* (Baltimore: Johns Hopkins University Press, 1990), 36; Michael Wallace, "Visiting the Past: History Museums in the United States," in Susan Porter Benson, Stephen Brier, and Roy Rosenzweig, eds., *Presenting the Past: Essays on History and the Public* (Philadelphia: Temple University Press, 1986), 140.
64. New York Genealogical Society, *Twenty-Fifth Anniversary, February 27, 1864* (New York: T. A. Wright, 1895), 10, 23.
65. Letter of Sherman, August 19, 1878, Isaac Sherman Papers, Huntington Library.
66. For details on this conflict, see Sven Beckert, "Democracy and Its Discontents: Contesting Suffrage Rights in Gilded Age New York," in *Past & Present* (February 2002), 114–155.
67. For a brilliant analysis of Boston's cultural history and its relationship to bourgeois class formation, see Paul DiMaggio, "Cultural Entrepreneurship in Nineteenth-Century Boston: The Creation of an Organizational Base of High Culture in America," in *Media, Culture and Society* (982), 33–50. For a discussion of the emergence of stratified cultural spheres in the course of the nineteenth century, see Lawrence W. Levine, *Highbrow, Lowbrow: The Emergence of Cultural Hierarchy in America* (Cambridge, MA: Harvard University Press, 1988), especially 17, 208, 231.
68. This argument, in reference to Boston, has also been made by Paul DiMaggio, "Cultural Entrepreneurship in Nineteenth-Century Boston: The Creation of an Organizational Base of High Culture in America," in *Media, Culture and Society* (982), 33–50. The middle class, according to DiMaggio, was attracted to such museums because they wanted to differentiate themselves culturally from the working class. Paul DiMaggio, "Cultural Entrepreneurship in Nineteenth-Century Boston," in Paul DiMaggio, ed., *Nonprofit Enterprise in the Arts* (New Haven, CT: Yale University Press, 1986), 49.
69. Quoted in Calvin Tompkins, *Merchants and Masterpieces: The Story of the Metropolitan Museum of Art* (New York: Henry Holt, 1989), 75. See also Tompkins, *Merchants and Masterpieces*, 17, 30, 47, 68, 73, 78. Defining and appropriating high culture, the Metropolitan Museum was an institution that brought different segments of New York's bourgeoisie together, transcending earlier divisions. Among the Metropolitan's trustees was a whole range of bourgeois New Yorkers, some of whom represented old mercantile capital, and others the newly made industrial fortunes. Old-time merchants such as William H. Aspinwall, William H. Astor, and Theodore Roosevelt joined with newcomers such as printing press manufacturer Robert Hoe Jr., banker John Pierpont Morgan, and railroad entrepreneur Cornelius Vanderbilt. For a list of trustees of the Metropolitan Museum, see Calvin Tomkins, *Merchants and Masterpieces: The Story of the Metropolitan Museum of Art*, Rev. and updated ed. (New York: Henry Holt and Company, 1989), 395–399.
70. Henry Edward Krehbiel, *The Philharmonic Society of New York* (New York and London: Novello, Ewer, 1892), 7.
71. Ibid., 28.
72. Ibid., 28–29.
73. Ibid., 83.
74. Ibid., 65, quoted from an 1857 report by the Philharmonic Society.
75. Krehbiel, *The Philharmonic Society of New York*, 60.
76. Ibid., 175–176.
77. For Switzerland, see Albert Tanner, *Arbeitsame Patrioten—Wohlanständige Damen: Bürgertum und Bürgerlichkeit in the Schweiz, 1830–1914* (Zürich: Orell Fuessli Verlag, 1995). For the Netherlands, see Boudien de Vries, *Electoraat en Elite: Sociale Structuur en Sociale Mobiliteit in Amsterdam, 1850–1895* (Amsterdam: Bataafsche Leeuw, 1986).
78. A notion shared by such diverse thinkers as Friedrich Engels, Max Weber, Antonio Gramsci, and Seymour Martin Lipset. See Seymour Martin Lipset, *Continental Divide: The Values and Institutions of the United States and Canada* (London: Routledge, 1990), 25.

7

The Steady Supporters of Order: American Mechanics' Institute Fairs as Icons of Bourgeois Culture

Ethan Robey

> The middling classes—our city's yeomanry, the steady supporters of order, law, and religion—enjoyed a rich feast.
>
> —*Report of the Third Annual Fair of the American Institute of the City of New-York, Held at Masonic Hall, October 1830*[1]

These steady supporters of order, these skilled artisans, shop masters, engineers, scientists, teachers, lawyers, and others involved with American mechanics' institutes in the first half of the nineteenth century were bound together by commercial ties and a shared interest in encouraging practical innovation. This essay examines the social norms, preoccupations, and aspirations promulgated by such organizations, and their role in defining a particular strain of the American bourgeoisie. Inasmuch as a bourgeoisie can perhaps be defined by a degree of control over capital, cultural, and political power, it is never a stable designation. Who might be considered bourgeois depends on the nature of cultural institutions and the structure of the economy. Changes over the course of the century—in the scale and organization of a craft shops, in retail strategies, in relations between commercial production and capital, and in the meaning of shop-made goods—created ever more complex economic interdependencies and cultural standards, redefining the makeup and shared beliefs of the American bourgeoisie.

Of primary concern here are the annual trade fairs hosted by urban artisan societies throughout the century. Celebrations of domestic industry and invention, these events can be seen as the embryonic form of a spectacle of consumption that would ultimately propagate bourgeois cultural assumptions across the social spectrum. Artisan societies, such as the American Institute of the City of New-York and the Massachusetts Charitable Mechanic Association, tended to be run by coalitions of manufacturers and politicians, and devoted to the promotion of local manufacturing and commerce. Their periodic trade fairs were more than presentations of commercial products; they were testaments to the social import of commercial goods themselves. Implicitly and explicitly, in the arrangement of the exhibition halls and in orations and publications, these fairs conflated commercial production and cultural production, mechanical ingenuity and aesthetic quality, lending the status of a cultural event to the act of inspection and purchase. Such fairs can therefore be seen as a cultural institution, temporary but repeated every year, an institution embodying the values of the artisan societies' leadership, of an increasingly coherent manufacturing elite. As has been noted in a previous essay, over the first decades of the nineteenth century this segment of the emergent American bourgeoisie was effectively excluded from the social networks of mercantile, professional, and financier leaders. The system of annual fairs can be understood as the manufacturers' attempt to make a claim to cultural authority and, in that sense, tracks their assimilation into the bourgeoisie.

The present study is, ultimately, a story of integration: how economic changes eroded the social distinctions of the early nineteenth century, and how the culture of the manufacturing elite became enmeshed with other aspects of American bourgeois culture. Already by the 1840s, the manufacturers' societies had interests in common with mercantile entrepreneurs, as they soon would with the professional and financial elite as well. Midcentury developments in shipping, advertising, and, especially, means of financing larger-scale production impelled commercial production and sales to increasingly intertwine with banking and capital. These economic changes, in turn, rendered as less significant older distinctions between elite social groups, resulting in the makeup of the American bourgeoisie growing ever more complex.

Initially, the managers of the artisan societies denied any firm social distinction between the fine and useful arts, in order to affirm the cultural relevance of artisanal production. This, in turn, gave rise to a set of aesthetic judgments asserting the cultural equality of all forms of production, which intentionally blurred differences between art and commercial production, and between the cultural status of artists and artisans. In the literature surrounding these fairs, salable qualities such as originality, inventiveness, and finish became the highest praise for works of fine arts, an aesthetic that, in turn, laid the groundwork for the spectacularization of consumerism in the later nineteenth century.

In 1844, a New York turner and chair maker named Benjamin Harrison tried his hand at watercolor and drew an elaborate view of the seventeenth annual fair of the American Institute of the City of New-York, which he then sent to be displayed at that same event (fig. 7.1). The colors, now slightly faded to muted earth tones on a yellowed ground, hint at what was once a brilliant spectacle of goods and decorations. Elaborate showcases on the main floor of Niblo's Garden, a pleasure garden and theater on Broadway, are filled with a wealth of household items: a large collection of top hats and bonnets takes up one side of the room; opposite it are displays of lamps, glassware, and cravats; ship models and portrait busts are arranged around the walls; and examples of gaily-colored textiles are suspended from the edge of the balcony. On the balcony itself is a varied display of small, framed works: oil paintings, engravings, examples of handwriting, embroidery, and the like. Precisely rendered (if slightly awkward) people mill about amidst this commercial splendor. They are all dressed as befits a dignified, festive occasion. Visitors to these fairs were typically workingmen and their families, and members of the newly emergent urban white-collar professions. The men in Harrison's drawing all sport dark frock coats and tall hats, the women are dressed in bonnets with jackets over their crinolines, and even the two children in the center foreground are well dressed and seemingly well mannered. All is in order on the fair's display floor, with items of everyday use artfully exhibited in glass vitrines and dignified by the serious attention of the audience.

The American Institute of the City of New-York was the most prominent artisans' society in what was already economic capital of the United States. It was founded in 1828 to encourage and promote domestic industry, commerce, agriculture, manufacturing, and the arts, by, in its members' words, "enlightened gentlemen of wealth and position and scientific attainments."[2] Its management consisted of shop masters and larger-scale manufacturers, men who might have been called industrialists later in the century. Allied with them were professionals devoted to the ideal that

Figure 7.1 Benjamin J. Harrison, Annual Fair of the American Institute at Niblo's Garden, ca. 1845. Watercolor on paper. Museum of the City of New York, Bequest of Mrs. J. Insley Blair.

production, rather than mercantilism or finance, was the highest calling of a man and the backbone of the American economy. In its first decades, the Institute's presidency was occupied by a series of politicians, professionals, and manufacturers, all united by their faith in protectionism. Whig politics defined the American Institute. As a supporter of internal improvement, the society was behind efforts to build the Erie Canal, and in 1831, Henry Clay and Daniel Webster were made honorary members.[3]

Many of the era's important inventors and entrepreneurs were also closely involved with the American Institute and other, similar artisan societies—men such as industrialist Peter Cooper, pioneer in cast iron buildings James Bogardus, arms manufacturer Samuel Colt, leather-tanning baron Zadock Pratt, steam-press innovators Richard and Robert M. Hoe, physicist James Renwick Sr. (father of the architect), and chemist James J. Mapes.

Beyond influencing policy, societies such as the American Institute existed to justify commercial production as a cultural endeavor. As such, they were steeped in a somewhat defensive rhetoric of the moral and cultural superiority of manufacturers over the financial industries. American Institute President Mahlon Dickerson noted in an 1846 speech that "from the earliest period to which history extends, mankind have been separated, as they still are, into two great divisions: those who labor, and those who do not." Dickerson then pointed out that, in seeming defiance of logic, those in the nonproductive classes control the wealth of most nations, casting bankers and financiers in the role of the *ancien-régime* aristocracy.[4] Such sentiments were commonly expounded within the walls of the various artisan societies; in oration after oration, utility, in the sense of any form of production, was elevated above commercial capitalism.

In the first half of the nineteenth century, cultural identification by trade was far stronger than class identification by economic rank. The managers of New York's artisan societies—men who formed, in effect, a manufacturing elite—identified themselves as members of what they would consider a producing class, and were quite sincere in their claim to champion the individual American mechanic. In an address before the New York Mechanics' Institute, Zadock Pratt of Prattsville, New York, who had established the largest tannery in the world and had founded a bank in the company town named after his family, could, without irony, call himself "a *working-man* and *Tanner*" and honor "we plain Mechanics."[5] For men like Pratt, the distinction between shop owner and journeyman was not as important as the distinction between a producer of products and a financier, speculator, or other non-producer. It was common for a shop master, however many employees he may have had, to call himself a mechanic, even if he no longer (or had never) worked with his hands.[6]

Production, however, did not exist independent of trade. For all their suspicion of the financial elite, the leaders of the American Institute worked closely with men who made their fortunes in shipping and retail. Domestic economic strength was considered a product of shared interests in the manufacture and distribution of goods. Even at the earliest of its fairs, the men of the Institute made a point of demonstrating the economic interdependence of production and trade. The closing ceremony of the American Institute's second annual fair, in 1829, for example, featured an elaborate symbolic temple to Alexander Hamilton, which included an ornate baldachin supported by four columns, representing commerce, agriculture, manufacturing, and the arts, each decorated with appropriate items from the fair.

Although they saw themselves as a mechanics' society, the pro-business ideals of the American Institute set it against anti-tariff Democrats and the emergent labor unions. William Cullen Bryant's Democratic *Evening Post* asserted after the Institute's first fair that "the cause of our mechanics cannot be identified with that of the manufacturers."[7] For the *Post*, this meant specifically that protective tariffs, while advantageous for domestic producers, impose a financial burden on individual consumers by raising prices. Many years later, the *Post* still chided the American Institute for being a "tool of the tariff party."[8] To its opponents, at least, it was clear that for all the public rhetoric of artisans' mutual assistance, the American Institute and like organizations primarily supported the interests of a manufacturing elite.

Nevertheless, the American Institute fairs managed to transcend a purely political message. The fairs were praised across the gamut of New York journals, from the Whig to the Democrat. Writing for the *Brooklyn Eagle* in 1846, Walt Whitman noted the essential ambiguity of a trades fair, and took from the American Institute fair a message exactly opposite that of the Whigs. In an editorial printed right under the paper's endorsement of the Democratic Republican ticket, Whitman argued that "these noble and plenteous exhibitions" were, in fact, the best argument against protectionism, and proved "we can give the rest of the world odds . . . and beat them then."[9] It was hard to find fault with the ideal of supporting the work of local artisans. Even George Henry Evans's radical paper, the *Working-man's Advocate,* carried notices of the American Institute fairs, without political commentary.[10]

The American Institute sponsored lectures and evening classes, and it published a short-lived journal; the annual fairs, however, were the main focus of the institute's activity. To the Institute's managers, the fairs were incitements to industrial competition in "all the departments of the workshop—from the owner to the journeyman, *down* to the humblest apprentice."[11] A typical fair would fill the main hall of one of the city's theaters or exhibition spaces, with samples of domestic production including models of new inventions, raw materials, a variety of consumer goods, furniture and ornamental art, and paintings and drawings: the great bounty of American production arrayed in largely undifferentiated splendor.

In the usual arrangement, shop- and factory-made commercial products were laid out on tables in the center of the hall, while needlework, paintings, and engravings were hung on the walls and, if one was available, in the gallery. The juxtaposition of categories invited visitors to compare works within and across categories of production, and to recognize the relationships between the fine arts, technologies and consumer goods on display. No one form of production could be considered self-sufficient. Published descriptions of these fairs reflect the visual cacophony of the exhibition halls and emphasize affinities between the various forms of production. From the first fairs early in the century, the organizers not only insisted that the fine arts be included but also that the commercial goods and the fine arts were each elevated by their relation to the other. In their very structure, thus, the fairs allied the fine and useful arts as parallel demonstrations of American skill and potential.

A preoccupation of early nineteenth-century American artisan rhetoric was the dignity of commercial production. Having achieved a significant economic position, manufacturers nevertheless had little claim on cultural authority. The conflation of the cultural status of the fine arts and commercial production as effected through the system of trades fairs helped define this segment of the American elite as patrons of taste as much as they were producers of basic utility. In fact, orators before mechanics' institutes tended to speak of the fine arts as a form of useful production. In his speech at the 1830 American Institute fair, the renowned lawyer Tristram Burges proposed a definition of utility that went beyond the production of goods to include intellectual capital. In his formulation, so amenable to the project of the Institute, "all employed in the high functions of instruction, whether of letters, arts, sciences, morals, [or] religion" could be considered producers of useful goods. Accordingly, Burges specifically defined "utility" to include moral instruction and the cultural advancements that make life enjoyable.[12] In this rhetorical formation, often repeated before mechanics' institute audiences, the fine arts were simply a useful enterprise that required a certain set of skills attainable by any who studied, and not a self-sufficient, esoteric sensibility reserved for an intellectual elite.

Thus, these manufacturers and politicians became patrons of the arts by insisting on the parallel between national economic improvement and aesthetic innovation, between manufacturing and art making. The mechanics' institutes displayed the work of amateurs and professionals alike; the works of engravers, lithographers, photographers, architects, painters, and even wax-figure makers were all exhibited on the undifferentiated walls of the many fairs departments of the fine arts. In their choice of judges, artists represented, and mode of display, the mechanics' institute fairs, especially those of the American Institute, kept vague the borders between artistic creativity, mechanical invention, and commercial showmanship.

In the 1830s and '40s, the fine arts establishment in New York was still able to accommodate a certain fluidity in these distinctions. Alliances existed between the National Academy of Design and the city's artisan societies. William Sidney Mount and many other artists exhibited each year at both the Academy salons and the mechanics' fairs.[13] Further, New York's American Institute and its rival, the Mechanics' Institute of the City of New-York, embarked on several joint projects with the National Academy to encourage artisan education in the fine arts for commercial purposes. In 1834, the Academy instituted a course in ornamental design in addition to its schools of live model and antique drawing.[14] The course was largely the brainchild of Samuel F. B. Morse, the painter turned inventor who presided over the Academy from its founding, in 1826, until 1845, and who was, from 1843 onward, also a member of the American Institute. Morse proposed in 1836 that the course be expanded into a "School of Ornament," arguing that such a school could "show the Public at once the direct connection between the Arts of Design and the Arts of Industry."[15] The proposal did not succeed, but several other cooperative ventures between the city's art establishment and its mechanics' institutes were initiated in this period. New York's Mechanics' Institute established an art curriculum in 1841 in the form of a suite of two drawing classes for its members: one for mechanical drawing and the other for drawing from the antique.[16] The Institute then announced a plan by which the National Academy would admit three pupils from the Mechanics' Institute class to the Academy, though it seems that the Institute never followed through on the plan.[17] The American Institute also established a course in industrial design, to be taught in conjunction with the National Academy.[18] (New York artisans were often encouraged to familiarize themselves with the National Academy. For example, an 1841 review in a mechanics' magazine of an Academy exhibition then on view urged its readers to see the paintings, noting "the present exhibition offers a good opportunity to those engaged in the mechanic arts, who wish to cultivate a classical taste."[19])

The practice of displaying fine arts alongside the decorative and applied arts at mechanics' fairs also helped enmesh the fine arts with commercial production and sales by engendering the development of a peculiar language of aesthetic appreciation that fused the concepts of beauty and utility. Commentators meted out praise and awards for work that was original, inventive, or well finished—categories equally serviceable to both art and commercial goods. On the whole, the exhibition managers and the invited speakers were the most invested in the cultural alliance of the arts and the trades, and it is from them that a true set of critical criteria emerged. However, because of the type of works on display and the eclecticism of the fairs itself, the judges, drawn from the ranks of the city's professional artists, worked, to a greater or lesser degree, within a set of expectations that paralleled the managers' vision—as did newspaper reporters.

In some instances, facility in art was less significant than a self-improving industriousness on the part of the artist. For example, an H. Lane was awarded the privileges of the New York Mechanics' Institute as "an incentive to improvement" at an 1838 fair for a specimen of painting deemed "not creditable" by the judges.[20] The judges' comments as well as managers' reports often agreed in their praise of amateur artists—indeed, the mechanics' institute fairs were the city's main outlet for amateur and beginners' art. A genre piece by William Tylee Ranney, exhibited at the same 1838 fair, was lauded in the managers' report as "executed by him after only six months' practice in the art, displaying in its composition an unusual degree of ingenuity," a phrasing borrowed from the language of mechanical invention.[21] The concept of process underlies the judgment: Art is seen not as transcendent effort but as a skillful mode of fabrication.

Such commendation of innate talent could have commercial significance, as well. When the Whiggish *New-York Commercial Advertiser* praised an exhibit of fancy work by a young woman at the 1833 American Institute fair as "the fruits of untaught ingenuity" and an "expression of native genius," the newspaper was also implicitly supporting the protectionist assertion that Americans have the skill and resources to produce goods of competitive quality.[22] Indeed, a metaphorical equation of youthful skill and the potential of the youthful country lurks behind the many reports lauding young successes in the arts.

Beyond praise for the self-taught, reports of the fairs often stressed the originality of the art. In fact, novelty was of primary importance in all departments of a mechanics' fair. Newspapers often critiqued commercial exhibitors for displaying the same articles twice. As the fair was a public lesson in the quality of American goods, such repetition was a liability. The same standards held for the artworks.

Aesthetic judgments in the official reports emphasized finish, likeness, and apparent effort over most considerations of subject matter or expression. An orator at the seventh American Institute fair averred that every item at the fair was admired for "the materials of its composition, the skill with which they have been fabricated, [and] the combined effect of both, in beauty of appearance," thus explicitly linking beauty with production value.[23]

Finish was a key element of this aesthetic. The word "finish" implied a sense of craftsmanship, and was associated with beauty for all classes of objects. Furniture, carpeting, articles of clothing, and even models of machines displayed at mechanics' institute fairs were all praised or condemned in terms of their neatness of preparation or degree of evident finish. A simple suitability to its purpose characterized a well-made tool, and, likewise, a well-made painting revealed a direct expression of its purpose: precision, accuracy, and a truthful representation of nature.The judges of the 1837 Mechanics' Institute fair in New York thought T.W. Whitley's landscapes too hastily done. "With more care and time," they maintained, "the artist could have given his pictures a finer finish."[24] Following similar criteria, the judges of the third annual American Institute fair commended a painting by Charles V. Ward as "a very natural and well-finished landscape."[25]

Even from the first decades of the fairs, however, there had been resistance to the cultural model implicitly proposed by the mechanics' fairs. In Benjamin Harrison's drawing of the 1844 American Institute fair (fig. 7.1), the fine arts section is ranged around the gallery of an otherwise largely undifferentiated exhibition space. Typically for these fairs, the fine arts, although frequently on a balcony or gallery, had little or no special exhibitionary advantage over the commercial goods: the furniture, musical instruments, ceramics, embroidery, millinery and the like filling the main exhibition hall. This arrangement was increasingly disturbing to the city's artists and art critics. Notes of frustration with the intentional leveling effect of this diversity of objects occasionally appear, even in the reports of judges hired by the fair's managers. In judging the fine arts at the American Institute's 1840 fair, the architect Minard Lafever complained in a letter to the managers that the commercial productions seemed to denigrate by association all of the fair's more intellectual exhibits, especially the fine arts. While "Candies, Shoe-blacking, *Ladies bonets* [sic] and many other articles of a-like luxurious class" were shown to the best advantage, Lafever complained, "*Fine Arts*, . . . are disposed of in a very unfavourable manner." Such a situation, he noted, naturally "disgusts the highest and noblest minds."[26] Lafever remarked that academicians increasingly avoided exhibiting at the mechanics' fairs, and recognized the growing divide between the manufacturers' ideal of a unified field of production and a more-exclusive high cultural model.

While commercial production and all it entailed was the *raison d'être* of an artisan society fair's art gallery, by midcentury evolving cultural distinctions put commerce and aesthetic production increasingly at odds. To take a prominent example, in his 1855 "Letters on Landscape Painting," Asher B. Durand, who had exhibited banknote engravings at American Institute fairs 20 years earlier, specifically condemns commercial production as antithetical to the purity of art. The love of money, he insists, "is one of the principle causes operating to the degradation of Art, perverting it to the servility of a mere trade," enforcing a distinction between the genius of Art and the mundanity of artisanship.[27] Such a hierarchy of forms of production paralleled the implied distinction between bourgeois of manufacturing backgrounds and those from the financial and mercantile realms. As manifestation of the cultural authority of a manufacturing elite, the fairs of the artisans' societies were bound to commercial production and unable to sublimate monetary power into something more abstract. The fairs thus represented a very different cultural model from the National Academy of Design and other increasingly prominent bourgeois-sponsored cultural institutions.

The National Academy, aided by its mercantile bourgeois patrons, helped professional artists in New York to distinguish their trade, both culturally and economically, from artisanal work. Artists and art critics implicitly treated the arts as a cultural manifestation completely separate from and superior to commercial culture, and the artist as a distinguished genius in a way an inventor or artisan could never be.[28]

The career of John Frazee serves as an example of this sort of self-conscious distinction. Frazee began his career as a bricklayer's apprentice and stonecutter, carving blocks for bridges and buildings, and occasionally testing his skill by chiselling letters. The work was surely skilled, but Frazee longed to be known as a fine artist. In his letters, he makes a clear distinction between such commercial tasks as "stone cutting" and "making chimney pieces and grave stones" and the refined production of "sculpture" and "statuary."[29]

Frazee was one of the founders of the National Academy of Design and became renowned for his neoclassical statuary; nevertheless, he still felt burdened not only by the gaps in his knowledge of the fine arts but also by the invisible social attributes of his artisanal background. In a telling passage, portraitist and historian of the Academy Thomas S. Cummings recalled that Frazee "was entirely self-educated, and therefore, perhaps, wanting in that exterior refinement which would have rendered him popular."[30] That is to say that Frazee could not easily fit into bourgeois society as it had by then defined itself.

Frazee served at least five times as a judge of the fine arts and sculpture for the American Institute fairs between 1832 and 1840, always in his capacity as a sculptor and an architect—despite the deliberate commingling of chimney pieces and sculpture on the exhibition floor. As the more exclusionary model of cultural space was gaining a stronger foothold among New York's bourgeoisie, the gulf between it and the commercialized space of the fairs grew increasingly evident. Artworks that the manufacturing elite were happy to champion as potential native genius were found lacking in the context of the academy. For example, Rosanna Purcell, the daughter of a drawing master, exhibited small watercolor views with such titles as "The Cottage Door" and "The Literary Retreat" at both the American Institute fairs and the salon of the National Academy of Design. She was awarded a diploma in 1835 by the American Institute, but a review of the Academy exhibition two years later asserted that her drawings "would be considered good at a young ladies' boarding school, but have no merit to give them a place here." This same review asserted that a life-size horse's head drawn by Frederick Swinton, whose work had been deemed "clever" at the 1837 Mechanics' Institute fair, was barely tolerated at the Academy salon: "About as appropriate here as a real horse would be."[31]

In the 1840s, the prominence of the American Institute as a site of display for original artwork began to decline, and the National Academy of Design was already shedding its connections with amateurism and commercial art. The proposed School of Ornament for artisans had never gotten off the ground, and by the end of Morse's tenure as president of the Academy in 1845, any lingering interactions between it and the American Institute seem to have fallen away. The boundaries of fine art and commercial products were solidified enough in New York by 1859 that a newspaper reviewer could denounce the exhibition managers at the National Academy for violating their "duty to the public" by "admitting machine and clock paintings" into the gallery.[32] By midcentury, the amateur paintings, wood engravings, and novelty work that had formed a part of the Academy's earlier exhibitions accounted for a tiny fraction of the art displayed at its annual salons.

New York's artisan societies' fairs represented the manufacturing elite's model of cultural leadership, and its gradual dissociation from the art academies supported by the more established branches of the bourgeoisie was of a pattern repeated in other cities across the country. In western cities, the establishment of a local art gallery or academy often dramatically reframed the cultural position of the local mechanics' institute. The St. Louis Agricultural and Mechanical Association fair, for example, provided the only art exhibition space in that city before midcentury. The organization's membership included a wider swath of the local bourgeoisie than the New York mechanics' institutes, and its fairs' art galleries were less eclectic. The "Fine Art Hall" of the annual fairs of the St. Louis Agricultural and Mechanical Association was run independently of the rest of the exhibition, by "gentlemen who were Connoisseurs of the Fine Arts." Local artists and collectors alike sent their best pieces to the annual fairs, including a great number of minor Dutch and Italian old master paintings. But with the opening of the Western Academy of Art in 1860, the fair was no longer the most elegant site of display in St. Louis, and it lost the attention of many collectors.[33] Similarly, the Ohio Mechanics' Institute was Cincinnati's main cultural organization until the establishment of the Cincinnati Academy of the Fine Arts in 1839, after which the Ohio Mechanics' Institute soon eliminated the fine arts department from its fairs.[34]

This rise of the academies and, later, art museums in cities across the nation in the mid-nineteenth century signaled a change in the makeup of the American bourgeoisie. As Alan Wallach has argued elsewhere in this volume, the institutionalized definitions of high culture established with the art academies, galleries, and museums of the 1860s-1880s represented the emergence of a more cohesive "national upper class."[35] Manufacturers had a place in this new national elite, but their heterogeneous definitions of cultural quality did not. Bourgeois cultural authority rested on the distinction of the arts from other, lower, forms of production. While heterogeneity had been politically effective for the manufacturing elite, it was proving culturally untenable by midcentury. An expectation increasingly prevalent among artists, critics, and patrons of the arts that art galleries not only be decorated with ferns and curtains but should also be closed off from the rest of the world was frustrated by the situation at the mechanics' fairs. The standards of high culture could never seem to be met in the cluttered, arbitrarily lit, eclectic art displays of the early-century mechanics' institute fairs.

Even in his 1840 complaint, architect and exhibition judge Minard Lafever had urged the American Institute to keep the art galleries separate from the rest of the exhibition. He surmised that if "more conspicuous, and tasteful apartments" could be had for the display of fine arts, which he defined as "Architectural drawings and designs, Paintings, [and] Engravings" (notably excluding furniture making, needlework, and other crafts usually deemed by the Institute to be in the "department of fine arts" as well), the fair might attract the best artists of the city.[36] The various artisan societies, however, did not make any real moves toward such a separation, with all of its implied hierarchization, for a generation. By the post-Civil War era, the managers of the mechanics' fairs in the eastern cities understood that a creditable art gallery—and with it, the claims to high cultural authority—could no longer be so tightly interwoven into the commercial fabric of the fair. In the 1860s and '70s, the period that saw the founding of the first great American art museums, mechanics' fairs were marked by their, somewhat halting, move toward segregating the fine arts as a privileged category of exhibition.

The Massachusetts Charitable Mechanic Association, Boston's main artisans' society, made the most successful such alteration to the structure of its fairs. Even more insistently than in New York, the judges for the Boston association's fairs had admonished the managers that the very nature of the exhibition degraded the fine arts to mere "decoration" relative to the more "useful" products. For example, in their 1847 report, the judges of the fine arts department noted that artworks, especially paintings, "require not only peculiar arrangement of light for their exhibition, but a peculiar state of mind for the right appreciation and judgment of their merits." Therefore, they argued, paintings were "entirely out of place . . . [in the exhibition] except as mere ornaments."[37]

However, the twelfth triennial exhibition of the Association, in 1874, featured a temporary, two-level wooden addition, linking Faneuil and Quincy Halls, with more than 10,000 square-feet of exhibition space on its two floors—all of which was given over exclusively to the art exhibition. These galleries were gotten up in high style, with attention given to the "proper covering of the walls, the coloring of the ceiling," and the arrangement of the articles.[38] The walls were draped with decorative fabrics, gilt moldings were applied, and skylights let in northerly light to the upper floor. Further, the Association had special circulars printed up asking Boston artists and collectors to contribute works to the exhibition. The circular noted that "an experienced and disinterested committee of gentlemen"—a phrase evoking an ideal of bourgeois dissociation from the world of commerce—would act as a selection and arrangement committee, and that "catalogues of the art-gallery [would] be a distinct and special feature." To preserve the proper display of the artworks, artists and collectors were informed that "All Pictures, Busts, &c. must be provided with suitable frames, pedestals, &c., as necessary, to render the exhibition complete."[39] In a literal expression of the hierarchy of the arts, the structure's skylit upper level was reserved for oil paintings, watercolors, and engravings. Statuary, ceramics, photographs, architectural drawings, and art-school productions were shown on the lower level. Newspaper reviews recognized the significance of the manifest isolation of the art exhibition. Even within the temporary art building, the different displays were separated by screens, "thus avoiding," in the words of one review, "the presence of extraneous objects, the effect of which is to disturb the view of the spectator."[40] Although not universally well received in the press, the exhibition was an unqualified success in terms of attracting a creditable selection of artists and artworks.[41]

Thus, only by segregating the fine arts from the other kinds of exhibits, by providing a carefully decorated and controlled space, and even by separating the higher arts from the decorative did the Massachusetts Charitable Mechanic Association earn favorable notice from Boston's artists and collectors. The relative acclaim for the art galleries of the Association's exhibitions in 1874 and its next few triennial fairs indicates the effectiveness of the segregation and embellishment of the spaces of art display.

At the American Institute, the tradition of equating the fine arts and useful production remained strong, yet, in this same period, from the late 1860s into the mid-1870s, the managers of the New York exhibitions made halting attempts to treat fine arts as a separate and self-sufficient, and make its art galleries as significant in the city's cultural life as its commercial displays already were. While still insisting on the alliance of the fine and the useful arts, the fairs increasingly treated the fine arts as a unique class of objects. In the wake of the 1867 *Éxposition Universelle* in Paris, the American Institute deemed its thirty-seventh annual fair the "Grand Exhibition." The official catalogue asserted that "art exhibitions were never more popular than at present," and the Institute claimed the task of fairly representing America's progress in a way impossible at the distant world's fair.[42] The art gallery took up the north end of the long hall of the 22nd Regiment Armory on Fourteenth Street, the site of the fair that year, and included genre scenes by Constant Mayer, a William Beard animal painting, and landscapes by Aaron Draper Shattuck, William Hart, and Albert Bierstadt—all in all, a generally more professional class of artist than was usually seen at the Institute fairs. The rhetorical connections between art exhibitions and skilled labor were still being touted in speeches, but the catalogue marks an early instance of the American Institute highlighting its fine arts gallery as a central feature of the fair. Under a new classification system, oil paintings were designated as group 1 of department 1, the first items listed in the catalogues.[43]

Even having aggrandized its art department after 1867, the American Institute, unlike the Massachusetts Charitable Mechanic Association, did not refine its broad definition of the "fine arts." Accounts of the exhibition in the press call the art department the "great attraction" of the 1867 fair, yet go on to note the clocks, mantelpieces, furniture, and chromolithographs on display, before even mentioning any of the oil paintings.[44] In later fairs, the art galleries, though prominent, were increasingly filled with the mechanically reproduced merchandise of the city's major photography studios and chromolithograph publishers, and the Institute's role in displaying the work of individual artists significantly declined.

During this same period, however, the American Institute made its boldest essay at becoming a significant cultural institution in the city. Beginning in the late 1860s, the Institute put into action plans to establish a permanent Palace of Art and Industry. The project got off to an auspicious start. Walt Whitman was hired to compose a poem celebrating the museum, "After All, Not to Create Only," which he delivered at the opening of the Institute's fortieth annual fair in 1871.[45] Following him on the podium, E. G. Squire, the orator delivering the annual address, put the poet's vision into more concrete terms. The proposed Palace of Art and Industry would comprise exhibits of American workmanship and of natural history, geology, and horticulture, along with "a permanent gallery of American paintings, a great hall of American statuary, and a vast musical conservatory."[46]

Many plans for the structure were proposed, the most dramatic of which involved reusing the walls of the recently emptied receiving reservoir at Fifth Avenue and 42nd Street. The plan involved adding four elaborate entrances to the massive granite walls of the Egyptian-revival structure and raising a dome of glass and iron above. The old reservoir was to have provided four acres of floor space for displaying all types of machinery and inventions. Underneath the central dome would be a grand gallery, 15 feet wide and a third of a mile long, "admirably suited for statuary, paintings, photographs, and other works of art"—the art galleries at the center of the building thus metaphorically confirming their place at the top of the cultural hierarchy.[47]

A shortage of ready capital following the Panic of 1873 ended this dream prematurely, but more than mere finances made the idea impractical. Although the plan predated the Metropolitan Museum of Art by a few years, had it been built, the Palace of Art and Industry would likely never have challenged the art museum as the city's cultural nucleus. The American Institute's deep-rooted ambivalence about isolating the fine arts as a privileged form of production was at odds with the cultural model favored by the gradually consolidating New York bourgeoisie: which defined the aesthetic experience as incompatible with commercial concerns.

Further, wealthy manufacturers were decreasingly motivated to defend the cultural superiority of useful production, or to distinguish themselves from the mercantile and financial elite. The American Institute and other artisans' societies began to represent less an isolated segment of the bourgeoisie and more a node in an increasingly complex web of professional and elite organizations. Ever more frequently over the middle decades of the nineteenth century, manufacturers and the owners of large workshops regarded merchants as integral to the honorable task of production. Even merchant-capitalists, men of rising economic importance who made money from warehousing, shipping, and trading goods, without owning an interest in a craft shop, were acknowledged in most American Institute speeches as respectable producers, not condemned along with the non-productive class. Toward the middle of the century, capital accumulation *per se* was much less stigmatized in artisans' rhetoric, becoming instead a mark of personal success and republican virtue, in a way that mastery of a craft had been earlier in the century.[48] The makeup of the American Institute and similar organizations reflected these developments. In fact, the Institute's second president was John Mason, a financier who founded Chemical Bank and owned several streetcar lines. His connection with the Institute was indicative of the collapsing social distinctions between the professional and manufacturing elite, as the several strains of the bourgeoisie moved toward achieving a cultural critical mass.

Although the alliance of the fine arts and commercial production did not engender a viable model for the display of art, it was integral to the development of commercial space as a site of bourgeois cultural authority. Retail goods, elegantly displayed, were transformed into spectacle in the halls of the mechanics' fairs, and became associated with proofs of fashion and taste. While the institutes' official publications and orations generally stressed the fairs' role as educational events, other commentators increasingly treated the mechanics' fair as a pleasure ground of merchandise. As early as the late 1830s, a New York journal reported "our exposition [in this case, the 1838 American Institute fair] has now become the centre of attraction for all the men, and the favorite promenade of every lady who has the least pretension to taste or discrimination."[49]

Decades before the establishment of the great department stores, the mechanics' institute fairs marked a link between women's culture and recreational shopping, and, for male visitors, one of the signal attractions of the fairs was the great numbers of women to be seen in the exhibition halls.[50] The large proportion of female visitors helped merge expectations of womanly propriety into an ideal of genteel behavior in the presence of purchasable goods. In this regard, the entire fair was gendered feminine.[51] A great measure of moral education was ascribed to the institute fairs. "These Fairs," claimed one lecturer at the 1847 American Institute fair, "not only operate directly upon individuals, but are also raising up children."[52] Such maternal overtones were also reflected in official notices reporting the presence of women at the fairs. Female visitors were understood as the keepers of the flame of propriety. "To their presence," one managers' report notes, "an influence may no doubt be ascribed, in a great measure, the perfect propriety and order which uniformly pervaded the great room."[53]

Propriety was a significant concern; the leadership of the American Institute and its sister societies were keenly aware of the moral hazards inherent in public entertainments. At a time when the theater was considered a danger to the morals of young apprentices and, according to sensationalist descriptions of New York City, even fine art galleries were known as strolling grounds for prostitutes, the manufacturing elite ensured that the image of the fair—in pictures, verbal descriptions, catalogues, reports, and the like—was always one of high purpose, and a site of restraint and order: witness the idealized well-dressed laborers shopping alongside the middling classes in Harrison's watercolor (fig. 7.1).[54] To the merchants' clerks, artisans, and laborers walking amidst the decorated displays of goods, the mechanics' fair was a training ground in bourgeois manners. As the public equivalent of the formal front parlor, where interactions were codified, and the inspecting glances of fellow visitors enforced self-regulation, the fair halls fueled the normalization of bourgeois morality. Published reports of the American Institute fairs relished the orderliness of the crowd at these events, applauding the fact that a "potent and salutary moral influence" could be found even in the commercial metropolis.[55] In reports of their very first fair, the Institute was proud to note that even with an estimated 20,000 visitors "of all classes" over the three days of the fair, not one article was stolen from the exhibitors' display cases.[56] Such self-regulation was helped along by the private security forces often employed by the mechanics' societies to ensure "proper order" and "to prevent offences against exhibiters and visiters [*sic*]" at its fairs.[57]

Within the exhibition hall an air of pageantry reigned, complete with orations, music, and other diversions.[58] Ultimately, the peculiar aesthetic of the mechanics' fairs impelled the transformation of products into entertainment. As aesthetic value was positioned as a subset of commercial applicability, productive value was understood in increasingly spectacular terms alone. Even the most functional of objects—a hammer or a tractor—were admired primarily for their visual effect. The most blandly functional machines were increasingly displayed at the fairs as consumer goods, and the grime of their actual operation was often obscured. As in the later world's fairs, working machinery continued to be an attraction of the mechanics' fairs, but largely as dramatic spectacle, not as any sort of lesson or spur to invention. Like the music and the fireworks, the machinery displays served to heighten the excitement surrounding the commercial goods.

By the middle of the century, the American Institute's and related fairs had become largely indistinguishable from retail showrooms in terms of the range and decorative quality of the commercial displays. The fairs' elegant profusions of American-made merchandise, accented by elaborate showpieces, marked the consolidation of bourgeois interests. Reflecting a growing interconnection of production, distribution, and finance, the artisan fairs demonstrated that the commercial system was not simply a concrete relation of production and purchase but a subtle play of the immaterial, of desire and capital. The claim of a particular high-cultural authority by the manufacturers and their allies ultimately had little traction. The real legacy of the American Institute and its sister organizations is not any ideal of the cultural equality of all forms of commercial and aesthetic production but the spectacularization of commerce itself. In transforming the site of commercial display into a pleasure ground and haunt of fashion, the mechanics' fairs were a major factor in the definition of bourgeois aspirations as a cultural norm up and down the economic scale.

Notes

1. *Report of the Third Annual Fair of the American Institute of the City of New-York, Held at Masonic Hall, October 1830* (New York: J. Seymour, 1830), 11.
2. American Institute of the City of New York, *Charter and By-laws of the American Institute* [adopted 1866] (New York: American Institute of the City of New York, 1872), 3; American Institute of the City of New York, *The American Institute and Its Mission* [pamphlet] (New York: American Institute of the City of New York, 1871), 3.

3. Henry Clay was appreciative enough of the policies of the American Institute to write to the managers: "Such an unsolicited association of my name with an Institute having in view an object so patriotic as that of the American System is inexpressibly gratifying to me" (June 3, 1831), quoted in Edwin Forrest Murdock, "The American Institute," in *A Century of Industrial Progress,* ed. Frederic William Wile (Garden City, NY: Doubleday, Doran, 1928), xiv.
4. Mahlon Dickerson, "Address, Delivered at the Opening of the Nineteenth Annual Fair of the American Institute, of the City of New-York, at Castle Garden, October 5, 1846," in *Fifth Annual Report of the American Institute* (Albany, NY: C. Van Benthuysen, 1847), 277.
5. Zadock Pratt, *Address Delivered Tuesday Evening, January 16th, 1849, before the Mechanics' Institute of the City of New-York* (New York: H. R. Piercy, Printer, 1849), 5 (emphasis in original).
6. Sven Beckert, *The Monied Metropolis: New York City and the Consolidation of the American Bourgeoisie, 1850–1896* (Cambridge: Cambridge University Press, 1993), 61–64; Stuart Blumin, *The Emergence of the Middle Class: Social Experience in the American City, 1760–1900* (Cambridge and New York: Cambridge University Press, 1989), 71–73.
7. "The Mechanics," *New York Evening Post,* October 25, 1828.
8. *New-York Evening Post,* October 27, 1843.
9. Walt Whitman, "What we thought at the Institute Fair, this morning," *Brooklyn Daily Eagle,* 6 October 1846.
10. "Fair of American Manufactures," *Working Man's Advocate* 2 (October 13, 1830): 3.
11. Thaddeus B. Wakeman, "Introductory Lecture Delivered Before the American Institute of the City of New-York, the Second Thursday in January, 1835," *Mechanics' Magazine* 5 (1835): 73 (emphasis in original).
12. Tristram Burges, *Address Delivered before the American Institute of the City of New-York at the Third Annual Fair* (New York: John M. Danforth, 1830), 14–15.
13. Mount displayed his painting *Rustic Dance after a Sleigh Ride* at the National Academy of Design in 1830 and at the American Institute fair later that same year.
14. Thomas Seir Cummings, *Historic Annals of the National Academy of Design, New York Drawing Association, Etc., with Occasional Dottings by the Way-side, from 1825 to the Present Time* (Philadelphia: G. W. Childs, 1865), 134.
15. "National Academy of Design Annual Meeting 4 May, 1836, Report of the Council," National Academy of Design Minute Books 1825–38, 78, Archives of American Art.
16. *American Repertory of Arts, Sciences, and Manufactures* 2 (1841): 438–39 (hereafter cited as *American Repertory*).
17. *American Repertory* 3 (1841): 36. *See also* Cummings, *Historic Annals*, 167–68: "January 25th. [1841] A resolution was passed for the purposes of disseminating a knowledge of the arts of design to the mechanic and artisan, and the privilege was granted to the Mechanics' Institute to send any three of their pupils to the Academy schools, of which they never availed themselves."
18. James J. Mapes, *Address, Delivered at the Opening of the 18th Annual fair of the American Institute, at Niblo's Garden, Tuesday, Oct. 7, 1845* (New York: James Van Norden, 1845), 6.
19. "National Academy of Design," *American Repertory* 3 (1841), 284.
20. *Report of the Managers of the Fourth Annual Fair of the Mechanics' Institute, Held at Castle Garden, September 1838* (New York: [The Institute], 1838), 16.
21. Ibid.
22. *New-York Commercial Advertiser,* November 1, 1833.
23. "Address by Judge Baldwin of Pennsylvania to the American Institute," reprinted in *First Exhibition and Fair of the Massachusetts Charitable Mechanic Association, at Faneuil and Quincy Halls, in the City of Boston, September 18, 1837* (Boston: Dutton and Wentworth, 1837), 5.
24. *Third Annual Fair of the Mechanics' Institute of the City of New York, September 1837* (New York: n.p., 1837), 14.
25. *Report of the Third Annual Fair of the American Institute*, 27.
26. Minard Lafever, "Judges' Report, 13th Annual Fair of the American Institute" [1840], manuscript, New-York Historical Society (emphasis in original).
27. Asher B. Durand, "Letters on Landscape Painting: Letter IV," *The Crayon* 1, no. 7 (1855): 97.
28. Dell Upton, "Inventing the Metropolis: Civilization and Urbanity," in *Art in the Empire City: New York, 1825–1861* (New York: The Metropolitan Museum of Art, 2000), 35–38.

29. John Frazee to Noah Frazee, February 2, 1835, John Frazee Papers, 1810–1964, Archives of American Art.
30. Cummings, *Historic Annals*, 230.
31. *New York Herald*, May 18, 1837. Another paper noted that Swinton's work was "judiciously hung high" (*New-York Mirror*, May 6, 1837).
32. *New York Herald*, May 8, 1859.
33. "Class F. Fine Art Hall. Paintings, Statuary, &c.," in *Report of the Fourth Annual Fair of the St. Louis Agricultural and Mechanical Association, of September, 1859*. (St. Louis: George Knapp & Co., Printers and Binders, 1860), 121–26; William McPherson, "Class F. Fine Art Hall," in *Report of the Fifth Annual Fair of the St. Louis Agricultural and Mechanical Association, of September, 1860* (St. Louis: George Knapp & Co., printers, 1861), 94.
34. Lillian Miller, *Patrons and Patriotism: The Encouragement of the Fine Arts in the United States, 1790–1860* (Chicago: University of Chicago Press, 1966), 194–95.
35. Alan Wallach, "Long-Term Visions, Short-Term Failures: Art Institutions in the United States, 1800–1860," in *Exhibiting Contradictions: Essays on the Art Museum in the United States* (Amherst: University of Massachusetts Press, 1998), 21. See also Wallach, "The Birth of the American Art Museum" in this volume.
36. Lafever, "Judges' Report, 13th Annual Fair of the American Institute."
37. William T. Andrews et al., "Fine Arts," in *Fifth Exhibition and Fair of the Massachusetts Charitable Mechanic Association, at Faneuil and Quincy Halls, in the City of Boston, September 1847* (Boston: Dutton and Wentworth, 1848), 20.
38. *The Twelfth Exhibition of the Massachusetts Charitable Mechanic Association, at Faneuil and Quincy Halls, in the City of Boston, September and October 1874* (Boston: A. Mudge and Son, Printers, 1874), 166–67.
39. Fine Art Department. Twelfth Exhibition of the Massachusetts Charitable Mechanic Association, 1874, "To Artists, Connoisseurs, and Art-lovers generally . . . ," handbill [1874], n.p., Rare Books Collection, Boston Public Library.
40. "The Great Art Exposition," *Boston Evening Transcript*, August 17, 1874.
41. William Morris Hunt, George Inness, James M. Hart, George Loring Brown, John G. Brown, M. F. H. De Haas, and A. F. Bellows all won awards at this exhibition. Their work was in the company of hundreds of other paintings and sculptures by American artists, as well as canvases by Leon Bonnat, James Tissot, and other contemporary French painters, lent by collectors in Boston, New York, Philadelphia, and elsewhere. On the lower floor, Sevrès vases and Prang chromolithographs accompanied sculptures by Thomas Ball and others.

    A few reports took the Massachusetts Charitable Mechanic Association to task for arranging the exhibition too late, thus missing most of the collectors before they left town for summer travels and the artists for sketching trips. Newspaper reporters also saw too many "shop-worn," familiar paintings, and further surmised that little had been excluded by the vaunted selection committee. See E. M., "Art in Boston: The Pictures at the Charitable Mechanic Association Exhibition—Why the Display Is Not Better," *New York Evening Post*, September 21, 1874; and "The Fine Arts Exhibition at the Mechanic Fair," *Boston Evening Transcript*, September 21, 1874.
42. *Grand Exhibition 1867* [pamphlet] (New York: American Institute of the City of New York, 1867), n.p.
43. In this the American Institute mirrors on a small scale the organizational hierarchies expressed in Frédéric Le Play's design for the main exhibition building of the 1867 Éxposition Universelle. Moving from the outer edges toward the center of the oval-shaped building, a visitor would encounter exhibits arranged on a scale of production, from raw materials to machinery to commercial goods. The art gallery was in the innermost aisles.
44. *New York Tribune*, September 17, 1867.
45. The poem is now more commonly known as "Song of the Exposition." Whitman was paid $100 for it, plus expenses.
46. E. G. Squire, address before the 1871 American Institute fair, reported in *New York Times*, September 3, 1871.
47. C. F. Chandler, "On Combustion," *Annual Report of the American Institute of the City of New York for the Years 1871–72* (Albany: The Argus Company, Printers, 1872), 237.
48. Gary J. Kornblith, "Self-Made Men: The Development of Middling-Class Consciousness in New England," *The Massachusetts Review* 26, nos. 2–3 (Summer/Autumn, 1985): 469–70. For models of earlier developments leading up to this consolidation, see Robert Babcock,

"The Decline of Artisan Republicanism in Portland, Maine, 1825–1850," *The New England Quarterly* 63, no. 1 (March 1990): 9; and Sean Wilentz, "Artisan Republican Festivals and the Rise of Class Conflict in New York City," in Michael H. Frisch and Daniel J. Walkowitz eds. *Working-Class America: Essays on Labor, Community and American Society* (Urbana: University of Illinois Press, 1983).

49. "The Fair," *New York Morning Herald,* October 19, 1838.
50. For example, a newspaper article titled "The Fair!—the beautiful Petticoat and the Pretty Petticoats," describes both the "beautiful works of art" and the "beautiful works of Nature" on display at the 1837 Mechanics' Institute fair in New York; see *New York Morning Herald,* September 26, 1837. In the same vein, describing the closing of the 1838 American Institute fair, the *Morning Herald* reported: "There was a great deal of fun, and a great many females; where they are, wit, good humor, cheerfulness, vivacity, and happiness uniformly exist" (November 2, 1838).
51. *New-York Commercial Advertiser,* October 14, 1831.
52. George Gifford, *An Address Delivered at Castle Garden, on Invitation of the American Institute, during its Twentieth Annual Fair* (New York: Joseph H. Jennings, 1847), 13.
53. *Report of the Third Annual Fair of the American Institute,* 4.
54. George G. Foster, *New York by Gaslight and Other Urban Sketches* (1850; repr., Berkeley and Los Angeles: University of California Press, 1990), 72. Perhaps in response to such reports, James Mapes, a scientist and former president of the New York Mechanics' Institute, insisted in an 1851 article that the fine arts were such a refining influence that one finds at exhibitions of Academies and Art Unions "youth of both sexes innocently enjoying each other's society" ("Usefulness of the Arts of Design," *Sartain's Union Magazine* 8, no. 3 [March 1851]: 213).
55. "New York American Institute," *Niles' Register,* October 31, 1829, 156.
56. *Reports of the American Institute, in the City of New-York, on the Subject of Fairs,* 2nd ed. (New York: J. Seymour, Printer, 1829), 9.
57. "Regulations of the Fair," *Minutes of the Board of Managers of the 27th Annual Fair,* [1855], manuscript, New-York Historical Society.
58. The 1837 fair of the American Institute, for example, featured "Mr. Coombs, Phrenologist from London, . . . Mr. Porter, the far famed Kentucky Giant, and the celebrated Major Stevens, the American Dwarf," as well as the display of a moving panorama; see *New-York Evening Post,* October 26, 1837.

8
A Noble Pursuit?: Bourgeois America's Uses of Lineage

Francesca Morgan

Across the world and since antiquity, people have practiced genealogy—the study of lineage. Prior to the 1800s, genealogy's most familiar incarnation in the Western world was as a monarchical and aristocratic practice. Indeed, premodern Europeans relied on lineage for the maintenance of social hierarchies. Genealogy constituted an ideology, a set of ideas or signs that expresses and reproduces social and other power relations.[1]

The urban upper classes, or bourgeoisie, of the nineteenth-century United States redefined genealogy. In bourgeois hands, genealogy expressed and helped reproduce contemporary power relations relating to class, gender, and race—prolonging, in the process, genealogy's ideological character.[2] The bourgeoisie remade descent—the relationships between ancestors and descendants as viewed by descendants—into a form of social capital, imparting prestige to those able to document their lineages. Throughout the nineteenth century, genealogy's "bourgeoisification" operated informally, notably in bourgeois households. Genealogy's evangelists in these private settings were typically female. Bourgeois men transformed genealogy further in formalizing it, in the form of organizations and publications. Organized genealogy was concentrated in the Northeast, especially New England, during the Early Republic. Later in the century, genealogical groups and publications developed throughout America, in places where industrial capitalism gave birth to bourgeoisies. By 1900, bourgeois uses of genealogy resulted in a potent, truly national community of hundreds of thousands of white Americans, including women. They practiced genealogy publicly and with a confidence fueled by new scientific theories regarding heredity.[3] Even though the American Revolution had severed the ties between lineage and political authority in America, and rejected hereditary government, bourgeois America in the nineteenth century prolonged the ties between lineage and social authority.[4] Although many bourgeois found genealogy insufficient to maintain class distinctions, in the end, genealogy was a key component of such distinctions.

In remaking genealogy, and in developing flourishing hereditary organizations during the Gilded Age, the American bourgeoisie simultaneously formed itself. As it did with dress, manners, and food, bourgeois America constituted genealogy as social glue that would mend internal divisions, and also as a badge of belonging that distinguished the bourgeoisie from others.[5] In bourgeois hands, the study of lineage could and did bridge intraclass differences in political opinions, ethnicity, religion, section, and gender. Class distinctions that set the bourgeoisie apart, as expressed in genealogical practices, took intangible and tangible forms. The intangible forms refer to the meanings that bourgeois Americans attached to lineage, particularly their attribution of prestige and stature to documented colonial ancestry.[6] The obstacles to practicing genealogy encountered by people who themselves lacked leisure time, and whose ancestors were neither leisured nor literate, signified class and other social distinctions past and present. Plebeian ancestors usually lacked the education, wealth, free time, and property holdings that enabled the generation of letters, diaries, and wills. Another form of evidence treasured by genealogists was records of marriages, and births within wedlock. But the marriages and births of lower-class Americans and slaves did not command the respect of contemporaries. The poor of early America had their common-law marriages and children inconsistently recorded by public and religious authorities. When enslaved people married, their marriages carried no legal weight; contemporary laws and practices proscribed the literacy of most; and, in the nineteenth century, the domestic slave trade vaporized many families by permanently separating children from parents, and spouses from spouses.[7] Bourgeois Americans added to genealogy's inherent exclusivity by praising their kin selectively—prizing them for their social prominence, wealth, and/or whiteness. When genealogical practices failed to screen out individuals who did manage to map their descent from the humble and the nonwhite, and individuals who seemed unworthy of illustrious lineages, bourgeois America developed additional, nongenealogical means of excluding such people from its circles.

At first glance, American bourgeois predilections for genealogy appear paradoxical. European genealogical practices and beliefs had been most obvious within nobilities; European bourgeoisies developed in conflict with those nobilities; and the United States itself originated in repudiation of hereditary government.[8] Following the War of 1812, pro-democracy commentators forcefully articulated that last point, denouncing interest in one's own "noble" origins as "not fitted to the genius of our country or its institutions."[9] Yet the absence of an official hereditary nobility in the United States helps explain Americans' penchant for genealogy. Genealogy had shed the stigma it would have retained in the presence of nobility. Intending no irony, a genealogy aficionado could defend Americans' interest in lineage as a "noble pursuit," without making any reference to nobles.[10] Americans' break with European-style aristocracy was decidedly incomplete. Many genealogists partook also of heraldry, studying family coats-of-arms and crests. By definition and in practice, nineteenth-century heraldry treasured relatedness to foreigners with titles.[11] Yet, in a country where no nobility frustrated the bourgeoisie's ascendance, the desire to map noble ancestry came to seem harmless—unable to undermine American republicanism. Especially when imparting a whiff of foreignness, genealogy's and heraldry's rituals developed into effective, emphatic methods used by the American upper classes to differentiate themselves from others.

Descent itself was difficult or impossible to purchase, to be sure, but the ability to document descent through multiple generations signified considerable financial means and leisure time on the part of descendants as well as of ancestors. Especially before the Civil War, genealogical and historical research was so time-consuming that it was hardly possible for those who needed to support themselves financially from day to day. Researchers operated in the absence of public libraries or, indeed, any research entities accessible to the public.[12] Such people relied on family and other class-specific connections to perform their time-consuming work. Access to historical texts depended on the personal collections of wealthy men; private associations and private libraries, depending on the location; and on the whims of town clerks, clergy, and others who controlled access to places where historic records were stored.[13] Where and when such records failed genealogists, or when they wished to reconfirm information in a written source, genealogists turned to "tradition"—oral and/or written family lore obtained from descendants.[14]

Informal Genealogy

Men and women alike produced and preserved family lore, orally and on paper. They operated within bourgeois households, outside or in the absence of genealogical institutions, and with family members as their audiences. Women contributed especially powerfully in this informal way to the bourgeoisie's appropriation of genealogy, as well as to the dynastic reinvention of the bourgeoisie. Even—and especially—when single and childless themselves, women reproduced a family's fame backward as well as forward.[15] Mothers, wives, and grandmothers also assumed the duty of reminding the next generation to praise their lineages. Compared to their male kin, such women lived in fragile relationships with financial capital—separated from poverty solely by a husband or a bequest. Especially before the Civil War, women lacked access to many forms of social capital such as college educations. Their forced financial dependence on men compelled some women to invest in forms of capital that were accessible to women. The ability to reckon one's ancestry was one such form of capital.

In 1831, a Virginia planter reflected on his elite lineage ("with the Teutonic knights we could count four descents"). A grandfather was a colonial governor of Virginia. He had obtained this information during his childhood "at the old manor house" from his "aged grand-mother, the garrulous historian of Indian wars, the wonders achieved by the pristine colonists."[16] Pacing the streets of Charleston, South Carolina, in 1836, a native of that city mused on the city's history. He, too, had "gathered" his information "from an ancient relative. My head is full of her stories of the revolution. She was one of the citizens during the [1780] siege by Clinton." Noting that his kinswoman had stored her reminiscences in her own head, as many antebellum women had done, and "thinking about the thousand anecdotes and legends of old time to which my young ears have listened, I feel a regret—a positive sorrow—that they should go unchronicled." Conflating the city's history with "family history," the South Carolinian concluded that local history and genealogy should pass out of "the cold hands of tradition" and into the hands of "heads of families"—men—who would commit them to writing. "We are proud of a family name—should we neglect the very material [public events] from which it may have derived all the pride and character which it may happen to possess?"[17]

The loquacious female relative with a zeal for family history appears also in the writings of Northerners. The New Hampshire state legislator John Kelly was certain of his Irishness because, he remarked in 1827, a "good old maiden aunt, who kept in her head the records and genealogy of the family, delivered it unto me, that long before either of us was born *we* came from the land of Shilalas [shillelaghs], buttermilk, and potatoes."[18] In neighboring Massachusetts, Mary Moody Emerson (1774–1863) anticipated her famous nephew's transcendentalism, and also passed on family history to him and his sister. As an adult, Ralph Waldo Emerson developed a vexed relationship with lineage. "The dead sleep in their moonless night; my business is with the living," he remarked in 1825.[19] Four years later, however, he cared enough to contact a genealogist to reconfirm the information provided by his redoubtable "Aunt Mary" on their descent from New England clergy five generations distant. He praised her as "a very accurate person generally."[20]

This pattern, in which bourgeois women orally transmitted considerable knowledge of family history to subsequent generations, endured well after the Civil War. Elizabeth Perkins Lee Shattuck of Boston descended from English gentry and also from those intertwined tribes of merchants and industrialists who dominated Boston's business scene. After marrying in 1876, she imparted her keen regard for her lineage to her children. She instilled in her son Henry Lee Shattuck, who later became a Massachusetts politico, "stories about her ancestors, so that the experiences of his great-grandmother . . . became as vivid to him as if they were his own," wrote his biographer. "(Quite unconsciously, in later years, referring to the acts of his colonial forebears, he would say, 'we thought,' or 'we said,' as if he, too, had been there.)"[21]

Women who evangelized their families about their lineages and, by extension, their families' social prominence occasionally committed their own words to paper. A good example is the commonplace books—compendiums of personal writings and other information usually intended for families' and intimate friends' viewing—and genealogical diaries kept by Deborah Norris Logan (1761–1839) and other women of the Quaker upper classes in and around Philadelphia.[22] Anna Henshaw (born 1778) of Leicester, Massachusetts, the daughter of a landowner and Revolutionary officer there, directed her own highly didactic 1839 compendium to "all the Descendants, unto the fourth and fifth generation, of my late Honerd [*sic*] Father." In it, she began the family's lineage with a list of lords of the same surnames in thirteenth-century England.[23] A Cambridgeport, Massachusetts, merchant's daughter named Caroline Frances Orne viewed her widowed mother as so valuable a source of information on her own family (Orne's maternal ancestors) that Orne dedicated herself to transcribing that information. To Orne, who published multiple articles on local history in area newspapers, her mother was the family's "real antiquarian" and Orne herself "not much more than her amanuensis, or assistant to her labors."[24]

Bourgeois women's enthusiasm for genealogy—as exemplified by daughters' and (in the case of Mary Moody Emerson) grandnieces' transmission of their female elders' knowledge—creates a paradox in that genealogical practices reinforced male supremacy.[25] To document forebears' marriages, births, and military service (the latter information required by many hereditary organizations at the end of the nineteenth century), genealogists necessarily depended on institutional records generated solely by men.[26] Other features of genealogy that reinforced female subjugation had to do with genealogy's own culture. It was female labor, in all senses of the word, that ensured new generations. Yet because Americans engaged in patrilineal naming and inheritance customs, genealogy stressed men's contributions to each individual, male or female, and eclipsed contributions by women. New brides' habitual adoption of their husbands' surnames, the assignment of those surnames to subsequent children, and single women's expected childlessness all explain many family trees' representation of adult women, whether married or unmarried, as leaves or fruitless stumps—the same iconographic representation as that of children who died before reaching maturity. The trees' branches carried the names of men. The early death or absence of males in any generation meant that a family name—and with it, the family—was "extinguished."[27] Nevertheless, many women from wealthy and prominent families conspicuously devoted themselves to transmitting genealogical information long before genealogical institutions existed, and long before such institutions admitted women.

The Formalization of Genealogy

Starting in the 1820s, bourgeois men in the North moved the study of lineage into public forums such as publications and new societies.[28] The leisured gentlemen of antebellum historical and genealogical organizations blurred the boundaries among genealogy, history, and biography.[29] The proliferation of historical societies in the early nineteenth century, such as in New Hampshire (1823) and Philadelphia (1824), was inspired by bicentenary celebrations of the beginnings of European settlement, and by the nationwide tour of the Revolutionary major general Marquis de Lafayette in 1824–25.[30] Later, Boston's New England Historic Genealogical Society (NEHGS), formed in 1845, represented the first private-sector organization, in post-Revolutionary times, devoted to genealogy per se. Among Southern gentlemen, though, the absence of organized genealogy (publications and institutions) was pronounced well before the Civil War destroyed many public buildings in the South and the early American records inside them.[31] Southern individuals—such as the two in Virginia and South Carolina who took inspiration from their grandmothers—considered their lineages important to who they were. But the antebellum South boasted few cities. Therefore, Southerners possessed even narrower access than Northerners to historical documents and other resources that would enable them to perform research.

In organizing genealogy before the Civil War, Northern men utilized it to signify their leisured status, and to constitute themselves as a class. Organized genealogy ameliorated some meaningful divisions among such men—occupations or sources of capital; political and partisan issues; Protestant, Northern European ethnicities; and Protestant religious denominations. The midcentury Boston bourgeoisie, the stratum that sustained NEHGS, rarely experienced tensions between merchants and manufacturers—in contrast to the New York bourgeoisie.[32] Differences among New Englanders were more obvious regarding politics. Debates of the 1840s and 1850s on antislavery divided the Boston business classes and their families. Whig-spirited industrialists and merchants desired continued commerce and comity with Southern planters, as cheap domestic cotton ensured the economic health of New England mills. Two leading Massachusetts "Cotton Whigs" in Congress, Representative Robert C. Winthrop and Senator Edward Everett, joined NEHGS early on.[33] Smaller numbers of manufacturers, merchants, and others (Republicans after 1854) resented slavery's potential proletarianization of the white male labor force. Among those antislavery businessmen were some leaders of NEHGS—the Boston banker Almon D. Hodges (president), Massachusetts governor John Albion Andrew (president), and the Boston and New Hampshire dry-goods merchant and banker William B. Towne (treasurer).[34] The merchant-industrialist Amos A. Lawrence was among those opponents of slavery who donated funds and weapons to John Brown's actions in Kansas's civil war.[35] Outside events ultimately brought former Whigs and Republicans in Boston together in opposition to slavery, most notably Congress's acceptance in 1854 of slavery's northward expansion and the coming of the U.S. Civil War. Expressing bourgeois Bostonians' newfound political unity as supporters of the Union were mutually pursued leisure activities, among them genealogy. In 1863, Lawrence purchased a $1,000 life membership in NEHGS.[36]

The leisure-time practice of genealogy helped unify the bourgeoisie across ethnic and religious lines as well as political ones. There was nothing inherently ethnically specific or nativist about genealogy, despite its accommodation of "Anglo-Saxon" exclusivity. Despite presuming an interest in Anglo, Protestant forebears, and not promoting Catholic or Irish genealogy in any sustained fashion until the twentieth century, the formation of NEHGS should not be considered a backlash against new immigrants' swift demographic transformation of Boston. NEHGS hatched (barely) in advance of Ireland's potato famine, and did not manifest much overt hostility against the incoming Irish in its first half century.[37] A likely reason was that organized nativism in 1850s Massachusetts expressed resentment of the upper classes.[38]

Organized genealogy accommodated ethnic differences more gracefully in places where the upper classes had long included non-Anglophones. Physicians, Union generals, and others directly inspired by NEHGS's example formed the New York

Genealogical and Biographical Society (NYGBS) in 1869, the country's second-oldest genealogical institution. Here, gentlemen—including the financier John Jay, the cotton merchant Benjamin Howland, Silvanus J. Macy, and various Brevoorts, Onderdonks, and Pierreponts—and the very occasional woman (Elizabeth Clarkson Jay) came together who treasured upper-class New York's polyglot past and their own blood connections to it.[39] Nearly every issue of NYGBS's periodical in the late nineteenth century featured Dutch and Huguenot (French Protestant) genealogies and reprinted historical documents, including untranslated marriage and death records of Manhattan's Reformed Dutch Church.[40]

Though a mainline Protestant redoubt, organized genealogy tolerated some religious diversity. Small numbers of Catholic and Jewish families traced their American lineages to colonial times.[41] Bourgeois forms of genealogy did not intrinsically favor any one denomination or sect. The practice of genealogy bridged divisions, among Protestants, that still mattered in the Early Republic. In Revolutionary New England, whether one practiced Anglicanism (later, Episcopalianism) or Congregationalism spoke volumes about one's British or American patriotism. Indeed, Congregational churches subscribing to Unitarianism, a relatively liberal sect preferred by upper-class Bostonians, remained tax-supported in Massachusetts until 1833. Seceding Orthodox or Trinitarian Congregationalists and other non-Unitarians had been compelled to subsist on laypeople's contributions. Yet Congregationalists, Unitarians, and Episcopalians alike, including clergy, populated the leadership of the midcentury NEHGS.[42]

"Race and Blood" in the Gilded Age

After the Civil War, upper-class Americans across the country infused genealogy with new, science-based confidence, and operated on a much larger scale. Genealogy's expansion constituted a delayed reaction to the war itself, since the war resulted in an extraordinary number of premature and violent deaths, and increasing awareness of death.[43] Discoveries in evolutionary biology also energized the study of lineage. Starting with the 1859 publication of Charles Darwin's *Origin of Species,* educated people on both sides of the Atlantic increasingly applied his and others' notions of inherited characteristics to humans. Eugenics, or the study of human breeding, developed as a shared Anglo-American interest starting in 1883.[44] Late-nineteenth-century genealogists altered their own practices to express more restrictive race and class distinctions, and combined race with documented lineage ("race and blood"). Starting in the 1870s, genealogy came increasingly to accommodate the new, science-based racisms—placing "Anglo-Saxons" above others—that accompanied educated Americans' escalating confidence in heredity to explain group phenomena.[45]

As the percentages of Americans in northern cities who had been born overseas (outside Britain's Protestant populations) or who possessed foreign-born parents grew to majorities by the end of the century, genealogists' characterizations of their derivations centered on race and heredity. Frank talk of noble inheritances faded from NEHGS's periodical by 1880. The desire to map the Englishness, per se, of New Englanders grew. Starting in 1883, in a quest for greater accuracy and comprehensiveness, and catering to individuals unable to afford the services of overseas genealogists, NEHGS raised funds to send to London a full-time researcher. In nearly every issue of the *Register* for the next 16 years, Henry FitzGilbert Waters of Salem, Massachusetts, published his "Genealogical Gleanings in England." His gleanings consisted largely of seventeenth-century wills that helpfully named relatives already in North America.[46] The pursuit of English ancestors became all the more racially specific once that pursuit focused on English descent per se and not just on the English aristocracy. Other genealogy aficionados took inspiration from animal breeding and pedigree keeping, as the "purebred" pet originated as a concept in these same decades of the Gilded Age. Since "*race* and *blood* are important" to the "intelligence and courage . . . and as to size, strength, speed, and endurance" of a given horse or dog, a New Yorker asserted in 1870, "then, must not race and blood be much more important, in both departments, for *man;* the highest class of all animals?"[47]

Simultaneously, bourgeois Americans outside the Northeast began publishing in genealogy and building new genealogical institutions. They launched both local initiatives and nationwide entities. Organized genealogy became national as a result of bourgeoisies' developing nationally—west of the Appalachians and in the South. In 1887 Chicago began sporting a research library that by 1900 stressed history and genealogy, and courted an elite clientele. Chicago business leaders of colonial New England lineage developed the Newberry Library and its genealogical mission.[48] After the South began industrializing in the 1880s, Southern state governments developed their departments of archives and history. They collected materials of interest to genealogists and newly enabled genealogical research.[49]

Such facilities found an eager clientele among propertied whites. Women everywhere and Southern men formalized their interest in lineage as new hereditary organizations emerged late in the century. Unlike earlier genealogical organizations such as NEHGS and NYGBS, hereditary organizations required genealogical documentation for membership. The Sons of Revolutionary Sires, organized in San Francisco in 1875 shortly before the country's centenary, was later absorbed into the Sons of the Revolution (formed 1883).[50] In 1885, Huguenot societies formed in New York City (as the Huguenot Society of America) and in South Carolina. Both groups required for admission proof of descent from colonial Huguenots.[51] The largest and best-known hereditary organizations, totaling hundreds of thousands of members nationwide, are the Sons of the American Revolution (SAR), founded in 1889; the Daughters of the American Revolution (DAR, 1890); the Daughters of the Revolution (1891); the invitation-only National Society of the Colonial Dames of America (NSCDA, 1891); the New York-based Colonial Dames of America (CDA, 1890), an unrelated and also invitation-only group; the mixed-sex General Society of Mayflower Descendants (1897); and the invitation-only, mixed-sex Order of First Families of Virginia (1912).[52] These Daughters, Dames, and Sons combined genealogy with other objectives, such as commemorations by means of monuments, holidays, and rituals; historic preservation; and the patriotic education of immigrants and/or schoolchildren.[53]

Hereditary organizations helped assemble a truly national upper class that united disparate sources of capital and types of power, including newer strata of professionals, corporate managers, their female kin, and female entrepreneurs; cities with towns, the white West with the white East, and the white North with the white South.[54] An important force for North-South reconciliation among white Americans, the new hereditary organizations bridged class, sectional, partisan, and cultural divisions that would otherwise have torn the national webs and impeded bourgeois class formation. Here, the bourgeoisie bundled genealogy with patriotism to a new degree.

Genealogy's expansion into hereditary groups brought about the public practice of genealogy by bourgeois women. Starting in the 1890s, women poured into organized genealogy well beyond the point of integrating the field. "Daughters" organizations quickly outstripped "Sons" organizations in numbers and in their intensity.[55]

Swimming with the tide, NEHGS began admitting women to its membership in 1898.[56] Women's now-public expression of interest in lineage was due to genealogy's continued effectiveness in proclaiming bourgeois class distinctions. Women perceived that their documented lineages conferred considerable public influence, if not power. Daughters and Dames constructed their ancestry into a perch from which they sought to uplift Americans at large, and to produce patriotism in the population. Active as clubwomen yet veiled in their husbands' names (in print), the women did not view male-centered naming customs as indicating women's unimportance. Studying lineage in the course of serving their families, such women knew that behind those naming customs lay a world of female endeavor with decidedly public and political consequences. The ability to name ancestors and trace lineages honored motherhood and, by extension, women's labor. Another reason for the late-nineteenth-century pattern in which women outnumbered men in hereditary organizations has to do with women's still-indirect relationships with their families' wealth. Women achieved social mobility through marriage, inheritance, or both. These women, as a group, therefore felt less attached than bourgeois men as a group to the fading archetype of the self-made man—and therefore more eager to freight lineage with profound class significance.[57]

"Personal Acceptability," or Genealogy's Limits

Despite genealogy's creation of formidable barriers around the bourgeoisie, the study of lineage proved overly exclusive to some bourgeois, and insufficiently exclusive to others. The study of lineage effectively snubbed families that had recently acquired their wealth and/or prominence, creating new divisions within the bourgeoisie. Therefore, genealogy's ability to foster unity within the upper classes proved limited. The adoption of class-specific fashions in dress, food, entertainment, and manners entailed only changes in behavior on the part of white Americans and required nothing of their ancestors. Bourgeois with humble antecedents who had arrived into the upper classes in their own or their parents' lifetimes found genealogy difficult. Consequently, the abovementioned fashions and rituals brought together larger numbers of people than did genealogy, and did more to promote bourgeois coalescence.

But genealogy's tendency to strengthen class distinctions was evident even from its own weaknesses in doing so. American bourgeois realized that they did not wish to pursue their genealogy work to its logical conclusion—valuing all kin for being kin—unless they wanted to diminish the social differences in which they believed. Hereditary organizations required that prospective members be "personally acceptable," in addition to possessing documented colonial or Revolutionary descent.[58] Relatedness, especially from a distance of multiple generations, did not guarantee like-mindedness. Genealogists most treasured their descent from ancestors whose actions and values harmonized with their own. Such acts of selection, especially when committed by those intent on reinforcing class distinctions, illustrate kinship's plasticity.[59] Selective readings of kinship also demonstrate the bourgeoisie's deployment of genealogy to signal its differences, as a class, from others.

Bourgeois America developed these uses of genealogy especially after it became more accessible to white Americans outside the bourgeoisie. In the 1870s and after, research facilities developed in more places, in part because of interest in the new hereditary organizations. Late-nineteenth-century Americans traveled and communicated over long distances faster, more easily, and more cheaply than previously, and genealogical and historical publications containing reprinted historical documents multiplied. To some extent, the largest hereditary organizations—the DAR and the SAR—accommodated middling Americans who could document their Revolutionary lineages. Daughters and Sons encouraged each other to research and praise their eighteenth-century forebears, even if they had been teenage drummer boys and not officers. The DAR "is, or should be, for the people, and should again be for all the people who have any claim to Revolutionary blood," a national officer proclaimed in 1894.[60]

In response, others in hereditary organizations combined genealogical membership requirements with other, nongenealogical requirements to preserve differences between the bourgeoisie and those outside it. A right-thinking, truly elite membership ultimately mattered more to such organizations than did the ability to document colonial or Revolutionary descent. Many Daughters of the American Revolution formed local chapters by first contacting women they wanted in the group and then beginning the task of documenting the women's lineages. In this way, Mary Beardsley Prince (born 1846), married to the New Mexico territorial governor L. Bradford Prince, organized the DAR there in the 1890s. She made repeated trips to the public library in Denver to map the Revolutionary descent of friends and acquaintances.[61] Like other hereditary organizations, the DAR required a prospective member to obtain the signatures of two current members to signify that she was "personally acceptable."[62] Suspecting rightly that some African Americans with free ancestors could prove Revolutionary or colonial descent—as the civil-rights pioneer W. E. B. Du Bois nearly did in a 1908 bid for membership in the Sons of the American Revolution—the early DAR added an internal statute that banned "colored" women outright.[63]

Other hereditary groups devised additional barriers against those able to meet steep genealogical criteria but who seemed otherwise objectionable. Having been asked to apply to the invitation-only, New York-based Colonial Dames of America, a prospective Dame was required to map her descent, via marriages and births within wedlock, from a colonial figure of sufficient prominence. After current Dames located in "the thirteen original states, through which we all claim ancestry" vetted the woman's pre-Revolutionary ancestor (for his wealth and importance) and her own genealogical research, her membership was then voted on by Dames in her own state.[64] Leaders of hereditary groups knew that genealogy in itself could not guarantee a membership "representative of the best and finest in conservative society today," as described by a president of the First Families of Virginia. She cautioned members, "[I]t is not enough that a casual acquaintance may have 1607–1620 ancestry . . . Guard your invitation privilege as you guard your personal honor."[65]

In studying their ancestors, members of Gilded Age hereditary organizations agreed to elide aspects of ancestors' lives that descendants found unpalatable. Within the Daughters of the American Revolution, the 1927 "Rules for D.A.R. Vital Statistics Workers" in copying historical records in Michigan libraries specified, "If the words 'illegitimate' or 'reputed father' appear in the original records, or there are words indicating the same, they should be copied, but will be omitted in printing," and, thus, kept from public view.[66] Genealogy owed its existence, after all, to acts of heterosexual congress. Yet bourgeois America believed in such activity's strict containment within marriage, especially when involving bourgeois women.[67] Although Daughters, Dames, and Sons found that genealogy was only partially effective in ensuring the group composition they sought, their efforts began with genealogy-based barriers.

When carried to its logical conclusion—in which all kin were valued for being kin—genealogy exposed the porousness of U.S. class boundaries. This same tendency helps explain genealogy's later popularization. Genealogy's democratization in America—its spread outside the white upper and middle classes, and its universalist justifications emphasizing self-knowledge and personal fulfillment—waited until the second half of the twentieth century. Then, genealogy expanded conspicuously among African Americans and among descendants of early twentieth-century immigrants. Members of both groups sought further information on their individual and collective "roots." Genealogy expanded also among older-stock white Americans who continued to view U.S. history through the prisms of their own family histories.[68] That popularization, with its multiplication of notions and methods of genealogy, resembles a backlash against genealogy's long history of reinforcing class distinctions. Yet genealogy's twentieth-century democratization was first made possible by the nineteenth-century bourgeoisie's uses of genealogy to set itself apart from others. Nobilities' and monarchs' monopolies of genealogical practice in the Western world weakened when bourgeois Americans began pursuing their lineages in the private sector, both informally and as institution builders, and viewed documented descent as social capital. These patterns enabled genealogy's compatibility with nonmonarchical, and antimonarchical, polities.

Notes

In completing this essay, I am indebted to Sven Beckert, Julia Rosenbaum, Mary Rhinelander McCarl, Charles R. Steinwedel, Karin A. Wulf, Susan Jennifer Pearson, a fellowship from the New England Regional Fellowship Consortium, and the Newberry Library's Scholars-in-Residence program. The Massachusetts Historical Society and the New England Historic Genealogical Society kindly permitted me to cite and quote from materials in their collections.

1. Christiane Klapisch-Zuber, "The Genesis of the Family Tree," *I Tatti Studies: Essays in the Renaissance* 4 (1991): 105–30, esp. 107–09; Anthony Molho et al., "Genealogy and Marriage Alliance: Memories of Power in Late Medieval Florence," in *Portraits of Medieval and Renaissance Living: Essays in Memory of David Herlihy,* ed. Samuel K. Cohn Jr., and Steven A. Epstein (Ann Arbor: University of Michigan Press, 1996), 39–70; David Lowenthal, *The Heritage Crusade and the Spoils of History* (1996; repr. Cambridge: Cambridge University Press, 1998), 193–94. Ideology "can also denote any significant conjuncture between discourse and political interests" (Terry Eagleton, *Ideology: An Introduction* [London and New York: Verso, 1991], 221).
2. My definition of the U.S. bourgeoisie starts with Sven Beckert's, which focuses on an economic elite that "owned and invested capital, employed wage workers" (including servants), "did not work for wages themselves, and did not work manually." See Sven Beckert, *The Monied Metropolis: New York City and the Consolidation of the American Bourgeoisie, 1850–1896* (Cambridge and New York: Cambridge University Press, 2001), 3, 6–7 (quotations).
3. Outside these processes, nineteenth-century Mormon communities were simultaneously reframing genealogy as a religious observance. James B. Allen, Jessie L. Embry, and Kahlile B. Mehr, *Hearts Turned to the Fathers: A History of the Genealogical Society of Utah, 1894–1994* (Provo, Utah: BYU Studies, Brigham Young University, 1995); Douglas J. Davies, *An Introduction to Mormonism* (Cambridge: Cambridge University Press, 2003), 91–115, 206–11; Richard Bushman with the assistance of Jed Woodworth, *Joseph Smith: Rough Stone Rolling: A Cultural Biography of Mormonism's Founder* (New York: Alfred A. Knopf, 2005), 421–23, 425, 477–78; Colleen McDannell and Bernhard Lang, "Modern Heaven . . . and a Theology," in *Mormons and Mormonism: An Introduction to an American World Religion,* ed. Eric A. Eliason (Urbana and Chicago: University of Illinois Press, 2001), 137–46; Michael Sweeney, "Ancestors, Avotaynu, Roots: An Inquiry into American Genealogical Discourse" (PhD diss., University of Kansas, 2010); Francesca Morgan, "A History of Genealogy in Mormon America" (presented at the 2006 meeting of the Mormon History Association, Casper, Wyo.).

On genealogy and the formation of national bourgeois communities, see Francesca Constance Morgan, "'Home and Country': Women, Nation, and the Daughters of the American Revolution, 1890–1939" (PhD diss., Columbia University, 1998), and Amanda Laugesen, *The Making of Public Historical Culture in the American West, 1880–1910: The Role of Historical Societies* (Lewiston, NY, and Lampeter [U.K.]: The Edwin Mellen Press, 2006).

4. Both the Articles of Confederation (1777), Article 6, and the U.S. Constitution (1787), Article I, section 9, specifically outlawed titles of nobility (personal communication, Sven Beckert, October 20, 2009). See also Karin A. Wulf, "Representing the Family to the State; or, Lineage in a New Nation" (presented at the 2006 meeting of the Organization of American Historians, Washington, DC); and Brendan McConville, *The King's Three Faces: The Rise and Fall of Royal America, 1688–1776* (Chapel Hill and London: University of North Carolina Press, 2006), 281–316.
5. Beckert, *Monied Metropolis*, 270–71.
6. I am indebted here to the sociologist Pierre Bourdieu's delineation of the importance of perceptions, such as taste, to forming class distinctions; see his *Distinction: A Social Critique of the Judgement of Taste*, trans. Richard Nice (Cambridge, MA: Harvard University Press, 1984), esp. 466.
7. Nancy F. Cott, *Public Vows: A History of Marriage and the Nation* (Cambridge, MA, and London: Harvard University Press, 2000), 4, 24–55; and Brenda E. Stevenson, *Life in Black and White: Family and Community in the Slave South* (1996; repr. New York and Oxford: Oxford University Press, 1997), 131–32, 159–65, 206–57, 275–77.
8. Eric J. Hobsbawm, *The Age of Capital, 1848–1875* (1975; repr. New York: Vintage Books, 1996), 242–50; Michel Foucault, *The History of Sexuality: An Introduction, Volume I,* trans. Robert Hurley (1978; repr. New York: Vintage Books, 1990), 123–27, 135–59 (on European bourgeoisies' adaptations of nobilities' genealogical and sexual practices).
9. Here, the Baltimore editor Hezekiah Niles was bemoaning President James Monroe's interest in heraldry. "Ancestry and Heraldry," *Niles' Weekly Register* 13 (September 6, 1817): 18. *See also* H. (pseud.), "English Genealogy—Sunday," *New Monthly Magazine and Literary Journal* 1, no. 4 (1821): 411–12. Numerous brief anecdotes also considered genealogy focused on noble descent to be un-American and/or to exemplify the sin of pride. See, for example, "Miscellaneous: Pride," *The Weekly Visitant: Moral, Poetical, Humorous, &c.* 1 (June 28, 1806): 207; "Anecdotes," *Ladies' Literary Cabinet, Being a Repository of Miscellaneous Literary Productions* 2 (September 30, 1820): 166. Some modern-day scholars also stress the Early Republic's repudiation of authority based on lineage: Joyce Appleby, *Inheriting the Revolution: The First Generation of Americans* (Cambridge, MA: Belknap Press of Harvard University Press, 2000); and Sean Wilentz, *The Rise of American Democracy: Jefferson to Lincoln* (New York: W. W. Norton, 2005).
10. John A. Schutz, *A Noble Pursuit: The Sesquicentennial History of the New England Historic Genealogical Society, 1845–1995* (Boston: NEHGS, 1995).
11. Heraldry's purposes have ranged far beyond signifying nobility. However, the form of heraldry that appealed most to nineteenth-century bourgeois "consists particularly in the appropriation of figurative representations, designed, by suitable emblems, to exhibit the achievements of valor, the descent of hereditary honors, and the distinctions appertaining to nobility" ("Heraldry," *New England Historical and Genealogical Register* 1 [July 1847]: 225, hereafter cited as *NEHGR*). Most who were interested in heraldry focused on trying to establish their descent from English families that had undergone "Visitations" by heralds during Henry VIII's reign (1509–47) in the regime's attempt "to better regulate the use of [family] arms" (David T. Thackery, *"Back to Adam": A Survey of Genealogy in the Western World, as Illustrated in the Collections of the Newberry Library* [Chicago: Newberry Library, 1992], 13–14).
12. The National Archives dates only from 1932, and the Library of Congress (created in 1802) remained relatively small in the nineteenth century. Public libraries developed in antebellum New England and spread nationally starting in the 1870s, but they did not usually emphasize the collection of sources favored by genealogical researchers. To fill such vacuums, historical societies and, later, genealogical societies created libraries intended for use by members and, later, researchers who met their approval. See Leslie W. Dunlap, *American Historical Societies, 1790–1860* (Madison, WI: privately printed, 1944), 4, 9; Haynes McMullen, *American Libraries before 1876* (Westport, CT, and London: Greenwood Press, 2000), 37, 123, 130; Hawthorne Daniel, *Public Libraries for Everyone: The Growth*

and Development of Library Services in the United States (Garden City, NY: Doubleday, 1961), 7–14; Pamela Spence Richards, *Scholars and Gentlemen: The Library of the New-York Historical Society, 1804–1982* (Hamden, CT: Archon Books, 1984), 7–8; Louis Leonard Tucker, *The Massachusetts Historical Society: A Bicentennial History, 1791–1991* (Boston: Published by the Society, 1995; distributed by Boston: Northeastern University Press), 80–89; and *Bulletin of the New York Genealogical and Biographical Society* 1 (December 1869): 4.

13. The nearly 500 surviving letters between the genealogist John Farmer and his colleagues vividly depict the logistical difficulties of performing genealogical and historical research in the 1820s and 1830s. John Farmer Papers, New Hampshire Historical Society, Concord (hereafter cited as Farmer Papers); Franccois Weil, "John Farmer and the Making of American Genealogy," *New England Quarterly* 80 (September 2007): 425–26; and Francesca Morgan, "Lineage as Capital: Genealogy in Antebellum New England," *New England Quarterly* 83 (June 2010): 250-262.
14. One historian remarked in 1835 that traditions "should be depended upon only as leading the investigator *towards* the truth, which, on further inquiry and comparison of different traditions with records, may be discovered" (Lemuel Shattuck, *A History of Concord; Middlesex County, Massachusetts, from Its Earliest Settlement to 1832, and of the Adjoining Towns, Bedford, Acton, Lincoln, and Carlisle* [Boston: Russell, Odiorne, and Company/Concord, MA: John Stacy, 1835], iv). *See also* Weil, "John Farmer," 425–26.
15. *See also* Morgan, "Lineage as Capital."
16. "The Describer," *Atkinson's Casket* 1 (December 1831): 562.
17. "The Idle Man—Number Four," *The Southern Literary Journal and Magazine of Arts* 3 (October 1836): 99–100.
18. John Kelly to John Farmer, January 12, 1827, 1, folder 15, box 2, Farmer Papers.
19. Phyllis Cole, *Mary Moody Emerson and the Origins of Transcendentalism: A Family History* (New York and Oxford: Oxford University Press, 1998); Ralph Waldo Emerson, *The Journals and Miscellaneous Notebooks of Ralph Waldo Emerson, Volume II, 1822–1826*, ed. William H. Gilman, Alfred R. Ferguson, and Merrell R. Davis (Cambridge, MA: Harvard University Press, 1961), 316, quoted in Cole, *Mary Moody Emerson*, 185.
20. Cole, *Mary Moody Emerson*, 11; Ralph Waldo Emerson to John Farmer, February 14, 1829 (quotation), folder 2, box 3, Farmer Papers.
21. Henry Lee Shattuck's later career fulfilled his mother's wishes for him. At a time when Massachusetts state politics were dominated by Irish Americans and largely shunned by his fellow Yankees, he resuscitated the nineteenth-century pattern of upper-class men's holding of political office. John T. Galvin, *The Gentleman Mr. Shattuck: A Biography of Henry Lee Shattuck, 1879–1971* (Boston: Tontine Press, 1996), 32, 46 (quotation).
22. Karin A. Wulf, "'Of the Old Stock': Quakerism and Transatlantic Genealogies in Colonial British America," in *The Creation of the British Atlantic World*, ed. Elizabeth Mancke and Carole Shammas (Baltimore and London: Johns Hopkins University Press, 2005), 304–20; Wulf, "*Milcah Martha Moore's Book*: Documenting Culture and Connection in the Revolutionary Era," in *Milcah Martha Moore's Book: A Commonplace Book from Revolutionary America*, ed. Catherine La Courreye Blecki and Karin A. Wulf (University Park: Pennsylvania State University Press, 1997), 14–19; Susan M. Stabile, *Memory's Daughters: The Material Culture of Remembrance in Eighteenth-Century America* (Ithaca, NY, and London: Cornell University Press, 2004), esp. 1, 6–16; Gary B. Nash, *First City: Philadelphia and the Forging of Historical Memory* (Philadelphia: University of Pennsylvania Press, 2002), 5–6, 133, 157–58, 205–09.
23. Anna Henshaw, historical notes, November 1839, Mellen Family Papers, Massachusetts Historical Society (MHS).
24. Caroline's father, and Ann Stone Orne's husband, was the merchant John Gerry Orne (d. 1838). Caroline F. Orne to Henry Bond, February 9, 1855, 1 (quotation), 13, folder 42, subgroup III, box 9, Henry Bond Papers, NEHGS, Boston (hereafter cited as Bond Papers). Another genealogy aficionado described Ann Stone Orne as having "the Stone genealogy at her tongue's end, & whose recollections & traditions go back many years" (Thaddeus William Harris to Henry Bond, June 16, 1854, folder 31, subgroup III, box 9, Bond Papers).
25. Ellen Tucker Emerson (1839–1909), daughter of Ralph Waldo Emerson, transcribed in 1861 "What I Can Remember of Stories of Our Ancestors Told Me by Aunt Mary Moody Emerson." Cole, *Mary Moody Emerson*, 11–12, 298–99, 313.
26. Shawn Michelle Smith, *American Archives: Gender, Race, and Class in Visual Culture* (Princeton, NJ: Princeton University Press, 1999), 140.

27. Edward Jarvis, M.D., "The Supposed Decay of Families," *NEHGR* 38 (October 1884): 387. *See also* Laurel Thatcher Ulrich, "Creating Lineages," in *The Art of Family: Genealogical Artifacts in New England,* ed. D. Brenton Simons and Peter Benes (Boston: NEHGS, 2002; distributed by Boston: Northeastern University Press), 5–6; and Maureen A. Taylor, "Tall Oaks from Little Acorns Grow: The Family Tree Lithograph in America," in Simons and Benes, eds., *The Art of Family,* 76.
28. After the American Revolution exiled genealogy to the private sector, the first genealogical publication aimed an audience broader than the author's own relatives was John Farmer's *A Genealogical Register of the First Settlers of New-England* (Lancaster, MA: Carter, Andrews, 1829). *See also* Weil, "John Farmer," 420–22, 428–30.
29. I refer to the organizations' members as leisured because, for example, the nineteenth-century New England Historic Genealogical Society of Boston held its meetings in daytime in the middle of the workweek—on the first Wednesday of each month, except during the vacation months of July and August; see "Donations to the Society," *NEHGR* 3 (January 1849), 104; "Constitution," *NEHGR* 24 (April 1870), 219. No wage earner could possibly have attended.
30. New-Hampshire Historical Society to Lemuel Shattuck, circular letter, June 9, 1831, Lemuel Shattuck Papers, MHS; Nash, *First City,* 207; Hampton L. Carson, *A History of the Historical Society of Pennsylvania* (Philadelphia: Published by the Society under the Special Centennial Publication Fund, 1940), 1:xv, 45; Susan Stitt, "Pennsylvania," in *Historical Consciousness in the Early Republic: The Origins of State Historical Societies, Museums, and Collections, 1791–1861,* ed. H. G. Jones (Chapel Hill: North Carolina Society, 1995), 61–62; Sarah J. Purcell, *Sealed with Blood: War, Sacrifice, and Memory in Revolutionary America* (Philadelphia: University of Pennsylvania Press, 2002), 171–209. In an exception to this pattern, the American Antiquarian Society (formed 1812) developed at its inland location of Worcester, Massachusetts, because it anticipated British threats to the coast; Dunlap, *American Historical Societies,* 16–17.

    Although the older, invitation-only Massachusetts Historical Society (established 1791) eschewed genealogical research for its own sake, many of its members, including president and Boston attorney James Savage and the Federalist Congressman Nahum Mitchell, took an interest in lineage. James Savage, *A Genealogical Dictionary of the First Settlers of New England, Showing Three Generations of Those Who Came Before May 1692, on the Basis of Farmer's* Register, 4 vols. (Boston: Little, Brown, 1860–62); Nahum Mitchell, *History of the Early Settlement of Bridgewater in Plymouth County, Massachusetts, Including an Extensive Family Register* (Boston: Kidder & Wright, 1840), most of which he devoted to the "family register" (85–390).
31. "Notices of Publications," *NEHGR* 10 (January 1856): 93; "Book-Notices," *NEHGR* 24 (January 1870): 95; W. Fitzhugh Brundage, *The Southern Past: A Clash of Race and Memory* (Cambridge, MA, and London: Harvard University Press, 2005), 107–8.
32. New England's first successful industrial mills, and the factory towns surrounding them, had been developed by merchants who continued in commerce even after the mills began to prosper. Robert F. Dalzell Jr., *Enterprising Elite: The Boston Associates and the World They Made* (Cambridge, MA, and London: Harvard University Press, 1987), 12, 61–63; Beckert, *Monied Metropolis,* 85–97.
33. *NEHGR* 9 (October 1855): 378; *Rolls of Membership of the New-England Historic Genealogical Society, 1844–1890* (Cambridge, MA: John Wilson and Son, 1891), 5.
34. Schutz, *Noble Pursuit,* 27, 29, 46–47; "Marriages and Deaths," *NEHGR* 14 (July 1860): 293.
35. In aiding Brown, Lawrence did not know about his plans for fostering slave insurrections in Virginia. Thomas H. O'Connor, *Civil War Boston: Home Front and Battlefield* (Boston: Northeastern University Press, 1997), 10–11, 14, 38–41, 46–47; Dalzell, *Enterprising Elite,* 164–224; Richard H. Abbott, *Cotton and Capital: Boston Businessmen and Antislavery Reform, 1854–1868* (Amherst: University of Massachusetts Press, 1991), 22–27, 40.
36. O'Connor, *Civil War Boston,* 13–14, 53–54, 109–13; *Rolls of Membership,* 6; "Life Members," *NEHGR* 19 (January 1865): 94. Thirty-five other men purchased life memberships that year.
37. A lonely exception is an 1848 review of Jesse Chickering's eight-volume work *Immigration into the United States.* By 1855, Irish comprised one-third of Boston's population. Irish and other immigrant groups, and the American-born children of immigrants, made up 64 percent of that population in 1880. "Notices of New Publications," *NEHGR* 2 (April 1848): 227; O'Connor, *Civil War Boston,* 4; Galvin, *The Gentleman Mr. Shattuck,* 38.

38. Galvin, *The Gentleman Mr. Shattuck*, xiv, 18–20; Paul DiMaggio, "Cultural Entrepreneurship in Nineteenth-Century Boston: The Creation of an Organizational Base for High Culture in America," *Media, Culture and Society* 3 (January 1982): 40. At least one Boston-area Know Nothing, however, treasured his own *Mayflower* lineage and researched it at length; see Solomon Bradford Morse, genealogical notes, Records of the East Boston Chapter of the American Party, vols. 1–3, 4 (1853–1858), MHS. I thank Dean Grodzins for drawing my attention to this material.
39. Five of the NYGBS's 29 resident (voting) members in its first year, 1869, were doctors (holders of M.D.'s), as were the organization's first president and first vice president. As of 1871, the NYGBS claimed a total of 152 members "in good standing." *Bulletin of the New York Genealogical and Biographical Society* 1 (December 1869): 1–3; "Our Society's Proceedings," *The New York Genealogical and Biographical Record* 2 (January 1871): 41 (hereafter cited as *NYGBR*); "Our Society's Proceedings," *NYGBR* 2 (April 1871): 104 (quotation); "Obituaries," *NYGBR* 6 (January 1875): 56; "Proceedings," *NYGBR* 10 (July 1879): 144–46. *See also* Beckert, *Monied Metropolis*, 254, 270–71.
40. "Ten Eyck Family Records," *NYGBR* 1 (October 1870): 31–32; C. B. Moore, "Biography of Ezra L'Hommedieu," *NYGBR* 2 (January 1871): 1–7; "Records of the Reformed Dutch Church in the City of New York," *NYGBR* 6 (January 1875): 32–47 (and also in subsequent issues).
41. "Master Sullivan of Berwick—His Ancestors and Descendants," *NEHGR* 19 (October 1865): 289–305, celebrated a powerful Irish family that had supported Catholic claimants to the English throne before taking refuge in Maine. I thank Mary Rhinelander McCarl for this reference.

    Annie Nathan Meyer (1867–1951), a physician's wife who helped found Barnard College, was born into a Jewish family of documented colonial lineage. She belonged to the Daughters of the American Revolution. See Barbara Sicherman et al., eds., *Notable American Women: The Modern Period* (Cambridge, MA, and London: Harvard University Press, 1980), 473–74.
42. Dalzell, *Enterprising Elite*, 179; Peter Dobkin Hall, "What the Merchants Did with Their Money: Charitable and Testamentary Trusts in Massachusetts, 1780–1880," in *Entrepreneurs: The Boston Business Community, 1700–1850*, ed. Conrad Edick Wright and Katheryn P. Viens (Boston: Massachusetts Historical Society, 1997; distributed by Boston: Northeastern University Press), 399–400, 408; Rev. Increase N. Tarbox, D.D., "William Cogswell, D.D.," *NEHGR* 37 (April 1883): 117–28; Schutz, *Noble Pursuit*, 53 (on Rev. Edmund Slafter's Episcopalianism), 65.
43. Drew Gilpin Faust, *This Republic of Suffering: Death and the American Civil War* (New York: Alfred A. Knopf, 2008).
44. Harriet Ritvo, foreword, to Charles Darwin, *The Variation of Animals and Plants Under Domestication, Vol. 2* (1868; repr. Baltimore: Johns Hopkins University Press, 1998). Works on the early eugenics movement include Diane B. Paul, *Controlling Human Heredity, 1865 to the Present* (Amherst, NY: Humanities Books, 1998), 27-48; Daniel J. Kevles, *In the Name of Eugenics: Genetics and the Uses of Human Heredity* (1985; repr. Cambridge, MA, and London: Harvard University Press, 1995), esp. 57–112; Ruth Schwartz Cowan, *Heredity and Hope: The Case for Genetic Screening* (Cambridge, MA, and London: Harvard University Press, 2008), 13–15, 45–46; and Margaret E. Derry, *Horses in Society: A Story of Animal Breeding and Marketing, 1800–1920* (Toronto and London: University of Toronto Press, 2006), 14–20.
45. John Higham, *Strangers in the Land: Patterns of American Nativism, 1860–1925*, rev. ed. (New York: Atheneum, 1963); Matthew Frye Jacobson, *Whiteness of a Different Color: European Immigrants and the Alchemy of Race* (Cambridge, MA, and London: Harvard University Press, 1998); and Paul A. Kramer, "Empires, Exceptions, and Anglo-Saxons: Race and Rule between the British and United States Empires, 1880–1910," *Journal of American History* 88 (March 2002): 1,315–53.
46. Henry F. Waters, "Genealogical Gleanings in England," *NEHGR* 37 (July 1883): 233–40, and in subsequent issues until 1899; "Notes and Queries," *NEHGR* 37 (July 1883): 305–6.
47. Charles B. Moore in "Plan of Genealogical Work," *NYGBR* 1 (April 1870): 9. Italics are his. The British Kennel Club issued the first known "public record book" for dogs in 1874. "Purebred" livestock are an older institution, dating from late-eighteenth-century England. Margaret E. Derry, *Bred for Perfection: Shorthorn Cattle, Collies, and Arabian Horses since 1800* (Baltimore: Johns Hopkins University Press, 2003) (Kennel Club on 56); Harriet Ritvo, *The*

Platypus and the Mermaid and Other Figments of the Classifying Imagination (Cambridge, MA: Harvard University Press, 1997), esp. 120–30; Katherine C. Grier, *Pets in America: A History* (Chapel Hill and London: University of North Carolina Press, 2006), 27–35, 207–12. I thank Susan Jennifer Pearson for directing me to this literature.

48. Eliphalet Wickes Blatchford (1826–1914) was a Chicago lead manufacturer and a family-history aficionado. As longtime chairman of the Newberry Library's board of trustees, Blatchford oversaw the hiring of the Newberry's first librarians and did much to shape the institution, including developing its commitment to genealogy. The Newberry Library originated as half of the $4 million estate of the railroad and real-estate magnate Walter Loomis Newberry (1804-1868). His nephew Walter C. Newberry (himself a library trustee) and other surviving relatives showed keen interest in colonial New England and English lineage. Galleys for Eliphalet Wickes Blatchford, comp., *Blatchford Memorial II: A Genealogical Record of the Family of Rev. Samuel Blatchford, D.D. with Some Mention of Allied Families* (privately printed, 1912), folder 997, box 14; Walter C. Newberry to E. W. Blatchford, February 24, 1908, folder 920, box 13; E. W. Blatchford Papers, Board of Trustees Personal Papers, 02/15/01, Newberry Library Archives, Newberry Library, Chicago. *See also* Rick J. Ashton, "Curators, Hobbyists, and Historians: Ninety Years of Genealogy at the Newberry Library," *Library Quarterly* 47 (April 1977): 149–62; Helen Lefkowitz Horowitz, *Culture and the City: Cultural Philanthropy in Chicago from the 1880s to 1917* (1976; repr. Chicago: University of Chicago Press, 1989), 35–36, 71–73, 98–99, 109.
49. Brundage, *Southern Past,* 105–37.
50. John St. Paul Jr., *The History of the National Society of the Sons of the American Revolution* (New Orleans: Pelican, 1962), 1–6, 156; Woden Sorrow Teachout, "Forging Memory: Hereditary Societies, Patriotism, and the American Past, 1876–1898" (PhD diss., Harvard University, 2003), 19-51.
51. "Societies and Their Proceedings," *NEHGR* 37 (October 1883): 411; Robert R. Davenport, ed., *Hereditary Society Blue Book* (Baltimore: Genealogical and Beverly Hills, CA: Eastwood, 1994), 31, 34.
52. The DAR became the largest, at 30,000 in 1900 and more than 100,000 a decade later; the SAR claimed fewer than 10,000 in 1900. In 1909, the Daughters of the Revolution counted just over 4,800 members. By the 1930s, the NSCDA numbered around 11,000. All other hereditary groups maintained memberships in the hundreds. Some Civil War commemoration organizations were also hereditary in character: the United Daughters of the Confederacy (1894), for the most part; the Sons of Confederate Veterans (1896); and the Ladies of the Grand Army of the Republic (1886). Wallace Evan Davies, *Patriotism on Parade: The Story of Veterans' Organizations and Hereditary Organizations in America, 1783–1900* (Cambridge, MA: Harvard University Press, 1955), 77. Also see Julie Des Jardins, *Women and the Historical Enterprise in America: Gender, Race, and the Politics of Memory, 1880–1945* (Chapel Hill and London: University of North Carolina Press, 2003), 20, 66–69; Mrs. Joseph Rucker Lamar (Clarinda Huntington Lamar), *A History of the National Society of the Colonial Dames of America from 1891 to 1933* (Atlanta: Walter W. Brown, 1934), 2; Charles B. Hosmer Jr., *Presence of the Past: A History of the Preservation Movement in the United States before Williamsburg* (New York: G. P. Putnam's Sons, 1965), 132–33; *Proceedings of the Eighteenth Annual Meeting of the General Society, Daughters of the Revolution* (Englewood, NJ: Englewood Press, 1909), 22–23; Francesca Morgan, *Women and Patriotism in Jim Crow America* (Chapel Hill and London: University of North Carolina Press, 2005).
53. Cecilia Elizabeth O'Leary, *To Die For: The Paradox of American Patriotism* (Princeton, NJ: Princeton University Press, 1999); Morgan, *Women and Patriotism in Jim Crow America;* Teachout, "Forging Memory"; Brundage, *Southern Past,* 12–54; Stuart McConnell, "Reading the Flag: A Reconsideration of the Patriotic Cults of the 1890s," in *Bonds of Affection: Americans Define Their Patriotism,* ed. John Bodnar (Princeton, NJ: Princeton University Press, 1996), 102–119; Des Jardins, *Women and the Historical Enterprise in America,* 13–51; Davies, *Patriotism on Parade*; Sweeney, "Ancestors, Avotaynu, Roots."
54. Morgan, "'Home and Country,'" 549–66.
55. The memberships of the two largest all-female hereditary organizations in 1900, the DAR and the NSCDA, totaled 34,000. The combined membership of the two largest all-male hereditary organizations, the SAR and the Sons of the Revolution, was less than 16,000. Davies, *Patriotism on Parade,* 77.

56. The organization subsequently contained meaningful numbers of women; see Schutz, *Noble Pursuit*, vii–viii, 62.
57. On perceptions of self-made men, see in particular Michael Kimmel, *Manhood in America: A Cultural History* (New York: The Free Press, 1996), 81–188.
58. *Constitution and By-Laws of the Daughters of the American Revolution* (Washington, DC: National Society Daughters of the American Revolution [NSDAR], 1890), 4; National Society, U.S. Daughters of 1812, "Circular of Information," n.d. [1930s], in scrapbook of state activities, vol. 2 (1933–1936), box 34, Papers of the Daughters of the American Revolution, Michigan Society, Michigan Historical Collections, Bentley Library, University of Michigan, Ann Arbor (hereafter cited as Michigan DAR). Membership in the SAR was open to any man older than 21 whose ancestor had rendered "material aid" to the Revolutionary cause, assuming the descendant was "a citizen of good repute." Nebraska Society of the SAR, Registrar's Circular (1899), 2, folder 6, box 1, Series 1: Correspondence, Nebraska Society of the Sons of the American Revolution collection, Manuscript Division, Nebraska State Historical Society, Lincoln (hereafter cited as Nebraska SAR). The constitution of the invitation-only CDA reserved the right to expel anyone for conduct unbecoming a "'gentlewoman.'" *Society of Colonial Dames of America, Colonial Dames of the State of New York, Annual Report* (1924–25): 51–52.
59. Morgan, "Lineage as Capital"; Donald Harman Akenson, *Some Family: The Mormons and How Humanity Keeps Track of Itself* (Montreal: McGill-Queen's University Press, 2007), 71-281; Janet Carsten, *After Kinship* (Cambridge: Cambridge University Press, 2004); *Relative Values: Reconfiguring Kinship Studies*, ed. Sarah Franklin and Susan McKinnon (Durham, NC, and London: Duke University Press, 2001).
60. Morgan, "'Home and Country,"' 49–62; Henrietta Nesmith Greely (wife of General A. W. Greely) in "Proceedings of the Third Continental Congress," *American Monthly Magazine* 4 (June 1894): 754; *Remembrance Book of the Daughters of the American Revolution* (Washington, DC: NSDAR, July 1918), 7–8.
61. Elizabeth Kimmick, comp. and ed., *History of the New Mexico State Organization of the National Society, Daughters of the American Revolution* (n.p., 1957), 14–15, 20–21; Isabel Anderson, "The Growth and Development of Our Library," *Daughters of the American Revolution Magazine* 58 (April 1924): 212–13. SAR leaders in Lincoln, Nebraska, organized a chapter similarly, by recruiting the town's "best men" and then performing genealogical research on their behalf. Correspondence by Clarence S. Paine and Edwin O. Halstead, 1913, folder 2, box 2, Series 1: Correspondence, Nebraska SAR.
62. *Constitution and By-Laws of the Daughters of the American Revolution*, 4; *Constitution and By-Laws of the Daughters of the American Revolution* (Washington, D.C.: Press of W. F. Roberts, 1894), 8.
63. David Levering Lewis, *W. E. B. Du Bois: Biography of a Race, 1868–1919* (New York: Henry Holt and Company, 1993), 13, 374–75, 660 (note 66); *Statutes of the National Society, Daughters of the American Revolution, 1890 to 1897* (Washington, D.C.: NSDAR, n.d. [1897]), 7. The DAR scrapped this statute by 1977, when it admitted its first known African American member, Karen Batchelor Farmer of Detroit; see "DAR Accepts a Black Member," *Philadelphia Inquirer*, December 4, 1977, 22A. For other examples of Revolutionary lineages mapped by early twentieth-century African Americans, see "Here and There," *Colored American Magazine* 2 (March 1901): 378–79; and "Social Uplift," *The Crisis* 11 (November 1915): 8.
64. Lamar, *History of the National Society of the Colonial Dames of America*, 41; membership certificate of Kate Singleton Conley, Missouri Society of the Colonial Dames of America, November 26, 1910; Juliet L. Finney to Kate Singleton Conley, December 7, 1910; folder 52; Finney to Conley, November 6, 1911, folder 53; box 2, Conley-Miller Family Papers, Western Historical Manuscript Collection, University of Missouri / State Historical Society of Missouri, Columbia (hereafter cited as MO); "Colonial Dames of America," www.cdamesusa.org (updated May 18, 2007; accessed July 24, 2007); Harriet Smith to Edwin O. Halstead, May 11, 1912 (quotation), folder 9, box 1, Series 1: Correspondence, Nebraska SAR.
65. Minnie G. Cook to "the Members," March 28, 1928, folder 77, box 3, Helm-Davidson Family Papers, MO.
66. Mary E. Frankhauser and Sue Silliman, "Rules for D.A.R. Vital Statistics Workers," 2, enclosed in a report of the state librarian, March 8, 1927, in a book of state executive board minutes, vol. 3 (1925–28), unpaginated, box 1, Michigan DAR.

67. Historians emphasize that such sexual ideals existed amidst a multiplicity of other ideals, not to mention sexual practices, in the nineteenth-century United States. See, for example, John D'Emilio and Estelle B. Freedman, *Intimate Matters: A History of Sexuality in America*, 2nd ed. (Chicago: University of Chicago Press, 1997), 55–167; and Helen Lefkowitz Horowitz, *Rereading Sex: Battles over Sexual Knowledge and Suppression in Nineteenth-Century America* (New York: Alfred A. Knopf, 2002). However, the censoring described above indicates that prohibitions on extramarital sexual activity were deeply felt in the staid circles in which genealogists moved.
68. Pauli Murray, *Proud Shoes: The Story of an American Family* (New York: Harper's, 1956); Alex Haley, *Roots* (Garden City, NY: Doubleday, 1976); David Chioni Moore, "Routes: Alex Haley's *Roots* and the Rhetoric of Genealogy," *Transition* no. 64 (1994): 4–21; Kathleen Neils Conzen et al., "The Invention of Ethnicity: A Perspective from the U.S.A.," *Journal of American Ethnic History* 12 (Fall 1992): 3–41; Matthew Frye Jacobson, *Roots Too: White Ethnic Revivals in Post Civil Rights America* (Cambridge, MA: Harvard University Press, 2006); and Roy Rosenzweig and David Thelen, *The Presence of the Past: Popular Uses of History in American Life* (New York: Columbia University Press, 1998), esp. 1–18.

9
Elite Women and Class Formation

Mary Rech Rockwell

It is telling that a 1906 *Buffalo Courier* article begins its listing of the social sets of the city of Buffalo, New York, with a tribute to women, calling them "Grande Dames" of Buffalo "society." Attributing to them the creation of "society" in Buffalo in the 1880s and 1890s, the article highlights their social activities, leisure pursuits, and founding of women's clubs and organizations.[1] Recognizing those women who were particularly intellectual and cultured, the *Courier* proceeds to name prominent residents of Buffalo, grouped by their social sets. Elite women, as the newspaper suggests, were powerful agents in this process of class formation and perpetuation in the period 1880 to 1910. In this essay, by focusing on the rituals and practices created to define an elite in the changing and uncertain social milieu of Buffalo, we see that these women's position as models for the young, arbiters of social taste, and creators of marriage mergers allowed them to create and perpetuate kin networks that would dominate Buffalo society and control access to business and political assets for subsequent generations.[2]

Between 1880 and 1910, Buffalo peaked as an industrial city. Eighth in the nation in population, Buffalo exploited its geographic location by serving as a center for grain exchange through Great Lakes shipping. As its economy matured, the city's emphasis shifted from the shipment of grain to manufacturing, relying on the coalfields of Pennsylvania and the iron ore of Minnesota as raw materials for the iron and steel industries.[3] Given its rapid change from a small town to a nationally important and extremely wealthy city, Buffalo provides an ideal laboratory for the study of class formation.

Profound social and economic changes occurred in Buffalo during the period 1860 to 1900. The population of Buffalo in 1860 was 81,000, and by 1900 it had reached 352,000, after a wave of immigration brought many new residents to Buffalo. One surveyor for the 1900 census concluded that scarcely more than one-fourth of the city's population was of native American stock.[4] Joining the immigrants were Americans who had left their farms for the cities. Social distinctions were difficult to discern due to population growth and newly acquired wealth. With traditional notions of social relations, manners, and appropriate behavior in a state of flux, traditional methods of displaying oneself and recognizing others of similar status became more difficult. In such a climate, elite women worked to monitor and control access to class status through intricate social rituals and conspicuous leisure activities and goods consumption.

Thorstein Veblen, in *The Theory of the Leisure Class*, characterized women's activities as frivolous and designed simply to advertise a husband's wealth and prestige.[5]

In truth, their activities influenced and maintained a family's economic power. Through their creation of kin networks and elaborate social protocols, which filtered the worthy from the unworthy in order to maximize economic advantage, women formed marriage "mergers and acquisitions" to perpetuate family wealth and dominance for generations. As Frederic Cople Jaher's work demonstrated, for the rising elite in New York City, "failure to meet accepted standards in domicile, dress, manner, and dinner table conversation blackballed anxious aspirants."[6] Elite women in Buffalo assured that only acceptable social aspirants would join Buffalo society, while simultaneously guarding an Anglo-Saxon heritage and preserving "pure" bloodlines through intermarriage.

Buffalo had not always been the site of such efforts. In the 1850s, the city's bourgeois class dominated society through its commonly held commercial interests and their mutually understood moral code that stressed individualism, self-reliance, and temperate rationalistic behavior. It also stressed decency and humility in social and personal relations.[7] David Gerber's study of Buffalo, *The Making of an American Pluralism: Buffalo, New York, 1825–60,* documents the basis on which the midcentury bourgeois class staked its supremacy—success in commerce or a profession, high-status social networks, voluntary association affiliations, church membership, and intangible qualities such as gentility and cultivation.[8] Within 50 years, the bourgeois had reconstituted themselves into an extremely rich upper class formed of interrelated family networks. Newcomers who accrued wealth in manufacturing joined old Buffalo families whose original fortunes had come from lake shipping and the grain trade. This elite relied less on gentility and church attendance to distinguish themselves, placing more emphasis on elaborate social events and other conspicuous displays of wealth.

Hosting balls in their city and country homes, enjoying leisure time at their country clubs, traveling extensively, they consumed on a scale hitherto unknown in American history. By 1900, a small set of elite families had become a surprisingly resilient upper class, building great mansions on Delaware Avenue, country homes for fox hunting in the Genesee Valley near Rochester, New York, and private clubs for exclusive social rituals. This essay focuses on women's role in the creation of the new upper class by examining two key elements in the training of elite girls: private education and the ritual of "coming out" in society, both essential steps in the formation of class boundaries at this time. Girls' education arose from the need to provide "discipline and culture" for those who would "mould the sentiments and character of society,"[9] while debutante balls and formal introductions into society assured success in the marriage market.

Each step in a girl's life introduced her to appropriate suitors, emphasized the skills necessary to make an advantageous marriage, and stressed her importance to the future of the family. Etiquette books advised a cultured lady to possess certain defining characteristics. She should play music with taste, have an understanding of European history and languages, and write fluently in a legible hand. More important, she must be comfortable in social situations, able to converse confidently with her acquaintances, and dance well.[10] Primarily designed to prepare her for marriage, motherhood, and her life in society, upper-class girls' education could be socially demanding but not physically demanding. It did not prepare her to attend college.

Elite families also placed emphasis on intergenerational family life. Large extended families provided models of social norms and enforcement of appropriate behavior. Children, raised within a world of grandparents, maiden aunts, uncles, and cousins, gathered often to socialize, have dinner, or ride in a coaching party. Frederic

Cople Jaher finds that kinship was crucial for the emergence and sustenance of an elite class:

> Households in the upper strata of these cities were nuclear in form but extended in substance. Although they generally did not live together, grandparents and grandchildren, uncles, nephews, and cousins, parents and married children constantly interacted.[11]

Maiden aunts often lived with their sisters, teaching younger children and helping to supervise them. Within this intergenerational milieu, young girls were relatively free. They explored the countryside on horseback or drove their pony carts around the city. After the age of ten, or 11, however, and as they entered puberty, they were physically separated from boys.

Elite girls inhabited the children's quarters, separated spatially from their parents and supervised by Irish or German nannies and nurses. Mabel Dodge Luhan in her autobiography *Intimate Memories,* discusses how her friends Nina and Frances Wilcox entertained their parents for a few moments after dinner each evening "because it was the custom to have the children after dinner."[12] After a half hour of interaction, Mrs. Wilcox would announce, "Well, children, I think you may be excused for tonight," and they returned to the care of the nanny.[13] Both Luhan and Evelyn Rumsey, daughters of socially prominent families, mentioned playing with male and female members of Buffalo's other elite families. Luhan remembers "rowboats in summer and skating in the winter and all manner of games."[14] The Rumsey compound, for example, included tennis courts, a small private lake that doubled as a skating rink in winter, and stables filled with horses. Boys and girls were raised alike in the early years.

Prior to 1900, both girls and boys received sporadic instruction before attending formal schools. Tutored at home by single women or maiden aunts, groups of cousins and neighbors gathered in the ballroom or library to learn rudimentary skills. With the approach of puberty began physical separation of girls from their brothers, male cousins, and friends. Relegated to single-sex environments in girls' academies and finishing schools, under the watchful eyes of their teachers, mothers, and maiden aunts, they were inducted into the world of women. In elementary schools such as Miss Hill's School or St. Margaret's (an Episcopal school) in Buffalo and, later, at secondary schools such as the Buffalo Female Academy, elite girls approached humanistic learning with an emphasis on foreign languages, the classics, and musical training. Although most of their classmates lived in the same neighborhood, social gradations became obvious and noticeable at school. Luhan reports that two German girls whose father became wealthy and moved into the neighborhood "never came out, they just came over."[15] In other words, the girls did not make a debut: they just moved into the neighborhood. Early formal schooling helped girls become cognizant of their social position while allowing them exposure to a wider, yet still protected, world.

Elegant education distinguished these girls from those of other classes. By restricting elite girls to secondary school and boarding school, and adding a European tour, parents proclaimed their class status. The girls formed a national network that carried out the mandates of upper-class behavior. They socialized only with one another and married men from similar backgrounds and families. The nature of the education they received prepared them for lives of leisure and recreation.

At the age of 14, girls left St. Margaret's or Miss Hill's and moved to the Buffalo Female Academy (BFA) for their secondary education. The BFA, founded in 1851 by a prominent group of male citizens, was one of the country's earliest schools for girls. By the 1890s, the curriculum had expanded to conform to the national curriculum standards developed by The Committee of Ten, a group of educators chaired by Harvard President Charles W. Eliot. The school now adopted rigorous courses in botany, Latin, psychology, English, history, and foreign languages.[16] The teachers, many of whom were first-generation women's college graduates, urged these students to make the most of their intellectual capabilities.

For most educators of this time, however, "the ideal female curriculum aimed at giving women the graces of a liberal, humanistic education" and an appreciation for "the productions of masculine genius."[17] Dr. G. Stanley Hall, who brought the theory of adolescence to the United States, suggested in 1905 that female education should focus on tact and taste and emphasize intuition rather than mental development. In his speech to the graduating class at BFA (now called the Buffalo Seminary) in 1894, Dr. Hall stressed "learning the lessons of rest."[18] He and other theorists of the time worried that too much mental exertion would severely affect the health of women.

Parents also desired a womanly education that prepared their daughters for marriage, and abhorred the idea of too much scholarship that could make girls "manly" and, therefore, ineligible for marriage. Some theorists maintained that rigorous scholarship might possibly make them sterile, as well.[19] Elite girls were challenged intellectually but pampered physically. Pulled between those who felt women deserved the same education as men and those who believed education and physical activity harmful to women, they pursued rigorous coursework, while adhering to the gender cautions of the day.

The BFA graduates marked themselves and their families as superior socially to girls who were educated at home or attended public school. Small graduating classes of just 20 to 30 girls attest to its selectivity. Formal course descriptions mirrored those of boys' schools in Buffalo, but the founders took great care to preserve the qualities in women that made them the keepers of the home and authorities in domestic affairs. The differing purposes of male and female education provides an important distinction, for there were reformers of women's education at the time—notably M. Carey Thomas of Bryn Mawr College—who advocated identical studies and encouraged identical aspirations for her female students.[20]

In Buffalo, it seems, most elite families were not willing to risk their daughters' prospects for marriage by overeducating them. Instead, as prominent educator Emma Willard complained:

> Among families, so rich as to be entirely above labour, the daughters are hurried through the routine of boarding school instruction, and at an early period introduced into the gay world; and, thenceforth, their only object is amusement. Mark the different treatment, which the sons of these families receive. While their sisters are gliding through the mazes of the midnight dance, they employ the lamp, to treasure up for future use the riches of ancient wisdom.[21]

Girls were offered high school subjects, a year at finishing school, and a tour of Europe, and then sent into the social world. Only those few who looked to support themselves sought college training—at least before 1900.

Families who aspired to rank themselves among a national elite removed their daughters from the BFA after two or three years and sent them to exclusive boarding schools on the East Coast, thus distinguishing them from the families of local industrialists whose wealth was more recently acquired or whose social position did not match their own. For example, Mabel Dodge Luhan went to Miss Graham's School in New York and the Chevy Chase School in Maryland; Evelyn Rumsey and Sallie Cary traveled to Miss Porter's School in Farmington, Connecticut.

Schools like Miss Porter's and Miss Dow's School for Young Ladies in Farmington, or the Rosemary Hall School in Greenwich, Connecticut, were typical destinations for nationally prominent girls, mirroring the elite prep schools for boys. E. Digby Baltzell maintains that these institutions were crucial to the creation of a national upper class: "These fashionable family surrogates taught the sons of new and old rich, whether Boston, Baltimore, Philadelphia or San Francisco [or Buffalo], the subtle nuances of an upper-class way of life."[22] The same holds true for East Coast finishing schools for girls.

Many elite girls spent a "finishing year" at one of these schools. The experience added the necessary patina to a young girl to make her ready for coming out in the social season. Girls from Chicago and the West Coast came East to refine manners and social skills, and to make contacts with others of similar station.[23] Finishing schools also provided a homosocial environment in which to explore their nascent sexuality and practice social forms, skills that would be crucial in the heterosocial marriage market.

Miss Porter, the sister of Noah Porter, president of Yale University, combined rigorous academic pursuits in her school, following Yale's curriculum with the social training necessary to function as society matrons.[24] For example, girls attended German cotillions every Friday night, organizing the themes, prizes, decoration, and food, and choosing partners from among the other girls. They learned to socialize and to plan social events. This training occurred in a homosocial atmosphere under the watchful eyes of matronly women chaperones, who minimized the risk of sexual experimentation or threat of pregnancy. A loss of virginity imperiled the continuation of an untainted family line and could not be risked by elite families. Girls also trained in elite sports such as tennis, golf, and horseback riding, which assured their confidence during country weekends and outings to the Country Club of Buffalo.[25]

A national network of elite girls was created, and they corresponded, visited, traveled, and socialized together during the years preceding—and in some cases, after—marriage: "Good friends visited each other and met each other's brothers. Romances bloomed and marriages often followed."[26] At St. Timothy's School in Catonsville, Maryland, Esther Goodyear became friends with Mary Forman, who later married Goodyear's brother, Conger. Evelyn Rumsey kept in touch with Evelyn Hay, daughter of the former secretary of state, from the time they attended finishing school together in France; they attended parties together in Albany and Buffalo.[27] Rumsey often socialized with friends in New York City when she visited there. She invited girls from across New York State and New England to her debutante party.[28]

Elite boarding schools never claimed to be colleges, thereby accommodating the upper-class idea that women should be educated, but not so rigorously as to ruin their health, make them unfit for domestic life, or create a desire to work for a living. The girls at Miss Porter's thought themselves superior to college women, as evidenced in these lyrics from the school's songbook:

> The Wellesley girl is out of joint
> The Vassar girl has lost her point
> The Farmington girl is all the go
> The Farmington girl is never slow
> To College, To College
> We'll never go there, anymore![29]

Elite boarding schools provided "culture" to the girls and demonstrated status by indicating that girls would live a life of leisure. A few of the daughters of the women in this study did go to college, such as Grace Rumsey Smith, who graduated from Vassar in the class of 1928. In her nineties she maintained that, before she went, "attending college just wasn't done. I was the first of the Rumsey women to attend college."[30] Etiquette books from the 1920s also commented on the recent enrollment of elite girls in colleges. Girls, until the time of their debuts, were "engaged in their different studies; in classes, finishing schools, and colleges (though it should be said here that, during the reign of the last generation, college was not the mode for daughters of the leisure classes)."[31] Not attending college, in fact, demonstrated privilege because it marked elite girls as economically self-sufficient and superior to those who needed to concern themselves with wage work.

Commencement from finishing school led to a grand tour of Europe to sample the wonders of Western civilization and absorb the lessons that great art and architecture could teach. In another moment of selection, those who made a grand tour may have been thought more accomplished than those who did not. Exposure to other cultures was essential to rounding out a young woman's education, so she traveled to scenic cities and country areas primarily in France, England, Germany, and Italy. Elite girls demonstrated their class status by staying at fine hotels and by frequenting the same restaurants and neighborhoods as their friends and acquaintances from home.

Elizabeth Wilkeson, a descendant of Samuel Wilkeson, a former mayor who brought the terminus of the Erie Canal to Buffalo, embarked on a European tour after secondary school. She spent four months on a voyage with five friends.[32] She left New York on a luxury liner, landing at Gibraltar. Her grand tour stretched from April 22 to August 6, 1897, with stops in Italy and Switzerland, continuing through Belgium, France, London, and Scotland before the return to New York.[33] Evelyn Rumsey traveled to Europe with her parents, siblings, and aunts. She and her younger sister and brother enrolled in a boarding school at the Château de Dieudonne in Oise, France, an hour from Paris.

An elite girl completed her experience abroad at age 18 or 19. She was now "finished," a peculiar term that can be interpreted in a number of ways. That a girl was "finished" implied an end to girlhood, an end of a phase in life in which she was surrounded by women and other girls. Because an ending had come in her life, few resources would be put toward further education. She had completed her training and fulfilled her expectations as a girl. She was accomplished in the skills she needed to succeed as an adult woman. Yet "finished" also represents a finishing coat, like varnish, that smoothed out her rough qualities but also protected her. She would operate from behind this shield as she moved forward into society. The boarding school smoothed the girl, but her European travels rubbed all the wonders of Western civilization into her, thereby polishing her to a lustrous sheen so she might shine as she stepped into the adult world.

Among the elite in Buffalo, marriage and the rituals surrounding it served a threefold function. Marriage perpetuated the economic continuity of families from one generation to the next. Advantageous marriage solidified the class position of elite families, linking wealthy families together socially, and proclaimed continuing economic dominance.

Only after they were "finished"—that is, having completed their schooling and acquiring the necessary amount of culture—were girls allowed to reenter the heterosocial world. They crossed a limen into adult life by completing a rite of passage known as a debut. Their liminal status during the debutante year found them abandoning the carefree life of the schoolgirl, surrounded by close girlfriends, and entering a world of intense socializing characterized by conspicuous display and competition for a suitable (male) mate.

Elite parents did not leave their daughters' futures to chance. By launching their daughters into the heterosexual marriage market through the vehicle of the "coming out" party and the accompanying season of social events, they carefully orchestrated engagements and marriages, drawing suitors from an accepted social circle and supervising courtship in their homes. To ensure the continuation of the family line, elite families quickly integrated their daughters into the adult social world. But they also preserved female solidarity and connection by ensuring that girls moved through the debutante ritual as a group, or debutante class. The debutantes of a given year formed a "deb class" and made the transition to adulthood in the company of 15 or 20 friends.[34] The experience of coming out distinguished elite girls from those of other classes, for only a few families had the resources and inclination to sponsor a debutante ball and costume a daughter for the social season. The ball provided an elaborate demonstration of the manners and wealth of a girl's family. It launched her into heterosocial society, while the rituals surrounding the ball carefully protected her from indiscretion or individuation from family.[35] Unlike some middle-class girls who worked before marriage, elite girls concentrated on the debut. They did not leave the house unbonneted or unchaperoned.[36] As Elizabeth Wilkeson, granddaughter of one of the founders of the city, remarked "[I] come home in October, come out into society (Oh, how I long to be a success!) I am filled with the desire to be a social success, I—even homely Bessie."[37] Anxiety about personal appearance and desire for a successful launch onto the marriage market characterized the feelings of elite girls at this time in their lives.

The first component of the debutante's rite of passage involved her mother holding an introductory tea for her daughter and inviting all of the mother's adult female friends. Friends sent hundreds of bouquets of flowers. Buffalo debutante Mabel Dodge Luhan, for example, received 72 dozen roses. The mother arrayed herself in black or dark violet, while the young girl shone in a white costume. Teas took place in a space controlled by women and symbolized a young girl's acceptance into the world of adult women. It also trained her in the niceties of the visiting ritual,—sending out cards, planning a menu, pouring tea. After the tea and the debutante ball, she was considered an adult woman.

A debutante "class" would hold their teas and coming-out balls one after another each year, during the Christmas social season, which historically corresponded to the closing of trade in Buffalo Harbor due to ice on Lake Erie. The social calendar was filled nightly. The girls maintained a schedule that began at noon with a luncheon, followed by an afternoon tea, an evening dinner party, and a ball that often lasted until three or four o'clock in the morning. The process of planning and carrying out the debutante ball was complicated. The first step called for a young girl, her mother, and her older sisters to visit or, failing that, to leave their cards at the houses of all the acquaintances whom they planned to invite to the party. The number of guests could range from 200 to 500 people. After the visits, a girl's mother mailed engraved invitations containing the card of the debutante, with the invitations arriving approximately ten days prior to the event. An accompanying newspaper announcement, sent by the mother to the society page editor, announced that invitations had been issued.

Grace Rumsey Smith remembered the protocol of leaving a specific number of cards at a given home, depending on the number of people in the family and whether they were male or female.[38] Each unmarried adult male in a household received a separate invitation. Females, however, received one card for all.[39] This may reflect their status as family members rather than as individuals in their own right.

The notice of the ball advertised a daughter's availability for marriage to both a local and a national social network. On December 10, 1893, an out-of-town newspaper reported on the reception and ball given by Mr. and Mrs. Samuel Wilkeson in honor of their daughter, Mary Juana Wilkeson: "The decorations were superb and Miss Wilkeson was the recipient of hundreds of dozens of roses, easily eclipsing those she received at her graduation last June. Her dress was of rare lace and was made in India." In a clear effort to delineate class position, the dinner given "to the fair debutante by her grandfather, Samuel Wilkeson, was notable from the fact that none but descendants of the founders of the city of Buffalo were present."[40]

Girls split dances into two and three parts near the conclusion of the ball in order to maximize their exposure to eligible men. Elizabeth Wilkeson noted that she danced halves and quarters with different men, for "one always splits at the end of the evening."[41] After another ball two years later, she commented: "I danced with so many different men that I can't remember half of them really. This splitting dances is fun but when you are having a love of a talk and dance and are called . . . and rush off with some chump it is hard and it's the same scrappy time all evening."[42]

Following the ball, mothers tended to their daughters' future prospects with great care. Eligible bachelors visited during "at home" hours in full view of the young woman's mother. Their conduct during visits could make or break their prospects for wooing the debutante. This formality led Wilkeson to wonder:

> Why is it that fellows will take the trouble to make a girl think he is passionately devoted to her, that she is the one girl in the world for him, tell her all his hopes and aspirations, hold the most tender conversations on the philosophy of love, haunt her footsteps, so to speak, when he doesn't care one bit for her and knows that she doesn't care for him more than a dozen others? I think there would be more life long friendships between men and women if this artificiality were dropped for . . . if you see a fellow every day for three months you get dreadfully tired of him.[43]

The intensive socializing forced young men and women to interact daily, and to adopt poses of love and express sincere interest. Wilkeson's remarks confirm that some girls hoped for more sincere relationships with young men.

While young men participated in a number of social seasons before seriously considering marriage, girls were allotted a short time to contract an engagement. If they did not marry "within a few years after their introduction, they had a mortified sense of having lost time—that the expectations of friends and of parents had not been fulfilled."[44] This abbreviated timetable demonstrates the anxiety felt by elite families to place girls safely into marriages before a social misstep. It also shows a desire for a return on the investment fathers had made in the education and social training of their daughters.

Marriage was the most important step in a young woman's life, not only for herself but also for her family. It could preserve economic continuity and serve as a conduit to class acceptance or rejection. For some, it meant upward social mobility; for others, it assured their continuing supremacy. The tie of marriage, which linked men and women of the elite through romantic love and class interest, was a powerful one; a poor decision could have dire and long-lasting ramifications.

Rules of etiquette required during courtship were vigilantly observed. Society matrons and their families would be "watching closely and criticizing severely any breach of good manners" on a debutante's part over the next year.[45] Public displays of affection were strictly forbidden; dignity and reserve were required in all relations with suitors. Demonstrative conduct of any kind was frowned upon, and an engagement could be abruptly terminated if a young lady failed to be circumspect. It was imperative that her public persona remain in place during courtship, during the period of her engagement, and during the festivities surrounding her wedding.

Post-debutante girls honed their marketable accomplishments until they had successfully contracted an engagement. Alice Evans studied music, dancing, and French in the morning and entertained calls from gentlemen in the afternoon, regularly receiving four suitors during the year before her marriage.[46] With three local beaux and one who visited from Toledo, Ohio, she was in a position to consider her options. After touring Europe with her sister in 1882, she returned to the United States and found George Hunter Bartlett, a suitor who had visited daily prior to her departure, waiting for her ship at the dock in New York Harbor. Accepted by her family as a suitable son-in-law due to his Anglo-Saxon lineage, his Yale degree, and his family's social position, the engagement took place shortly thereafter.[47]

Other activities that facilitated courtship and engagements include carriage driving and country outings. The Carys and Rumseys were dedicated equestrians, and both Evelyn Rumsey and Mabel Dodge Luhan drove with Seward Cary, Evelyn's uncle.[48] He formed coaching parties of young people, and drove 65 miles east of Buffalo to the Genesee Valley, where the Cary relatives lived.

The extent to which summer outings provided a marriage market can be seen by the activities of the country weekend. The Rumseys, for example, moved to their summer residence on the Niagara River. Young gentlemen visited Evelyn and her cousins, often staying the night.[49] Socializing through playing tennis, boating, carriage driving, and swimming brought young women and men together in acceptable venues that allowed them to display their athletic prowess and good manners. Mothers created the social dynamics by inviting eligible bachelors as houseguests. Summer leisure activities also allowed young people some rare moments of privacy, for they could stroll about the grounds together. Girls also found courtship opportunities and gained national exposure through their spring and summer travels. Evelyn Rumsey visited the summer home of her friend, Evelyn Hay, outside of Newbury, New Hampshire. A printed card instructed her to board a special train car at Boston's Union Station. In Newbury, a boat ferried her to the estate.[50]

After her debut, Evelyn Rumsey entertained visits from suitors for the next few seasons. Family descendants recount that David Gray, the son of the editor of the *Buffalo Courier,* emerged as her favorite. When he asked for Evelyn's hand, however, her father refused to allow him to propose. Mr. Rumsey did not think he would amount to much. Evelyn accepted this decision but did not choose another young man. She did not marry until 21 years later.

The marriage ceremony mirrored the debut in its opulence and its conspicuous display of wealth. Often, weddings were held in the morning and a luncheon followed. In the case of Gertrude Rumsey, Evelyn's sister, 300 guests attended and enjoyed a sumptuous wedding breakfast. Both mothers and daughters donned elaborate gowns crafted by Parisian dressmakers and fitted locally. Many couples observed the English tradition of morning weddings, holding a wedding breakfast following the service. The opulence and lavishness confirmed the economic position of the family. The breakfast was as formal as an evening dinner party, with a hierarchical entrance into the dining room based on status, assigned seating, and a strict protocol of toasting.

For Gertrude Rumsey's wedding breakfast, held in June 1903, the family invited 325 guests to the house for a noon breakfast. They ordered 300 rolls, three gallons of lobster salad, three boned turkeys, three hams, two cold salmon, five gallons of cold bouillon, and 35 quarts of strawberries. Guests consumed six gallons of ice cream and ices, 300 small cakes, and five cases of champagne.[51] One of Buffalo's most celebrated connections to the national elite was the marriage of Charles Cary Rumsey to Mary Harriman, daughter of E. H. Harriman. Mary Harriman, reputed to be "the favorite daughter of the late king of finance," ran her own horse farm in northern New York. Cary was a brilliant horseman, polo player, and sculptor. The couple announced their engagement in May and married before the summer ended.[52]

Members of a wedding party were thrown together in a series of social events that fostered future connections. At the wedding of Frank Baird of Buffalo and Flora Cameron of Waco, Texas, Frank's sister, Faith, fell in love with Flora's brother, William. They were married shortly thereafter. Such ties between families were often reinforced by the social events surrounding weddings.[53]

This summary of the key events in the training and marriage of elite girls demonstrates the steps society mothers took to smooth a daughter's transition through the adolescent years. The social training, the tight circles of suitors, and the qualifying social events ensured that a girl met only young men of suitable stature, and the watchful eyes of her mother and maiden aunts ensured she did not make a false move or a bad decision at this crucial time. Social activities in summer colonies, country clubs, and resorts reinforced residential concentration and city social clubs as the means of enhancing social position and defining an upper-class marriage market. According to Betty Farrell, "The insularity of the social circles made it unnecessary for parents to intervene directly in order to ensure that their children's marriages would be socially and economically endogamous."[54] Her education and training prepared a girl for one fate only: marriage to a man who would add to the fortune and status of the family. Mothers were present at every step to assure their daughters married well.

Yet there are instances of a few rebellious daughters who deviated from the prescribed rituals. Their experiences provide insight into how violations were received. Buffalo socialite and memoirist Mabel Dodge Luhan eloped with a young man named Karl Evans in 1901. Despite his being heir to a considerable fortune from his family's steamship company, Mabel's parents, for some reason, considered Evans an unsuitable match for their daughter. Her father expressly forbade her to see him: "I won't have you carrying on with that Evans boy. He's no good. If I catch you speaking to him again, I'll lock you up."[55] Her father's dictum seemed to strengthen her resolve, and she thought of herself as engaged to Evans.

According to Luhan's memoirs, Evans tricked her into marriage on the pretense of showing her his summer home in Canada; instead, he led her to a church. She went through with the impromptu nuptials. Eventually, the couple informed her parents of the marriage. The Luhans had no choice but to accept it, and her mother immediately planned a lavish church wedding to legitimize the union.[56]

Luhan probably had not intended to defy her father by marrying against his wishes. She did, however, defy his orders to see Evans. A limited rebellion turned into a much larger one because she placed herself outside the protection of her mother's eyes. She went unchaperoned on the outing to Canada and ended up married. It seems she suffered from the pitfalls of stepping outside her prescribed role. Her father refused to attend her formal wedding ceremony. Her mother covered up the embarrassment as best she could. The quick birth of her first child and Evans's unfortunate death in a hunting accident led Luhan to a nervous breakdown. Her mother sent her off to Europe for "a change," but partly to avoid the ostracism of

Buffalo society. Defiance of the rules of society led to exclusion and, in this case, self-imposed exile.[57]

Because of their relative economic independence, it is difficult to determine whether or not elite women divorced at higher rates than other women. Historian Elaine Tyler May claims that between 1867 and 1929 the divorce rate in America rose by 2,000 percent, while the national population grew by only 300 percent and the number of marriages by only 400 percent. By the end of the 1920s, one in every six marriages ended in divorce.[58] Mary Rumsey Movius, daughter of Bronson Rumsey, filed a separation agreement with Edward Movius in 1893 and received custody of the children. Interestingly, she sought no economic support. She kept the home and all properties that she brought to the marriage, terminating her dowry interest in any lands owned or acquired by her husband. In Rumsey's case, her own income could support her family without the financial assistance of her former husband.[59]

This case and others indicate that elite women's economic position allowed them to retain their homes and incomes after marriage. Elite women rarely stayed in unsuccessful marriages simply because of economic dependence. Most produced children prior to suing for divorce, thereby insuring the continuance of the family line. Divorce did not seem to result in a loss of status for a woman, as long as she had produced heirs. It seems that, as a result of their financial independence, elite women were freer than middle-class women to make decisions about their lives and the lives of their children. Most elite children, however, conformed to their parents' wishes in marriage and family life, spending their entire lives within the boundaries of their families' (and society's) expectations. A phalanx of mothers, grandmothers, and maiden aunts inculcated values in each generation well before the critical marriage decision arrived, thereby guaranteeing compliance at the important moment of betrothal. As historian T. J. Jackson Lears recognized, the Victorian family was the focal point for moral and social development: "The family marked the chief arena for the creation of a modern superego, the chief agent of acculturation in a volatile culture."[60] Rituals conducted by elite matriarchs reinforced the concepts of duty to family, self-sacrifice for family harmony, and self-control in the face of personal inclination. This ethos seems to have effectively curbed the natural desires, including sexual desires, of wealthy young men and women, even after marriage.[61]

Women's roles in creating a circumscribed social world also demonstrate the misconception of the separate-spheres ideology in characterizing the lives of elite women during this period. As Lears asserts, "Unlike the relative domestic insularity of middle-class women in nuclear families, upper-class women experienced domesticity in the context of extended family systems and a milieu that emphasized intense sociability."[62] Home, the sphere of women in the late nineteenth century, while idealized as a haven for men away from the rigors of industrial society, was actually dominated by social relations, and was not private or cut off from the economic world of men. As Betty Farrell has noted, "privatization" of family life did not occur. It was impossible for the home to remain isolated from the values of the heartless world outside. If the home was meant to be a refuge from the marketplace, it was also meant to socialize people, both men and women, to succeed in the competitive realm. It taught the aggressive traits of the acquisitive capitalist and the discreet authority of the society matron, and it was the mother, in the homes of the elite, who assured that these lessons were learned.

The structure of power among the elite becomes obvious in tracing the web of extended kinship relations and overlapping business ties within the group. Sociologists and historians have noted the breakup of "family capitalism" and the rise of the managerial revolution at this time.[63] But in Buffalo, the elite continued to control the banking industry as well as the top industrial and commercial concerns—steelworks, railroads, lumber firms, electric power plants, automobile factories, department stores, paper mills, shoe factories, and real-estate brokerages. [64]

Kinship ties provided a bridge between men and women's spheres, placing the bonds of family loyalty and kin solidarity at the service of collective economic interests.[65] Ensuring class endogamy was an integral part of the role of women, and the kinship networks they set in place reinforced the economic position of their families.

A statistical study of intermarriage patterns among Buffalo's elite confirms the solidification of class position through family connections. Among 54 families characterized as elite by the Buffalo Courier and appearing in social listings such as Buffalo's blue books, school yearbooks, club membership lists, and the social section of the newspaper, 97 percent married within the social register. The rate of social registry for the United States population for all years is less than one-tenth of 1 percent (.001). Even more revealing, in 50 percent of the cases, the elite in Buffalo married within the same 54 families. A related study on the founding families of Nichols School, the first independent school for boys in Buffalo, corroborates the evidence, finding an intermarriage rate of 54 percent.[66] In Buffalo, families who had made their money in the grain trade in the 1850s and 1860s consolidated wealth and position by joining with newly wealthy families in the 1880s and 1890s. The newer money came from investment in street railways, real estate, steel, iron, railroads, and banking.

Eric Hobsbawm, in *The Invention of Tradition,* maintains that establishing a class presence of an upper-class elite was difficult when the number of people aspiring to the elite was increasing rapidly. The fluidity of borders increasingly obscured any clear criteria of social distinction: "The problem was that the marks of class in stable local communities had been eroded and descent, kinship, intermarriage, local networks of business, private sociability, and politics no longer provided firm guidance."[67] The case of Buffalo complicates this assertion since the bourgeoisie were,in fact, entrenched here through kinship and intermarriage. Kin networks provided a bastion of power for elites allowing them to retain their economic dominance into the first decades of the twentieth century.

Elite women created and solidified class position serving as gatekeepers to entry and arbiters of fashion and manners. Moreover, many kept their own monetary resources after marriage, supporting and sustaining daughters through gift-giving and inheritance. In this way, Buffalo's society matrons secured both generational continuity and economic dominance.

In succeeding decades, kinship networks and intermarriage became less important in Buffalo. The rise of corporations diffused wealth and a managerial strata displaced individual capitalists. In this corporatization, these elite women moved from guarding the gates of access to improving society through charitable pursuits, including engaging in political activity as women gained suffrage.

Notes

1. *Buffalo Courier,* February 11, 1906.
2. Following the work of G. William Domhoff and E. Digby Baltzell, I use the term "upper class" to define a broad group who exercises authority and accumulates wealth but also assumes generalized hegemony and shapes all facets of its members' lives. The term "elite" refers to individuals who hold central positions of power in the local economy at any one point in time and who exercise authority, accumulate wealth, and command respect

within their group. In Buffalo, a group of 50 to 60 families formed the core of society at the turn of the last century.

3. Mark Goldman, *High Hopes: The Rise and Decline of Buffalo, New York* (Albany: State University of New York Press, 1983), 21.
4. J. N. Larned, *A History of Buffalo Delineating the Evolution of the City* (New York: The Program of the Empire State Co., 1911), 94.
5. Thorstein Veblen, *The Theory of the Leisure Class* (1899; repr., New Brunswick, NJ: Transaction Publishers, 1992), 36.
6. Frederic Cople Jaher, "Style and Status: High Society in Late Nineteenth Century New York," in *The Rich, the Well Born, and the Powerful: Elites and Upper Classes in History*, ed. Frederic Cople Jaher (Urbana: University of Illinois Press, 1973), 272.
7. David A. Gerber, *The Making of an American Pluralism: Buffalo, New York, 1825–60* (Urbana: University of Illinois Press, 1989), 75–76.
8. Ibid., 80.
9. Buffalo Female Academy, *Twenty-Fifth Anniversary Catalogue and Circular, 1875–6* (Buffalo, NY: A. L. Freeman, 1876), 8.
10. Florence Hartley, *The Ladies' Book of Etiquette and Manual of Politeness* (Boston: DeWolfe, Fiske, 1879), 184.
11. Frederic Cople Jaher, *The Urban Establishment: Upper Strata in Boston, New York, Charlestown, Chicago, and L.A.* (Urbana: University of Illinois Press, 1973), 9.
12. Mabel Dodge Luhan, *Intimate Memories*, vol. 1 (New York: Harcourt Brace, 1933), 72–73.
13. Ibid.
14. Ibid., 89–90.
15. Ibid., 3.
16. Buffalo Seminary circular, 1895–96 (Buffalo, NY: James D. Warren's Sons, 1895), 8.
17. Janice Law Trecker, "Sex, Science and Education," in *History of Women in the United States*, ed. Nancy Cott (Munich: K. G. Saur, 1993), 201.
18. "Sixteen Graduate," *Buffalo Courier*, June 8, 1894.
19. Sara Delamont, "The Contradictions in Ladies' Education," in *The Nineteenth-Century Woman: Her Cultural and Physical Worlds*, ed. Sara Delamont and Lorna Duffin (New York: Barnes and Noble Books, 1978), 144.
20. Ibid., 154–55.
21. Aileen S. Kraditor, ed., *Up from the Pedestal* (New York: Quadrangle, 1975), 79.
22. E. Digby Baltzell, *Philadelphia Gentlemen: The Making of a National Upper Class* (Glencoe, IL: Free Press, 1958), 10.
23. Nancy Davis and Barbara Donahue, *Miss Porter's School, A History* (Farmington: Miss Porter's School, 1992), 15–16.
24. Louise L. Stevenson, "Sarah Porter Educates Useful Ladies, 1847–1900" *Winterthur Portfolio* 18 (1983), 39.
25. Ibid., 57.
26. Nancy Davis and Barbara Donahue, *Miss Porter's School: A History* (Farmington, CT: Miss Porter's School, 1992), 22–23.
27. Rumsey diary, November 27, 1896.
28. Rumsey diary, April 19, 1898.
29. Grace Stoddard, "New Girl, Old Girl Song," Songbook 1891, Student Activities, Box 6, Miss Porter's School Archive; quoted in Stevenson, "Sarah Porter," 56.
30. Grace Rumsey Smith, interview by the author, October 1995.
31. *Vogue's Book of Etiquette: Present Day Customs of Social Intercourse with the Rules for Their Correct Observance* (New York: Condé Nast Publications, 1925), 385.
32. For a description of the careers of Wilkeson and his sons, see Gerber, *Making of an American Pluralism*, 32–33, 64.
33. Elizabeth Wilkeson, travel diary, C67–4, Wilkeson Family Papers, Buffalo and Erie County Historical Society (BECHS), 1–59 (hereafter cited as Wilkeson diary).
34. The *Buffalo Evening News* of November 21, 1900 lists the debutantes of the 1900–1901 social season.
35. Arthur S. Reber,*Dictionary of Psychology* (New York: Penguin, 1985), 366.
36. Both Alice Evans Bartlett's and Elizabeth Wilkeson's diaries attest to these pursuits.
37. Wilkeson diary, October 16, 1894.
38. Grace Rumsey Smith, interview by the author, October 1996.

39. *Social Etiquette of New York* (New York: D. Appleton, 1878), 41.
40. Wilkeson diary, December 10, 1893.
41. Wilkeson diary, December 21, 1894.
42. Wilkeson diary, January 1, 1896.
43. Wilkeson, diary, 1892.
44. Hartley, *Ladies Book of Etiquette,* 244–45.
45. Lillian Eichler, *Book of Etiquette* (Oyster Bay, NY: Nelson Doubleday, 1922), 1:20.
46. Alice Evans Bartlett, diary, September 1881, Ellicott-Evans-Bartlett Family Papers, C66–1, BECHS (hereafter cited as Bartlett diary).
47. Bartlett diary, September 25, 1882.
48. Mabel Dodge Luhan discusses her experiences with Seward Cary in Luhan, *Intimate Memories,* vol. 2 (New York: Harcourt, Brace, 1935), 16–17.
49. Jennie Cary Rumsey, Lewiston guest book, 1886–1905, A81–36, BECHS.
50. The printed card was pasted into Evelyn Rumsey's diary of 1899.
51. Scrapbook and account book of the Rumsey family, Waverly Ball and other events, private collection of Grace Rumsey Smith, 34.
52. *Buffalo Evening News,* May 5, 1910; May 9, 1910, 3.
53. *Buffalo Evening News,* November 20, 1900; January 10, 1901.
54. Betty G. Farrell, *Elite Families: Class and Power in Nineteenth-Century Boston* (Albany: State University of New York Press, 1993), 83.
55. Luhan, *Intimate Memories,* 2:29.
56. Ibid., 38–40.
57. Ibid., 56.
58. Elaine Tyler May,*Great Expectations: Marriage and Divorce in Post-Victorian America* (Chicago: University of Chicago Press, 1980), 2.
59. Separation agreement between Mary Rumsey Movius and Edward Movius, September 22, 1893, Rumsey Family Papers, B93–2, Box 1, Folder 4, BECHS.
60. T. J. Jackson Lears, *No Place of Grace: Antimodernism and the Transformation of American Culture, 1880–1920* (New York: Pantheon Books, 1981), 16–17.
61. Ibid., 16.
62. Farrell, *Elite Families,* 79.
63. Ibid., 12.
64. Broad, "Upper Class Cohesion," 273.
65. Farrell, *Elite Families,* 82.
66. Broad, "Upper Class Cohesion," 273.
67. Eric Hobsbawm, "Mass Producing Traditions: Europe, 1870–1914," in *The Invention of Tradition,* ed. Eric Hobsbawm and Terrence Ranger (Cambridge: Cambridge University Press, 1983), 291–93.

10

Rediscovering the Bourgeoisie: Higher Education and Governing-Class Formation in the United States, 1870–1914

Peter Dobkin Hall

The voluntary association was the central instrument of America's bourgeois revolution. In the decades following the Civil War, associations in a variety of forms—ranging from government-chartered joint stock and nonstock corporations to informal entities—became the dominant mode of collective action throughout the country in every significant domain of activity. Arts and culture, commerce, education, finance, health care, manufacturing, politics, recreation, and social welfare were overwhelmingly organized as voluntary associations.

The board of directors was the core of the voluntary association. Almost all associations delegated the basic tasks of governance to officers and directors, some of them elected by members, others co-opted by the boards themselves. Boards not only administered the affairs of particular organizations but also—because directors and trustees often sat on multiple boards—served as arenas for setting community agendas and for negotiating the interrelationships of economy, polity, and society.

As early as the 1820s, business leaders understood that service on multiple boards both enlarged their influence in the business community and enabled them to manage the political and social environments in which business operated. Later in the century, they came to understand how service on the boards of educational, charitable, and cultural institutions positioned them to influence the production of technology and the recruitment and training of skilled personnel needed for their expanding enterprises. In the decades following the Civil War, as corporations became the dominant actors in American life, service on governing boards became the desideratum of membership in the emergent bourgeoisie. Preparing young men for service in governing and administering corporate institutions became one of the central tasks of higher education.

Effective use of associational forms of collective action had to be taught and learned. Because of their familiarity with municipal and ecclesiastical corporations, New Englanders were uniquely well positioned to learn the art and science of association.[1] By 1800, the region led the nation in the granting of corporate charters: 200 of the nation's 333 corporations had been chartered in New England.[2] In view of this, it is hardly surprising that Harvard and Yale, two of the nation's oldest corporations, became major centers for teaching young Americans how to "use and enjoy" associations; that graduates of these colleges should play preeminent roles in establishing and directing these enterprises; or that alumni should act as vectors in spreading models of associational organization throughout the country and extending their reach into every area of American life.

This chapter examines the roles of Harvard and Yale—the nation's preeminent colleges—in the process of recruiting and training the men who would, through their service on governing boards, constitute a key element of the bourgeoisie: the decision makers who both guided the activities of particular social, cultural, and political enterprises and who, through interlocking directorships across these major domains, were able to shape their interrelationships. Because of the unusual prominence and influence of these private institutions, their board members were positioned not only to determine the allocation of the pooled resources of donors but also—to the extent that public institutions tended to follow the lead of private ones—the collective resources of the whole society. In utilizing this capacity, the boards of these institutions exercised the directive and boundary-spanning roles that define the bourgeoisie as a class—a group with collective identity and intentionality.

Harvard, Yale, and the Ethos of National Leadership

The rousing lyrics of Civil War songster Henry Clay Work's "Who Shall Rule This American Nation?" posed the central question raised by the Union's victory. In the decades following the war, Harvard and Yale offered assertive but distinctly different answers to this question, with detailed expositions of their visions of the kind of leadership the nation needed, how it should be recruited, how it should be instructed, and the kinds of activities that would best prepare them for their responsibilities.

Harvard used its graduates' heroism in the Civil War to vindicate its national mission. Citing the heroic sacrifices of Harvard alumni who gave their lives for the Union, the triumphalist rhetoric of the *Harvard Memorial Biographies* declared: "If there is any one inference to be fairly drawn from these memoirs, as a whole, it is this: that there is no class of men in this republic from whom the response of patriotism comes more promptly and surely than from its most highly educated class."[3] Members of a class "which would elsewhere form an aristocracy," these young men, "favored by worldly fortune," "threw themselves promptly and heartily into the war" not out of bravado or ambition but "evidently governed, above all things else, by solid conviction and the absolute law of conscience."[4] "Our system of collegiate education must be on the whole healthy and sound, when it sends forth a race of young men who are prepared, at the most sudden summons, to transfer their energies to a new and alien sphere, and to prove the worth of their training in wholly unexpected applications."[5] Harvard's Memorial Hall, constructed 1866–78, paid tribute to the sacrifices of graduates who gave their lives for the Union cause.

Charles W. Eliot, soon to be selected as Harvard's president, built on these sentiments in the pages of the *Atlantic Monthly,* urging the transformation of American higher education: "The American people are fighting a wilderness, physical and moral, on the one hand, and on the other are struggling to work out the awful problem of self-government. For this fight they must be trained and armed."[6] Under Eliot's leadership, Harvard set out to recruit, train, and arm the managers, administrators, and specialists who would "work out the awful problem of self-government."

Eliot envisioned a nation of great public and private enterprises, guided by leaders in America's growing metropolitan centers. To this end, he began administering Harvard admissions examinations in major cities throughout the country and replaced the ancient prescribed classical curriculum with an "elective system" that maximized choice in the expectation that students would discover their specialized vocations. These would lead some to graduate and professional schools, which would train them to be "commissioned officers in the army of industry."[7] Others would learn the practical lessons of leadership in the real world of enterprise.

Having spent the war years touring Europe investigating the relationships between higher education and national power, it is hardly surprising to find in Eliot's pronouncements a vision of national rather than local leadership. His views resonated with those of Boston's economic and political leaders—the magnates who yearned "to see the banks of the Upper Mississippi connected by iron bands to State Street."[8]

Yale responded to the Civil War very differently. It issued no self-congratulatory publications, though more than a thousand graduates had served the Union cause.[9] No equivalent of Harvard's monumental Memorial Hall was built on the Yale campus—and, indeed, no war memorial of any kind would be built until the early twentieth century, when the names of those who fell in the Civil War would be inscribed in the buildings constructed to celebrate Yale's bicentennial, along with the names of graduates who had died in all the nation's conflicts, from the Revolution to the first World War. Yale did not regard the Union's victory as a Northern triumph, but as a national tragedy.

Yale defined national leadership in a very different way. Its course had been set by the Yale Report of 1828, which stated its intent to provide its students—nearly half of whom by 1830 were born beyond the borders of Connecticut—with "the *discipline* and the *furniture* of the mind." Its proclaimed mission was to furnish a student with the shared values and "balance of character" that would enable him not only to successfully pursue their occupations but also to fulfill a broad range of duties "to his family, to his fellow citizens, to his country" in ways enabling "to diffuse the light of science among all classes of the community" in town and cities throughout America.[10]

Evoking a peculiarly democratic and egalitarian conception of leadership, the Report declared:

> Our republican form of government renders it highly important, that great numbers should enjoy the advantage of a thorough education . . . In this country, where offices are accessible to all who are qualified for them, superior intellectual attainments ought not to be confined to any description of persons. *Merchants, manufacturers*, and *farmers*, as well as professional gentlemen, take their places in our public councils. A thorough education ought therefore to be extended to all these classes. It is not sufficient that they be men of sound judgment, who can decide correctly, and give a silent vote, on great national questions. Their influence upon the minds of others is needed; an influence to be produced by extent of knowledge, and the force of eloquence.[11]

For Yale's leaders, the goal was not only to make higher education accessible but also to make it broadly influential. "The active, enterprising character of our population," the Report concluded,

> renders it highly important, that this bustle and energy should be directed by sound intelligence, the result of deep thought and early discipline . . . Light and moderate learning is but poorly fitted to direct the energies of a nation, so widely extended, so intelligent, so powerful in resources, so rapidly advancing in population, strength, and opulence. Where a free government gives full liberty to the human intellect to expand and operate, education should be proportionally liberal and ample.[12]

Both Harvard and Yale viewed corporations and voluntary associations as the most suitable instrumentalities for exercising leadership, but where Harvard's ideal of leadership would be exercised through powerful centralized institutions located in metropolitan centers, Yale's ideal, modeled on evangelical Protestantism, would work through broadly disseminated networks of community luminaries guiding organizations in villages and towns across the country.

Curriculum and Extracurriculum at Harvard and Yale

The differences between Harvard's and Yale's conceptions of leadership were embodied in curriculum (what students were taught), pedagogy (how they were taught), and extracurriculum (student activities outside the classroom).

Within the framework of Eliot's "new education," Harvard's curriculum became a mechanism for leading students to discover specialized callings that would enable them to become "commissioned officers of the army of industry" who would take their places in enterprises created and controlled on State Street.[13] "We need engineers who thoroughly understand what is already known at home and abroad about mining, road and bridge building, railways, canals, water-powers, and steam machinery," Eliot proclaimed, along with,

> architects who have thoroughly studied their art; builders who can at least construct buildings which will not fall down; chemists and metallurgists who will know what the world has done and is doing in the chemical arts, and in the extraction and working of metals; manufacturers who appreciate what science and technical skill can do for the works which they superintend.[14]

Mere technical competence was not enough, Eliot stressed. Harvard graduates would have to combine the highest levels of expertise with the highest values of public service in order—as Eliot's protégé, reform journalist Herbert Croly (Class of 1890) would put it 40 years later—to perfect themselves as instruments "for the fulfillment of the American national promise."[15]

Although his methods were pragmatic, Eliot's ultimate goal, like those of the secularized Puritanism of the Boston elite, was a spiritual one. The spiritual desideratum was not otherworldly. It was embedded in the material world and consisted of measurable progress of the human spirit toward mastery of human intelligence over nature—the "moral and spiritual wilderness." While this mastery depended on each individual fully realizing his capacities, it was ultimately a collective achievement and the product of institutions that established the conditions for both individual and collective achievement. Like the Union victory in the Civil War, triumph over the moral and physical wilderness, and the establishment of mastery, required a joining of industrial and cultural forces.

While he proposed the reform of professional schools, the development of research faculties, and, in general, a huge broadening of the curriculum, his proposals for undergraduate education in crucial ways preserved—and even enhanced—its traditional functions of molding character and values. Echoing Emerson, Eliot believed that every individual mind had "its own peculiar constitution." The problem, both in terms of fully developing an individual's capacities and in maximizing his social utility, was to present him with a course of study sufficiently representative so as "to reveal to him, or at least to his teachers and parents, his capacities and tastes." An informed choice, once made, would enable the individual to pursue whatever specialized branch of knowledge he found congenial.

individual vocation and fulfilling the collective purposes of the nation were not incompatible. Having found his vocation, Eliot declared, the student

> thereafter . . . knows his way to happy, enthusiastic work, and, God willing, to usefulness and success. The civilization of a people may be inferred from the variety of its tools . . . As tools multiply, each is more ingeniously adapted to its own exclusive purpose. So with the men that make the State. For the individual, concentration, and the highest development of his own peculiar faculty, is the only prudence. But for the State, it is variety, not uniformity, of intellectual product, which is needful.[16]

The "elective system," which vastly expanded the range of courses offered and permitted undergraduates unrestricted choice in selecting their courses of study, promoted an unprecedented intellectual individualism. Students strove for individual distinction and were rewarded for doing so by scholarships, prizes, and other forms of public recognition. Accompanying this was a shift in pedagogy from recitations and lectures toward classes that put students' achievements to the test and, through a revised grading system, rigorously assessed individual performance.

Student life at Harvard—the extracurriculum of athletic teams, clubs, publications, musical and literary societies, and other student organizations—mirrored broader institutional trends. Before 1860, Harvard's student life had been inclusive and democratic. Students formed clubs and teams to serve their own needs. The majority of students were involved in some organized extracurricular activity. But as the expansion of the university after 1869 brought in increasing numbers of students from beyond Boston and the city's elite, student activities became more exclusive and elitist, emphasizing excellence rather than broad participation. By the last quarter of the nineteenth century, the majority of undergraduates were "unclubbed," if not "unclubbable."

University historian and Boston Brahmin Samuel Eliot Morison (Class of 1908) wrote with brutal candor about the exclusiveness of Harvard's student life. Preoccupied with building the intellectual side of Harvard, Morison wrote, Eliot paid little attention to the extracurriculum and left the students to fend for themselves as far as living arrangements were concerned. Traditional student housing in the Yard retained an eighteenth-century primitiveness, while private developers, recognizing that the affluent scions of new industrial wealth desired such amenities as flush toilets and hot and cold running water, built luxurious private dormitories—the "Gold Coast"—along Mount Auburn Street.

This produced a social cleavage between the affluent undergraduates, usually products of the new boarding schools, and middle-class students, usually the products of rural academies and public schools. This divide was reinforced by relationships that developed between undergraduates and elite Boston families "as the Boston mammas suddenly became aware that Harvard contained many appetizing young gentlemen from New York, Philadelphia, and elsewhere."[17] "Obviously," Morison noted, writing in the present tense for Harvard's 1936 tercentennial history,

> you could not room with a man in College or be very intimate with those you could not well ask to meet your sister, and naturally you got your friends into your club in preference to others . . . The social sets of metropolitan Boston became increasingly the dictators of social sets in Cambridge. This has baulked all attempts to make Harvard a social democracy.[18]

The impact of this dynamic was evident not only on Harvard's student clubs, which became far more exclusive than they had ever been: Nearly 90 percent of members of the Harvard Class of 1880 belonged to a club or participated in a student organization or activity; only 27 percent of members of the Class of 1910 did so.

In contrast with Harvard's elite individualism, Yale—in line with its evangelical roots—offered a vision of leadership that was egalitarian and decentralized, that sought to influence the nation by recruiting its students nationally and, once equipped with the "discipline and furniture of the mind," sent them back to the towns and cities from which they had come. Rather than transforming its students into "commissioned officers of the army of industry," Yale sought to imbue them with convictions that enabled them, regardless of whether they were businessmen, lawyers, physicians, teachers, or farmers, to regard their callings as ministries and themselves as moral agents empowered by their faith to influence their neighbors, colleagues, and fellow citizens wherever they happened to find themselves.[19] Beyond this notion of spiritualized leadership, the body of ideas developed by the "New Haven Theologians" of the antebellum decades stressed the importance of voluntary associations as instruments of collective moral agency—a fact expressed not only in the extraordinarily high levels of associational engagement by Yale graduates but also in the intensely associational character of student life, which evidently served as a school of learning civic values and organizational skills.[20]

Unlike Harvard, which was closely tied to urban commercial and industrial elites, and strove to serve their needs, Yale's leaders were openly suspicious of wealth, a suspicion that ripened into open conflict in the late 1860s, when elite New Yorkers, under the banner of the "Young Yale" movement, attempted to wrest control of the college from the Connecticut ministers who had controlled it since its establishment.[21]

The rebellious alumni were keenly aware of Harvard's and Yale's competing claims for national leadership and urged inclusion of laymen on the college's governing board as the first step toward bringing Yale up to speed. Addressing a meeting of alumni in the fall of 1869, William Walter Phelps, a scion of the Phelps-Dodge copper dynasty, declared, "Lawyers and clergymen, physicians and capitalists, judges and editors, representing all the interests of the varied civilization, from whose fiercest current we step for the moment aside are not satisfied with the management of the college." "The college wants a living connection with the world without," Phelps exclaimed.

> This great want can be supplied only by the Alumni. Put them into your government. Get them from some other State than Connecticut—from some other profession than the ministry . . . Let her own alumni, from Maine to California, be Yale College—the bounding blood of youth will throb in every one of its ancient members . . . Yale men, who got their training here, and are as able to manage its affairs as Rev. Mr. Pickering, of Squashville, who is exhausted with keeping a few sheep in the wilderness, or Hon. Mr. Domuch, of Oldport, who seeks to annul the charter on the only railway that benefits his constituency.[22]

"Don't let Harvard, our great rival, alone have the benefit of it," Phelps pled.

Yale's Old Guard fought back, led by professor of moral philosophy, the Rev. Noah Porter. In a widely circulated counterattack, *American Colleges and the American Public,* which appeared first as a series of articles and subsequently as a book, Porter harshly criticized secular economic and political leadership. Porter was well aware of the differences between Harvard and Yale alumni, and the implications of these differences for college governance. "The graduates of Yale do not, like those of Harvard, live in its immediate neighborhood," he wrote, "but are scattered all over the country."[23]

Pointing first to the indifferent participation of the laity already on the Yale Corporation—the six ex officio state-elected officials who had served as members since 1792—Porter went on to claim that governance by gentlemen "residing in Chicago or Cincinnati," who had no ongoing direct knowledge of college affairs, left much to be desired. Besides being ignorant of the college's best interests and, at best, poorly positioned to give its affairs their full attention, a lay board elected by the alumni would bring to college governance the deplorable morality of politics and business. The Corporation, so constituted, Porter argued, could:

> be very easily "packed"—to use the language of politics—in favor of particular candidates, or even by the candidates themselves. They would be liable to have their harmony and good feeling—so large a part of the usefulness and enjoyment of such meetings—broken up by the pressing of "party-tickets" and "excitements and ill-feeling."[24]

The battle over Yale governance ended in a lopsided compromise. Conservative champion Noah Porter was elected president. As a sop to the alumni, Yale's charter was amended to replace six of the eight ex officio members with men elected by the alumni, and to open the ten "successor trustee" positions to the laity. (Under this scheme, laymen would not become a majority on the board until 1910). Young Yale's leaders, understandably unhappy with this arrangement, withheld their donations during Porter's regime—relenting only in 1899, when the college (now calling itself a university) finally elected its first lay president, economist Arthur Twining Hadley.

As Eliot moved Harvard's curriculum toward rich diversity and its pedagogy toward the cultivation of individual excellence, Porter defended Yale's attachment to the prescribed classical curriculum and a traditional pedagogy based on collective rather than individual achievement. His sentiments were echoed by conservative alumni like Lyman Hotchkiss Bagg, who was unembarrassed in defending the educational vision first articulated in the Yale Report of 1828. "The chief value of a college course lies not in the scholarship or absolute knowledge with which it supplies a man," Bagg wrote,

> but rather in that intangible thing called culture, or discipline, or mental balance, which only its possessor can appreciate, and which he cannot describe, certainly no one can say that the peculiar life and customs which the students themselves adopt form an unimportant, even though it be an unrecognized, part of that course. Exactly how important this part is I will not attempt to determine, but this I will say, that were it possible for it to be removed, I think the value of the curriculum would thereby be diminished by at least one half.[25]

Given the relatively undemanding pace of the college's prescribed classical curriculum, through which undergraduates moved in lockstep through group recitations, it may well be that the rich possibilities of the extracurriculum had as much or more to offer than its official counterpart. Many student "societies" and many of the early fraternities were devoted to "literary pursuits," accumulating their own libraries and featuring debates and discussions of papers written by their members.[26]

Certainly, if Bagg's detailed description of the extracurriculum is to be believed, the complex "society system" of freshman, sophomore, junior, and senior clubs, "society institutions" (literary societies like Linonia and Brothers in Unity, which had their own libraries), publications (the college newspaper, literary magazine, and class book), athletic teams (which would become increasingly important in the last decades of the century), and dramatic and musical organizations, as well as the intricate bonding rituals of the classes and the college, served not only to inculcate shared values but also to teach invaluable lessons in self-government. The societies, publications, teams, and cultural organizations were initiated by students, and, even after they had acquired official or quasi-official status, students retained the power to elect officers and directors and decide organizational policies.[27]

As can well be imagined, the power of students in such a setting was extraordinary—and sometimes broke out into murderous violence, riotous encounters between Town and Gown, and cheating scandals. The students' extraordinary autonomy frequently placed them at odds with college and municipal authorities, and with one another in interclass and intersociety rivalries. At the same time, they provided students opportunities to develop practical skills in negotiation, persuasion, and financial management of a sort that could not be found in the classroom.

College photographs of the period depict the distinctive style of college men in the last quarter of the nineteenth century. Their bearing, clothing, jewelry, and hats set them apart from their less privileged contemporaries, while at the same time giving them more in common with men in other colleges. The homogenization of college life and the emergence of the stereotype of the "college man" after the Civil War was driven by a number of forces, including the growth of intercollegiate athletics, the rise of national fraternities, the standardization of secondary school curricula, and the founding of boarding schools, which became major feeders to Harvard, Yale, and other elite institutions.[28] These constituted essential aspects of a bourgeois style that enabled members of the class both to assert their shared identity and to recognize one another.

This was the period in which the classic college songs were written. "Bright College Years," penned by a member of the Yale Class of 1881, perfectly expresses both the centrality of the college experience to the lives of these young men and their emerging sense of themselves as a distinct group—with the last line affirming their awareness of the responsibilities they bore as future leaders.

> Bright college years, with pleasure rife,
> The shortest, gladdest years of life,
> How swiftly are ye gliding by,
> O, why doth time so quickly fly?
> The seasons come, the seasons go,
> The earth is green, or white with snow:
> But time and change shall naught avail
> To break the friendships formed at Yale. . . .
>
> In after-years, should troubles rise
> To cloud the blue of sunny skies,
> How bright will seem, through mem'ry's haze,
> Those happy, golden by-gone days!
> So let us strive that ever we
> May let these words our watch-cry be,
> Where'er upon life's sea we sail:
> "For God, for Country, and for Yale!"[29]

Harvard and Yale Alumni as Civic Leaders

Each university's ethos of national leadership and their distinctive expressions in their curricula, pedagogies, and extracurricula appear to have profoundly shaped the postgraduate careers of their alumni.[30] In some respects, the two groups were very similar: both embraced professionalism and the value of trained expertise; both sought and obtained top positions in business and the learned professions; they also served in disproportionate numbers on nonprofit and public boards. Together, they represented the bourgeois ideal as the avant-garde of economic, political, and cultural transformation.

At the same time, there were noteworthy differences between Harvard and Yale alumni. The most notable of these involved their service on corporate and non-profit boards and nonelective public boards and commissions. As table 10.1 shows, Yale alumni were nearly twice as likely as their Harvard counterparts to serve on governing boards.

Not only were Yale alumni more likely than their Harvard counterparts to serve on boards, but they were also two to three times more likely to serve on multiple boards. In most instances, multiple board memberships spanned domains of activity. Thus, for example, it was not uncommon for businessmen to serve on several business boards and nonprofit boards, on several public boards or commissions, and as a vestryman, deacon, or trustee of his religious congregation. Significantly, as table 10.2 indicates, businessmen were more likely than their classmates in other occupations to serve on multiple boards and, as such, were strategically positioned to influence and coordinate relations between major domains of public activity.

What accounts for these differences between Harvard and Yale alumni? One factor may have been variations in the extracurricula of the colleges. Harvard's elitism, particularly the emphasis on individual academic achievement, was reflected in its extracurriculum: clubs, teams, publications, and other student activities tended to include only the best, brightest, and most talented. Despite Harvard's size (Harvard classes were much larger than Yale's), there were far fewer student organizations—and those permitted to exist were far more selective in admitting members. As a result, Harvard students had relatively few opportunities for extracurricular activity.

Yale, in contrast, nurtured its extracurriculum. Besides its complex "society system," which included associations and fraternities for members of every class, and many publications (including, during the 1870s, two weekly newspapers), a wide range of informal and ephemeral organizations flourished at the college. As table 10.3 shows, the level of student participation in the extracurriculum was consistently higher at Yale than at Harvard, offering abundant opportunities

Table 10.1 Percent of members of Harvard and Yale classes of 1890, 1900, 1910, and 1920 serving on business, nonprofit, and nonelective public boards and commissions

	HARVARD (%)	YALE (%)
1870	40	41
1880	39	59
1890	28	47
1900	35	51
1910	35	54

Table 10.2 Percent of Harvard and Yale graduates entering major occupations and percent of alumni serving on three or more boards, by class year, 1890–1910

CLASS YEAR	1890		1900		1910	
	HARVARD	YALE	HARVARD	YALE	HARVARD	YALE
BUSINESS (%)	28	42	33	49	47	57
BUSINESS ON >3 BOARDS (%)	46	42	54	64	61	59
LAW (%)	21	25	14	16	10	10
LAW ON >3 BOARDS (%)	27	47	22	22	14	21
MEDICINE(%)	10	9	7	8	5	4
MEDICINE ON >3 BOARDS(%)	0	5	0	0	4	3
CLERGY(%)	4	3	2	2	2	3
CLERGY ON >3 BOARDS(%)	0	0	0	0	0.06	0.03
EDUCATION(%)	11	7	13	8	10	0
EDUCATION ON >3 BOARDS(%)	9	0	16	7	6	10
OTHER(%)	26	14	31	17	26	26
OTHER ON >3 BOARDS(%)	18	6	9	7	10	4

Table 10.3 Percent of Harvard and Yale alumni who participated in undergraduate clubs, teams, publications, and other student activities.

CLASS YEAR	HARVARD (%)	YALE (%)
1870	59	100
1880	87	92
1890	76	80
1900	62	69
1910	27	84

for acquiring civic and leadership skills that would, evidently, be carried into postgraduate life.

As table 10.4 suggests, participation in the extracurriculum appears to have been powerfully associated with civic engagement later in life for both Harvard and Yale alumni—though the impact on Yale alumni appears particularly striking, with extracurricular participants nearly twice as likely to serve on boards after graduation than participants.

Another factor that may have influenced postgraduate board membership by Harvard and Yale alumni may be differences in occupational choice. Businessmen were more likely to serve on boards than clergymen, lawyers, physicians, and other professionals—and, as table 10.2 shows, Yale graduates were consistently more likely to enter business than their Harvard counterparts.

Table 10.4 Percent extracurricular participants and non-participants ("clubbed" and "unclubbed") who served on governing boards after graduation, by class year.

CLASS YEAR	HARVARD		YALE	
	Clubbed on Boards	Unclubbed on Boards	Clubbed on Boards	Unclubbed on Boards
1870	38	42	41	0
1880	40	30	60	44
1890	30	22	54	20
1900	40	27	56	30
1910	38	31	60	30

Table 10.5 Residency of living Harvard and Yale alumni, 1910

	TOTAL	NORTH ATLANTIC	SOUTH ATLANTIC	NORTH CENTRAL	SOUTH CENTRAL	WEST	OTHER OR UNKNOWN
YALE ALUMNI							
N	14,806	9,723	650	2,532	384	804	713
%		0.66	0.04	0.17	0.03	0.05	0.05
HARVARD ALUMNI							
N	32,188	21,991	1,239	1,467	695	1,467	5,329
%		0.68	0.04	0.05	0.022	0.05	0.17

Source: Harvard Alumni Association, *Harvard University Directory* (Cambridge, MA: Harvard University Press, 1910; Yale University, *Directory of Living Graduates* (New Haven, CT: Yale University Press, 1910).

A third factor may involve where alumni ultimately settled. As table 10.5 shows, two-thirds of Harvard and Yale alumni resided in the North Atlantic region (New England, New Jersey, New York, and Pennsylvania). Of Harvard alumni living outside the North Atlantic region, the vast majority lived in the South Atlantic region (Delaware, District of Columbia, Florida, Maryland, Virginia, and the Carolinas). In contrast, most of the Yale alumni living outside the North Atlantic states had settled in the North Central region (the Dakotas, Illinois, Indiana, Iowa, Kansas, Michigan, Minnesota, Missouri, Nebraska, Ohio, and Wisconsin). The Harvard alumni tended to concentrate in and around large cities: 25 percent in the greater Boston area, 15 percent in New York; Yale alumni were more likely to work and reside in smaller towns and cities. In places like New York, Boston, and Philadelphia, the number of places on boards was smaller and competition for leadership positions was more intense; consequently, the Harvard alumni who concentrated in those cities may have been less likely to be elected to governing boards. The many smaller cities and towns where Yale alumni were more likely to settle had, in the aggregate, many more organizations and boards, and a smaller pool of competitors for leadership positions. In addition, the North Central region, where so many Yale alumni resided, was especially rich in for-profit and nonprofit corporations—far more so than the Southeastern states favored by Harvard alumni.[31]

It is worth noting that, despite their relatively small number in relation to the whole population of college graduates in the United States, Ivy League graduates are overrepresented on governing boards. A recent study of the educational backgrounds of members of nonprofit boards in seven American cities (Atlanta, Boston, Cleveland, Los Angeles, Minneapolis, St. Paul, and Philadelphia) found that in the period 1931–91, Ivy League graduates comprised 37 percent of all hospital trustees, 37 percent of trustees of cultural organizations, 29 percent of trustees of community foundations, and 53 percent of trustees of colleges and universities.[32] In the period 1870–1910, when Ivy Leaguers represented a far larger proportion of the educated population than they do today, this overrepresentation was undoubtedly even more pronounced.[33]

Creating "The College Life" and the Convergence of Wall Street and Main Street

The data on Harvard and Yale alumni indicate that, for much of the nineteenth century, America had parallel bourgeois systems, one anchored in centralized metropolitan power, the other casting a broad decentralized network across the nation and exercising sway in smaller cities and towns. By the turn of the century, these two systems were converging. A key indicator of this convergence was the surge in the founding of national membership associations (including fraternal/sororal organizations, college fraternities and sororities, professional societies, service clubs, religious denominations, and trade associations), which peaked in the period 1880–1910.[34] Many of these were federated structures, which brought state and local chapters into larger national organizations and, in doing so, served to integrate local and national elites.

Higher education played a central in this process not only by recruiting and training elites but also by providing civic leaders with shared manners and mores and self-awareness. By the turn of the century, eligibility for civic leadership had less to do with nativity and ancestry than with education and occupation. The portability of educational credentials made graduates of national institutions like Harvard and Yale candidates for civic eminence wherever their careers carried them and, as such, constituted the connective tissue of the emergent national governing class: America's twentieth-century bourgeoisie.

In his 1936 memoir, Henry Seidel Canby (Yale Class of 1899) gave a particularly insightful account of the relationship between the excurriculum—which he termed "the college life"—and the postgraduate lives of his fellow alumni. He began by sketching the distinctive undergraduate subculture that emerged in the post-Civil War decades. The "college life" involved more than yearning to look "collegiate." It offered undergraduates opportunities to remake themselves, free from the burdens of their families, their hometowns, and their boarding schools. An undergraduate, Canby wrote, "was no longer a boy from Rochester, he was [an] undergraduate, admitted to the rights and privileges of college life, and this consciousness went to the roots of his being."[35]

"There never was a more strenuous preparation for active life anywhere than the American college of those days," Canby wrote.

> The cry in our undergraduate world was always "do something," "what does he *do?*" Freshmen hurried up and down entry stairs seeking news for the college paper, athletes, often with drawn, worried faces, struggled daily to get or

> hold places on the teams, boys with the rudiments of business ability were managers of magazines, orchestras, teams, or co-operative pants pressing companies. Those who had a voice sang, not for sweet music's sake, but to "make" the glee club . . . The toil was supposed to be fun, but the rewards were serious. No one that I remember did anything that was regarded as doing, for its own sake. No, the goal was prestige, social preferment, a senior society which would be a springboard to Success in Life.[36]

The intensity of Yale's extracurriculum as an arena in which individuals had to prove themselves undercut the authority of conventional hierarchies of wealth and power. "College life burnt up old social distinctions and made new ones," Canby wrote:

> After the sons and heirs who might have formed an American aristocracy of wealth and privilege had been shuffled in the college competitions with the shrewd children of parvenus and the good baseball players whose fathers were Irish policemen, cards were redealt in new social categories. . . . We were not impressed by the Great Names of plutocracy—by Vanderbilts, Astors, Rockefellers as such—since we saw them at first hand. And thus, with our realistic experience in the qualified democracy of the colleges died the possibility of adding to the economic privileges of the very rich the respect given elsewhere to rank.[37]

Canby's use of the term "qualified democracy" to describe the college life is significant, since he makes clear at the outset of his reminiscence that he is describing the experience of a privileged group—"golden boys and girls" who had been "sent to this pleasant place to work a little and to play hard until our time came."[38] He and his classmates were being trained for leadership, whether they knew it or not—and their postgraduate careers, in which they carried their hustling competitiveness and civic skills from the campus into America's communities, suggests just how successful this process was.

The Campus as Didactic Landscape

Canby's focus on the college experience rather than on the institutional structures and dynamics that shaped it should not obscure the extent to which Harvard, Yale, and other educational institutions carefully crafted the "college life" and used it as a mechanism for preparing "college men" to become a class of leaders equipped with the knowledge, skills, and values for leadership.

One measure of this is the physical transformation of college/university campuses beginning in the 1890s. The "old campuses" of Harvard and Yale were randomly constructed, crumbling monuments to their colonial pasts and to the idiosyncracies of donors.[39] The new campuses were both carefully planned and architecturally coherent efforts to embody and express institutional values. While classroom buildings, laboratories, and libraries became increasingly specialized to serve the universities' role in producing research and expertise, structures serving the social and recreational needs of students—dormitories, clubs, and athletic facilities—became increasingly elaborate and lavishly appointed. In place of privies and woodpiles, the creators of the new campuses placed iconic public art, like Daniel Chester French's famous statue of John Harvard (1884) and Bela Pratt's idealized rendering of Nathan Hale (1898–1913).

Because Harvard's leaders both led and enthusiastically articulated the relationship between higher education and the national order they hoped to create, their motives and actions are far more transparent than those of other educational leaders. As Boston investment banker Henry Lee Higginson, a key figure in the physical and social transformation of Harvard, put it in an 1886 letter to a relative, "How else are we going to save our country if not by education in all ways and on all sides?"

> Democracy has got fast hold of the world, and *will* rule. Let us see that she does it more wisely and humanely than the kings and nobles have done! Our chance is *now*—before the country is full and the struggle for bread becomes intense and bitter. Educate, and save ourselves and our families and our money from mobs!

"I would have the gentlemen of this country," he concluded, "lead the new men, who are trying to become gentlemen, in their gifts and in their efforts to promote education."[40]

If his intentions are to be judged from his actions, Higginson evidently understood that the extracurriculum was as important as the classroom in shaping the college experience. His two greatest contributions to Harvard—Soldiers Field (1890) and the Harvard Union (1901)—were components of a series of three important structures intended to shape the identity and values of the Harvard community through shaping college life.

The first of these structures, Memorial Hall (fig. 10.1), was an impressive shrine erected to the memory of the university's Civil War dead. Completed in 1878, it housed Harvard's largest public spaces: the Sanders Theater, a banqueting hall

Figure 10.1 Memorial Hall's magnificent banquet room. Alumni Hall, served as a common dining hall for undergraduates during the academic year and as a gathering place for old grads at commencement. Source: Harvard Yearbook (1904).

Figure 10.2 Harvard-Yale football game ("The Game"), first played at the new Harvard Stadium on Soldier's Field, November 21, 1903. Yale won. Source: Harvard Yearbook (1904).

("Alumni Hall"), and the great memorial chamber, with its solemn stained glass, statuary, and the names of the honored dead. Memorial Hall, writes architectural historian Douglass Shand-Tucci, was "the great symbol of Boston's commitment to the Unionist cause and the abolitionist movement in America which also crested in the Civil War, a war Harvard took up with almost a religious fervor."[41]

Once completed, Memorial Hall became the center of university life: here, students lined up to register when they entered college; here, graduation and major performances were held; here, the alumni convened at commencement and for reunions. Memorial Hall, Shand-Tucci notes, represents "an attempt to restore the old Hall of Harvard College" and, as such, is an obvious effort to impose a unified institutional identity—and one suffused with an ethos of service—on its increasingly heterogeneous students and alumni.[42]

Higginson's first major gift to the university was Soldiers Field (fig. 10.2), the broad expanse across the Charles River that would house Harvard Stadium (1902) and other athletic facilities. In dedicating his gift to friends and classmates with whom he had served during the Civil War, Higginson spoke of his "dear friends who gave their lives, and all that they had or hoped for, to their country and to their fellow men in the hour of great need—the War of the Rebellion."[43] In pondering the lessons to be learned from his friends' sacrifices, Higginson evoked their character as leaders, referring to "the beauty and the holiness of work, and of utter, unselfish, thoughtful devotion to the right cause, to our country, and to mankind." Referring to the power of the extracurriculum in molding their characters, Higginson declared that "they loved study and work, and loved play too." He hoped that his gift, as a space for play, would help students become "full-grown, well-developed men, able and ready to do good work of all kinds—steadfastly, devotedly, thoughtfully," and that it would remind them of the reason for living, and of their "duties as men and citizens of the Republic."[44]

In his closing remarks, Higginson suggested how well he understood the central importance of institutions like Harvard, Yale, and Princeton in creating a national leadership class and in fulfilling America's national promise:

> Lately I traveled with an ex-Southern artillery officer. . . . I asked him of his family, and he said, "I've just sent a boy to Yale, after teaching him all in my power. I told him to go away, and not to return with any provincial notions. Remember," I said, "there is no Kentucky, no Virginia, no Massachusetts, but one great country."[45]

Figure 10.3 Completed in 1901, the Harvard Union was more splendid than any of the final clubs and rivaled the grandeur of the "Gold Coast's" private dormitories, Source: Official Guide to Harvard University (1904).

A key figure in organization such great national corporations as American Telephone & Telegraph and General Electric, Higginson envisioned the athletic competitions between Harvard, Yale, and Princeton students as activity—like the Civil War itself—that would forge them them into a unified moral force in the life of the nation and its economy.

The Harvard Union (fig. 10.3) was built at a time when the lines between the wealthy and pedigreed, and students of more humble—or ethnic—origins, had been sharply drawn. The former lived in luxurious private dormitories—the so-called "Gold Coast—and dominated the college's clubs, teams, and publications, while the former were scattered through boardinghouses and rented rooms. Many local boys lived at home. Higginson intended the Union "to provide an attractive gathering place for students not wealthy enough to afford the luxuries of a Gold Coast club."[46]

As in his Soldier's Field dedication, Higginson affirmed the importance of the extracurriculum in a Harvard education. In transforming itself from a college into a great university, he suggested, Harvard had "unwittingly imperiled the comradeship and social life" of the university, allowing the spread of "habits of exclusiveness and of luxury in living which hurt our democratic university."[47] "We cannot bear such a result," he declared. "we must see to it that young men entering our University stand on a footing equal in all respects, until they themselves, by their merits or faults, have raised or lowered it. Any other basis implies a failure in the system of our University, which, in the name of true civilization, we will strive to avert."[48]

The Union, with its stately architecture (designed by Charles McKim) and impressive interiors (which would do justice to any upper-crust metropolitan club of the

Figure 10.4 The "Living Room" of the Harvard Union, in its scale and luxurious appointments, resembled the grand spaces of elite metropolitan men's clubs. Source: Harvard Yearbook (1904).

period), was a huge success (fig. 10.4, 10.5). Within two years of its opening, more than two-thirds of undergraduates were members and it was hosting some three dozen student organizations and 19 "entertainments" concerts, plays, and public lectures.[49]

Harvard opted for a Georgian/colonial style in constructing its new campus, while Yale embraced the Gothic. The overall effect was the same: the physical setting of the undergraduate experience for students at both institutions became magnificent stage sets for the enactment of the "college life" and the formation of new identities and ambitions. Ultimately, in the late 1920s, the universities would completely institutionalize the process by gathering all undergraduates into campus structures that served both as dormitories and as social centers: Harvard's "houses" and Yale's "residential colleges"—both made possible through the generosity of Standard Oil heir Edward S. Harkness (Yale Class of 1897).

Alumni Associations, Graduates Clubs, and the National Organization of the Alumni

The era of campus reconstruction was also marked by the creation of national alumni organizations and a national network of graduates' clubs.[50] Since the 1830s, Harvard and Yale alumni had maintained ad hoc organizations that convened periodically and issued occasional publications. By the 1860s, these organizations became more formally institutionalized, appointing class secretaries, who received correspondence and donations; holding regular reunions; and compiling and publishing volumes of class biographies every five years. In the 1890s graduates at both universities formed general associations of alumni, which took increasingly active roles in college fund raising and governance. The founding of alumni magazines (in the '90s) and alumni directories (in 1910) and the establishment of Harvard and Yale clubs in New York and other major cities not only reflected the increasingly national

Figure 10.5 The fireplaces at either end of the Union's Living Room were truly baronial in scale. A bust of Daniel: Chester French's famous John Harvard statue presides over the mantel. Source: Harvard Yearbook (1904).

character of the alumni but also helped to sustain the alumni's sense of themselves as a distinctly bounded group throughout their adult lives.

Superficially, the growth of these organizations served to intensify intercollegiate rivalries, especially as athletic competition became an increasingly central feature of the public profile of higher education (and an increasingly important venue for alumni gatherings). At the same time, they helped to erase the more fundamental differences between institutions. Harvard's and Yale's football and baseball teams and crews might sport different colors, sing their own songs, and cheer their own cheers, but they were playing the same games by the same rules, while the contests themselves became rituals for displaying the growing homogeneity of the university-educated as a group. "The Game" (the Harvard-Yale football game) and the Harvard-Yale rowing races became major occasions not only for displays of athletic prowess and gentlemanly standards of conduct but also for convivial gatherings of the alumni, with the attendant ceremonies and rituals of America's new bourgeoisie.

Although alumni would continue to insist on the distinctiveness of Harvard and Yale, the reality, by the first decade of the twentieth century, was that the two institutions—and, indeed, elite higher education generally—was becoming increasingly homogenized. By the late 1920s, the differences in undergraduate life would begin to disappear, as Harvard's "houses" and Yale's "residential colleges" enabled institutional administrators to supplant the old student-controlled extracurriculum and to manipulate it to their own egalitarian ends.[51] The members of Yale's residential colleges and Harvard's houses represented a cross section of intellectual interests and backgrounds. The colleges and houses had their own athletic teams, cultural groups, and social events, which supplemented the activities of campuswide organizations.[52] This assured that virtually any student interested in participating in an activity had an opportunity to do so.

Not surprisingly, the differences in alumni careers, civic engagement, and residence so evident in the period 1870–1910 began to disappear—and, by 1940, the profiles of alumni of the two institutions would be almost indistinguishable. They were trained to be—and in large measure succeeded in becoming—members of a governing class whose influence was evident not only in their overrepresentation in the top ranks of government, industry, education, philanthropy, and the professions nationally, but also in their prominence on the boards of directors of local organizations. In his 1969 study *The Education of American Leaders,* Yale historian George W. Pierson found that, of the 347 individuals comprising the "National Executive" (presidents, vice presidents, and cabinet members) serving between 1789 and 1962, 120 (35 percent) were alumni of Harvard, Yale, or Princeton; of the 332 executives of top American corporations in 1950, 170 (51 percent) were graduates of these institutions; and, of the 455 deceased university graduate members of the American Academy and the National Institute of Arts and Letters in 1963, 163 (36 percent) were Harvard, Yale, or Princeton alumni.[53] A more recent study of the educational backgrounds of trustees and directors of local nonprofit organizations in the period 1930–90 found that Ivy League graduates comprised between a quarter and a third of board members.[54]

There is no more powerful testament to the successful integration of the two bourgeois systems than the suburban enclaves that began to form on the periphery of American cities by the 1920s. Their planned architecture and streetscapes, inspired by the Cities Beautiful movement, echoed the campuses where their residents had spent their "shortest gladdest years"—much as the institutionalization of leisure and recreation mirrored college and university extracurricula.

Conclusion

One of Marx's most powerful ideas was his notion of the bourgeoisie as a revolutionary avant-garde that relentlessly extended its power geographically and across all domains of public and private life. But Marx's vision of the bourgeoisie was flawed by his economic reductionism. Economic motives are not always dominant; actions with economic outcomes may be unintended consequences.[55]

Ultimately, the usefulness of the bourgeoisie as a concept is its capacity to describe and explain relationships and flows of resources across specialized domains of activity. American historians have tended to resist examining these crosscurrents, preferring instead to analytically and descriptively mirror the specialized character of the institutions and activities to which they have devoted their attention. Thus, for example, business historians have viewed economic development as a product of the drive for profits coupled with rational utilization of resources and technology, ignoring the social and cultural dimensions of capitalism. Alfred D. Chandler's *The Visible Hand,* for example, calls attention to the central role of middle managers in the emergence of multidivisional firms but, curiously, makes no effort to investigate how and why the large pool of persons possessing the skills and values needed to create and administer these complex, technology-intensive, geographically extensive enterprises happened to be on hand to take on the task of organizing the modern American economy.[56] Was it mere happenstance? Or was this cadre of talented administrators the product of strategic investments in education, culture, and social institutions by entrepreneurs who understood that capitalism was more than an economic system?

A broadened concept of the American bourgeoisie enables us to understand capitalism as both a system of economic organization and a universe of interconnected and interdependent organizations linked not only by common interests but also by human actors. Recent scholarship has refocused the attention paid to members of governing boards, from their role within organizations to their function as boundary spanners who, in connecting organizations to needed resources and sources of information, effectively enact organizational environments.[57] The social characteristics of board members, especially the ways in which they may interconnect a variety of organizations, determines not only organizational standing, but the standing of board members themselves. Civic leadership, as J. Alan Whitt has noted, inheres in "big linkers" who interconnect the major domains of community activity through their board memberships.[58] To the extent that alumni of Harvard, Yale, and similar institutions were overrepresented on boards—national and local—is, in these terms, a measure of the role that these colleges and universities played in creating the bourgeoisie not merely as an economic group, but as a governing class.

American scholarship has generally resisted investigating these interconnections: business history not only gives scant attention to noneconomic factors in accounting for the expansion of modern enterprise but also generally regards the philanthropic and civic activities of business leaders as extraneous. Historians of education pay more attention to ideas, pedagogy, and curriculum than to the business and civic leaders whose political and financial support for expanding the educational system made possible the modern educational enterprise; until recently, social historians have had little to say about associations and their significance in the modernization of American public culture.

Nonetheless, it is indisputable that modern business enterprise, dependent on ever-advancing technology and geographically extensive administrative structures staffed by trained experts and managers, required educational institutions, professional societies, and other nonbusiness organizations to produce the intellectual, human, and social capital on which their operations depended. It is equally indisputable that the development of the educational, occupational, and social infrastructures depended on large-scale financial investments and political commitments by business firms and those who controlled them.

Our capacity to grasp these interrelationships and interdependencies—along with our ability to candidly address issues of power—is immeasurably advanced by a conception of a bourgeoisie, which enables us to track large patterns and trends, and to use them to contextualize the artifacts and practices of everyday life. In doing so, it enriches our understanding of modernity.

Note on Sources

The primary sources of data on Harvard and Yale alumni are the class reports published by graduating classes, usually at five-year intervals, from their year of graduation on. These books contain biographies (often autobiographies), photographs, and statistics of occupation and residence, as well as accounts of class dinners and other events.

These volumes began to appear regularly in the 1850s. Though class books exist for classes graduating as early as the 1820s, most of these volumes are retrospective—in contrast to the post-1850 reports, which provide information on class members current to the time of publication.

The quality of information in class reports varies in quality and quantity before the early 1880s. At this point they began to assume a more or less standardized format. This format seems to have been embraced by both Harvard and Yale classes.

This study used 25th-reunion (Yale) or sixth-reunion (Harvard) reports for accounts of board memberships (or "offices held," as Harvard's reports have it). These volumes caught men in their early forties—at the peak of their careers—giving the richest possible panorama of their activities. Club, team, and publication participation was tracked through reports published in the graduation year.

The reader will note my preference for the term "alumni" rather than "graduates." This is because my samples include not only graduates but also members of classes who left before graduation but were nonetheless acknowledged by class publications as members.

Notes

1. Tocqueville, in *Democracy in America* (New York: Vintage Books, 1835), I: 63, declares that New England town meetings "are to liberty what primary schools are to science; they bring it within people's reach, they teach men how to use and enjoy it." It is no less accurate to say that New Englanders' voluntary associations served a similar function.
2. Joseph S. Davis, *Essays in the Earlier History of American Corporations* (Cambridge: Harvard University Press, 1917), 1:349.
3. Thomas Wentworth Higginson, *Harvard Memorial Biographies* (Cambridge: Sever and Francis, 1866), I: iv–v.
4. Ibid., v.
5. Ibid., v–vi.
6. Charles W. Eliot, "The New Education," *Atlantic Monthly* 23 (February 1869): 203.
7. Ibid., 202.
8. Hamilton Andrews Hill, *Memoir of Abbott Lawrence* (Boston: Little, Brown, 1884), 13. State Street was Boston's financial center—its equivalent of New York's Wall Street.
9. The authoritative compendium on Yale alumni's Civil War service, Ellsworth Eliot Jr.'s *Yale in the Civil War* (New Haven: Yale University Press and London, Oxford University Press, 1932), did not appear until nearly 80 years after the end of the war.
10. The actual title of the Yale Report of 1828 is *Reports on the Course of Instruction in Yale College; by a Committee of the Corporation, and the Academical Faculty* (New Haven: Hezekiah Howe, Printer, 1828).
11. Ibid., 23.
12. Ibid., 35.
13. Eliot, "New Education," 202.
14. Ibid., 366.
15. Herbert Croly, *The Promise of American Life* (New York: Macmillan, 1909), 439.
16. Charles W. Eliot, "Inaugural Address as President of Harvard College, October 19, 1869," in Eliot, *Educational Reform: Essays and Addresses* (New York: Century, 1898), 12–13.
17. Samuel Eliot Morison, *Three Centuries of Harvard, 1636–1936* (Cambridge: Harvard University Press, 1936), 420.
18. Ibid., 421.
19. On this, see Leonard Bacon, *The Christian Doctrine of Stewardship in Respect of Property* (New Haven: Nathan Whiting, Printer, 1832). Bacon, a member of Yale's faculty and pastor of New Haven's venerable Center Church, was a pioneer theorist of voluntary associations. In this influential sermon, he called on Christians to regard their occupations as ministries and associations as vehicles for the "the business of doing good."
20. In a later essay, Bacon suggested that participation on governing boards offered invaluable opportunities for spiritual development. On this, see Leonard Bacon, "Responsibility in

the Management of Societies," *The New Englander* 5, no. 1 (1847), 28–41. This was the first serious study of board governance ever written.

21. For an account of the laicization of governance at Harvard and Yale, see Peter Dobkin Hall, "'Noah Porter writ large': Reflections on the Modernization of American Education and Its Critics, 1866–1916," in *The American College in the Nineteenth Century,* ed. Roger L. Geiger (Nashville: Vanderbilt University Press, 2000), 196–220.
22. William Walter Phelps, "Speech of W.W. Phelps," *The College Courant* (July 23, 1870), 71–72.
23. Noah Porter, *American Colleges and the American Public* (New Haven: Charles C. Chatfield, 1870), 289.
24. Ibid., 232.
25. Lyman Hotchkiss Bagg, *Four Years at Yale* (New Haven: Charles C. Chatfield, 1871), 702.
26. Loomis Havemeyer, *"Go to your room": A Story of Undergraduate Societies and Fraternities at Yale* (New Haven: privately published, 1960).
27. College faculties, however, retained the power to rule on the existence of student organizations. Harvard banned national fraternity chapters in the 1850s. Yale banned the sophomore societies in 1900.
28. The standardization of secondary school curricula was driven, in turn, by the adoption of standardized admissions examinations—an innovation championed by Harvard's Charles W. Eliot. the College Board, which Eliot helped to found, had produced and was administering standardized tests nationally by the turn of the century.
29. H. S. Durand and Carl Wilhelm. "Bright College Years" (1881). http://www.yale.edu/yaleband/ypmb/music/yale.html.
30. I use the term "alumni" to include both graduates and nongraduates. Although dropouts were not listed in the college's alumni directories or necrologies, their biographies were included in Harvard and Yale class books. The data used in this study include both graduates and nongraduates.
31. On the geography of American philanthropy, see William G. Bowen et al., *The Charitable Nonprofits: An Analysis of Institutional Dynamics and Characteristics* (San Francisco: Jossey-Bass, 1994). *See also* Peter Dobkin Hall, "A Historical Overview of Philanthropy, Voluntary Associations, and Nonprofit Organizations in the United States, 1600–2000," in *The Nonprofit Sector: A Research Handbook,* 2nd edition, ed. Richard Steinberg and Walter W. Powell (New Haven: Yale University Press, 2006).
32. Rikki Abzug and Jeffrey S. Simonoff, *Nonprofit Trusteeship in Different Contexts* (Aldershot: Ashgate, 2004), 92.
33. According to George W. Pierson, in 1940 Yale and Harvard alumni comprised 1.62 percent of the college educated population over 25. By 1975, they comprised only 0.92 percent. See Pierson, *A Yale Book of Numbers: Historical Statistics of the College and University, 1701–1976* (New Haven: Yale University Press, 1976), 54.
34. Theda Skocpol, "How Americans Became Civic," in *Civic Engagement in American Democracy,* ed. Theda Skocpol and Morris Fiorina (Washington: Brookings Institution Press, 1999), 54.
35. Henry Seidel Canby, *Alma Mater: The Gothic Age of the American College* (New York: Farrar & Rinehart, 1936), 32.
36. Ibid., 37–38.
37. Ibid., 49–51.
38. Ibid., 36.
39. On the evolution of campuses, see Paul Venable Turner, *Campus: An American Planning Tradition* (New York: Architectural History Foundation and Cambridge, MIT Press, 1984). On Harvard's campus, see Bainbridge Bunting, *Harvard: An Architectural History* (Cambridge: Belknap Press of Harvard University Press, 1985); and Douglass Shand-Tucci, *Harvard University: The Campus Guide* (New York: Princeton Architectural Press, 2001). On Yale, see Vincent Scully et al., *Yale in New Haven: Architecture and Urbanism* (New Haven: Yale University Press, 2004); Patrick L. Pennell, *Yale University: The Campus Guide* (New York: Princeton Architectural Press, 1999); and Aaron Betsky, *James Gamble Rogers and the Architecture of Pragmatism,* ed. David G. De Long (New York: Architectural History Foundation and Cambridge, MIT Press, 1994).
40. Bliss Perry, *Life and Letters of Henry Lee Higginson* (Boston: Atlantic Monthly Press, 1921), 329.
41. Shand-Tucci, *Harvard University,* 158.
42. Ibid., 160.

43. Perry, *Life and Letters,* 532.
44. Ibid., 535.
45. Ibid., 536.
46. Bunting, *Harvard,* 84.
47. Perry, *Life and Letters,* 354.
48. Ibid., 354.
49. John Daniels, Reginald Foster, and Ralph Sanger, eds., *The Harvard Year Book* (Cambridge: Harvard University, 1904), 92–98. *See also* William Garrott Brown, ed., *Official Guide to Harvard University* (Cambridge: Harvard University Press, 1903).
50. For a valuable account of the motives driving the organization of alumni clubs, see Ormande de Kay, *From the Age That Is Past: Harvard Club of New York City, a History* (New York: The Club, 1994). *See also* Association of Harvard Clubs, *Handbook for Harvard Clubs* (Garden City, NY: Doubleday, Page, 1924).
51. On this, see Havemeyer, *"Go to your room,"* 101-105.
52. Although fraternities and other social organizations for underclassmen had disappeared at both Harvard and Yale by 1950, Harvard's final clubs and Yale's senior societies survived, though greatly diminished in influence and notoriety. Other elite organizations also survived, including the college daily newspapers (the *Crimson* and the *Yale Daily News)* and such musical organizations as the Whiffenpoofs and the Pierian Sodality.
53. George W. Pierson, *The Education of American Leaders: Comparative Contributions of U.S. Colleges and Universities* (New York: Praeger, 1969), 21, 89, 157.
54. Abzug and Siminoff, *Nonprofit Trusteeship,* 92.
55. Max Weber argued persuasively that the triumph of the modern economic order was a by-product of religious belief and practice, and showed how specialization, professionalism, and bureaucracy became fundamental organizing characteristics of all modern institutions. Building on Weber, Talcott Parsons argued that these universalistic institutions coexisted with—and were dependent on—particularistic ties of kinship, friendship, and loyalty. More recently, Robert Putnam and Theda Skocpol have explored the interrelationships of social networks and formal organizations: Putnam argues that the efficacy of formal institutions of government and commerce depend on trust, reciprocity, and interpersonal networks; Skocpol shows how membership organizations gave Americans the values, skills, and connections that facilitated modern politics and government. See Robert D. Putnam, *Making Democracy Work: Civic Traditions in Modern Italy* (Princeton: Princeton University Press, 1993); and Theda Skocpol,*Diminished Democracy: From Membership to Management in American Civic Life* (Norman: University of Oklahoma Press, 2003).
56. Alfred D. Chandler Jr., *The Visible Hand: The Managerial Revolution in American Business* (Cambridge: Harvard University Press, 1977).
57. Melissa Middleton, "Nonprofit Boards of Directors: Beyond the Governance Function," in *The Nonprofit Sector: A Research Handbook,* ed. W. W. Powell (New Haven: Yale University Press, 1987), 143.
58. J. Allen Whitt and Mark S. Mizruchi, "The Local Inner Circle," *Journal of Political and Military Sociology* (1986): 14 (Spring), 115–25.

Part III

The Public Sphere

11

Ordering the Social Sphere: Public Art and Boston's Bourgeoisie

Julia B. Rosenbaum

In the fall of 1896, the well-respected architect Charles F. McKim made one last addition to his recently completed Boston Public Library. He donated a bronze statue for the interior courtyard fountain, and unwittingly he set off a major civic battle. For more than a year, controversy raged as opponents fought to expel the statue from the city and supporters fought just as ardently to keep it. Denounced as "debauched," "vice-ridden," a memorial to "reckless abandon" and "the worst type of harlotry," McKim's gift was a three-quarter life-size female nude in mid-skip holding a cluster of grapes in one hand and a young child in the other (fig. 11.1). McKim had envisioned it as the perfect complement to his Renaissance, palazzo-style building. Set on a pedestal in the courtyard pool, the work would unify architectural structure and open space (fig. 11.2). But within a year, the statue was banned from Boston and McKim's artistic vision abandoned. This essay addresses how a seemingly innocuous bronze statue succeeded so effectively in not just dividing Boston society but galvanizing class interests.

By November, debate among citizens over Frederick MacMonnies's *Bacchante and Infant Faun* had reached fever pitch. One incensed opponent in a public talk entitled "Treason in the Boston Public Library" went so far as to accuse library trustees, who defended the statue, of treason to purity and treason to the city as well as "treason to Almighty God."[1] In their turn, McKim, library trustees, and supporters regarded such accusations as reactionary and uninformed. In his journal, Thomas Sullivan, a Boston playwright, best summed up thc situation brewing in Boston:

> Both cats have their backs well up, and the fur is likely to fly before the spring comes . . . and we [Sullivan and other supporters] hope to overwhelm the howling dervishes by our numbers, if not by rational arguments. Against the group are arrayed President Eliot, H.U. [Harvard University], Professor Norton, Robert Grant, Barrett Wendell, and others, who regard it as 'a menace to the Commonwealth.' Their allies, the sensational clergy, go a few steps further, and declare that this begins a righteous crusade against the intolerable indecencies of the antique in the Art Museum. Verily, impropriety makes strange bedfellows![2]

Through the winter and spring of 1897, local citizens organized meetings for and against the statue, petitions and counter petitions were filed, and news-papers in Boston and in cities across the country took up positions on the subject. Articles on the latest developments in the uproar appeared regularly in papers from Los Angeles to Milwaukee to Philadelphia.

Figure 11.1 Frederick MacMonnies (1863–1937). *Bacchante and Infant Faun,* 1893. Gift of Charles F. McKim, 1897 (97.19) The Metropolitan Museum of Art, New York, NY, U.S.A.

Figure 11.2 Photographer unknown, *Bacchante* Installed in Courtyard Pool, 1896. Courtesy of the Boston Public Library, Print Department.

In the course of these exchanges, MacMonnies's statue assumed two distinct personalities. For the president of the library trustees, the *Bacchante* was "simply glorious, a beautiful work of art." Others similarly described the statue as an innocent expression of grace and joy. But while supporters praised the *Bacchante* for its vital image of life and delighted in what McKim called the "spirit of joyousness and spontaneity," opponents denounced the statue as a wanton woman, "unclothed, unquiet, and vile." In the words of one expert appointed by the Boston Art Commission, the work portrayed no innocent joy but only "a drunken revel of debased civilization."[3] Critics personified the statue so frequently she even acquired a voice of her own. A New York paper imagined hearing the *Bacchante*'s poetic lament: "Although I have a joyous air / I'm really feeling sad; / When I am so divinely fair / How can they call me bad?"[4]

Ultimately, MacMonnies's statue did not find a home in Boston, despite the groundswell of popular support and the endorsement of the library's trustees and later the Boston Art Commission. Back in July 1896, when McKim had first offered the work as a gift, the library's trustees had enthusiastically accepted. But their acceptance could only be conditional, because all public works of art had to win the approval of the city's art commission. Following procedure, the trustees later that summer submitted a smaller model of the *Bacchante* to the commission for evaluation. At first, the commission voted against the statue after conferring with a committee of experts. Then, the commission reversed itself and accepted the work, prompting those opposed to the *Bacchante* to launch a more vehement and concerted opposition. Nearly a year later in June 1897, after months of bitter debate, the commission moved once again to reject the *Bacchante*. Charles McKim reported to a colleague that "petitions were circulated by a certain element in the [Boston] community, which chose to find in Macmonnaies' [sic] masterpiece that which neither the Trustees nor the Art Commission were able to discover, and which Macmonnaies never intended."[5] Chagrined and dismayed by the references to the statue's unsuitability and degeneracy, McKim took back the statue to end the controversy and spare the library and its trustees any further humiliation. In June he offered it to the Metropolitan Museum of Art in New York City—which immediately accepted.

What so powerfully disturbed particular Boston citizens about the *Bacchante* and gave common cause to social groups that otherwise had little to do with one another? Many critics, especially those in other cities, ascribed the commotion to Boston prudery and primness, fodder for endless ridicule of the city (critics' own apprehensions about the public display of nudity no doubt fanning the flames). As the *New York Sun* put it, "The people there [in Boston] do not believe that such trifling with the terrible gravity of life as the Bacchante delighted in is proper. They don't do it themselves, and they object to anybody's doing it or having done it." Modern scholars have also tended to regard the incident as a less enlightened moment in Boston's relationship with the arts.[6]

But squeamishness over nudity or overzealous sobriety cannot fully explain the explosive battle over the *Bacchante*. What happened in Boston at the end of 1896 and into 1897 exposes fundamental issues about class-consciousness and the organization of public space in the late nineteenth century, and it particularly speaks to a move on the part of Boston's bourgeoisie (an Anglo-Saxon, Protestant elite) to consolidate its interests and affirm power. Its opposition to the statue, along with protests by anti-vice and religious organizations (typically of middle- and upper-middle-class membership), suggests deep anxiety about shifting social hierarchies and changing demographics within the city. Both groups fought the sculpture not so much because they found it offensive as because they feared its potential corrupting power over others; it would become a catalyst to social anarchy. Behind a seemingly decorative *Bacchante* lurked a basic question: Whose civic values would shape public life?

In proposing to place the statue in such a prominent public building as the city's library, McKim inadvertently thrust MacMonnies's *Bacchante* into the center of contemporary concerns about class and cultural authority, not to mention the nature of women's roles and leisure activities. Drunken nude or bronze goddess—such divergent interpretations fit into a larger context of class and social conflicts in late-nineteenth-century America. As the *Bacchante* story suggests, public art brought class and ethnic struggles into the open and played a pivotal role in mobilizing citizens around perceived social and political issues.

Joyous Nymph or Wanton Woman?

From the beginning, McKim thought he had presented to the city of Boston a splendid gift. Not only had the *Bacchante* been well received upon its completion in 1893, but also MacMonnies himself had earned by the turn of the century numerous awards and commissions, both in Paris where he had studied and worked and in the United States. One of his most renowned projects was the *Barge of State* fountain, the sculptural centerpiece at the Chicago World's Fair of 1893. When McKim received the statue from Frederick MacMonnies—a thank you for the architect's generosity in helping finance the young sculptor's first study trip to Paris back in 1884—he thought of his newly constructed library building. He had planned a courtyard fountain as a memorial to his recently deceased wife, and the *Bacchante* not only seemed ideal for the setting but also had garnered international acclaim.

When the statue first went on display in Paris at the Salon of 1894, artists and audiences on both sides of the Atlantic found much to applaud. The French government indeed contacted the sculptor about purchasing it for the Luxembourg Museum—a singular honor for an American artist. (Having already promised the statue to McKim in June, MacMonnies ended up making a replica for the Luxembourg.) Encouraged perhaps by the reception in France, MacMonnies began producing reductions of the *Bacchante* in 1895, which were exhibited and sold in the United States. American art critic Royal Cortissoz singled out the statuette for praise, declaring after a New York showing: "It is deft, compact, a little triumph of concision, yet it has all the expansive grace, all the intimations of endless movement, which belong to a dancing figure."[7]

Two of the United States' most illustrious sculptors, Daniel Chester French and Augustus Saint-Gaudens, greatly admired the statue. Saint-Gaudens, writing to a French friend after seeing the *Bacchante* (presumably one of the reductions exhibited in New York), spoke of the deep impression that it had made on him and proclaimed it a masterpiece, "the *dernier mot* of grace and life. No one had ever done better. No one will ever do better."[8] Solicited by the Boston Art Commission for their expert opinions less than two years later, Saint-Gaudens and French both sent letters of support in the summer of 1896. They wrote again in the fall after the Art Commission's initial rejection of the statue, expressing dismay at the decision and urging reconsideration. They emphasized that the name "bacchante" and its allusion to Greek mythology and the god Bacchus should not prejudice the commission.[9]

In employing a mythological theme, MacMonnies' statue drew on works by nineteenth-century French sculptors. To demonstrate the Bacchante's distinguished genealogy, Saint-Gaudens had specifically mentioned in his June letter to the commission a series of Pompeiian bronzes by various artists. He had pointed out that the *Bacchante and Infant Faun* echoed, for example, the pose of Hippolyte-Alexandre Julien Moulin's *A Lucky Find at Pompeii*, which won a medal at the Salon of 1864, and the *Hunting Nymph* (1884), exhibited in 1884, 1885, and 1888, by Jean Alexandre Falguière, one of MacMonnies' teachers in Paris.[10]

Like Moulin and Falguière, MacMonnies avoided a strictly columnar or vertical composition in favor of a more open and lively one with the extension of limbs and counterpoint balance; the *Bacchante*, on tiptoe, arches slightly backward and to the side, left leg bent, right arm outstretched. Like Falguière, MacMonnies also explored mythological subjects in his work; his *Diana* won him an honorable mention at the Salon of 1889. In the 1890s, he executed not only *Bacchante and Infant Faun* but also *Pan of Rohallion*, *Running Cupid*, and *Young Faun with Heron*, a laughing young boy wrestling a large heron that MacMonnies made for Joseph Choate's estate in Stockbridge, Massachusetts, and showed in the salon of 1890. In their emphasis on movement and playfulness, these works hearkened back to a French tradition of lighthearted sculptural figures such as those with a fisher-boy theme by François Rude, François-Joseph Duret, and Jean-Baptiste Carpeaux.

It was the vitality of the work that struck advocates of the *Bacchante* as its great charm, the feature that made it a highly decorative and desirable addition to the courtyard of the Boston Public Library. As one critic commented, McKim and MacMonnies "will give Boston one of the few admirable examples of imaginative sculpture in public places in America."[11] Although the courtyard was shielded from the street, large windows on the upper floors of the library looked out onto the grassy inner sanctum. Visitors could also stroll into the courtyard either directly from the carriage entrance on Boylston Street or through the Grand Staircase via the Dartmouth Street doors to stretch their legs, relax, read, and enjoy the outdoor pool and fountain.

Artists and critics were not alone in their appreciation. Approval for the *Bacchante* ran high among Boston citizens in general. A local poll showed majority acceptance, and after the statue went on public display at the library in November 1896, the local papers, from the *Boston Evening Transcript* to the *Boston Herald* and the *Boston Post*, all reported that among the great number of viewers nobody appeared to be offended. "'Not so bad after all!' sighed the crowd rather disappointedly," one reporter for the *Boston Record* wrote. As the *Herald* noted, many who came "prepared to see a figure that was inappropriate to the courtyard of the Public Library were struck by its beauty and fitness for the fountain."[12] Viewers admired the statue as a joyous image of life, and many demanded that democratic procedures should determine the fate of MacMonnies' nymph; if the majority of Boston citizens approved, then the sculpture should stay.[13] But once the Art Commission voted to accept the statue, those against it launched an all-out attack, seeing the *Bacchante* as nothing less than "a menace to the Commonwealth."

Leading the charge was a formidable set of Boston figures, among them Harvard President Charles W. Eliot, Harvard professors and critics Barrett Wendell and Charles Eliot Norton, and Judge Robert Grant. All were men of impeccable bourgeois status, perfect examples of Boston Brahmins—a relatively homogenous, Anglo-Saxon, Protestant elite that had perpetuated itself over generations through family ties, old money, and multi-faceted involvement in the political and cultural institutions of the city. By the late nineteenth century, Harvard University was a bastion of Brahmin power. Of 40 individuals identified as *the* Brahmin leaders of the era by historians, at least 93 percent held Harvard degrees.[14] The elevated social and economic status the group above distinguished them from well-known Boston citizens who firmly registered their support of the *Bacchante*, such as Boston's former mayor, Frederick O. Prince, Edward Robinson, a curator at the Boston Museum of Fine Arts, Francis A. Walker, the president of the Massachusetts Institute of Technology, and the playwright Thomas Sullivan, for example.[15]

Like the other major anti-*Bacchante* bloc, the religious and anti-vice organizations such as the Watch and Ward Society and the Women's Christian Temperance Union, Boston's outspoken Brahmin bourgeoisie held fast to the conviction that the act of looking had the power to transform human behavior. Both sets of opponents believed in the ennobling and moral influences of art, but where the religious and anti-vice organizations focused more on concerns about morality and intemperance, the language of Boston's most prominent points to anxiety, above all, about the preservation of class distinction and social order.

To them MacMonnies' *Bacchante* stood out as singularly inappropriate and unsuitable for the library. Nudity, Barrett Wendell and other leading Brahmins insisted, was not the problem. What was objectionable about the *Bacchante,* in the words of Robert Grant, was "the artistic unworthiness of the entire composition as a keynote to the [library]—a place in an educational sense sacred and which should be reserved for a work of art intrinsically noble."[16] This notion of "want of sympathy," or element of aesthetic disruption, had a thoroughly social dimension. Charles Eliot Norton suggested a clear link between aesthetically inappropriate and dangerous to the community when he warned that "to a public who look not always from an artistic standpoint, more harm is apt to be worked than good."[17] Such statements hinged on the certitude that what people saw in a work of art had the power to affect their behavior—for better, or, in the Bacchante's case, for worse. From this perspective, uplifting visual models not only reinforced but were also required by the educational mission of a public library, a mission that for Norton and his circle confirmed and perpetuated clear class distinctions and hierarchies.

Public Space/Public Interests

By the late nineteenth century, public libraries were heralded as an instrument for social control and reform. Members of the public library movement, underway since 1876, looked to this public venue as a potential solution to pressing social problems such as alcoholism, penury, and the assimilation of diverse ethnic groups. Stocked with collections of good reading materials and fine art, libraries provided patrons with resources to improve themselves, to become better, more responsible citizens. A prominent librarian summed up this view: "Free corn in old Rome bribed a mob and kept it passive. By free books and what goes with them in modern America we mean to erase the mob from existence."[18] For library proponents and Boston Brahmins, the "public" in public institution did not imply an open place in which to congregate or bring together heterogeneous groups as we might think of such a site today. What mattered was not fulfilling an individual desire but absorbing prescribed communal values (in this case determined by a political and social elite).

Spurred by a belief in public libraries to mold an edifying civic culture—or, as art historian Sally Promey has noted in her study of the library's John Singer Sargent murals, to promote "enlightened" democracy through education—Boston city officials in the late 1880s had drawn up plans for a grand, new building.[19] Their efforts resulted not only in one of the largest public libraries in the country but also in an impressive union of architecture, painting, and sculpture: an environment to inspire both heart and mind (fig 11.3). The inscription above the main entrance on the Dartmouth Street side, which read "The Public Library of the City of Boston Built by the People and Dedicated to the Advancement of Learning," beckoned visitors, who entered the library through massive bronze portals that opened onto a grand marble staircase guarded by two sculpted lions. An imposing, barrel-vaulted reading room—218 feet long, 42 feet wide, and 50 feet high—served library patrons. Throughout the building, elaborate mural cycles by some of the era's most prominent artists decorated the walls and ceilings. Sargent, for example, depicted the

Figure 11.3 Baldwin Coolidge, Boston Public Library, c.1896. Courtesy of the Boston Public Library, Print Department.

history of religion in the vaulted hall of the third-floor gallery, while the legend of the Holy Grail by Edwin A. Abbey ornamented the Book Delivery Room. The French painter Puvis de Chavannes illustrated the realms of human knowledge along the walls of the Grand Staircase.

In its union of texts and images, the library was meant to offer a complete aesthetic and uplifting experience. Frederick M. Crunden, an active member and past president of the American Library Association, elaborated on the beneficial role of a library building: "Is not its mere beholding educative and inspiring? Can the thousands who see it every month fail to imbibe a truer taste for beauty? And is not a pervading love of beauty one of the corner stones of civic improvement?"[20] When the new Boston Public Library opened its doors in 1895, New York art critic Mariana Van Rensselaer described it as a "civic monument," and of the courtyard in particular, she wrote that it was "a place owned by the public of a great city, where hours or even moments of repose or study will be doubly fruitful, feeding the most careless or unconscious eye with the food of high artistic loveliness?"[21] Dubbed a "palace for the people," the library could equally have been termed a temple of refinement, a secular counterpart to the church.

The Boston Public Library was not alone in its cultural mission. A network of bourgeois institutions dedicated to the arts had emerged within the city. Beginning in the 1870s, in response to popular political assaults on Brahmin institutions and the flow of immigrants (with their seemingly improper social customs) into Boston, the city's elite had attempted to strengthen itself by erecting cultural barriers. Unlike the bourgeoisie in New York and Philadelphia, which concentrated less of their money and effort on cultural enterprises, Boston leaders, as sociologist Paul DiMaggio has written, "retreated from the public sector to found a system of nonprofit organizations that permitted them to maintain some control over the community even as they lost their command of its political institutions."[22] Both the Boston Museum of Fine Arts and the Boston Symphony, for example, were founded in this period. While the public library fit into this network of bourgeois social structures, it specifically reached out to a lower-class constituency. The institution's backers had high hopes that the library would counter what they perceived as the dangerous influence of establishments such as the saloon. Concerns about the use of alcohol and leisure time indeed made the Bacchante controversy all the more explosive.

In the bourgeois world of the late nineteenth century, the library and the saloon represented opposing moral and social poles. Associated with alcohol and often called the "workingmen's club," the saloon was essentially a stronghold for immigrant as well as lower-class culture. By the 1890s, temperance groups such as the Women's Christian Temperance Union, Boston's Citizens' Law and Order League, founded in the 1880s, and the Anti-Saloon League, which came into force in the mid-1890s, launched a frontal attack on places of drink, using the law to regulate alcohol consumption and hours of business. Battles over the saloon's existence, according to historian Roy Rosenzweig, "often took on aspects of a 'class war' over the recreational world of the industrial working class."[23] Although saloons provided certain amenities such as socializing space that were not readily available elsewhere in public, from a temperance perspective, saloons meant alcohol, and alcohol was a scourge. Ideals espoused by temperance organizations about leisure time and family life clashed with the circumstances of immigrant life and lower-class uses of urban areas.

For proponents, libraries offered social comforts but without the alcohol. In the civilizing space of the public library, patrons imbibed culture, not booze. That libraries and bars met the same social needs and could be easily exchanged, and would be by those given the choice, was presumed. Crunden, the passionate spokesman for the library association, explicitly described the library's role as antidote to the saloon: "It is fair to assume," he wrote, "that saloons and resorts of a demoralizing character . . . are nightly frequented by men and boys who would go to a free reading room, if one was found in the neighborhood. Prohibition will not do: substitution is the true remedy."[24] Libraries, from this perspective, extended the work of public schools. They assumed the role of literary shepherd, guiding their flock to the wholesome pastures of the written word. The library, envisioned as a structure of enlightenment, and the saloon, a site of iniquity, thus stood at opposite ends of the cultural spectrum.

While the grapes the *Bacchante* holds, her pose, and her title do not necessarily convey drunkenness or licentiousness, the image, as a whole, does not strongly counter such associations. The statue, in the eyes of temperance unions, left too much open to individual interpretation, particularly the role of women. Organizations such as the Women's Christian Temperance Union saw women as defending one of the bastions of moral society, the home, and viewed the abuse of alcohol as a serious threat. Drinking squandered precious family funds and disrupted family relationships in part by encouraging greater sexual freedom. The Women's Christian Temperance Union consequently centered its temperance activities on "home values," or more generally what it called the "white life." An attempt to fortify women's authority both inside and outside the home, living the white life meant, as historian Barbara Epstein has noted, "elevating the position of women by placing restraints on sexuality, supposedly a primarily male interest, and valorizing the moral role of women in family and society."[25]

The statue's lighthearted air thus strained against Victorian notions of public female behavior, according to which a good woman was modest and responsible. Chavannes's partially nude figure of *Chemistry*, painted in the grand stairwell of the library, for example, constituted a traditional and acceptable display of the female form: nudity cloaked by allegorical context. An image of civilized society, she represents rational, scientific endeavor and humankind's successful efforts to domesticate natural forces. The deployment of the figure—solid, columnar, and balanced—underscores that control. This sense of discipline was equally true for other nude statues, like those of Venus, which graced the library halls. A copy of Venus de Medici, prominently placed in a corridor to the Children's Room, had a contained pose: feet together, arms modestly placed before her body, gaze averted.

By contrast, MacMonnies' *Bacchante* portrays female nudity without the shield of edifying allegory. There is no pretense toward modesty or restraint; her open arms, her wide grin, and her head thrown back express pure delight. The lively composition and MacMonnies' naturalistic rendering of her head further distance the statue from the safe haven of the idealized world. Not only does she sport a loose, unstyled hairdo, but her face is rendered realistically, so much so that newspapers at the time consumed much ink speculating about the identity of the model. Free-spirited and exuberant in her nakedness, the *Bacchante* touched nerves made raw not only by shifting attitudes toward the use of alcohol but also by changing women's roles. In short, to install the statue in the courtyard would have meant for some the dissolution of class structure and civic order. An article in the *Boston Globe* expressed it most bluntly: "Vices which fill our prisons should not be exalted in our library."[26]

Civic Order and Class Distinctions

In challenging mores, the *Bacchante* threatened to collapse boundaries between elite and mass purviews. An incident involving the Boston Public Library before its move to the new building in 1895 illuminates the reliance of Boston citizens on class codes and their sensitivity to social position. Several local papers released a story in 1892 that the library was not planning to arrange for a separate space for the collection of popular books and magazines housed in the old library's "Lower Hall." The *Boston Globe* wrote of the "indignities" that the Lower Hall readers—a lower-class constituency—would suffer if they had to go to "the [new] enormous Bates Hall along with everyone else, and rub elbows with the Beacon st. [sic] swell, the teacher, and all varying classes of people who are now accommodated in the [old] Bates Hall, upstairs, and are away from the plain people, who are glad to avail themselves of the 'lower hall."[27]

Although library officials went ahead with the plans for one hall, the newspaper coverage underscores the role that public space played in maintaining class distinctions. The Brahmin bourgeoisie's charge of inappropriateness against the *Bacchante* registered fears about the potential upending of the city's social stratification and specifically the absorption of lower class and, by extension, immigrant groups such as the Irish into Boston society. Associated as they often were with drunkenness and crime, the immigrant working class appeared to constitute a social powder keg. At the height of the *Bacchante* controversy, for example, the *Boston Evening Transcript* ran an article arguing for a correlation between alcohol consumption and crime, pauperism, and insanity. In listing the statistics for each category, the report broke down figures into "citizen born" and "alien"; percentages ran significantly higher for the latter.[28]

The immigrant group that appeared to pose the greatest threat to the social hierarchy was the Irish. Middle-class and bourgeois perceptions of them focused on their poverty and the supposed inability of even American-born Irish to be productive. Magazines such as *Atlantic Monthly* and *Century Magazine*, for instance, circulated reports about the degeneracy of second-generation immigrants. Catholic and culturally distinct, the Irish had started arriving in Boston in the 1840s; by 1895, estimates put the Irish population in the city at 60 percent.[29] The Irish had increasingly exercised their electoral muscle, challenging the political hegemony of Boston's elite. In 1884, for example, for the first time, an Irishman became mayor; from 1900 on, the Irish would consistently control the mayoralty. In the face of their move into political life, many of Boston's Anglo-Saxon, Protestant bourgeoisie felt themselves and the values they believed in under assault by an alien people.

The remarks of *Bacchante* opponent Charles Eliot Norton just after the statue's expulsion reveals the level of tension and unease particularly among Boston's Brahmins. Norton declared in an 1897 letter, "I fancy that there has never been a community on a higher and pleasanter level than that of New England during the first thirty years of this century, before the coming in of Jacksonian Democracy, and the invasion of the Irish."[30] For many of Boston's bourgeoisie, the Irish continued to be viewed as outsiders, dangerous and impossible to control or assimilate.

A Boston newspaper cartoon, entitled "A Suggestion for a Pedestal for the Bacchante," suggests how deeply the debate over the statue and its placement into public space tapped into contemporary class and ethnic conflicts. Although ambiguous in its stance toward MacMonnies' statue, the cartoon categorized types of alcohol to set up a clear visual hierarchy. Grouped with the harder alcohols at the bottom of the pedestal is Irish whiskey. Four books occupy the middle tier. Identified by titles on their spines such as *Vintner's Guide* and *The Art of Brewing*, they suggest a middle class with more refined taste. A layer of lush grape leaves, a reference perhaps to a natural order, leads to the top of the pedestal. Above stands the *Bacchante* herself holding a cluster of grapes, the union of art and discriminating taste that could be interpreted as representing a cultivated and sophisticated bourgeoisie.

In the climate of 1896—a time of deepening recession, labor unrest, the rise of a populist movement in the West, and agitation for a silver standard that galvanized the presidential election debates that year—signs of unconventional behavior and nontraditional values proved especially intimidating. For a Brahmin bourgeoisie, an unsophisticated public might see in an officially sanctioned sculpture that broke the bounds of convention and freed inhibition a license for irregular behavior. Another cartoon, this one from the *Boston Journal* in November 1896, entitled "Bacchante Skip Will Be the Rage: The Lame, the Halt and the Blind Will Make This Their Fad Now That the Statue Has Been Accepted," illustrates the possible chaos and loss of control that the statue could inspire (fig. 11.4). A crudely drawn *Bacchante* lurks in the left corner of the cartoon. Imitating her pose, a cross section of Boston citizens prance down the street, arms thrown above their heads, legs kicked out in front of them. Even the animal kingdom gets mixed up in the potential anarchy, as the little dog in the drawing suggests.

To immortalize in bronze and enshrine in a public space—a public library, no less—a statue that the bourgeoisie saw as legitimating civic disorder was tantamount to backing that class's own demise. Impelled to fight against the statue, Boston's prominent fastened on the question of suitability. By establishing themselves

The Lame, the Halt and the Blind Will Mace This Their Fad Now That the Statue Has Been Accepted.

Figure 11.4 "Bacchante Skip Will Be the Rage: The Lame, the Halt, and the Blind Will Make This Their Fad Now That the Statue Has Been Accepted," cartoon from the *Boston Journal* (18 November 1896). Reproduced in Walter Whitehill, "The Vicissitudes of the *Bacchante* in Boston," *New England Quarterly* 27 (December 1954).

as purveyors of good taste, they staked out cultural ground. From their position, the *Bacchante,* while perhaps artistic, failed as a model of social order and behavior.

The *Bacchante* incident speaks to ways of seeing and the mediation through art of social tensions. Opponents described the statue as intoxicated, but sympathetic viewers, including a library janitor who had helped to install the statue, saw nothing of the kind. A columnist who was favorably inclined toward the statue, for example, pointed out a fallacy in the argument of the opposition: "No one who has made the slightest study of the outward symptoms of inebriety could charge this Bacchante, who is standing on the tip of one toe and carrying a baby safely and comfortably on one shoulder, of being under the influence of the bunch of grapes which she dangles over the baby's mouth."[31]

The conflicting visions of MacMonnies' statue as "wanton woman" or "joyous nymph" emphasize the role that public space played in regulating social and particularly class interaction. The art that shaped such space participated in that process. In the fall of 1896, opponents saw danger stalking in the form of a bronze Bacchante. The efforts by both a Brahmin bourgeoisie and temperance and anti-vice groups to consolidate their own social position, as well as prescribe a cultural model for alien, lower-class groups, made issues of appropriateness and abstinence—and by extension the *Bacchante* itself—symbolically loaded. Alone, the crusade organizations might not have been enough to banish MacMonnies' statue. But the union of moral mission and social authority translated into clout. By the summer of 1897, enough pressure had been exerted to convince McKim to relinquish his vision for the courtyard fountain. Perhaps the most telling event of the *Bacchante* debacle is a coda to the uproar. Several years later, a Boston collector purchased a bronze replica of the statue and presented it to the Boston Museum of Fine Arts. No one raised the slightest fuss. In the confines of an elite institution, dedicated to artistic taste and high culture, the *Bacchante*'s blissful abandon could cause no harm.

Brahmin leaders, like the anti-vice groups, sought to mold a public in their own image, and they turned to art and culture to transmit and inculcate the values they esteemed. The expulsion of the MacMonnies' *Bacchante* marked a small victory in a campaign waged by Boston's bourgeoisie stretching back to the 1870s to resist the increasing transformation of public life. As Barrett Wendell, one of the social elite, commented several years after the incident, "[T]he future of our New England must depend on the standards of culture which we maintain and preserve here. The College, the Institute, the Library, the Orchestra . . . are the real bases of our strength and dignity in the years to come."[32] With the rejection of the statue in 1897, Wendell could claim that, for the moment those standards had been preserved. But the lead of a social elite presumed, of course, a people compliant and desiring guidance. By the end of the late nineteenth century, patrician dominance was giving way to mass politics and competing claims to cultural expression. MacMonnies' *Bacchante* had arrived in the city just as the terms of "the public" were being challenged and reconstituted.

After the *Bacchante* debacle, and through many generations, the courtyard pool in the Boston Public Library remained unadorned. But in 1992, in celebration of the 100th anniversary of the building, thoughts turned back to MacMonnies's *Bacchante*, and city officials moved to fulfill McKim's original vision, to welcome the statue back after "an error of hundred years ago."[33] Formally installed in 2000, the *Bacchante* joyously—and now innocently—skips on her pedestal in the courtyard pool. Over the course of a century, the uses of public space and the presumed power of public art have changed. Once an emblem for the Boston bourgeoisie's consolidation of class interests, the statue today takes form only as an object of beauty and aesthetic significance.

Notes

A version of this essay was originally published in the Fall 2000 issue of *American Art*.

1. Rev. James Brady, "Dr. Brady Breaks Loose," *Newark Advertiser,* November 1896, exact date unclear, Frederick MacMonnies Papers, Archives of American Art (hereafter AAA) roll D245, fr. 130. See also *Boston Globe*, 23 November report in the scrapbook of newspaper clippings, January 3, 1895 to January 25, 1897, Trustees Library, Boston Public Library. MacMonnies' papers and the Boston Public Library's scrapbook of newspaper clippings contain a wealth of contemporary commentary on the *Bacchante* controversy.

2. Thomas Russell Sullivan, *Passages from the Journal of Thomas Sullivan, 1891–1903* (Boston: Houghton Mifflin, 1917), 188–89.
3. The remarks by the president of the library trustees, Frederick Prince, are quoted in Walter Muir Whitehill, "The Vicissitudes of Bacchante in Boston," *New England Quarterly* 27 (December 1954): 449. For McKim's assessment, see his letter to the library trustees of July 6, 1896, Art Correspondence File, Trustees Library, Boston Public Library. For the opposing views, see "At Intervals," *Boston Evening Transcript*, October 22, 1896, 6 and the letter of H. L. Warren, August, 1896, Correspondence File of the Boston Art Commission, Boston City Hall.
4. The seven-stanza poem, "The Bacchante's Plaint" appeared in *New York Town Topics*, June 10, 1897, Frederick MacMonnies Papers, AAA roll D245, fr. 80.
5. Letter of June 1, 1897 to Metropolitan Museum trustee Frederic W. Rhinelander, Charles McKim file, Metropolitan Museum of Art Archives.
6. The *New York Sun* article is quoted in Whitehill, "Vicissitudes of Bacchante," p. 440. In a show of journalistic mudslinging and regional rivalry, the *Boston Evening Transcript* of October 24, 1896 (p. 16) indignantly responded to what it called the "blackguarding of Boston" by the *New York Sun*: The Sun has been morally perverted and bent on public mischief for more than twenty years. . . . So nobody knows whether the Sun is serious in a given matter and nobody really cares." For current scholarship, see Tom Armstrong, et al., *200 Years of American Sculpture* (New York: Whitney Museum of American Art, 1976); Albert TenEyck Gardner, *American Sculpture: A Catalogue of the Collection of the Metropolitan Museum of Art* (Greenwich, CT: New York Graphic Society, 1965); Hildegard Cummings, "Chasing a Bronze Bacchante," *Bulletin of the William Benton Museum of Art, The University of Connecticut* 12 (1984): 3–19, as well as Mary Smart, *A Flight with Fame: The Life and Art of Frederick MacMonnies* (Madison, CT: Sound View Press, 1996). Joy S. Kasson in *Marble Queens and Captives: Women in Nineteenth-Century American Sculpture* (New Haven, CT: Yale University Press, 1990) speaks of the fraught attitudes of nineteenth-century audiences toward nudity.
7. See Royal Cortissoz, "Some Imaginative Types in American Art," *Harper's New Monthly Magazine* 91 (July 1895): 174. Cummings in "Chasing a Bronze Bacchante" details the various reproductions and reductions made of the statue.
8. Saint-Gaudens's letter to Paul Bion is cited in Charles Meltzer, "Frederick MacMonnies—Sculptor," *Cosmopolitan* 53 (July 1912): 210. Similar compliments appear in letters to the Art Commission, July 21, 1896 and June 26, 1896, Correspondence File of the Boston Art Commission, Boston City Hall.
9. Joint letter by Daniel Chester French and Augustus Saint-Gaudens, October 26, 1896, Correspondence File of the Boston Art Commission, Boston City Hall.
10. Kathryn Greenthal in *Augustus Saint Gaudens: Master Sculptor* (New York: Metropolitan Museum of Art, 1985), 42 compares the works of Moulin and MacMonnies. Interestingly, Moulin had found inspiration in an antique sculpture from Pompeii known as *Dancing Faun;* see *The Romantics to Rodin: French Nineteenth-Century Sculpture from North American Collections,* Peter Fusco and H. W. Janson, eds. (Los Angeles County Museum of Art in association with George Braziller, 1980), 308.
11. W. T. Parker, cited in Whitehill, "Vicissitudes of *Bacchante* in Boston," 438.
12. "Not Bad," *Boston Record*, November 16, 1896, scrapbook of newspaper clippings, January 3, 1895 to January 25, 1897, Trustees Library, Boston Public Library. For the *Herald* report, see "The Bacchante on Exhibition," *Boston Herald*, November 16, 1896, scrapbook of newspaper clippings, January 3, 1895 to January 25, 1897, Trustees Library, Boston Public Library.
13. See Whitehill, "Vicissitudes of *Bacchante* in Boston," 445, and the *Boston Traveller* clipping from December 11, 1896 in MacMonnies Papers, AAA, roll D245, fr.64.
14. These figures are cited in Ronald Story, *The Forging of an Aristocracy: Harvard and the Boston Upper Class, 1800–1870* (Middletown, CT: Wesleyan University Press, 1980), 177.
15. This group, for example, had less august family lineages, maintained fewer ties to Harvard, and had fewer affiliations with Boston's exclusive social clubs. For a detailed discussion of the status and background of key opponents and supporters, see Julia B. Rosenbaum, *Visions of Belonging: New England Art and the Making of American Identity* (Ithaca, NY: Cornell University Press, 2006), 45–47.

16. Robert Grant had his protagonist make this comment in his novel *The Chippendales* (New York: Scribner's, 1909), 365. See also his comments in *Fourscore: An Autobiography* (Boston: Houghton Mifflin, 1934), 292.
17. *Boston Evening Record*, November 16, 1896, Frederick MacMonnies Papers, AAA, roll D245, fr. 125. See also the *Boston Post*, November 16, 1896, 5.
18. Josephus N. Lamed, "The Freedom of Books," *Why Do We Need a Public Library*. Library Tract, no.1 (American Library Association, 1902), 18. See also Joseph L. Harrison, "The Public Library Movement in the United States," *New England Magazine*, n.s. 10 (August 1894): 709–22, as well as such useful histories as Dee Garrison, *Apostles of Culture: The Public Librarian and American Society, 1876–1920* (New York: Free Press, 1979) and Rosemary Ruhig Du Mont, *Reform and Reaction: The Big City Public Library in American Life* (Westport, CT: Greenwood Press, 1977). In addition, see Richard Sennett, *The Conscience of the Eye: The Design and Social Life of Cities* (New York: Alfred Knopf, 1990), and Jeff Weintraub, "The Theory and Politics of the Public/ Private Distinction" in *Public and Private in Thought and Practice: Perspectives on a Grand Dichotomy*, Jeff Weintraub and Krishan Kumar, eds. (Chicago: University of Chicago Press, 1997).
19. Sally M. Promey, *Painting Religion in Public: John Singer Sargent's Triumph of Religion at the Boston Public Library* (Princeton, NJ: Princeton University Press, 1999).
20. Frederick Crunden, "The Public Library and Civic Improvement," *The Chautauquan* (June 1906), 336.
21. Mariana G. Van Rensselaer, "The New Public Library in Boston: Its Artistic Aspects," *Century Magazine* 50 (June 1895), 262.
22. "Cultural Entrepreneurship in Nineteenth-Century Boston: The Creation of an Organizational Base for High Culture in America," *Media, Culture and Society* 4 (1982): 40. On the broader topic of the "sacralization of culture," see Lawrence W. Levine, *Highbrow, Lowbrow: The Emergence of Cultural Hierarchy in America* (Cambridge, MA: Harvard University Press, 1988), and Pierre Bourdieu, *Distinction: A Social Critique of the Judgment of Taste*, Richard Nice, trans. (Cambridge, MA: Harvard University Press, 1984).
23. Roy Rosenzweig, *Eight Hours for What We Will: Workers and Leisure in an Industrial City, 1870–1920* (Cambridge: Cambridge University Press, 1983), 95. See also Jon M. Kingsdale, "The 'Poor Man's Club': Social Functions of the Urban Working-Class Saloon," *American Quarterly* 25 (October 1975): 472–89; Ruth Bordin in *Woman and Temperance: The Quest for Power and Liberty, 1873–1900* (Philadelphia: Temple University Press, 1981); and John S. Blocker. Jr. in *American Temperance Movements: Cycles of Reform* (Boston: Twayne Publishers, 1989) discuss the class composition of the Women's Christian Temperance Union and other temperance groups. As Nicola Beisel has shown, upper-class individuals typically organized and led anti-vice movements such as Boston's Watch and Ward Society, while members came from the middle and upper classes. See her "Class, Culture, and Campaigns against Vice in Three American Cities, 1872–1892," *American Sociological Review* 55:1 (February1990): 44–62.
24. Crunden, "The Value of a Free Library," *The Library Journal* 15 (March 1890): 80.
25. Barbara L. Epstein, *The Politics of Domesticity: Women, Evangelism, and Temperance* (Middletown, CT: Wesleyan University Press, 1981). On the subject of home values, see also Nicola Beisel, *Imperiled Innocents: Anthony Comstock and Family Reproduction in Victorian America* (Princeton, NJ: Princeton University Press, 1997).
26. *Boston Globe*, November 24, 1896, 5.
27. *Boston Globe*, 1 January 1892, cited in Whitehill, *Boston Public Library: A Centennial History* (Cambridge: Harvard University Press, 1956),153.
28. "Influence of the Liquor Traffic," *Boston Evening Transcript*, November 18, 1896, 6.
29. See, for example, H. C. Merwin, "The Irish in American Life," *Atlantic Monthly* 77 (March 1896): 289–99 and "The Foreign Elements in Our Population," *Century Illustrated Monthly Magazine*, n.s., 6 (September 1884): 765. While in Boston the Irish did not tend to translate their political power into economic or occupational achievement, statistics suggest that second-generation Irish did do better than their parents; see Stephan Thernstrom, *The Other Bostonians: Poverty and Progress in the American Metropolis, 1880–1970* (Cambridge, MA: Harvard University Press, 1973), 130–35. For an ethnic breakdown of the population, see Geoffrey Blodgett, *The Gentle Reformers: Massachusetts Democrats in the Cleveland Era* (Cambridge, MA: Harvard University Press, 1966), 148–49. Blodgett's estimate presumably includes first- and second- generation Irish as well as third and fourth generations. As

James Connolly comments in *The Triumph of Ethnic Progressivism: Urban Political Culture in Boston, 1900–1925* (Cambridge, MA: Harvard University Press, 1998), 217, n. 4, census data from the period show that the number of first- and second-generation Irish alone totaled 41.7 percent of the city's population in 1885; adding third and fourth generations to that would greatly increase the percentage.

30. Letter to Samuel Ward, July 14, 1897, *Letters of Charles Eliot Norton*, vol. 2, eds. Sara Norton and Mark Anthony De Wolfe Howe (Boston: Houghton Mifflin, 1913), 254.
31. "The Listener," *Boston Evening Transcript*, October 28, 1896, p. 4. See also the *Boston Post*, November 16, 1896, front page.
32. Mark Anthony De Wolfe Howe, *Barrett Wendell and His Letters* (Boston: Atlantic Monthly Press, 1924), 145.
33. Boston's Art and Humanities commissioner made this statement back in 1992; see Greg Reibman, "The *Bacchante* That Got Left Behind," *Artnews* (May 1992): 40. Renovations to the courtyard and pool then needed to be completed before the statue, a casting from the original, which remains at the Metropolitan Museum of Art, could be installed.

12
The Problem of Chicago

Paul DiMaggio

The nineteenth century was marked by what historian Lawrence Levine has called a "sea change" in American culture. During the first part of the century, urban Americans shared a common culture, which they experienced at home and in a relatively undifferentiated set of public entertainments. By 1900, the arts were becoming sharply stratified. Works that just a few decades before had been presented in mixed programs to mixed audiences were now enclosed in nonprofit art museums and orchestras, part of an upper-class culture set off by a distinctive ideology and etiquette of appropriation. This classification and sacralization of the arts was accomplished by urban elites, members of a new industrial and commercial upper class actively engaged in transforming itself into a status group, with command over authoritative cultural resources.[1]

In emphasizing the grand contours of change, accounts of this transformation have stinted the importance of differences among cities in styles of cultural entrepreneurship. Cultural hierarchy did not emerge in precisely the same manner, or to the same extent, throughout the United States. Differences among cities are interesting in their own right, offer hints about correspondences between ways of organizing and classifying the arts and dimensions of social structure, and provide materials for developing a more general theory of the influence of urban social organization on institutional development in prenational societies.[2]

Notable differences in cultural entrepreneurship, classification, and sacralization distinguished Boston from New York. The cohesiveness of Boston's Brahmin class enabled its members to build hegemonic cultural organizations with relative ease, and to elaborate a distinctive artistic status culture that was impregnable to profane culture, commercial temptation, and, for the most part, the masses of Bostonians. By contrast, New York's size and the fragmentation of its upper class induced intra-elite status competition that delayed the establishment of hegemonic institutions and dissipated their authority. For 50 years after the founding of the Boston Symphony Orchestra (BSO) in 1881, commercial or weakly patronized ensembles competed in New York, forestalling the stabilization of a fine-arts musical canon until the consolidation of the major ensembles into the New York Philharmonic Symphony in 1929. The Metropolitan Museum of Art established artistic preeminence early on but compromised far more than Boston's Museum of Fine Arts (MFA) with commercial and popular interests. By the 1930s, a host of modernist competitors had begun challenging its cultural authority. The contrast between the two cities is striking and suggests a simple hypothesis: *ceteris paribus,* art worlds in cities with solidary upper classes have a high capacity for organizational entrepreneurship and a low capacity for aesthetic innovation; those in cities with fragmented upper classes have a low capacity for institutional innovation and a high capacity for aesthetic originality.[3]

The case of Boston illustrates the capacity of an old, cohesive upper class to organize a high culture. New York exemplifies the way in which elite fragmentation, by strengthening the hands of artists and impresarios and imposing on cultural enterprises greater dependence upon the commercial market, weakens the grip of cultural authority.

A third kind of relationship between wealth and art is evident in Chicago, where a cohesive bourgeoisie incorporated the arts not just into the life of their own class but also into a larger civic culture.[4] Chicago conforms poorly to generalizations drawn from Boston's and New York's experiences. The problem of Chicago is this: Given the cohesiveness and capacity of that city's upper class, why did its cultural institutions remain relatively open—to commerce, to the public, and to modernism in art—far longer than Boston's? Why, in other words, did Chicago's upper class lack the Brahmin's fervor in classifying and sacralizing the high culture they and the artists they employed began to define?

Chicago: Civic Culture in a Business City

In the most significant ways, the development of Chicago's high-culture institutions mimicked that of Boston's, by which they were influenced. By 1891, Chicago had a single patron-supported orchestra, the Chicago Symphony Orchestra (CSO), and a major trustee-governed museum, the Art Institute, each of which would classify and sacralize the art within it in much the same way the BSO and the MFA had done. These institutions and their programs were built and nurtured by a compact, cohesive upper class of cultural entrepreneurs eager to educate a community that they defined narrowly and, in so doing, to serve the interests of art.

Yet Chicago differed from Boston in intriguing respects. Although equal to the Brahmins in their capacity for cohesive action, Chicago's upper class lacked the Brahmins' historical maturity and numerous family ties to aesthetic specialists. The creation of artistic institutions was for them as much a project of civic mobility—an attempt to establish Chicago as central in culture, as in commerce, to an emerging national city system—as it was an effort to define and maintain social boundaries. Chicago's bourgeoisie was a business class in which bankers and manufacturers reigned, without the leavening influence of the ministers or scholars who instructed the Brahmins, or the lawyers who played a brokering role in New York. The men and women who built the Chicago Symphony Orchestra and the Art Institute lacked the almost instinctive commitment to standard-setting and social exclusion that characterized Boston. Consequently, the institutions they created were open both to commercialism and to the public to a greater extent than in many other places.

The growth of Chicago as an urban center

Unlike Boston or New York, whose histories began in the early colonial era, Chicago was a city of the nineteenth century. In 1829, it had fewer than 50 residents; in 1846, its population remained less than 15,000. Thereafter, the number of Chicagoans swelled rapidly, from just over 100,000 at the onset of the Civil War to nearly 1.7 million by 1900.[5] The city's economy grew apace: by the 1850s, Chicago had become a center of trade in grain and lumber; by the 1860s, it was an important railroad hub; by the 1870s, it had become the "merchandising emporium of the west"; by the 1880s, it was a center of manufacturing and, once Congress made it a central reserve city in 1887, of finance. By 1900, only New York exceeded Chicago in population or industrial output.[6] As its economy expanded, so did Chicago's size, from nine square miles in 1852 to 180 square miles in 1891. Despite the increased availability of property over that period, land values rose by 1,200 percent.[7]

As in Boston and New York, growth and industrialization brought population diversity, social problems, and labor conflict. By 1870, nearly half the city's residents were immigrants; in 1890, more than three-quarters were of foreign birth or parentage.[8] After the great fire of 1871, the city was rebuilt along class-stratified lines. As immigrant districts separated from middle-class and wealthy neighborhoods, hunger, poverty, and alcoholism became less visible but more widespread.[9] Bitter strikes nearly shut down the city in 1877, and management-labor violence flared again in the mid-1880s and in 1894. Historian Kathleen McCarthy has written, "Frightened and repulsed by the continual threat of the poor, wealthy Chicagoans began to insulate themselves from the rest of the urbanscape through barriers of privacy and certification. Clubs, private schools, and social registers, heralded their retreat."[10]

Cultural entrepreneurship: The Symphony and the Art Institute

In Chicago, as in other cities, elite estrangement was expressed in the cultivation of distinctive forms of art and music. When wealthy Chicagoans were ready to form a symphony orchestra, they called on Theodore Thomas, perhaps the leading U.S. conductor of his age and already popular among the city's music lovers. Thomas first performed in Chicago in 1870 and, from 1877 to 1891, presented light summer concerts on the lakefront; in 1882 and 1884 he organized and headed two mammoth music festivals. As early as 1879, Charles Norman Fay, a local utilities executive, tried to persuade Thomas to head an association of players and guarantors along the lines of New York's Philharmonic Society. In 1889, Fay and his allies proposed something better: a permanent, full-season, trustee-governed orchestra of national stature, comprising the best players the conductor could recruit, following "the model that had already been set in Boston." When Fay asked Thomas if he would come to Chicago to organize the enterprise, the response was swift: "I would go to hell if they would give me a permanent orchestra."[11]

Thomas's contract vested unusual authority in the musical director, giving him sole right "to determine the character and standard of all performances given by the Association, and to that end make all programmes, select all soloists, and take the initiative in arranging for choral and festival performances."[12] Why did Chicago's wealthy accept such terms? For one thing, the language did not mean much, however greatly it appealed to Thomas's vanity. The backers offered an annual guarantee, not an endowment, and could end the experiment at any time. Moreover, Thomas's relationship to his supporters was unusually intimate. He had worked for years with many of them, including the active trustees, Fay and banker Charles Hamill, on the festivals and summer concerts. His bond with Fay, reinforced when he gave Fay's pianist sister Amy her orchestral debut in New York, was sealed by his betrothal to Fay's other sister, Rose.[13]

Thomas's power stemmed from his national reputation as well as his personal ties. The city's commercial elite wanted Chicago's cultural prestige to be commensurate with its business achievements. Chicago's distance from the lucrative eastern touring market made it difficult to attract a luminary conductor, and Thomas's stock was high among the Easterners whom Chicagoans longed to impress. No less a figure than Harvard's John Knowles Paine had written him from Europe, "I hear no orchestra in London, Paris, Dresden or Berlin that played with the precision or fire that I have enjoyed under your direction."[14]

Thomas, for his part, was ready to leave New York for Chicago. A singularly ineffective businessman and musical politician, he had squandered the opportunities for wealth that his acclaim as a conductor offered, through a series of ill-conceived orchestral and operatic ventures. Although he was a favorite of classical-music sophisticates, in New York he had lost political and commercial ground to the garrulous Walter Damrosch at just the moment when Anton Sidl, an accomplished newcomer, Wagnerian, and champion of romanticism, was challenging his musical preeminence.

Chicagoans had founded a museum and art school several years before. In 1869, the city's artists created an Academy of Design to offer courses and stage exhibitions. After the 1871 fire destroyed most of its assets, the Academy's organizers permitted laypersons to join as contributing, but nonvoting, members. Many of the men who participated were also on the Art Committee of the Inter-State Industrial Exposition, an association of business leaders that sponsored annual industrial shows in which exhibitions of American and European art were included. Old and new members did not mesh easily: "While the artist founders wanted primarily to sell their own works, the businessmen trustees preferred showing their own collections for an admission charge." The latter founded a competing institution, the Academy of Fine Arts. In 1882 they changed its name to the Art Institute of Chicago and focused on creating a permanent museum and school.[15]

The Institute's organizers included both art collectors of substantial but not enormous wealth and business titans who favored civic improvement for its own sake—men like manufacturer and grain trader Nathaniel Fairbank and retailer/investor Marshall Field, both of whom would also play central roles in the Chicago Symphony. One founder, Charles L. Hutchinson, son of a wealthy grain speculator, was both titan *and* aficionado. Just 28 when he became the Art Institute's first president in 1882, Hutchinson was already an avid collector. Before turning 35, he would inherit the presidency of the Corn Exchange Bank from his father and become head of the Chicago Board of Trade. During more than 40 years as president of the Art Institute, Hutchinson placed his stamp on that institution and participated actively in nearly every civic undertaking of Chicago's bourgeoisie.[16]

Like museum men in other cities, the Art Institute's founders believed in art's potential for social improvement and were touched by the example of London's South Kensington Museum, which Hutchinson called "the greatest of all modern institutions for the advancement of art." In pursuing wealth, asked Hutchinson in 1882, "are we not losing sight of the being created in the image of God, with heart and intellect and soul?" Art, he felt, could "discover and present the ideal." An art museum was at once an instrument of economic growth, providing examples for emulation, an antidote to the moral abrasions of materialism, and a visible symbol of civic maturity.[17]

The museum grew slowly; until 1887 its small rented quarters housed paintings loaned by local collectors, and a few French academic pieces; in 1887 it moved to a larger site, where it added plaster reproductions of classical sculpture. Only after the 1893 Columbian Exposition did the Institute move to its present location, create an endowment, and obtain the core of a permanent collection.[18]

The Art Institute's trajectory, although not its pace, followed that of Boston's Museum of Fine Arts. At first, trustees and their wives ran the museum; exhibitions were varied, extending to flower arrangement and home decoration. Plaster and architectural casts dominated the permanent collection. As in Boston, the acquisition of original works of art hastened professionalization, and new staff enunciated new and higher standards. In 1921, the trustees hired as director Robert Harshe, former head of the department of fine arts at Pittsburgh's Carnegie Institute, and revised the charter to place acquisition and exhibition ahead of public service and artist training as museum goals. During his term of service, Harshe added millions to the endowment, expanded the acquisitions budget several fold, completed the reorganization of the collections into the by-then conventional art-historical format, distanced the Institute from local artists, and reduced the number of temporary exhibitions. As in other cities, such "reforms" were accompanied by declining attendance.[19]

The CSO likewise went through a transformation similar to that of its Boston model. Thomas stood fast in the face of resistance from local musicians and their sympathizers, who resented his importation of players from New York and Europe. His successor, Frederick Stock, clamped down on musicians' outside performance dates.[20] The early concerts contained much light music. After a while, Thomas segregated less classical works into special "popular" concerts. Eventually, as in Boston, they were banished into a separate summer series.[21] Thomas lectured his audiences on their deportment and resisted encores,[22] and the CSO's concert notes embraced Anglo-German aestheticism as fully as had Boston's, describing symphonic music as "the purest, the noblest and the most beautiful in tonal art."[23] No wonder that when the Chicago Symphony performed in Boston in 1911, the *Transcript,* ever the Brahmin house organ, hailed the orchestra's resemblance to the BSO in its "middle-aged aspect and self-possessed bearing."[24]

Like Boston's institutions, Chicago's art museum and symphony orchestra both participated in a process of cultural classification and sacralization, a separation of "serious art" from "popular entertainment," and a separation as well of the publics that favored each; and, as in Boston, these organizations were the handiwork of a unified upper class, supported by aesthetic specialists. Each institution was in the business of defining canons, the Institute by its purchase of works for the permanent collection, the CSO in the selection of compositions for its winter concert series. So brightly did the Institute and the Orchestra shine as symbols of civic and aesthetic virtue that their backers viewed them as a pair, the luster of which dimmed alternative cultural expressions from view. Thus Philo Otis could write, "In our city there are two institutions of a public nature, and only two, which represent the artistic side of life—the Art Institute and the Chicago Symphony Orchestra."[25]

Yet, if the development of public art in Chicago resembled, in both sponsorship and outcome, Boston more than New York, Chicago's business elite exhibited a more ambivalent and mechanical allegiance to the aesthetic doctrines that drove Bostonians like T. S. Dwight and Henry Lee Higginson, Samuel Warren and Benjamin Ives Gilman. In Chicago, as in Boston, the orchestra and the museum would come to use each other as models. But when Thomas defended the austerity of his symphony programs by stating that popular music "would be as wholly unsuited to our winter concerts as a chromo hung among the Dutch masterpieces of the Art Institute," he may have been unaware that the Institute had hung not just one chromolithograph, but a whole exhibit of them.[26] Chicago's cultural institutions evinced an openness—to commerce, to the public, and to modernism—that Boston's lacked.

Culture in a business city

Henry Lee Higginson did not like deficits, but he came to accept them as the price of realizing his aesthetic vision. The trustees of the Chicago Symphony relied on their conductors for artistic conviction, and strove to assimilate aesthetic aims to commercial realities. Unwilling either to make the orchestra a popular institution or to accept the inevitability of financial loss, Chicago's patrons, through compromise and innovation, pulled out of the red after just over a decade, and ran operating surpluses well into the 1920s.

The prospects of turning a profit on a permanent orchestra were not promising when Thomas arrived in Chicago.[27] The CSO's guarantors lost almost all of the $50,000 they pledged in each of the first four years. Some were unwilling to sustain such losses: Board President Nathaniel Fairbank and two of the other four original trustees resigned after the third season.[28]

During the rest of the decade, the board worked successfully to erase the deficits. In 1898 an accumulated debt of just over $28,000—almost one-quarter of it owed to Thomas—was retired with a single fund-raising dinner at the Chicago Club. The trustees determined to eliminate altogether the operating deficits, by then about $25,000 per year, and to build up a cash reserve.[29]

The CSO's managers were unusual in their commercial ingenuity. They pioneered subscription canvassing, membership plans, and option tickets, and increased advertising sales in the orchestra programs. One of their greatest innovations was to make tours profitable by organizing them through host-city women's clubs, which would provide guarantees, rather than through local concert managers, who offered only a percentage of the gate.[30] Such strategies increased the viability of the orchestra without directly influencing musical decision making.

Inevitably, however, the search for financial stability trespassed upon the programs.[31] In the second year, the directors asked Thomas for "one concession"—that he make a quarter of his concerts popular, comprising "miscellaneous numbers without a symphony." Worried by the deficit and "the forlorn little audiences scattered through the vast empty reaches of the Auditorium all winter," Thomas agreed. The popular concerts continued for as long as deficits ran high: the next season, Thomas, who opposed soloists on principle, presented English baritone Plunkett Greene, "who delighted the audience by his singing of a set of old country songs."[32]

Even as losses declined, Thomas remained under polite but persistent pressure. During the fifth season, CSO Treasurer Philo Otis and Trustee Charles Hamill "had many conferences with Mr. Thomas . . . to consider some plan for interesting the general public in our concerts." If the number of soloists on the next year's concert programs is any sign, the discussions had the desired effect.[33]

Finally, Thomas had had enough. In 1897, he told his patrons to stop using the repertoire as a means to boost receipts. Chicagoans had already proved willing to attend serious concerts "in a ratio greater than that shown by the people of the great European art centers." Should programs of an "inferior quality" be offered, "the howl which the critics of Eastern papers would instantly raise . . . would react upon our guarantors and subscribers in the most disastrous manner." Nor would he tolerate it:

> If you feel that the Association can no longer be maintained upon so high an artistic plane as heretofore, I am ready at any moment to resign my position as musical director, and give you the opportunity to try the experiment of interesting the public more generally by popularizing the programmes.

Faced with the prospect of losing their conductor and earning the scorn of Easterners in the bargain, the trustees assured Thomas that they shared his ideals and would support his efforts.[34]

Thomas threatened to resign once again, in 1899, citing a hostile press, Chicago's inclement weather, and the absence of an appropriate concert hall. In the prickly issue of the hall, which Thomas and his allies had kept on the trustees' agenda since the Orchestra's founding, lay the key to the CSO's commercial prospects. From its inception, the Chicago Symphony had performed in the Auditorium, a 4,300-seat concert hall that was connected to a hotel, office building, and banquet facilities. More than 150 of the city's business leaders had subscribed more than $3 million to build the Auditorium; it opened in 1889, and proved both a profitable investment for its subscribers and a source of civic pride.[35]

The Auditorium provided a natural setting for the new orchestra, but there was one problem: Thomas detested it. The difficulty lay not in the acoustics—contemporaries regarded it as one of six great American opera houses—but in business considerations. Auditorium managers, anxious for profits, occasionally cancelled CSO rehearsals when more lucrative bookings presented themselves. Thomas boiled when his ensemble was ousted to make room for Loie Fuller, a celebrated skirt dancer.[36]

More important, the Auditorium's vast size discouraged the growth of a subscription audience for the winter series. Bostonians attended symphony concerts because they had subscribed, and they subscribed because single tickets were unlikely to be available when they wanted them. In the Auditorium, tickets could always be purchased at short notice. Consequently, complained Thomas, "our audience" is "dependent on the weather, special attractions, [and] the season of the year." In other words, the CSO needed a hall in order to create artificial scarcity that might boost demand.[37] Thomas understood better than his directors that exclusive culture required a reversal of the economic logic articulated by Barnum and his peers: instead of packing 'em in, orchestras could boost revenues by shutting 'em out.[38]

The CSO's backers eventually realized that a new hall presented an opportunity to persuade a broader slice of the public to contribute to the Orchestra on a paying basis. Although some Auditorium guarantors opposed the campaign, donations began to mount once the Orchestra's trustees, with Thomas's support, threatened to disband the CSO if $750,000 could not be raised.[39] Thomas died almost immediately after opening the new hall in December 1905. Had he lived, he would have seen the hopes of the hall's backers realized. Due to revenues produced by hall and office rentals, for most of the next 25 years, the Chicago Symphony would operate at a profit.[40]

In Frederick Stock, Thomas's understudy and successor, the Orchestra's business supporters found a pliant conductor whose commercial sensibilities matched their own. Where Thomas jealously guarded his control of the repertoire, Stock routinely designed his programs in consultation with the CSO's business manager, Frederick Wessels. Where Thomas took Boston and Europe as his cultural models, Stock boasted, "There was never anything like this city in commerce, in building itself up from nothing. It is doing something the same in music." Where Thomas attempted to purge soloists, Stock enthused, "We hit upon the idea that . . . has made the orchestra pay—soloists, great soloists. People will pay money to hear stars—the opera shows that—so we have engaged soloists wherever possible." By 1924, Otis could write with pride that under Stock and Wessel's direction, the Orchestra "was assuming the character of a well established business, in routine, detail and system."[41]

If American orchestras have from the beginning been tempted by commerce in their efforts to make ends meet, museums have more typically sought public subsidy of their educational goals. Nonetheless, the commercial instincts of Chicago's patrons were visible in the Art Institute as well as the CSO. Whereas the MFA and the Metropolitan purged commercial transactions from their galleries early on, the Art

Institute maintained close relations with Chicago artists and their patrons, permitting them to use the Institute as a sales gallery, at first regularly, and, later, at annual salons. As late as 1920, these were crucial means by which local painters cultivated a buying public.[42]

The logic of commerce is also visible in the financial management of the Art Institute. Throughout the 1920s, most of the Art Institute's activities—its school, lectures, concerts, and special exhibits—operated on a fee-for-service basis and were largely self-supporting. In the 1930s, Chicago would become the first museum to institute a "dual directorship," whereby the director of fine arts, a professional art historian, shared power with a salaried director of administration.[43]

Chicago's institutions and the middle class

Although Chicago's upper class was as cohesive as Boston's, it displayed New York's willingness to include the middle class in art's relevant constituency. Indeed, before 1900, Chicago's patrons evinced a broader concern with serving the community—defined largely as the Anglo-Saxon elite and the middle class—than did New York's. Whereas in 1883 the Metropolitan Opera's house was built for the boxes, the creators of Chicago's Auditorium, opened just six years later, concentrated on the comfort of the middle class, viewing the Metropolitan, "where the whole structure is sacrificed to boxes, with infinite scorn and patriotic distaste."[44]

In the case of the Chicago Symphony Orchestra, such openness was, under Thomas, largely a matter of show. Ticket prices were high; and despite weak attendance in the early years, the CSO failed to publicize its concerts in Chicago's German community, which represented a natural audience for the predominantly German ensemble.[45] But it is notable that the trustees demonstrated concern for the public at all. The Orchestra's leadership addressed the 1903–04 fund drive for a new hall to the public at large, appointing a Committee of 1200, representing "much of the important religious, educational, professional, social and commercial life of Chicago," to assist in the effort. Much was made of the fact that the several thousand donors included "janitors, scrubwomen, seamstresses, clerks, and wage-earners of all sorts, as well as the wealthy and cultivated."[46] When the hall was completed and the orchestra rewrote its bylaws, some major donors insisted that all the subscribers be invited to vote on the new plan at a public meeting. Although the gesture had little substance, such democratic symbolism would not have occurred to Boston's Higginson or his peers.[47]

The Orchestra's concert notes offer a curious combination of appeals to dreams of opulence, civic pride, and business values, and the thirst for cultural instruction.[48] Critic W. S. B. Mathews, who wrote the notes, sought to domesticate classical music to its Chicago listeners. Beethoven, first prized by Americans as a democrat, later portrayed as a tortured genius, was shorn of such unsettling associations. "There is a great deal of fictitious worship of Beethoven in modern musical writing, which finds in him a disposition to represent all sorts of torn-up and complicated states of the soul," wrote Mathews. "More than twenty years ago, I commenced to maintain the exact opposite of this doctrine. I believe that the essential Beethoven nature was one of peace.[49] Mathews instructed his readers, cajoled them, exhorted them to greater effort. Noting that Thomas would perform a Tchaikovsky symphony only that year premiered in Berlin, he bragged, "It is plain that we are quite up with the procession, in so far as regards the presentation of musical novelties." Reporting that Chicago's audience selected a Bach fugue when polled for a request program,

Mathews congratulated his readers: "This is one instance where the voice of the people is also the voice of truth and intelligence." [50]

Many of Mathews's essays aim to tell diffident listeners the right way to experience the music Thomas played.[51] Others are purely didactic: reading Mathews, one learns the difference between lyric and thematic music, what a song form is, a variation, a fugue, a rondo, a sonata. Pure program music, which aims to tell a story, is of less value than compositions embodying a completely musical idea. A piece by Smetana might occasion an account of the "Bohemian Amazons," but, Mathews assured his readers, "The question is not whether it represents so and so, but whether it is good music."[52]

In contrast to William Foster Apthorp's contemporary concert notes for the Boston Symphony, Mathews's are more literal, more didactic, more earnest in their efforts at instruction. Apthorp's Boston notes differ not in the opinions expressed—both Mathews and Apthorp subscribed to German aesthetic doctrine, and both belittled representational music—but in the manner of their expression.[53] A New England native, Mathews studied in Boston and wrote for *Dwight's Journal* before moving to Chicago.[54] The difference in tone reflects not the men but the audiences they addressed. Whereas Apthorp's readers were on intimate terms with culture and willing to concede little to the middle class, Chicago's business elite and their middle-class employees were on much the same ground in their appreciation of art.

If the CSO's openness to the middle-class community at times had a grudging quality, the Art Institute's was more genuine. The Institute was built downtown; its 1888 annual report criticized the example of cities where "art has, as it were, set itself apart, and the Art Museum has been placed in a remote park where comparatively few of the people can visit it."[55] Unlike the MFA and the Metropolitan, the Institute remained an arts center as much as a museum, a presenter of concerts and lectures, and a meeting place for clubs and societies of amateur art lovers and professional artists. By 1914, 80 such groups met at the Art Institute each week. Whereas the MFA barely tolerated its school of art, by 1910, Chicago's taught art and industrial design to some 4,000 students.

The Art Institute's attendance figures reflected this open stance. By 1901, 861,000 Chicagoans visited their museum; by contrast, the Metropolitan, with its much larger local market, attracted slightly more than 700,000, and the MFA admitted only 225,000. Although the number of visitors, which reached one million in 1911, did not increase sharply thereafter, and even declined somewhat under Harshe, the Art Institute continued to lead American museums in attendance for another three decades.[56]

Attendance totals reflect repeat visits and the patronage of all groups, including Art Institute students. Membership figures are better measures of the commitment of the middle class. Here, the Art Institute also led American museums, with 14,000 members by 1924. As late as 1940, Boston had only 2,000 members, the Metropolitan just 4,600. Again, the Institute was more consistent and effective in its efforts at providing service to the middle class.[57]

Chicago's art institutions were characterized as well by an unusual degree of interest in the aesthetic welfare of the working class, at least after 1900. In this, they were touched by a progressive movement, epitomized by Jane Addams and Ellen Gates Starr's activities at Hull House, that was stronger and more closely articulated to upper-class philanthropy in Chicago than in most other cities.[58] What distinguishes both institutions is their participation in programs backed by coalitions of wealthy and middle-class Chicagoans that brought music and art into the neighborhoods.

The Art Institute's Hutchinson, who joined the CSO board in 1914, was central to the community activities of both the Civic Music Association (CMA) and the Art Institute. The CMA, spearheaded by the Chicago Women's Club, sought to provide "musical entertainment and instruction gratuitously or at little expense, in the small parks and playgrounds and other civic centers." Their programs combined a hierarchical and Eurocentric notion of musical art with a pluralist model of civil society, often juxtaposing classical music by composers from Chicago's various European immigrant groups in rituals of democratic incorporation. (Repertoires shifted toward American song with the United States' entry into the First World War.) The Association sponsored an amateur youth orchestra, several of whose members graduated into the Chicago Symphony or into symphony orchestras in other cities. With strong support from conductor Stock, the CSO cooperated with the Civic Music Association, loaning its players, conductor, and music library for the latter's activities. CSO members also accompanied concerts by the large and active choral society that Marshall Field established to provide wholesome music-making opportunities for his firm's employees.[59]

The Art Institute was even more active and more consistent in its efforts at outreach. Like the Metropolitan but with less strife, it instituted Sunday openings over the opposition of some trustees, in order, in Hutchinson's words, to "make our fine collection a source of pure and refreshing divertissement and refining instruction of the masses." Hutchinson loaned paintings from his personal collection to Hull House (of which he was a trustee) in the 1890s and, as a commissioner of the Chicago park district that held title to the Institute building, led the drive for neighborhood field houses. After 1909, the Art Institute provided traveling exhibitions at these and other community sites. In 1914 the Art Institute collaborated with the Board of Education, the Public School Art Society (in which Hutchinson was active), the Municipal Art League, and the General Federation of Women's Clubs in an ambitious effort to bring art exhibitions into the public schools.[60]

In 1927, the Art Institute reached out to Chicago's African American community with a special exhibition on "The Negro in Art," which featured paintings by contemporary American artists as well as tribal works from Africa. The exhibition, among the first in a U.S. museum to feature contemporary African American art, was widely publicized and well attended, with programs including lectures by James Weldon Johnson and Alain Locke, major figures in the Harlem Renaissance. Although stimulus for the program came from the Chicago Women's Club, a meliorist organization that brought together professional women and wives of the city's business class, this was not the first evidence of Chicago's arts institutions' openness to African American art. In 1893 Henry Ossawa Tanner lectured and showed his work at the Columbian Exposition; and several of the African American artists whose works appeared in the 1927 exhibit had studied at the Art Institute's school.[61]

Chicago's arts patrons were active, as well, in national efforts to employ art education and art museums as means to improve the quality of industrial design. Art Institute President Hutchinson co-founded the American Federation of Arts, the first significant effort to promote aesthetic awareness on a national scale, and Chicagoans played central roles in creating the American Association of Museums to foster professional standards in the museum field.[62] When the General Education Board, a Rockefeller-supported philanthropy located in New York, sponsored a national survey of methods of education in the industrial arts in 1919, Art Institute Trustee Martin Ryerson was an instigator of the project, and President Hutchinson was an enthusiastic backer. When the General Education Board created an Industrial

Arts Division, one of its first large grants supported the School of the Art Institute's program in industrial design.[63]

Openness to the new in art

Chicago also differed from Boston in the relative permeability of its art institutions to innovation. As early as the 1890s, modernist authors, poets, artists, and dancers mingled with forward-looking upper-class women over tea after Friday symphony matinees.[64] At the Symphony itself, Thomas's commitment to the classical canon kept the barriers to modernist music high, but his successor, Frederick Stock, displayed a more open disposition, especially early in his tenure. Like Damrosch's orchestra in New York, the CSO accompanied Isadora Duncan. The CSO performed Scriabin's "Prometheus" (though without the color organ that projected colored lights upon a screen during some performances, according to the composer's notation) in 1915, the year of its American premiere in New York. Stock also presented works by other modernists such as Debussy and Stravinsky, programmed more work by American composers than was typical of U.S. orchestras, and premiered some compositions, including Chicagoan John Alden Carpenter's "Krazy Kat" ballet, that were strongly influenced by jazz. Again like Damrosch, but unlike most of their contemporaries, Stock was ambivalent but open-minded in his attitude toward jazz.[65]

Chicago's bourgeoisie was also progressive in its attitude toward theater, creating the United States' first philanthropically supported art theater (the New Theatre) in 1906. Ten of the trustees were on the board of the Art Institute (including three—Arthur Aldis, Frederick Bartlett and Martin Ryerson—who were prominent allies of modernism at the Art Institute) and six were trustees of the CSO. The position of the stage in the cultural firmament was ambiguous: a canon of Shakespearian and classical works had been established, but actual theater houses were still highly commercial and often disreputable. The idea of building theaters on the model of the orchestra, which would blossom over the next two decades, remained inchoate. The New Theatre combined organizational innovations (philanthropic investment, short runs, and a focus on the company rather than on stars) with conventional commercial repertoire, met with mixed reviews, and folded within a year.[66]

Chicago art collectors were among the first Americans to purchase works by the Impressionists, and these found their way into the Art Institute more quickly than into other American museums. Like New York's Gertrude Vanderbilt Whitney, Mrs. Potter Palmer, the queen of Chicago society, was influenced by her friend Mary Cassat. Her hand, and that of the Institute's vice president, Martin Ryerson, lay behind early exhibitions of Monet, Renoir, and the Ashcan School, as well as the Art Institute's acquisition (by 1913) of works by Manet, Monet, and Cassatt for its permanent collection. The Art Institute also presented works by Kandinsky, Kollwitz, and Munch in two special exhibitions in 1913.[67]

Later that year, Art Institute trustee Arthur Aldis, a Harvard-trained lawyer, real-estate investor, and art patron and collector, persuaded the Art Institute's board to host the Armory Show. It was the only public museum to do so. The exhibition drew huge crowds and made tempers flare. After students at the Institute's school threatened to burn Matisse in effigy (they burned some copies of his works instead), the Institute's director wondered if "an established art museum ought . . . to adhere to recognized standards and refuse to exhibit works which at best represent but a small and eccentric group"; but in the end, he concluded that it was best "to give a hearing to strange and even heretical doctrines, relying upon the inherent ability of the *truth* ultimately to prevail." His attitude reflected an unusual interest in modernism among a portion of Chicago's business elite, and an equally unusual willingness of the rest to tolerate their associates' departures from orthodoxy. Just 20 years later, in 1933, the Art Institute's Century of Progress exhibition included paintings by Picasso and Duchamp in a canonical review of art history, an unprecedented step for a generalist American art museum.[68]

The Problem of Chicago

Chicago's cultural entrepreneurs created hegemonic institutions that defined, classified, and sacralized a distinctive high culture in the fields of music and art, just as did Boston's Brahmins and New York's fragmented elite. Yet there were significant differences between their efforts and those of their contemporaries in Boston and New York. They were as efficacious as the Brahmins in creating dominant organizations that possessed relatively uncontested cultural authority. Once the CSO and the Art Institute came into being, however, they were less strongly impelled to classify and sacralize the culture those organizations embodied. In the continued permeability of Chicago's cultural institutions to the logic of the marketplace, in the relative openness of the CSO and, especially, the Art Institute to the middle and working classes, and in the readiness of their patrons and artistic leaders to explore (if not to embrace) the modern, Chicago's institutions were more similar to New York's than to Boston's.

The cases of Boston and New York demonstrate that the cohesion of a city's elite—the extent to which its members constituted a unified class as opposed to a fragmented collection of plutocrats—as well as the brute effects of size, accounted for the speed and rigor with which cultural entrepreneurs could create institutions and define a distinct high culture insulated socially and aesthetically from popular forms. The case of Chicago reinforces the view that manageable size and bourgeois solidarity made it possible to create hegemonic nonprofit cultural institutions, but it suggests that these factors, although necessary, were not sufficient to generate the classificatory fervor that the Brahmins exhibited. Chicago's cultural entrepreneurs clearly possessed the *capacity* to make their institutions as exclusive, aesthetically rigid, and independent of the marketplace as Boston's. The puzzle is why they apparently lacked the *will* to do so. The solution requires an understanding of not just the structure but also the culture of Chicago's bourgeoisie, and of the historical circumstances that produced it.

The dominant forces in Chicago's nineteenth-century history, the factors that made that city different from its eastern counterparts, were its youth and the rapidity of its ascent. Boston and New York had grown organically; they were subject to elite attempts to change, manipulate, and control them, but their physical and institutional characters were products of gradual development. By contrast, Chicago was barely a city before 1860. For the men and women who came to prominence after the Civil War, Chicago was not so much an environment as a project.

During the period in which the Chicago Symphony and the Art Institute were formed, Chicago's upper class was defined less by lineage or even wealth (though wealth was a prerequisite) than by continuous collaboration in civic enterprise. In the 1880s, to be sure, these organizational bases of solidarity were supplemented by the familiar trappings of upper-class status. Chicago's bourgeoisie intermarried, lived in distinctive neighborhoods, created social clubs and annual social rituals, and identified one another through the *Social Register*.[69] But Chicago's business leadership remained notable for its unity, efficacy, and fund-raising prowess. "Those foolish enough to criticize their techniques or challenge their hegemony," writes Kathleen McCarthy, "were dealt with quickly, effectively, and as mercilessly as the most irksome business competitor."[70]

Their ability to act served them well in competition with elites in other American cities. During the competition for the 1893 Columbian Exposition, Chicago's "businessmen pledged five million dollars even while other cities were still holding discussions on how to raise the money."[71] The investment paid off: Harvard's Charles Eliot Norton, the leading figure among Boston's aesthetes and previously a harsh if distant critic of Chicago's commercial ethos, reported from the fair, "I like Chicago. I like the spirit, the civic power of the place."[72] More than upper-class leaders in Eastern cities, Chicago's upper class played to an external audience.

Chicago's bourgeoisie was astonishingly compact, even by Boston standards, with relatively little differentiation at the apex between sponsors of cultural, social, or reform enterprises. Hutchinson's interests spanned the gamut from the Art Institute to Hull House. The CSO's first president, Nathaniel Fairbank, served on the boards of the Relief Association, the University of Chicago, St. Luke's Hospital, and the American Opera Company. Even Charles Fay, a lesser light in Chicago's philanthropic firmament, served as a trustee of St. Luke's and Children's Memorial Hospitals as well as playing the central role in the Orchestra.

In the cultural realm, the city's leadership was even more intertwined. Most of the first CSO activists were veterans of the Apollo Club, the Biennial Music Festival Association, the Auditorium Association, or other musical ventures. Most of the early leaders of the Art Institute had participated in the Art Committee of the Inter-State Industrial Exposition or the Chicago Academy of Design. Many were active in both musical and artistic enterprises. Twenty-seven of 34 leading cultural activists identified by historian Helen Horowitz served on the boards of the CSO or the Art Institute, and of these, 14 were trustees of both institutions.[73]

Given the unity of its upper class, why did Chicago not simply duplicate Boston's pattern? One explanation can be dispensed with readily: Chicago's cultural entrepreneurs were neither naive nor uninformed. Fay's own roots were in Boston; Thomas, of course, corresponded regularly with many of Europe's musical notables, and his backers were well acquainted with Higginson's operation.[74] The Art Institute's Charles Hutchinson and Martin Ryerson traveled extensively in Europe, visiting museums and purchasing art. Hutchinson was himself a New Englander by birth (Ryerson, Chicago born, had graduated from Harvard Law School), and was at the forefront of national initiatives in the arts. He and Director William M.R. French discussed in detail the programs of eastern museums.[75]

Nor can the concern of Chicago's institutions with service beyond the upper class be attributed to reformist political sympathies on the part of their supporters. Except for Hutchinson, Chicago's cultural entrepreneurs were a reactionary lot, frightened by labor unrest and suspicious of democratic institutions. To be sure, the conservatism of Chicago's businessmen was leavened with a commitment to stewardship and noblesse oblige, but this did not distinguish them from their Boston peers.[76]

Vera Zolberg has suggested that the Art Institute's commitment to public service reflected the poor quality of its collection. This argument has some merit: With most of Chicago's collections destroyed by the fire of 1871, the Art Institute had little to work with; as late as 1914, New York dealer Germain Seligman found its collection "a dreary one." Nonetheless, this explanation cannot explain why, given their wealth, Chicagoans waited so long to build a major collection, nor why the CSO's trustees exhibited similar, if less consistent, concerns for public service.[77]

Might Chicago's institutions' greater openness, especially to modernism, reflect the timing of their creation? This is hardly likely: the Art Institute was organized just six years after the opening of the Boston Museum, and the founders of each acknowledged the same models and espoused the same goals. The CSO was conceived just eight years after the opening of Boston's orchestra, opening under the leadership of a conductor at least as artistically conservative as Boston's leadership.

Chicago's differences from Boston flowed not from rusticity, philosophy, founding dates, or factors peculiar to specific institutions. Rather, they reflected social structure, ideology, generational dynamics, and the interactions among them.

The political dominance of Chicago's cohesive business classes

First, Chicago's leadership group was very distinctly a business class. Although a few hailed from wealthy Boston families, most of Chicago's civic leaders were raised in families where neither art nor scholarship was a prominent interest. The division of labor within Brahmin families between commercial and cultural specialists, reinforced by the intimate relations between Boston's elite and Harvard, provided a model for a social division of labor between commercial and eleemosynary institutions, with the latter carefully insulated from the former. By contrast, Chicago's philanthropic and business leaders were essentially the same: men of new wealth or second-generation heirs who had increased the fortunes they inherited.[78]

Such men were impatient with calls for aesthetic purity. Although they were shrewd enough to recognize the importance of guarantee and endowment for certain civic enterprises, they lacked the Brahmin leadership's visceral sense of culture as a sacred sphere from which the market should be held at bay.[79] Indeed, many Chicago business leaders, including titans like Pullman, Field, and Fairbank, had little formal schooling. Some distrusted universities and elite culture. Richard Teller Crane, a leading supporter of the Chicago Relief Association and a founder of the Chicago Manual Training School, believed philanthropy should focus on workers—"the ones we must reach and control if we would be sure of the permanency of our social institutions"—and hoped that his children would never waste their money on "higher education, higher music, or higher art."[80]

Despite these convictions, Crane was a member of the Art Committee of the Inter-State Industrial Exposition and the board of the Chicago Academy of Design, a guarantor of the 1882 May Music Festival, a director of the 1884 Opera Association, and an early guarantor of the Chicago Symphony Orchestra. Each of these enterprises promised something beyond mere aesthetic uplift: the Art Committee and Academy might contribute to the quality of manufactures, the musical associations provided occasions for community-wide celebration, and the CSO offered prestige on a national scale. And it may have been difficult for a man of Crane's stature to turn down his associates' requests. Although these commitments did not loom large among his panoramic civic activities, the participation of Crane and others like him shaped the climate in which Chicago's cultural enterprises operated.

Men like Crane were schooled in the practical logic of business organization, and to this logic they turned in confronting the problems posed by philanthropic ventures. Thus, Chicago's cultural institutions were more frankly commercial and less concerned with establishing claims of disinterested connoisseurship than their counterparts in Boston. Observers were quick to comment on the occasionally ham-fisted generosity of Chicago's business leaders. "Chicago is not after all grossly material," the journal of the American Guild of Organists teased its readers: "The story that the local managers insist that Saint-Saens' air, *'Amour, vous adier ma faiblesse'* should be spelled '*Armour*,' etc., we have learned, after painstaking investigation, is the base fabrication of some flippant journalist."[81]

Although they dominated local government more decisively than did their peers in Boston or New York, Chicago's businessmen, ironically, faced more direct challenges from the city's working classes. The city's cultural institutions rose up alongside a vigorous trade union movement that threatened the bases of their fortunes. In 1886, the year the Chicago Auditorium Association announced its plans for civic betterment, Illinois labor unions called more than 1,000 strikes. Of 100,000 Americans who took part in a general strike that year to support the eight-hour workday, more than 42,000 were from Chicago. The Haymarket riots offered chilling evidence of the fragility of civil order. Less dramatic reminders of class conflict abounded, as well: in 1889, as the Auditorium neared completion, skilled craftsmen finishing details on raised scaffolds, rained spit and tobacco on an Auditorium official as he spoke to the press.[82]

The restiveness of Chicago's workingmen could not have been far from the minds of the city's cultural entrepreneurs. After organizing a successful opera festival in 1885 that featured low-price seats in a large concert hall, Ferdinand Peck, who in 1886 would spearhead the Auditorium project, wrote that "the continuation of this annual festival, with magnificent music, at prices within the reach of all, would have a tendency to diminish crime and Socialism in our city by educating the masses to higher things."[83]

The impact of Chicago's progressive movement

A second key to Chicago's distinctiveness is the paradoxical coexistence with business political hegemony of a vigorous progressive movement. In part, this reflected the influence of the new University of Chicago: whereas Harvard was a temple of orthodoxy, Chicago tolerated, at least temporarily, such figures as Thorstein Veblen and John Dewey. Common ties to the university linked patrons like Hutchinson to reformers like Jane Addams, creating a milieu in which progressive ideas could spread.[84]

The more active role of women in Chicago's philanthropy in comparison to those in other cities and the prominence of women among the city's leading progressives were especially important: working alongside of men, albeit usually in their own associations, in the interest of art, women formed the core constituency for social and cultural progressivism.[85] Moreover, they brought to their cultural philanthropy a sensibility formed in the Women's Club, the Women's City Club, and other associations in which upper-class volunteers collaborated with middle-class professional women in the interests of social reform.[86]

This in itself did not make Chicago unique. New York's bourgeoisie doubtless harbored many more progressives than Chicago's, and many wealthy Chicagoans viewed Addams and her allies with reserve. New York had as many reform-minded efforts aimed at using the arts to reach the city's poor—ventures like Frank Damrosch's Lower East Side musical settlement or David Mannes's Harlem Music School. But New York had nothing like the Art Institute, with scores of independent clubs meeting within its walls, or the Fine Arts Building, constructed by piano manufacturer Charles Curtis, which housed theaters, amateur art societies, artists' studios, and women's clubs under one roof. Whereas the fragmentation of New York's diverse elites kept the Philharmonic and the Metropolitan Museum largely buffered from progressive initiatives (save for Robert DeForest's influence on the latter), Chicago's compactness created conditions under which mutual influence flourished.[87]

Generational succession

A third factor accounts for Chicago's distinctiveness. The effects of Chicago's business culture and its progressive movement were extended and reinforced by the peculiar generational dynamics of the city's philanthropic leadership. The fire of 1871 rendered Chicago a clean slate upon which a new generation of urban leaders could exercise its imagination. The old business elite largely made way for a younger cohort of civic leaders.[88] The first generation of Chicago business leaders had created a range of cultural enterprises, most commercial but a few like the Chicago Academy of Design, embodying a collective mission, while the city was still small and young.[89] These might have constrained later efforts, but in the arts as in everything else, the fire swept away all that had been built. Crosby's Opera House (which housed a gallery and artists' studios as well as a concert hall), the McVickers Theater, the Dearborn Theater, Wood's Museum, Turner Hall, German Hall: all were rubble.

Equally important, the businessmen who created the Inter-State Industrial Exposition after the fire to celebrate Chicago's resurgence recruited a cohort of younger activists to their ranks who, over the next decade, would build the cultural enterprises that defined Chicago's cultural identity.[90] The young philanthropists behind the Chicago Symphony and Art Institute, a cohort forged in the crucible of the great fire, would collaborate for many years. Whereas death and retirement swept away a generation of patrons in Boston and New York around the turn of the century, Chicago's younger philanthropic elite remained active until the 1920s. The retreat into aestheticism that marked the MFA and, to a lesser extent, the Metropolitan in the first decade of the twentieth century did not reach Chicago until generational succession had taken place.[91]

In sum, then, the differences between Chicago and Boston's cultural development—the greater openness of the former to commercial influence, modernism, and social reform—reflect features of Chicago's social structure that moderated the drive toward cultural exclusivity that characterized the Boston case. Chicago's bourgeoisie was equal to Boston's in its capacity for action, but it lacked the Brahmins' historical depth and institutional breadth.

Boston composer George Chadwick, a student of Harvard's John K. Paine and head of the New England Conservatory, sensed this difference when he visited Chicago to conduct the CSO during the teens. Chicagoans, he observed, had not made:

> music an everyday affair, as we do . . . Chicago may be a musical center in a way, but I feel that the music here is regarded more as a luxurious toy or a syncopated lozenge for the digestion. It's different in Boston, where the populace inherits its musical taste along with other sacred family possessions.[92]

The "we" to whom Paine referred was, of course, the Brahmins and their intellectual auxiliaries. Given this, and looking beyond the insufferable snobbery of Paine's pronouncement, there is a grain of truth here. The arts in Chicago were knit less firmly into the inner life of the upper class than they were in Boston; more than in Boston, they would remain instruments of civic aggrandizement and social amelioration.

Notes

1. See Paul DiMaggio, "Cultural Entrepreneurship in Nineteenth-Century Boston," parts 1 and 2, *Media, Culture and Society* 4 (1982): 33–50, 303–22; John F. Kasson, "Civility and Rudeness: Urban Etiquette and the Bourgeois Social Order in Nineteenth-Century

America," *Prospects* 9 (1984): 143–67; Lawrence W. Levine, "William Shakespeare and the American People: A Study in Cultural Transformation," *American Historical Review* 89 (1984): 34–66; and Levine, *Highbrow/Lowbrow: The Emergence of Cultural Hierarchy in America* (Cambridge, MA: Harvard University Press, 1988).

2. By "prenational" I mean societies in which the impetus for organizing remains focused in urban social structures rather than in national private or public agencies. Nineteenth-century America was prenational in comparison to the United States after the First World War, although national in comparison, for example, to Italian city-states. The comparative historical study of urban social structure and institution building has made progress in recent years. Significant works include Thomas Bender, *Community and Social Change in America* (1978; repr. Baltimore: Johns Hopkins University Press, 1982); David C. Hammack, *Power and Society: Greater New York at the Turn of the Century* (New York: Russell Sage Foundation, 1982); Frederic Cople Jaher, *The Urban Establishment: Upper Strata in Boston, New York, Charleston, Chicago, and Los Angeles* (Urbana: University of Illinois Press, 1982); Martin Green's classic and implicitly comparative book on Boston, *The Problem of Boston: Some Readings in Cultural History* (New York: W. W. Norton, 1966); Peter Dobkin Hall, "Cultures of Trusteeship in the United States," in Hall, *Inventing the Nonprofit Sector and Other Essays on Philanthropy, Voluntarism, and Nonprofit Organizations* (Baltimore: Johns Hopkins University Press, 1992); and Sven Beckert, *The Monied Metropolis: New York City and the Consolidation of the American Bourgeoisie, 1850–1896* (Cambridge and New York: Cambridge University Press, 2001). On Europe, see William M. Weber, *Music and the Middle Class in Nineteenth-Century Europe* (New York: Holmes and Meier, 1976); and *Civil Society, Associations, and Urban Places: Class, Nation, and Culture in Nineteenth-Century Europe*, ed. Graeme Morton, Robert J. Morris, and Boudien de Vries (Burlington, VT: Ashgate, 2006.) Work by sociologists includes E. Digby Baltzell's trailblazing but flawed *Puritan Boston and Quaker Philadelphia: Two Protestant Ethics and the Spirit of Class Authority and Leadership* (New York: Free Press, 1979); Nicola Beisel, *Imperiled Innocents: Anthony Comstock and Family Reproduction in Victorian America* (Princeton, NJ: Princeton University Press, 1997); and Betty G. Farrell, *Elite Families: Class and Power in Nineteenth-Century Boston* (Albany: State University of New York Press, 1993).

3. On the contrast between New York and Boston, see Paul DiMaggio, "Social Structure, Institutions and Cultural Goods: The Case of the United States," in *Social Theory for a Changing Society*, ed. Pierre Bourdieu and James Coleman (Boulder, CO: Westview Press and New York: Russell Sage Society, 1991), 133–55.

4. Here I follow Beckert in using the term "bourgeoisie" to refer to Chicagoans whose wealth derived from their or their families' ownership of capital, including "the city's substantial merchants, industrialists, and bankers, along with rentiers . . . , real estate speculators," and "owners of service enterprises." (The definition appears on p. 118 of Beckert's "Democracy and its Discontents: Contesting Suffrage Rights in Gilded Age New York," *Past and Present* No. 174 [2001]: 116–57.) I exclude professionals, a portion of whom Beckert includes, but that is largely a consequence of their peculiar rarity among Chicago's cultural entrepreneurs. I depart from the conventional structural definition of the bourgeoisie (as does Beckert in *Monied Metropolis*, 2002, who emphasizes "the creation of a bourgeoisie as an active process of class formation" [9]) in that I use it to refer to a particular set of persons—a network that represents the union of a social class and a social elite in an urban elite status group (to use Max Weber's term for a collectivity defined by shared identity and a common sense of honor)—who collectively controlled Chicago's leading business and nonprofit institutions during the period about which I write. Beckert's use of "bourgeoisie" bears a family resemblance to what sociologists mean when they write of the "upper class" or "economic elite"; see E. Digby Baltzell, *The Protestant Establishment: Aristocracy and Class in America* (New York: Random House, 1964); and G. William Domhoff, *The Powers That Be* (New York: Random House, 1978). Of course, members of any effective leadership cadre draw on some combination of structural position, wealth, social centrality, and institutional affiliation to effect their influence, and the mix differs by time and place, rendering none of these terms satisfactory (Jaher, *Upper Establishment*, 2–3). Thus, I follow Beckert (6) in using these and kindred terms interchangeably.

5. Jaher, *Urban Establishment*, 453; Vera Zolberg, "Art Institute of Chicago: The Sociology of a Cultural Institution" (Ph.D. Diss., University of Chicago, 1974). Zolberg's fine dissertation is the indispensable source on the Art Institute.

6. Jaher, *Urban Establishment,* 454, 472–77; Hammack, *Power and Society,* 44.
7. Kathleen D. McCarthy, *Noblesse Oblige: Charity & Cultural Philanthropy in Chicago, 1849–1929* (Chicago: University of Chicago Press, 1982), 56; Hugh Dalziel Duncan, *Culture and Democracy: The Struggle for Form in Society and Architecture in Chicago and the Middle West during the Life and Times of Louis H. Sullivan* (Totowa, NJ: Bedminster Press, 1965), 385; Jaher, *Urban Establishment,* 473.
8. Zolberg, "Art Institute of Chicago," 33; McCarthy, *Noblesse Oblige,* 26.
9. McCarthy, *Noblesse Oblige,* 26–28.
10. Ibid., 30–31. *See also* Helen Lefkowitz Horowitz, *Culture and the City: Cultural Philanthropy in Chicago from the 1880s to 1917* (Lexington: University of Kentucky Press, 1976).
11. Rose Fay Thomas, *Memoirs of Theodore Thomas* (New York: Moffat, Yard, 1911), 52–54; Ellis A. Johnson, "The Chicago Symphony Orchestra, 1891–1941: A Study in American Cultural History" (Ph.D. dissertation, University of Chicago, 1955), 33.
12. Thomas, *Memoirs,* 356.
13. Johnson, "Chicago Symphony," 38; Florence Ffrench, ed., *Music and Musicians in Chicago* (New York: Da Capo Press, 1979 [1899]). Ffrench reports that Rose was from 1882 a mainstay of the Amateur Musical Club, an influential women's association devoted "to stimulating musical interest in Chicago" (60).
14. Chicagoans' hunger for prestige is reflected in the reaction to Thomas's marriage to Rose Fay; as one local newspaper put it, "Chicago felt honored . . . that this notable man should seek a bride from within her borders" (Johnson, "Chicago Symphony," 38, 41). By contrast, Walter Damrosch's wedding to Miss Blaine set Eastern sensitivities on end.
15. Zolberg, "Art Institute of Chicago," 40; Horowitz, *Culture and the City,* 37; McCarthy, *Noblesse Oblige,* 84–85.
16. Horowitz, *Culture and the City,* 49-51; Zolberg, "Art Institute of Chicago," 26.
17. James Sloan Allen, *The Romance of Commerce and Culture: Capitalism, Modernism, and the Chicago-Aspen Crusade for Cultural Reform* (Chicago: University of Chicago Press, 1983), 14; McCarthy, *Noblesse Oblige,* 85. *See also* Horowitz, *Culture and the City,* 74.
18. Nathaniel Burt, *Palaces for the People: A Social History of the American Art Museum* (Boston: Little, Brown, 1977), 179–81.
19. I rely heavily here on Zolberg's excellent dissertation, "Art Institute of Chicago," 30, 35–36, 40–42,60–65, 68–72, 75–76, 109–11, 115–18. *See also* Horowitz, *Culture and the City,* 88; and McCarthy, *Noblesse Oblige,* 159.
20. On resistance by the local musicians and their allies, see Johnson, "Chicago Symphony," 71, 78; Charles Edward Russell, *The American Orchestra and Theodore Thomas* (Garden City, NY: Doubleday, Page, 1927), 214–30; Thomas, *Memoirs;* Philo Adams Otis, *The Chicago Symphony Orchestra: Its Organization, Growth and Development, 1891–1924* (Chicago: Clayton F. Summy, 1925), 44–53. Enforcement of rules against outside employment came later than in Boston and was apparently aimed at preventing members, many of whom supplemented their incomes by playing in restaurants and similar venues, from straying too far into popular genres; the *Chicago Journal* headed its report of the new policy "Ragtime Barred in Thomas Orchestra" (cited in Johnson, "Chicago Symphony," 193–95).
21. Otis, *Chicago Symphony,* 185; Russell, *American Orchestra,* 258; Theodore Thomas, *Theodore Thomas: A Musical Autobiography,* ed. George P. Upton (Chicago: A.C. McClurg, 1905), 104; Thomas, *Memoirs,* 130, 196, 420.
22. Otis, *Chicago Symphony,* 169, 230, 263.
23. W. S. B. Mathews, *Program Notes* (Chicago: Chicago Symphony Orchestra, 1895–96), 41.
24. Johnson, "Chicago Symphony," 192.
25. Otis, *Chicago Symphony,* 272; Horowitz, *Culture and the City,* 199.
26. Zolberg, "Art Institute of Chicago," 40–42, 115.
27. Thomas himself noted commercial disadvantages in Chicago's isolation, which made musicians difficult to recruit and touring less remunerative, the lack of a suitable hall, the fact that such a large proportion of the city's inhabitants belonged "to the class employed in the mills, factories, and at all kinds of manual labor," and "the indifference of the mass of people to the higher forms of music" (Thomas, *Memoirs,* 101–5).
28. The turnover does not seem to reflect a serious crisis: those who resigned remained supportive of the orchestra in later years. Rather, it is likely that the original commitments were for three years and that financial considerations, not disenchantment with Thomas in the wake of the Columbian Exposition, were behind the resignations. (The Panic of

1893 had hurt many Chicago businessmen, and had swelled welfare roles and the claims of social agencies on philanthropic dollars.)

29. Otis, *Chicago Symphony,* 93, 100–05, 127; Ezra Schabas, *Theodore Thomas: America's Conductor and Builder of Orchestras* (Urbana: University of Illinois Press, 1989), 218.
30. Otis, *Chicago Symphony,* 39, 67; Thomas, *Memoirs,* 372. The importance of touring to the Orchestra's bottom line was evident in the aggressiveness with which the management reacted to attempts by other orchestras to play in cities on the CSO's tour circuit; see Robert F. Schmalz, "Paur and the Pittsburgh: Requium for an Orchestra," *American Music* 12 (1994): 138.
31. In the early years, the severe classicism of Thomas's programs "did not interest the people; the attendance at the concerts depended mainly on the soloists." Hawkers who canvassed neighborhoods for subscriptions reported that their efforts met with cries of "Too much Wagner! Too many symphonies! Will not Mr. Thomas give us some 'Ball Room' and 'Request Programs?' " Johnson, "Chicago Symphony," 53. Even W. S. B. Mathews, a local critic loyal to the Orchestra, complained that the CSO's course was commercially imprudent: the concerts were too few, the selections too similar and too long, Thomas's interpretation too spare. Moreover, he wrote, "experience testifies that it has been almost exclusively for the rich, the prices having averaged higher here than in any other amusement place in town." Otis, *Chicago Symphony,* 36–38. Memoirs of participants emphasize the trustees' hands-off policy—the board, wrote Philo Otis, "never interfered in these matters, the judgment of the Conductor was final" (96)—but such protestations are little more than *post hoc* myth-making. In fact, Thomas compromised his standards constantly. Indeed, Otis himself notes that he and Charles Hamill selected choral numbers from a list Thomas provided, and Thomas played "The Star Spangled Banner" at the trustees' request.
32. Otis, *Chicago Symphony,* 55, 84, 126; Thomas, *Memoirs,* 374. The concert notes were characteristically deferential to public demands, even when Thomas was not. Popular music was avoided not because the conductor disliked it (which he did) but because to "set this orchestra of nearly a hundred to play selections from 'Pinafore,' would be too much like setting a locomotive to hauling a baby wagon." When Thomas enraged the public by refusing to play an encore of "Ride of the Valkyries," they were told, "Theodore Thomas is not opposed to encores as a matter of principle" (although he was) and "was sorry that he was unable to gratify the hearers"; rather, the piece was "exceedingly taxing upon the violin players," and had they repeated it, "their wrists would not have been in condition for the delicate number which followed" (Mathews, *Program Notes,* 96, 176).
33. Otis, *Chicago Symphony,* 63, 82. Much as the CSO's backers appreciated the prestige Thomas brought to their city, few of them understood his aesthetic philosophy. Otis complained, "The people know what they want and will have what they want. . . . They will not be treated like 'dumb, driven cattle,' nor have they the slightest intention of becoming 'heroes' in the 'fight' for the musical uplift of the community" (ibid., 189).
34. Thomas, *Memoirs,* 455–58.
35. Horowitz, *Culture and the City,* 39–41; Duncan, *Culture and Democracy,* 237; Ffrench, *Music and Musicians,* 31. The estimate of 4,800 seats comes from Johnson, "Chicago Symphony," 28. Horowitz reports that the Auditorium seated 4,000; Duncan says 5,000, and Ffrench gives the number as 6,000. Mrs. Thomas, perhaps reflecting her husband's subjective impression of the hall's enormity, puts the figure at 8,000. Robert Twombly writes that it seated 4,237 ordinarily but with wooden flooring laid over the orchestra pit could accommodate 7,500, with another 1,500 persons standing, for conventions; see Twombly, "Cuds and Snipes: Labor at Chicago's Auditorium Building, 1887–1889," *Journal of American Studies* 31 (1997): 86.
36. Skirt dancing was a commercial precursor of modern dance, combining ballet and acrobatic steps and ordinarily performed in vaudeville houses by women in colorful and revealing clothing. Although Fuller is now celebrated as an important figure in the emergence of modern dance, at the time, most Chicagoans would have regarded her performances as artistically and morally questionable.
37. Thomas, *Memoirs,* 102–04; Otis, *Chicago Symphony,* 80–81. On contemporary evaluations, see Quaintance Eaton, *The Boston Opera Company: The Story of a Unique Musical Institution* (New York: Appleton-Century, 1965), 10.
38. It was not easy for the trustees to turn their backs on the Auditorium. Many of them had invested in it and the rest were close to others who had done so. As the CSO's president,

George Adams, explained, "Many friends of the Orchestra were largely interested in the Auditorium. In deference to their wishes the proposition for the New Music Hall was abandoned" (Otis, *Chicago Symphony,* 81–82).

39. Thomas, *Memoirs,* 510–16; Otis, *Chicago Symphony,* 134, 171. The degree of dissension aroused by the campaign may be reflected in the fact that the CSO board went to a Boston bank to secure the $330,000 loan necessary to begin construction.
40. Otis, *Chicago Symphony,* 182, 191, 202, 211, 225, 233, 246, 256, 265, 273, 287, 291, 313, 321, 331, 341, 360; Margaret Grant and Herman S. Hettinger, *America's Symphony Orchestras and How They Are Supported* (New York: W.W. Norton, 1940), 70. Unlike the Bostonians who clamored to keep Barnum out of their Music Hall, the Chicago trustees were willing to take on all payers. Johnson, in "Chicago Symphony," reports that the hall was rented out not just for chamber concerts, choral performances, and charity affairs but also for band concerts, temperance meetings, policemen's vaudeville benefits, and druggists' conventions; see 202–5. Not all Chicagoans were pleased with the Symphony's new home. One local journalist called it "a limited hall, to which few save the holders of season tickets, may have access"; another accused the CSO president of being out of touch "with the real people and music lovers," instead taking "his cue from the boxes." Ironically, the thousands of middle-class Chicagoans who contributed to the building fund were supporting a venture designed to make symphonic music less available to people like themselves. Ibid., 164–69.
41. Ibid., 176, 205–6, 293; Otis, *Chicago Symphony,* 22.
42. Zolberg, "Art Institute of Chicago," 234.
43. Ibid., 46, 74.
44. Quoted in Jaher, *Urban Establishment,* 528.
45. Joseph Horowitz, *Classical Music in America: A History of Its Rise and Fall* (New York: Norton, 2005), 173–74. Germans were prominent in the audiences for Thomas's garden concerts in the 1870s, and even after the CSO was founded, Hans Balatka and other conductors led German bands in Chicago's parks, which played classical music to enthusiastic crowds of their countrymen. See Derek Vaillant, *Sounds of Reform: Progressivism and Music in Chicago, 1873–1935* (Chapel Hill: University of North Carolina Press, 2003), 76–79.
46. At the new hall's opening, the president of the Orchestra Association said the "poorest contributor of the smallest sum has the same right as any other to look on this beautiful building with pride and a sense of ownership," and boasted that "the most effective patron of Art is an association like this, in which rich and poor, learned and unlearned men and women, merchants and bankers, professional men and workingmen, join hands to serve the higher life of the community in which they live." Jaher, *Urban Establishment,* 529. Such declamations exaggerate the breadth of the orchestra's base: approximately two-thirds of the funds raised came from just 1 percent of the orchestra's donors, almost all of them trustees or "governing members."Otis, *Chicago Symphony,* 137–42, 164.
47. The meeting was held on a weekday morning and only donors of $100 or more were notified; of several thousand public contributors, only three attended, and it "passed along as we had hoped, with no objections or comments" (Otis, 164). Governance of the orchestra was turned over to a self-perpetuating membership of 40 men, from whom 15 trustees would be selected. (In 1918, power was concentrated further in the hands of a seven-member executive committee, operating with a quorum of three, in which was vested all the powers of the board as a whole.) See Otis, *Chicago Symphony,* 314.
48. With respect to the former, the imagination of even the wealthiest Chicagoan may have been stimulated by Liszt's comment on Chopin's "Rand Polonaise in A Flat": "We see passing at intervals before us brocades of gold, velvets, damasked satins, silvery soft and flexible sables . . . gorgeous carpet from Persia . . . , filigreed furniture from Constantinople . . . ; all is marked by the sumptuous prodigality of the magnates who drew, in ruby goblets and embossed with medallions, wine from the fountains of Tokay, and shod their fleet Arabian steeds with silver" (quoted in Mathews, *Program Notes,* 55). Such pictorial evocations of material wealth were rare in the BSO's notes.
49. Ibid., 273.
50. Ibid., 2, 6, 15.
51. "Into a life drawn helpless by chain of cause and effect," he proclaimed, "the symphony breaks with its magic horn, awakening echoes of the ideal, and for a moment carrying us out of commerce and toil, raising the hearer into the realm of the peaceful and the

eternal. All of which comes not from striving . . . , but by taking that which stands at our ear. . . . It is simply a question of hearing, of listening quietly and of hearing. . . . To enjoy a symphony . . . is a privilege and pleasure, but never a duty." Frequently, directions are more specific. Schumann's Symphony in E Flat "is to be taken enjoyably, as a pleasant and almost jocular experience." Beethoven's Seventh "is so delightfully elf-like that the idea of monotony never occurs to the listener," who "gazes and gazes at the flitting procession of sprites, and only when it finally vanishes into the world of silence is he conscious of things earthly." Ibid., 23, 42, 68.

52. Ibid., 7, 98, 236–39.
53. William Foster Apthorp, *By the Way, I: About Music* (Boston: Copeland and Day, 1898), 3–12, 16–27, 30.Apthorp's essays are more learned than didactic: they put forth a point of view rather than defining a norm. Rather than explain musical forms, he takes his readership's familiarity with them for granted, using them as illustrations in discussions of such art movements as realism and naturalism, comparing a Strauss piece to works of impressionists in the visual arts.
54. Ffrench, *Music and Musicians,* 154.
55. The trustees went on to say that "proximity to the heart of the city is an overwhelming recommendation in the eyes of the Trustees, for no object is more distinctly entertained by them than the benefit of the great masses of people." McCarthy, *Nobless Oblige,* 87. As Helen Horowitz has noted, the inspection of programs, hours, and fees suggests that "the 'masses' were understood to be the middle classes who did go downtown to shop and to transact business" (*Culture and the City,* 117). But even in this modest commitment, the Art Institute distinguished itself from the MFA, which, by the turn of the century, had become a kind of solitary fortress.
56. Zolberg, "Art Institute of Chicago," 43, 151.
57. Ibid., 143.
58. McCarthy, *Noblesse Oblige;* Horowitz, *Culture and the City*; and Vaillant, *Sounds of Reform,* though differing in particulars, are invaluable sources for understanding the influence of the progressive movement on Chicago institutions. Hull House's Ellen Gates Starr was influenced by her aunt, Eliza Allen Starr, an artist who edited the first Chicago publication devoted to the arts in the late 1860s; see William H. Gerdts, "Chicago Is Rushing Past Everything': The Rise of American Arts Journalism in the Midwest, from the Development of the Railroad to the Chicago Fire," *American Art Journal* 27 (1995–96): 55–56. Starr was actively involved in the arts until her death in 1901. Jane Addams, profoundly influenced by John Ruskin, shared Starr's conviction that the arts were important instruments of social betterment; see Addams, "A Function of the Social Settlement," *Annals of the American Academy of Political and Social Science* 13 (1899): 33–55. The Hull House Music School was a special project of Addams's close friend and companion Mary Rozet Smith, who taught in the program and subsidized it financially as well. See Shannon Louise Green, *'Art for Life's Sake': Music Schools and Activities in United States Social Settlements, 1892–1942* (Ph.D. Dissertation, University of Wisconsin, 1998), 204–5; and Vaillant, *Sounds of Reform,* Chapter 3.
59. Vaillant, *Sounds of Reform,* Chapter 5; Linda L. Tyler, "'Commerce and Poetry Hand in Hand': Music in American Department Stores, 1880–1930," *Journal of the American Musicological Society* 45 (1992): 89; Peter W. Dykema, "The Spread of the Community Music Idea," *Annals of the American Academy of Political and Social Science* 67 (1916): 220. Elite worries about the assimilation of new immigrants lay close to the surface of some of these programs. In the early teens, the Association sponsored a "melting pot of music," in which choral societies of Chicago's diverse immigrant groups "sang songs of its own nationality and then from the music thrown upon the screen, one song of each nation was sung in English translation by the entire audience," after which "all of the elements joined in the singing of a number of American patriotic and folk songs" (ibid., 222–23). In its 1915 report, a CMA trustee wrote, "Every social center should have its own choral club, orchestra, children's chorus and series of artist concerts. Every factory should have its choral club, orchestra and band." The Civic Music Association's classical-music concerts in neighborhood field houses at popular prices attracted large and enthusiastic audiences; see Vaillant, *Sounds of Reform,*Chapter 5. The CSO also provided low-price tickets for occasional popular concerts on Michigan Avenue, where the atmosphere was less welcoming: In case attendees did not realize that they were objects of charity, CSO Vice President Charles Hamill

lectured them during the intermission: "You are hearing one of the great orchestras of the world at prices of admission which hardly meet one-third of the cost." See McCarthy, *Noblesse Oblige,* 112; See also, Otis, *Chicago Symphony,* 257–60, 322–23; and Horowitz, *Culture and the City,* 211–12.

60. The breadth of this commitment must not be exaggerated: as Zolberg notes, "If the much-vaunted educational project of the Art Institute is scrutinized, it is found to consist of a rather small, though varied program" ("Art Institute of Chicago," 153). What is notable is less the extent of such out-reaching activities than their very existence; see Horowitz, *Culture and the City,* 159, 197, 212–14, 217.
61. Lisa Meyerowitz, "The Negro in Art Week: Defining the 'New Negro' through Art Exhibition," *African American Review* 31 (1997): 75–89; Jennifer J. Harper, "The Early Religious Paintings of Henry Ossawa Tanner: A Study of the Influences of Church, Family, and Era," *American Art* 6 (1992): 74.
62. Barbara Jaffee, "Before the New Bauhaus: From Industrial Drawing to Art and Design Education in Chicago," *Design Issues* 21 (2005): 47.
63. Frank W. Hart, Executive Secretary, National Society for Vocational Education, to "Gentlemen," July 1, 1919; Abraham Flexner to Martin Ryerson, September 18, 1919; Ryerson to Flexner (telegram), September 24, 1919; folder 2780: "Industrial Art Survey, 1919–21," box 269, General Education Board, Rockefeller Archives Center.
64. Steven Watson, *Strange Bedfellows: The First American Avant-Garde* (New York: Abbeville Press, 1991), 13–14.
65. "Some of it is just vulgarity and noise," he told the press in 1922, "but real jazz properly played—well, I don't mind saying that I like it." Stock even took Igor Stravinsky to a Chicago jazz club, believing that jazz study would improve his compositions. Johnson, "Chicago Symphony," 282, 289; Dena Epstein, "Frederick Stock and American Music," *American Music* 10 (1992): 32; Otis, *Chicago Symphony,* 268. On Stock's repertoire, see Epstein, "Frederick Stock," 20–52; and Horowitz, *Classical Music in America,* 307. On "Prometheus," see Carol Oja, *Making Music Modern: New York in the 1920s* (New York: Oxford University Press, 2000), 50; and James M. Baker, "Prometheus in America: The Significance of the World Premiere of Scriabin's Poem of Fire as Color-Music, New York, 20 March 1915," in *Over Here: Modernism, The First Exile, 1914–19,* ed. Kermit Champa, Nancy Versaci, and Judith E. Tolnick (Providence, RI: David Winton Bell Gallery, Brown University, 1989), 90–111.
66. On the New Theatre, see J. Dennis Rich and Kevin L. Seligman, "The New Theatre of Chicago, 1906–1907," *Educational Theatre Journal* 26 (1974): 53–68; and Kathy Privatt, "The New Theatre of Chicago: Democracy 1; Aristocracy 0," *Theatre History Studies* 24 (2004): 97–108. On canonization in theater, see Levine, "William Shakespeare and the American People." On the annexation of the stage to the institutional model for high culture, see Paul DiMaggio, "Cultural Boundaries and Structural Change: The Extension of the High Culture Model to Theater, Opera, and the Dance, 1900–1940," in *Cultivating Differences: Symbolic Boundaries and the Making of Inequality,* ed. Michèle Lamont and Marcel Fournier (Chicago: University of Chicago Press, 1992), 21–57.
67. Andrew Martinez, "A Mixed Reception for Modernism: The 1913 Armory Show at the Art Institute of Chicago," *Art Institute of Chicago Museum Studies* 19 (1993): 32.
68. Art Institute of Chicago, *Annual Report of the Trustees of the Art Institute of Chicago, 1911,* 37. See also Zolberg, "Art Institute of Chicago," 50–54, 120–21. Martinez, "Mixed Reception," 53; Horowitz, *Culture and the City,*197–203, notes the surprising willingness of wealthy Chicagoans to patronize modernism in poetry and drama, as well as music and the visual arts. Stefan Germer, "Traditions and Trends: Taste Patterns in Chicago Collecting," in *The Old Guard and the Avant Garde: Modernism in Chicago 1910–1940* (Chicago: University Chicago Press, 1990), 171–91, describes the significance of the 1933 exhibition, as well as the contributions of the five patrons who built the Art Institute's collection of modern art.
69. Jaher, *Urban Establishment,* 468, 531–34. The club system served not to create Chicago's business class, which drew its unity from continuous collaboration, but as a theater of operations. Of 34 elite cultural leaders identified by Helen Horowitz as particularly active between 1880 and the First World War, nearly all were members of the Chicago Club and two-thirds belonged to the Commercial Club, which limited membership to 60. Many others belonged to the Union League. The Commercial Club provided a forum for organizing fund drives for the Auditorium, the University of Chicago, the Art Institute permanent

building, and other civic ventures. The Chicago Club was the focus for the creation of the Chicago Symphony, and hosted the fund-raising dinner that retired the CSO's deficit. The Union League launched the Civic Association, a reform group in which two-thirds of Horowitz's cultural leaders were active. See Horowitz, *Culture and the City,* 56–57; and Jaher, *Urban Establishment,* 501, 530–37.

70. McCarthy, *Noblesse Oblige,* 71.
71. Duncan, *Culture and Democracy,* 386.
72. Horowitz, *Culture and the City,* 43; Duncan, *Culture and Democracy,* 401–2.
73. Horowitz, *Culture and the City*. By contrast, only 6 of 37 officers during the first 40 years of the Metropolitan Museum of Art's existence, and only 2 of the 50 members of the committee that organized the Metropolitan, had any significant involvement with music during their philanthropic careers.
74. George Adams, a CSO president, was a member of the Harvard board of overseers. Amy Fay made her musical career in Boston, and her brother Charles retired there. Concert note authors Mathews and George Upton were both veterans of *Dwight's Journal.*
75. Indeed, Chicagoans exerted leadership in creating the national framework of museum professionalism. The Art Institute was a founding member of the American Association of Museums in 1906. In addition to Hutchinson, who was one of its first presidents, Bryan Lathrop and Franklin MacVeagh, the former a president of the CSO and both trustees of the Art Institute, were early trustees of the American Federation of Arts. The Association of Art Museum Directors was launched at the Art Institute in 1916. If Chicago diverged from Eastern models, ignorance was not the reason. Horowitz, *Culture and the City,* 96, 219; Zolberg, "Art Institute of Chicago," 29, 36; McCarthy, *Noblesse Oblige,* 32.
76. Marshall Field demanded the heads of the Haymarket rioters. George Pullman repressed his striking workers brutally. Franklin MacVeagh questioned the wisdom of universal suffrage. Charles Fay retired to Cambridge, where he spent his last years penning rightist tracks. Johnson, "Chicago Symphony," 221; Horowitz, *Culture and the City,* 66–67; Otis, *Chicago Symphony,* 60.
77. Zolberg, "Art Institute of Chicago," 40, 47, 62.
78. Jaher, *Urban Establishment,* 517.
79. Otis, *Chicago Symphony,* 128, 213, 335.
80. McCarthy, *Noblesse Oblige,* 117. Crane's views did not prevail, even within his own family. One son, Charles, attended Yale and became a noted diplomat, eventually serving as U.S. Ambassador to China. Another, Richard Jr., avoided college but was seduced by extravagance in later life, building a 40-room European-style estate in Ipswich, Massachusetts, where he was attended by a butler in livery (a degree of extravagance to which even his wealthy neighbors objected), and giving his daughter's hand in marriage to a Russian prince. See Richard Jay Hutto, June Hall McCash, and Stillman Rockefeller, *Their Gilded Cage: The Jekyll Island Club Members* (Macon, GA: Henchard Press, 2006).
81. Quoted in *New Music Review and Church Music Review* 7 (January 1908): 76.
82. Twombly, "Cuds and Snipes," 80–81, 92–93.
83. Joseph M. Siry, "Chicago's Auditorium Building: Opera or Anarchism," *Journal of the Society of Architectural Historians* 57 (1998): 137.
84. Duncan, *Culture and Democracy,* 195; Horowitz, *Culture and the City,* 133–38.
85. On the role of women in Chicago's philanthropy, see McCarthy, *Noblesse Oblige;* and Duncan, *Culture and Democracy,* 98.
86. Maureen Flanagan, "Gender and Urban Political Reform: The City Club and the Women's City Club of Chicago in the Progressive Era," *American Historical Review* 95 (1990): 1032–50; Dorothy Rogers and Therese B. Dykeman, "Introduction: Women in the American Philosophical Tradition, 1800–1930," *Hypatia* 19 (2004): xiv. The Chicago Women's Club that induced the Art Institute to sponsor its exhibition of African American art in 1927 had opened its membership to African American women in 1905, well before its counterparts in most other cities. Vaillant, in *Sounds of Reform,* makes the case persuasively that Chicago's musical progressives were a different group, not just in background and occupation but also, and especially, in ideology from the sacralizers of the "cultured generation."
87. On Frank Damrosch, see Lucy Poate Stebbins and Richard Poate Stebbins, *Frank Damrosch: Let the People Sing* (Durham, NC: Duke University Press, 1945); on Mannes, see George Martin, *The Damrosch Dynasty: America's First Family of Music* (Boston: Houghton Mifflin, 1983).

88. I draw here on McCarthy's compelling account of the fire's effects, in *Noblesse Oblige,* 53–71; and Jaher, *Urban Establishment,* 496, who notes that only 6 percent of the city's millionaires in 1892 had been born in Chicago.
89. Ffrench, *Music and Musicians;* Allan McNab, "The School of the Art Institute: A Brief History," *The Art Institute of Chicago Quarterly* 55 (1961): 24–28.
90. Not one of the eight business leaders convened to discuss the future of the troubled Crosby's Opera House (Chicago's most ambitious cultural institution at the time) just before the fire was centrally involved in organizing the Art Institute or the Chicago Symphony Orchestra; see Eugene H. Cropsy, *Crosby's Opera House: Symbol of Chicago's Cultural Awakening* (Madison, NJ: Fairleigh Dickinson University Press), 302. On early Chicago cultural enterprise, see also Ffrench, *Music and Musicians,* 19; McCarthy, *Noblesse Oblige,* 82; and Horowitz, *Culture and the City,* 36.
91. Zolberg, "Art Institute of Chicago," 31, 57, 64. And, as Germer points out in "Traditions and Trends," by then the aesthetic creed had expanded to endorse modern art as well as the traditional canon.
92. Johnson, "Chicago Symphony," 233.

13
Bourgeois Appropriation of Music: Challenging Ethnicity, Class, and Gender

Michael Broyles

At the beginning of the nineteenth century, the American upper class displayed scant interest in music. Unlike literature or the visual arts, both of whose artistic value had begun to be recognized, music was considered strictly entertainment, a means of recreation but little else. Even within those parameters, the bourgeoisie in each of the three principal urban areas of Federal America—Boston, New York, and Philadelphia—held varying attitudes toward music according to both tradition and to the prevailing social, religious, and ethnic makeup of the different regions. During the course of the nineteenth century, however, the bourgeoisie in each of these cities discovered how music could serve to consolidate their power as well as vindicate their social positions. Befitting the unique situation found in each city, the manner in which this occured was equally different; but by the end of the nineteenth century, certain types of music had achieved a similar position all three urban areas as symbol of status and means of class differentiation.

The bourgeoisie in Boston were particularly notorious for their lack of interest in music. Their Puritan heritage led them to deem it a frivolity, appropriate as an occasional recreation but unheard of as an art or object of serious contemplation. Amateur members of the elite did perform in the early nineteenth century, sometimes at home, sometimes in public alongside professionals, but even then, it was relatively rare and often met with approbation. When Samuel Atkins Eliot, mayor of Boston from 1837 to 1839, chose to participate in the Unitarian West Church Chapel Choir, his brother-in-law George Ticknor found it thoroughly unacceptable, even though this was strictly an amateur effort. When Eliot invited the choir home to rehearse, Ticknor was appalled.[1]

Hostility to opera was so strong in Boston that it was banned from 1750 to 1790, and even to this day opera does not enjoy the prestige or enthusiasm found in other major cities. The one enduring musical organization in early-nineteenth-century Boston, the Boston Handel and Haydn Society, had virtually no bourgeois support. One nineteenth-century report attests that "first families were not much represented in [the Handel and Haydn Society's] ranks," and a number of the working class tried out but were dismissed, ostensibly for musical reasons. It should be added that only men could become members, although the Society needed women's voices. Gradually, the church connections dissolved, and the organization became an important concert-giving body. It remains active today.[2]

Music fared scarcely better in New York. The bourgeoisie made several attempts to establish a culture for "scientific music" (as the Federal equivalent of classical was called), but all efforts died quickly from apathy and want of patronage. In 1824, a group of wealthy patrons founded the Philharmonic Society, which sponsored orchestral concerts typical of the time. Such concerts consisted of a potpourri of orchestral works, solos, glees, songs, and virtuoso showcase pieces. The Philharmonic was managed by a board of governors, who drew a hard and fast line between themselves and professional musicians: "No Professor of Music, or Teacher of Music shall be a Governor of the Institution," read their constitution. Professional musicians could not even be regular members of the society but were labeled "Associates." The society could not, however, sustain interest among New York's elite, and by 1827 ceased to exist.[3]

New York differed from Boston in one important sense, however: of all the musical genres, opera elicited the most enthusiasm among the upper class, a pattern that held throughout the 1800s. It was not a sentiment that could be sustained earlier in the century. In 1825, Dominick Lynch, a wealthy New York wine merchant, secured the Manuel Garcia Opera Troup, who opened the fall season with Italian opera at the Park Theatre—in Italian.[4] Prior to that, Italian opera had been performed in the United States in heavily adapted English versions, which often went so far as to substitute English ballads for the original arias. Opera, as such, was theatrical entertainment. At first, the Garcia venture garnered widespread support, creating a sudden interest in opera among the bourgeoisie, but the fad was brief. Within two months, New Yorkers had tired of the novelty, and by 1826 Garcia had left New York.

The New York elite's disdain for musicians, evident in the Philharmonic Society, had tragic consequences for George Templeton Strong, a devoted music enthusiast and member of New York's bourgeois society. Strong attended several concerts every week for some 40 years, served as president of the Philharmonic Society (a later manifestation, not the above one), and from 1835 to 1875 kept a detailed diary of musical observations. Yet, when his son George Templeton Strong II (1856–1948) decided to follow a career in music, Templeton not only disowned him but also refused to write his name in his diary, referring to him only as XY.[5]

The bourgeoisie of Philadelphia, despite that city's Quaker background, supported local musical activity. In the colonial and early Federal period, most of the activity occurred in homes rather than in public, however; hence, public concerts were relatively rare—a pattern that carried well into the nineteenth century. The city's large German population, which began arriving one year after the city's founding in 1683 and which increased significantly in the eighteenth century, may have contributed to the amount of domestic music making, even though most Germans were not of the upper classes. Private music making is much more difficult to document than public concerts, but that Michael Hillegas opened Philadelphia's first music store in 1759, sustaining it for many years, suggests both a flourishing musical culture and, in contrast to Boston, support for music by the elite. Hillegas was a member of that group, a merchant sufficiently successful and respected to be named the first treasurer of the United States. Records of Hillegas's shop indicate a preference by Philadelphians for stringed instruments, especially the violin, and for popular eighteenth-century composers, including Tomaso Albinoni, William Boyce, Arcangello Corelli, George Frederick Handel, Johann Adolph Hasse, Padre Martini, Henry Purcell, Domenico Scarlatti, Johan Stamitz, Giuseppe Tartini, and Antonio Vivaldi. These are the same composers then popular in England—confirming that, socially and culturally, Philadelphia in many ways both resembled and emulated London.[6] The preference for amateur performances on stringed instruments, however, probably demonstrates the strong Teutonic influence and suggests that bourgeois men were involved in amateur performances of chamber music.

Overall, the sheer amount of home music making set Philadelphia apart from other American cities.

One institution dominated musical life in Philadelphia in the early nineteenth century: the Musical Fund Society. It was founded in 1820 and still exists today, making it and the Boston Handel and Haydn Society (founded 1815) the oldest musical organizations in the country. The Musical Fund Society sponsored concerts; built one of the important halls in Philadelphia, the Musical Fund Society Hall, which remained until 1982; and founded an orchestra.

The Musical Fund Society was an outgrowth of the private music making that predominated in Federal Philadelphia. It began with "practices," where players would assemble to play string quartets. When the Society was formally announced in 1820, the list of members included names from a number of elite families in Philadelphia: Fisher, Harrison, Hopkinson, Roberts, and Sergeant.[7] Two physicians, Dr. William P. De Wees and Dr. Robert M. Patterson, were chosen president and vice president, respectively. Bourgeois interest in the society, as well as the choice of officers, may have had to do with its original benevolent purpose, to "institute a society for the relief and support of decayed musicians and their families." In addition, two physicians were to minister to the needs of members (musicians) and their families free of charge.[8]

Attitudes toward music began to change in the 1830s, and with the change came a new relationship between the bourgeoisie and music. This development may be traced to Boston; specifically, to 1835, when Samuel Atkins Eliot, one of the few members of the upper class interested in music, wrested control of the Boston Academy of Music from Lowell Mason. He changed it from an organization devoted to the improvement of church psalmody to a secular institution with a focus on orchestral music. At the same time, Eliot began a campaign through lectures, annual reports of the Academy, and anonymous articles in literary journals to convince Bostonians, and Americans in general, that secular instrumental music had a worth far beyond entertainment.[9] This led to what Paul DiMaggio has called the "sacralization of art," an ideal later adopted by Lawrence Levine as the "sacralization of culture."[10] Eliot quickly found an ally in John S. Dwight, previously a Unitarian minister, who began writing on music in Transcendental journals in the 1840s and founded his own *Dwight's Journal of Music* in 1852. For 30 years, *Dwight's Journal* was the most influential American magazine devoted to music. Together, Dwight and Eliot enshrined instrumental music, particularly classical orchestral music, as a form deserving sacred reverence. Dwight was explicit: the more abstract the piece, the more sacred it was. In regard to Beethoven's instrumental music, he asked, "Is it not almost the very essence of prayer?—not formal prayer, I grant, but earnest, deep, unspeakable aspiration? Is not his music pervaded by such prayer?"[11]

Later, the bourgeoisie would use the idea of a sacralized art to define their station and distance themselves from the rest of society. At first, however, some members of the bourgeoisie saw music both as a means to unify society and as a model for how society should be. Whig Republicanism had envisioned a homogenous society in which each individual contributed to the public good and, equally important, assumed the place assigned to him.[12] Members of the elite believed that if workers and immigrants were exposed to art music, especially orchestral music, they would come to prefer it, and society would be brought into a harmonious whole. Samuel Eliot was one of the first to articulate this point of view. Eliot believed there was a hierarchy of musical taste, with his music at the apex, and that, given the opportunity, everyone would ascend that hierarchy. That people might have different preferences seemed an alien concept to Eliot.

Music also provided a prime metaphor for the Whig belief that the duty of each person was to remain within their station. To this end, the orchestra proved a perfect example. Eliot argued this point explicitly: that within both an orchestra and politics, not everyone can be a leader, but everyone has a part to play—although for some it may be a supporting part. "Music," he wrote, "is the only art which, requiring the concerted action of members, in different spheres, can exemplify and enforce that principle of order and subordination of one thing to another, and of one man to another, without which harmony, whether in music or politics, cannot exist." How that part was chosen was clear to Eliot: "Every man must be willing to take the place for which nature has fitted him, and for which others, rather than he himself, think him qualified."[13]

Eliot's thinking harkened back to the notion of the eighteenth-century gentry that those at the top are most capable of determining what was best for the rest of society. Even though Jacksonian democracy had destroyed Whig Republicanism as a viable political medium, republicanism persisted throughout much of the nineteenth century as a set of cultural beliefs, encoded and reinforced by symbols and rituals, both in the home and in public. Jean Baker has argued that "republican ideas were encoded into the institutional life of the community, not as precise postulates of formal doctrine, but as vague behaviors."[14]

With the general acceptance of a clear musical canon, music gained in prestige, and it was only a small step to convert aesthetic values to social values. In the second half of the nineteenth century, Eliot's values were completely inverted as the bourgeoise discovered that a musical hierarchy derived from the notion of sacralization could become a means to distance themselves from other segments of society. As even Eliot and Dwight recognized, the masses continued to prefer music at the bottom of this hierarchy to the more refined styles that the upper categories represented, and a new tone crept into musical thinking: music of a higher class was for people of a higher class.[15] Although the notion that music could be used for the moral improvement of everyone persisted among some members of the elite, after the Civil War the bourgeoisie began to see certain types of music as rightfully belonging to them, and, as the attendant social rituals emerged, music could be used as a mark of social distinction.

Throughout this history, two issues of ethnicity and class intertwine in myriad ways. Instrumental art music, particularly symphonic, began to flourish only with the immigration of large numbers of Germans toward midcentury, and throughout most of the nineteenth century German musicians dominated virtually all orchestras. This had two consequences: First, a supply of well-trained professional musicians, necessary to a thriving musical culture, existed; and second, because they were clearly foreign in manner and language as well as in immigrant status, an obvious social distance was firmly in place. Musicians were viewed by many bourgeois Americans as the equivalent of immigrant servants, further weakening any idea of a society unified through an appreciation of art music.

Given the emphasis on orchestral music in the emergence of a musical canon and the stress upon large, abstract instrumental works as especially sacred, it is not surprising that the creation of symphony orchestras was one of the principal musical developments of the late nineteenth century, and that well into the late twentieth century a symphony orchestra remained a symbol of prestige for a community, an important cultural monument. In the East Coast cities of Boston, New York, and Philadelphia, and in the newly emerging Midwestern metropolis of Chicago, the route to the founding of a symphony orchestra was quite different. The one constant was the important role played by the bourgeoisie.

Orchestras existed in all three East Coast cities throughout most of the nineteenth century, and in some cases, even earlier. These earlier orchestras were often loosely amalgamated, even pickup groups of random instrumentation, combining both amateurs and professionals, drawing on any available musicians in town, and presenting mainly popourri concerts only irregularly, if they performed publicly at all. As we have seen, the first attempt to change that approach occurred in Boston when Samuel Eliot created the Boston Academy Orchestra in the 1830s. For several reasons this orchestra lasted only until 1847, but the Academy was hurt in its later years less because of lack of interest than the appearance of rival ensembles. Competition came from the Boston Philharmonic Society, founded in 1843, and the Harvard Musical Association, which sponsored chamber music.[16] Chamber music, being abstract and instrumental, was considered equally sacralized. Viewing chamber music as a more esoteric genre, Dwight advanced the argument that such music was not for everyone, only those capable of understanding its refinements.[17] This point directly contradicted Eliot's vision and was one of the first justifications of the idea of elite music for the elite.

In the early 1880s there were two orchestras in Boston, but each was struggling. The Harvard Musical Association had begun to offer orchestral concerts in 1866. The avowed purpose of this move was, according to the music critic and historian W. L. Hubbard, not "to make money but . . . to promote the taste for good music and to advance the progress of the art in Boston."[18] By the late 1870s, however, the conservative programming of the Harvard Musical Association Orchestra led to the formation of a second orchestra, the Philharmonic Society, in 1879. The rivalry between these two groups was acute, but given the limited musical resources, good orchestral musicians, and size of the potential audience, neither was able to thrive. Soon, it appeared that both would flounder, and the fate of orchestral music, and, by extension, the fate of a sacralized musical art, appeared to be in trouble.

In the midst of this chaotic situation, Henry Lee Higginson suddenly appeared as *deus ex machina*. In 1881 Higginson, a wealthy banker, announced the formation of the Boston Symphony Orchestra (BSO), to be funded out of his own pocket. Some of Higginson's ideas were revolutionary. He gave the musicians an annual contract, as opposed to the per performance arrangements that most orchestras had, and in return he expected their complete dedication: they were to play for the BSO and no other ensemble. Higginson sought the best conductor that he could find in Europe, in essence presenting him with a group of musicians totally at his disposal. Georg Henschel, the first conductor, could demand adequate rehearsals and, more important, be relatively certain that the entire orchestra would be there for a performance.In addition, continuity of personnel over a period of time allowed a precision of ensemble playing not easily matched. For 40 years, from 1882 until his death in 1919, Higginson managed the affairs of the BSO in detail, negotiating all contracts, hiring and firing musicians, and building an audience. This was in no way a democratic institution; it was a Gilded Age solution by a Boston Brahmin. Befitting Higginson's lofty ideals, the music itself was only of the most serious kind.

Higginson's plan worked, and the two other orchestras quickly folded. The Boston Symphony offered 24 concerts a year, far exceeding the half dozen or so that most other symphonic organizations managed, and in the Gilded Age Boston, more than any other city, exemplified the principle that a symphony orchestra was a cultural lynchpin of the social order. In 1900 Symphony Hall, the building in which the Boston Symphony still performs, was erected specifically for the orchestra, and in 1908 Hubbard could claim, "In the 27 years of its existence the Boston Symphony has come to stand for the highest and noblest in the orchestral art and it is doubtful if it now is surpassed by any like organization in the whole world."[19]

The multiethnic demography of New York created a set of conditions different from those in Boston. Even before the increased immigration resulting from the 1848 unrest in Europe, and in Germany in particular, a German bourgeois community had developed that sponsored musical events essentially for its own constituency. Although they shared the same halls as other organizations, German orchestras played Beethoven and other German music for ethnic audiences that included few Anglo-Americans.

In retrospect, the most significant event in New York was the founding of the New York Philharmonic Orchestra in 1842. This makes the New York Philharmonic the oldest established orchestra in the United States. It was only in the early twentieth century, however, when the bourgeoisie reorganized it and took control of it, that the orchestra began to assume the shape and position within New York culture that it has today. It was founded by 53 musicians and remained essentially a democratic institution throughout the nineteenth century. It was a cooperative run by the musicians, who did not receive a salary but, instead, paid an initiation fee and annual dues, and shared in the profits from the concerts—three per year at first, a number that gradually expanded to six.

The German influence is apparent in the organization. When it was founded, 22 of the 53 founding members were German, including Anthony Philip Heinrich, who was elected chairman of the organizational committee. By 1855, the orchestra had expanded to include 67 members, 53 of whom were German, and, beginning with the appointment of Theodore Eisfeld as the first full-time conductor, every conductor during the nineteenth century was German.[20] These statistics are not unusual for an American orchestra of the period, as German immigrants or their descendents dominated American classical music throughout the 1800s. The German impact on American music was so strong that study in Germany became de rigueur for any aspiring American musician. Douglas Bomberger has estimated that as many as 5,000 American musicians studied in Germany during the nineteenth century, and in the 1890s the Leipzig Conservatory alone admitted 455 students.[21]

In Boston, the bourgeoisie embraced the symphony as the defining symbol of their stature. One reason the symphony languished in New York was because that honor, as the apex of a musical and, by extension, social hierarchy, went to opera. By 1850, opera had separated itself from theater, principally by the physical removal of opera from theatrical buildings to halls constructed specifically for that purpose. This move was more about the establishment of a distinctive environment for the upper class than the suitability of existing theaters for operatic productions. Design of the building was crucial, from the size of the stage and orchestra pit, allowing a visual monumentality, to the position of the audience and the number, size, and elaborateness of the boxes, even to the outside doors themselves—in some cases, including a separate, segregated entrance for the gallery.[22] The grandiosity of Romantic opera, particularly Verdi and Wagner, contributed musically to what was apparent architecturally.

In 1847, a group of wealthy New Yorkers agreed to invest sufficient funds to build a new opera house at Astor Place, a spot convenient to the wealthy but remote to most others.[23] The house was visually and acoustically a disaster; a giant chandelier obscured any view of the stage for most of the gallery and the sound was poor throughout the house. But the boxes were sumptuous and served their intended purpose as a backdrop for personal and sartorial display. The *Home Journal* referred to the opera house specifically as a "movement of the Aristocracy."[24] Plagued by poor attendance and internecine quarrels among management and performers, however, Astor Place survived as an opera house only until 1852. Soon an even grander house was built, the Academy of Music, which opened in 1854. Like Astor Place, it was funded by a group of wealthy bourgeois, who bought shares, creating a stock company. With ownership came free admission and control of the most desirable boxes. While the boxes were as opulent as those of Astor Place, the Academy aimed to attract a wide audience; it seated 4,600 compared to the 1,800 that Astor Place had held, and it boasted having the largest stage in the world.

In spite of constant changes in management, the Academy survived until challenged by a new organization. Matters came to a head in the late 1870s, when Mrs. William K. Vanderbilt applied for a box at the Academy and was rejected. In 1880, other families who had been similarly turned down met on April 28, 1880, to organize the "Metropolitan Opera-house Company of New-York." It was also a stock company, with 55 members, each holding 100 shares. The Metropolitan Opera was launched on October 22, 1883. The clash has been viewed as a struggle between the older merchant wealth and the new industrial wealth, but it was more complex than that, for among the founders of the Met were members of some of the oldest New York bourgeois families: Roosevelts, Rhinelanders, Wetmores.[25] More likely, the Academy simply could not accommodate more boxes, and with the newly emerging industrial wealth, there were many more families with the wealth and the desire to demonstrate their status and position.[26] The sheer cost of a box at the Met precluded all but the most elite from obtaining one. Altogether, there were 110 boxes, and the shareholders, who had contributed $15,000 apiece, were first given boxes, the order chosen by lot. The remaining boxes went to those willing to pay $1,200 per year, with the probability of an additional $600 being levied annually.[27]

The Academy could not compete with the financial resources pumped into the Met, and within two years had folded. The Met itself, however, immediately ran into financial problems. Beyond the boxes, there was a 3,900-seat auditorium to fill. Henry E. Abbey, the first manager of the Met, had misjudged New Yorkers' willingness to pay for opera, charging between $3 and $6 for seats. This opened the door to a different kind of challenge to the elite—an ethnic one. The presence of many bourgeois Americans in New York of German origin, as well as large numbers of German immigrants who held music in high regard, had been a factor in musical circles throughout the nineteenth century, particularly as some of the German bourgeois attempted to maintain separate cultural circles. The Metropolitan Opera itself went through a German phase in the 1880s, after the first season. Management abandoned the practice of doing all opera, including Wagner, in Italian, slashed prices to between $.50 and $3, and began offering all operas in German. For seven years the Met was a German house, drawing large segments of the German population, but eventually alienating other ethnic groups as well as some box holders. The German phase ended in 1891, when the directors brought back Henry Abbey as manager and, with him, Italian and French opera.[28]

Major music halls were built in both Boston and Philadelphia in the 1850s, but, reflecting the different musical interests of the bourgeoisie of each city, they had different purposes. The Harvard Musical Association in Boston led the drive for a new hall, and in 1852 the Music Hall, seating 2,700, was opened. It was essentially a concert hall; opera continued to be performed in theaters, and an opera house, the Boston Opera House, was not built until 1909. By the 1850s, elites in Philadelphia recognized the need for a large music house in which opera could be performed, and the Academy of Music was built in 1857. Unlike the later Metropolitan in New York, this was not exclusively an opera house. The Academy of Music quickly eclipsed the Musical Fund Society Hall as the most prestigious space for musical events, and later became the home of the Philadelphia Orchestra, until Verizon Hall was built in 2001.

Surprisingly, Philadelphia had no permanent orchestra until 1900. Because of its location and prominence, many orchestras visited Philadelphia, and an active theater and operatic tradition meant that for much of the nineteenth century a local, permanent orchestra was not a priority. One local orchestra, the Germania Orchestra, a different group from the one that emigrated from Germany in 1848, remained in existence from 1856 to 1895.

In 1891 a group of Chicago businessmen, wanting to improve the cultural climate of their city, decided to create a symphony orchestra. They were fortunate in that Theodore Thomas, the most visible conductor in the nineteenth century was interested. Thomas, born in Germany but brought to America as a child, had formed his own orchestra in New York in 1862. From 1869 to 1888, he traveled extensively with the orchestra, each year playing in dozens of cities. When offered ample money and carte blanche to build an orchestra in Chicago, he leapt at the opportunity. The bourgeoisie of Chicago instantly had an orchestra that could rival any in the country.[29]

The most important social issue relating to bourgeois music in the late nineteenth century involved gender, particularly the persistent belief in the separation of the public and private spheres. Music became an arena in which the two spheres overlapped in ways that both forced a reconsideration of the nature of those spheres and provided opportunity for the culture to test the distinctions that it made. Music, of course, operated in both the public and the private sphere, but in the home, music was clearly a female province.

In the early part of the nineteenth century, the piano was almost strictly an upper-class instrument. Virtually all were imported from Europe and were consequently very expensive. By the late 1880s, virtually every bourgeois American home had a piano, which was usually located in the parlor. The lady of the house, if anyone, was expected to play it. Daughters were taught to play the piano as part of their upbringing; sons were not. If a young man learned a musical instrument, it was usually a band instrument, acceptable because of its association with the military and the outdoors.

The piano grew in importance as the role of women evolved in the nineteenth century. Throughout the eighteenth century a patriarchal system based on the extended family predominated, in which even adult males were governed by the elder patriarch of the family. With the "opening of American society" in the early 1800s, brought on by greater mobility and the beginning of mass migration inland, this patriarchal model gave way to a nuclear family model in which gender roles were clearly defined. The role of women, especially, changed in this model. Church and community could no longer enforce morality with the same authority that they had in the eighteenth century, when families remained within close proximity for generations and in some places the authority of the church was backed by law. In the nineteenth century, the burden of upholding moral standards fell primarily upon the adult female—that is, upon the mistress of the house.[30]

The sacralization of music only strengthened the importance of music to the "cult of true womanhood," a set of values that society inculcated in young girls throughout much of the nineteenth century.[31] These values were summarized as piety, purity, submissiveness, and domesticity. Of them, piety was particularly important, as the revolution in values in the early nineteenth century brought on by the decline of the influence of the extended family and the rise of the nuclear family put a special burden on women—that is, wives—to be the guardians of society's moral virtues.[32] Thus, as music morphed beyond entertainment to acquire moral capital of its own, its value to women increased. Not only could music do much to create domestic harmony, but it could also elevate and instill moral values in listeners.

Several strands interwove to create conditions that allowed music to become an important element in women's lives. It helped created a pleasant home and, with sacralization, it came to symbolize a set of values conducive with moral uplift and dignity. Beyond these, however, were equally important, if more subversive, qualities, although it is doubtful, in a pre-Freudian age, if the full psychological implications were realized. Music, particularly Wagner, provided an attractive emotional outlet bordering on a sublimated sensuality, as Joseph Horowitz has demonstrated, in a time when emotional repression and strictures were severe for bourgeois women.[33] Finally, when all of the rhetoric, justifications, and explanations were stripped away, music had an intrinsic aesthetic appeal that transcended class and location.

As the thriving concert world confirmed, however, music also had a public face, and the public sphere was supposed to be the male arena. Performance was, with few exceptions, male dominated.[34] The polymorphous nature of music, however, challenged the status quo in a way that undermined notions of public and private and gender. This happened primarily at the upper levels of society, for the position that music enjoyed in bourgeois society by the end of the nineteenth century is largely attributable to the role that women assumed in the public sphere. Throughout the country, women assumed the roles of impresario and, in several prominent cases, orchestral manager, usually with great success. They were shrewd in business, and men in the musical world recognized their talents. Tradition, which had placed music in general in women's sphere, provided the opening needed for women to prove their executive abilities publicly, in at least this one area of the very male world of business entrepreneuship.

This development occurred in three stages. First was the spread of women's musical clubs throughout the country. Many began as a means to allow women to get together, listen to one another perform, and in some cases form ensembles. In the second stage, they began to organize public concerts, which often became the central focus for musical activity in their municipality. Officers in clubs found themselves securing performing venues, negotiating contracts with agents, selling the concerts to the public, and managing them when they occurred. In many cases, they became the dominant force in the musical life of a town or city, and impresarios feared and respected the business acumen of these women. In the third stage, a number of women moved on to become impresarios on their own, or to administer major performance organizations, such as symphony orchestras. Their positions were fully recognized and quite public.

The women's club movement took shape after the Civil War, with the founding, in 1868, of the Sorosis Club in New York and the New England Woman's Club of Boston seen as the beginning. By 1898, Mrs. J. C. Croly, in her magisterial 1,200-page compendium of women's clubs, could list more than 700, in virtually every state.[35] The first women's music club was the Rossini Club of Portland, Maine, founded in 1869, although it existed informally several years prior.[36] In addition to the music clubs per se, many other women's clubs had music divisions that functioned much as music clubs did.

The club movement did not reach its apogee until the early twentieth century, although by the end of the nineteenth they had become a recognized national force. In 1898 the National Federation of Music Clubs was founded in Chicago. Its purpose was "to bring into communication with one another the various musical clubs of the country, that they may compare methods of work and become mutually helpful," and to encourage "musical education and developing and maintaining high musical standards throughout America."[37] In 1899, there were 76 clubs, a number that had risen to 124 by 1901. The number peaked in 1930, with 5,000 clubs.[38]

While most of these clubs were open to middle-class women, they functioned primarily for women who were members of the economic elite, and their success depended on bourgeois leadership. At first, the clubs were for the benefit of the members themselves. Later, members of the clubs envisioned a broader mission: to bring music to the community as a whole. As these clubs began assume the role of concert presentation, bourgeois leadership became even more critical, for success depended on women with sufficient social standing to gain entrée to the homes of the wealthiest men in the town, and then to persuade them to support their endeavors.

In many communities, women's music clubs became the town's principal concert-sponsoring organizations. Linda Whitesitt has estimated that three-fourths of the concerts booked outside the large cities were arranged by women's music clubs.[39] This put them in contact with artists, agents, building owners, and the public in general, as they undertook complex sets of arrangements to bring music to their areas. They had to book artists with agents, negotiate fees, arrange for concert halls, interest the public, sell tickets, and in many cases go out on a financial limb with guarantees to secure the needed arrangements. Social status and family wealth mattered. Few women were in business at this time, but if ever they were competing with men in the rough and tumble of business dealings and negotiations, this was one area.

In large cities the clubs did not have the influence that they had in smaller towns, but by the late Gilded Age many women played important roles in the business of music. A number of women who had inherited wealth established themselves as independent patrons. Their work often encompassed both art and music, as, for example, in the cases of Isabella Stewart Gardner of Boston and Gertrude Vanderbilt Whitney of New York. Some women went beyond supplying funds to worthy artists to actively creating or managing musical organizations; they were in every respect impresarios. According to Emanuel Rubin, New Yorker Jeanette Thurber "exerted as great an influence on the musical life of the United States as any other figure of her generation."[40] Thurber, the daughter of Danish immigrants, married a wealthy wholesale food merchant. Like Eliot and others earlier in the century, she believed that music should be democratized, and strongly opposed what it had become, an emblem of elitism and social status. She then struck where she felt this tendency was most obvious: the opera, particularly the Metropolitan Opera. She created an American Opera Company, with the avowed intention of bringing opera to the American people at affordable prices. Grand opera is, however, one of the most expensive ventures in the arts, and Thurber's vision, in terms of sheer spectacle, was especially grand. Even though she had the backing of wealthy donors such as Andrew Carnegie, and even though the productions were received enthusiastically in many cities, Thurber could not stave off the huge debts that the company accumulated, and within two years was forced to declare the company bankrupt.

This did not deter Thurber. She had another vision. She created the National Conservatory in 1885, and again persuaded many of the wealthiest men in America to back her, including Andrew Carnegie, William K. Vanderbilt, Joseph W. Drexel, and August Belmont, among others. Thurber herself served as president. The Conservatory survived until 1930, but the 1890s was its heyday. Thurber's greatest coup was to recruit Antonin Dvorak as director of the Conservatory from 1892 to 1995, but one of her greatest legacies was in providing an institution that welcomed women, minorities, and disabled students.

Thurber's vision was not unique. Use of music as a means of unifying culture persisted well into the twentieth century among some of the bourgeoisie. Frank Damrosch, the son of Leopold and the brother of Walter, embraced much the same viewpoint as Thurber when he founded the Institute of Musical Arts in New York in 1905. In 1892, he had established the People's Singing Classes and People's Choral Union, and in 1893 the Musical Art Society, an a capella vocal ensemble that specialized in Renaissance and Baroque music. All three organizations were meant to engage workers and immigrants in a morally uplifting activity. Claire Reis, née Raphael, aspired to be a concert pianist. According to Reis, however, who was from a wealthy family, "playing for charity was my mother's idea of bringing up a musical daughter." Reis, who later became involved in the management of several musical organizations in New York, organized the People's Music League in 1911, "for the purpose of bringing classical music to the new arrived immigrants.[41] The most well-known example of the use of music as a means of integrating society is Hull House in Chicago. Tying aesthetic choices with moral improvement, Jane Addams and Ellen Gates Starr, the cofounders, offered regular concerts and lessons as an integral part of their program.[42]

Bourgeois women played a significant role in either the creation or the continuance of all ten of the major symphony orchestras that were established between 1842 and 1919, and in Cincinnati, Philadelphia, New York, and Cleveland their work was crucial.[43] After several failed attempts by different individuals, the Ladies' Musical Club of Cincinnati created a governing board led by Helen Herron Taft, wife of William Howard Taft, to establish a symphony orchestra. In a role reversal, the governing board of women created an advisory board made up of men, mainly to act as a liaison to the business community. *Musical Courier* scoffed at the idea: "Any orchestra gotten up by a committee of ladies of good intention will not flourish."[44] Yet under Taft and then, when Taft left for Washington, Bettie Fleishmann Holmes, the orchestra did. Somewhat later, the Cleveland Orchestra was established mainly through the work of Adella Prentiss Hughes, who worked first through the Cleveland Fortnightly Music Club. A descendent of one of the founding settlers of Cleveland, she created interest in symphony music by sponsoring visits of several orchestras through the club. She then helped found the Cleveland Musical Arts Association, used it to secure funding for an orchestra, engaged Nicolai Sokolaff as conductor, and transformed the organization into the Cleveland Orchestra in 1918. Hughes then served as manager for 15 years.[45]

The New York Philharmonic and the Philadelpha Orchestra both owe their survival to bourgeois women. By 1900, it was apparent to many that Philadelphia needed a permanent orchestra. Earlier efforts had either failed or succeeded only briefly. In particular, efforts to lure Theodore Thomas and then Walter Damrosch and the New York Philharmonic Society to Philadelphia had come to naught.[46] Finally, in 1900, a group of wealthy Philadelphians put up $15,000 to fund a permanent orchestra. By 1904, the orchestra needed additional financing, and Frances Anne Wister, head of the women's committee, proposed that the committee be given the job. Skeptical, the male executive committee gave them one month to succeed. By the end of the month, they had raised $10,000 outright and secured an additional $5,000 in new subscriptions.[47] A similar pattern occurred in New York. By the early twentieth century, the New York Philharmonic was in serious financial trouble, and its directors had all but conceded bankruptcy. Mary Seney Sheldon convinced them that reorganization as a corporation was feasible, then headed a women's guarantors committee that led a successful drive to secure financial backing. The women's committee then assumed management of the orchestra, contracted a full complement of musicians, planned a season of 46 concerts, and secured Gustav Mahler as conductor.[48]

The bourgeois appropriation of concert music and opera in the second half of the nineteenth century had resonance well beyond the roles that elite men and women played, however. Through the support of the bourgeoise, music moved from the position of entertainment to art, and, in particular, through bourgeois financing the monumental aspect of nineteenth-century Romantic music became a reality—in large ensembles both orchestral and operatic, and in massive halls designed to reflect the grandeur of both the music and its patrons. To this day, the symphony, the opera, and the halls built to accommodate them stand—metaphorically in the first two instances, literally in the third—in most cities as prime symbols of civic pride and culture.

Notes

1. See Michael Broyles, *"Music of the Highest Class": Elitism and Populism in Antebellum Boston* (New Haven, CT: Yale University Press, 1992), 120–22, 186–88.
2. Ibid., 140–48.
3. Vera Brodsky Lawrence, *Strong on Music: The New York Music Scene in the Days of George Templeton Strong, 1836–1875* (New York: Oxford University Press, 1988), 1:xl.
4. Katherine K. Preston, *Opera on the Road: Traveling Opera Troupes in the United States, 1825–1860* (Urbana: University of Illinois Press, 1993),101.
5. Lawrence, *Strong on Music,* 1:xiii.
6. Joanne Taricani, "Music in Colonial Philadelphia: Some New Documents," *Musical Quarterly* 65, no. 2 (April 1979): 192–93, 198.
7. The complete list of officers and members is in Louis C. Maderia, *Annals of Music in Philadelphia and History of the Musical Fund Society, from its Organization in 1820 to the Year 1858* (Philadelphia: J. B. Lippincott, 1896), 59–61.
8. Robert A. Gerson, *Music in Philadelphia* (Westport, CT: Greenwood Press, 1940), 56–57.
9. See Broyles, *"Music of the Highest Class,"* 366, for a list of lectures and publications by Eliot.
10. Paul DiMaggio, "Cultural Entrepreneurship in Nineteenth-Century Boston," parts 1 and 2, *Media, Culture and Society* 4 (1982): 33–50, 303–22; Lawrence Levine, *Highbrow/Lowbrow: The Emergence of Cultural Hierarchy in America* (Cambridge, MA: Harvard University Press, 1988), 83–168.
11. John S. Dwight, "Address Delivered before the Harvard Musical Association, August 25, 1841," *Musical Magazine* 3 (August 28, 1841): 263–64.
12. Reflecting eighteenth-century thinking, the gender-specific pronoun is intentional.
13. Samuel Atkins Eliot, "Music and Politics," *Dwight's Journal of Music* 18 (1860): 345.
14. Jean Baker, "From Belief into Culture: Republicanism in the Antebellum North," *American Quarterly* 37 (Fall 1985): 539; Clifford Geertz, *The Interpretation of Culture: Selected Essays* (New York: Basic Books, 1973,) 192–93, 201.
15. Alan Trachtenberg, in discussing the "custodianship of culture," observed a "hierarchy of values corresponding to a social hierarchy of stations or classes" (Trachtenberg, *The Incorporation of America: Culture and Society in the Gilded Age* [New York: Hill and Wang, 1982], 140–81).
16. Although the Harvard Musical Association began as an outgrowth of a musical society for Harvard undergraduates, it soon severed all ties with Harvard and moved from Cambridge to Boston.
17. John S. Dwight, "Music in Boston during the Past Winter," *Harbinger* 1, no. 3 (1842): 123–24.
18. W. L. Hubbard, ed., *History of American Music,* with introductions by George W. Chadwick and Frank Damrosch (New York: AMS Press, 1976), 275; originally published as vol. 8 of *The American History and Encyclopedia of Music,* ed. Hubbard (Toledo, NY: I. Squire, 1908).
19. Hubbard, *History of American Music,* 276.

20. Howard Shanet, *Philharmonic: A History of New York's Orchestra* (New York: Doubleday, 1975), 109.
21. Douglas Bomberger, "American Music Students in Germany," paper presented at the 57th Annual Meeting of the American Musicological Society, Chicago, November 7–10, 1991.
22. The gallery was the area of the cheapest seats, located in the upper balcony.
23. The exact amount invested is not clear. Karen Ahlquist, *Democracy at the Opera* (Urbana: University of Illinois Press, 1997), 134–35, states that 200 investors agreed to invest $75 per year for 5 years; Lawrence, *Strong on Music,* 1:454, states that 150 investors ultimately agreed to the $75 plan. According to John Dizikes, *Opera in America: A Cultural History* (New Haven, CT: Yale University Press, 1993), 159, 50 stockholders put up $1,000 each to fund the opera.
24. *Home Journal,* December 11, 1847; quoted in Ahlquist, *Democracy at the Opera,* 137
25. "The New Opera-House, Formal Organization of the Company—the Officers Elected," *New York Times,* April 29, 1880, 8, lists the members present for the organizational meeting, as well as the officers elected.
26. There is some dispute regarding the number of boxes that the Academy had. Joseph Horowitz, *Wagner Nights: an American History* (Berkeley: University of California Press), 74, lists 18, as does Sven Beckert, *The Monied Metropolis: New York City and the Consolidation of the American Bourgeoisie, 1850–1896* (Cambridge: Cambridge University Press, 1993) 247. Dizikes, *Opera in America,* 216 states 30. The picture in Lawrence, *Strong on Music,* 2:528, suggests that 18 may have been for the first tier only, and that there were 3 tiers. According to John S. Dwight, in *Dwight's Journal of Music,* 26, no. 25 (March 2, 1867), 408 the Academy had 28 proscenium boxes. In addition, the mezzanine consisted of 22 boxes. I want to thank Adrienne Fried Block for pointing out the Dwight citation to me.
27. "Mr. Abbey Dispells a Cloud," *New York Times,* September 21, 1883, 5.
28. Horowitz, *Wagner Nights,* 76, 152–56.
29. For a discussion of Thomas's career as well as the founding of the Chicago Symphony Orchestra, see Ezra Schabas, *Theodore Thomas—America's Conductor and Builder of Orchestras, 1835–1905* (Urbana: University of Illinois Press, 1989).
30. Robert Wiebe, *The Opening of American Society: From the Adoption of the Constitution to the Eve of Disunion* (New York: Knopf, 1984), 268–74.
31. According to Barbara Welter, in "The Cult of True Womanhood: 1820–1860," *American Quarterly* 18, no. 2, part 1 (Summer 1966): 161, "Authors who addressed themselves to the subject of women in the mid-nineteenth century used this phrase as frequently as writers on religion mentioned God."
32. Wiebe, *Opening of American Society,* 274–79.
33. Horowitz, *Wagner Nights,* 213–17.
34. The few exceptions were singers and some pianists. Most of the pianists were foreign, however.
35. Mrs. J. C. (Jeane June) Croly, *The History of the Women's Club Movement in America* (New York: Henry G. Allen, 1898).
36. Linda Whitesitt, "'The Most Potent Force' in American Music: The Role of Women's Music Clubs in American Concert Life," in *The Musical Woman: An International Perspective, Vol. 3 : 1986–1990,* ed. Judith Lang Zaimont et al. (Westport, CT:Greenwood Press, 1991), 664.
37. Karen J. Blair, *The Torchbearers: Women and Their Amateur Arts Associations in America, 1890–1930* (Bloomington: Indiana University Press, 1994), 49.
38. Ibid., 213.
39. Whitesitt, "Most Potent Force," 162.
40. Emanual Rubin, "Jeanette Meyer Thurber (1850–1949): Music for a Democracy," in *Cultivating Music in America: Women Patrons and Activists since 1860,* ed. Ralph Locke and Cyrilla Barr (Berkeley: University of California Press, 1997), 135.
41. Information about Reis, including this quotation, is taken from Carol Oja, "Women Patrons and Crusaders for Modernist Music: New York in the 1920s," in Locke and Barr, *Cultivating Music,* 245–46.
42. For a discussion of musical activities at Hull House, see Derek Vaillant, *Sounds of Reform: Progressivism and Music in Chicago, 1873–1935* (Chapel Hill: University of North Carolina Press, 2003), 91–125.
43. Linda Whitesitt, "Women as 'Keepers of Culture,' " in Locke and Barr, *Cultivating Music,* 77.

44. Ibid., 74.
45. Adella Prentiss Hughes, *Music Is My Life* (Cleveland: World Publishing, 1947), 246–62.
46. Frances Anne Wister, *Twenty-Five Years of the Philadelphia Orchestra, 1900–1925* (1925; repr. Freeport, NY: Books for Libraries Press, 1970), 13–14.
47. Whitesitt, "Women as 'Keepers of Culture,'" 76.
48. Ibid., 76–77.

14
The Birth of the American Art Museum

Alan Wallach

Introduction

Before the Civil War, the United States could not boast of a single institution that could properly be called an art museum. After the war, the situation changed dramatically, with the opening in the 1870s of the Metropolitan Museum of Art in New York, the Museum of Fine Arts in Boston, and the Corcoran Gallery of Art in Washington, D.C. Commentators at the time saw the new museums as proof of the cultural progress of the nation as a whole. Later observers would describe them in similar, nationalist terms as symbols of American democracy.[1] But democracy was probably the least of the impulses underlying the creation of art museums in the period immediately following the Civil War. Instead, the new museums were a project of an emerging bourgeoisie intent upon founding institutions of high art as part of its drive toward cultural hegemony. Indeed, the very process of creating art museums contributed to the bourgeoisie's developing awareness of itself as a class.

That the situation changed so rapidly after the Civil War suggests that the creation of art museums was a necessary stage in the bourgeoisie's postwar consolidation of its economic, political, and cultural power. The art museum helped to validate the class's claims to represent the public interest and, simultaneously, to answer its need for what Pierre Bourdieu calls "distinction."[2] Thus, the class could emphasize the apparently democratic and benevolent aspects of the institutions it was creating, and, at the same time, the new institutions reinforced its developing sense of its inherent cultural superiority—the "distinction" that in part justified its growing hegemony.[3]

Motives

In 1867, Henry Theodore Tuckerman, a poet, travel essayist, literary critic, and spokesman for elite New York taste, published his magisterial *Book of the Artists: American Artist Life*. Tuckerman had been a close observer of art and artists in New York for more than two decades, and his book was the most authoritative contemporary pronouncement on the condition of the visual arts in the United States. Yet, as Tuckerman acknowledged, despite recent progress, American artist life was especially deficient in one area:

> Within the last few years the advance of public taste and the increased recognition of art in this country, have been among the most interesting phenomena

> of the times. A score of eminent and original landscape painters have achieved the highest reputations; private collections of pictures have become a new social attraction; exhibitions of works of art have become lucrative and popular; buildings expressly for studios have been erected; sales of pictures by auction have produced unprecedented sums of money . . .
>
> These and many other facts indicate too plainly to be mistaken, that the time has come to establish permanent and standard galleries of art, on the most liberal scale, in our large cities.[4]

Tuckerman's readers may have found his logic unassailable, but note the assumption governing the passage: "advances" in the arts necessitate the creation of "permanent and standard galleries of art"—in other words, museums of art of the sort that had over the previous 70 years appeared in many of the principal cities of Europe.

This assumption was widely shared by Tuckerman's upper-class contemporaries. For example, in 1865—that is, two years before the publication of *Book of the Artists*—John Jay, a wealthy New Yorker and, according to museum historian Winifred Howe, "a man ceaseless in good works," addressed the topic of an American art museum in an after-dinner speech at an elaborate Fourth of July celebration held at a Paris restaurant called the Pré Catalan.[5] According to the *London Times,* the "fête was organized through the active agency of some patriotic gentlemen" and brought together such notables as the U.S. minister to France, the assistant secretary of war, the U.S. commissioner to the Éxposition Universelle of 1867, and no less than six prominent American clergymen.[6] As he later recalled, Jay said in his address that "it was time for the American people to lay the foundation of a National Institution and Gallery of Art and that the American gentlemen then in Europe were the men to inaugurate the plan."[7] Jay's words spurred some of those present to form a committee that went on to lobby the powerful and fiercely nationalistic Union League Club "for the foundation of a permanent national gallery of art and museum of historical relics" to be located in New York.[8]

The committee's labors had their effect. In November 1869, the League (whose president at the time happened to be John Jay) organized a meeting at which 300 of the city's wealthiest men gathered over dinner to hear some stirring oratory from William Cullen Bryant, who called for the founding of a museum of art in New York. The gathering resulted in the creation of a provisional committee that went on to lay the organizational framework for the Metropolitan Museum. Through the efforts of a board of trustees, which included leading merchants, industrialists, and financiers as well as a number of artists, the museum received its charter in 1870. The museum boom of the 1870s began in earnest on February 20, 1872, when the Metropolitan held a gala to mark the opening of its galleries in a brownstone on lower Fifth Avenue that had previously served as the home of Dodsworth's Dancing Academy. The museum later occupied the Douglas Mansion on Fourteenth Street before taking up permanent residence in Central Park in March 1880, in a "Venetian" gothic building designed by Calvert Vaux and Jacob Wrey Mould.[9]

The founding of Boston's Museum of Fine Arts followed a somewhat similar route. In 1869 Charles Callahan Perkins, scion of a great merchant family and the author of two books on Italian Renaissance sculpture, formed a special committee for the American Scientific Association to consider the problem of art education. With the committee's help, Perkins prepared a report on "the feasibility of establishing a regular Museum of Art [in Boston] at a moderate expense."[10] A year later, the committee had grown into a board of trustees that included members of Boston's most powerful families as well as, ex officio, Boston's mayor and representatives of Harvard, the

Massachusetts Institute of Technology, the Boston Public Library, and the Lowell Institute. After receiving its charter of incorporation in 1870, the museum began holding exhibitions in temporary quarters at the Boston Athenaeum. Six years later, the museum opened in its new building in Copley Square, with an address by Perkins, now a trustee and the honorary director, who remarked, "It [is] not the building which makes the Museum, but the works of art you place in it"[11]—perhaps an apology for the museum's "Ruskin Gothic" design, which, as the historian Walter Muir Whitehill noted, had already been the object of severe criticism.[12]

As we have observed, collective efforts to establish the Museum of Fine Arts and the Metropolitan Museum date to the years immediately following the Civil War. By contrast, as early as the mid-1850s, the financier and art collector William Wilson Corcoran had on his own begun formulating plans for a National Gallery in Washington, D.C. A cosmopolitan banker and consummate political operator—early on, he had acquired the nickname "the American Rothschild"—Corcoran made a fortune during the Mexican War in the risky business of selling treasury bonds on Wall Street and in Europe. Corcoran was the one man in the United States who, during the 1850s, possessed the knowledge, ambition, and, most important, means to create a European-style art museum in the United States. A lone bourgeois acting in the place of the federal government or a local bourgeoisie, he hired James Renwick, architect of the Smithsonian Institution Building ("The Castle"), to design a building to house his ever-growing collection. Work began in 1859 and was almost completed by 1861. During the Civil War, the Federal Government requisitioned Corcoran's gallery for use as a clothing depot. At war's end, a radical Republican administration had little use for Corcoran, a Confederate sympathizer who had moved both his fortune and himself abroad shortly after the outbreak of hostilities, and took its time restoring the building to its owner. Like the Metropolitan Museum and the Museum of Fine Arts, the Corcoran Gallery of Art received its charter in 1870, but only after Corcoran had turned over nominal control of the gallery to a board of trustees. In February 1871, Corcoran celebrated the completion of the gallery building with a ball that was, according to a contemporary newspaper account, "the most magnificent . . . ever held in Washington."[13] The event, which took place on Washington's birthday, marked the reconciliation of Republican officialdom and Washington's indigenous elite, who, like Corcoran, had sided with the South during the war. Three years later, the Corcoran Gallery opened its first exhibition, with President Ulysses S. Grant and other high government officials again in attendance.[14]

What might be called "the museum boom of the 1870s" thus amounted to the opening of three art museums—not a large number, but enormous considering that before the 1870s there was no institution in the United States that could be considered a museum of art. An observer of the American cultural scene before the Civil War might have noted, along with Tuckerman, the presence of athenaeums, art academies, art galleries, and art unions. But as Tuckerman and his upper-class readers understood, an art museum was not the same thing. What an art museum might actually be was perhaps a matter for debate, yet, like Tuckerman, American elites, long practiced in the anxious business of comparing America with Europe, were acutely aware that Europeans could take pride in institutions that made their nations' cultural riches available to various publics, while Americans could not. Here is William Cullen Bryant addressing the November 1869 meeting that led to the founding of the Metropolitan:

> The little kingdom of Saxony, which, with an area less than that of Massachusetts, and a population but little larger, possesses a Museum of the Fine

> Arts marvellously rich, which no man who visits the continent of Europe is willing to own that he has not seen. There is Spain, a third-rate power of Europe and poor besides, with a Museum of Fine Arts at her capital, the opulence and extent of which absolutely bewilder the visitor.[15]

Envy explains little when it comes to assessing the motives that led to the creation of art museums in New York, Boston, and Washington; still, Bryant furnishes an important clue in the equation he drew between wealth, military might, and nationhood. Thus, he is, at least for rhetorical purposes, scandalized that Spain, "a third-rate power of Europe and poor besides," could boast a splendid art museum when the United States could not.

But what accounts for the almost automatic comparison that Bryant and his contemporaries so often made? Why was it imperative for bourgeois groupings in New York, Boston, and elsewhere in the United States to establish art museums that might eventually compare favorably with their European counterparts?

Here it is necessary to distinguish between the implicit and the explicit—between what was assumed or taken for granted, and what was overtly proclaimed. Such figures as Jay and Bryant agreed on the necessity of creating an art museum in New York—indeed, it almost went without saying that a museum would be of inestimable public benefit and, thus, a worthy goal for members of a civic-minded upper-classmen like Jay who were "ceaseless in good works." As so often happens, the interests of a ruling class or class faction took on the ideological guise of a universal social good. Still, if we examine what is implicit in the process of post-Civil War museum formation, we may begin to find possible explanations for the zeal with which a Jay, a Perkins, or a Corcoran labored to create his museum.

From the vantage point of the 1860s, the public art museum was a relatively new social institution. A number of European art museums predated the French Revolution—the Vatican Museums, for example, established in the second half of the eighteenth century, or the Uffizi, which became a museum in the 1740s. Still, the paradigmatic art museum was the Louvre, the former royal palace that opened its doors as a museum in 1793. We might, in a general way, say that at its inception, the Louvre symbolized the historical triumph of the French bourgeoisie.[16] Yet if this was the case—and I believe it was—we must ask why did the newly triumphant French state need a Musée du Louvre? Indeed, why would any state or municipal authority want an art museum? Here we are obliged to come to grips with a body of scholarly literature that I can only briefly gloss. One might maintain, as Carol Duncan and I did some years ago in an article titled "The Universal Survey Museum," that the invention of the art museum can be understood as a response to a new set of social needs: that the art museum was a new type of ritual structure, in effect replacing the earlier princely gallery. In the princely gallery, the sovereign represented himself as a latter-day Apollo, a bringer of art and enlightenment to his subjects. With the public art museum, the bourgeois-dominated state exhibited its benevolence as well as the necessity of its role as guardian of civilized values via a new form of display in which paintings and sculptures represented or exemplified a history of art. This new form of display prompted the citizen-visitor to act out, and thereby internalize, a redemptive history of culture in which, by implication, the state stood at the summit of humankind's greatest attainments.[17]

Because of its role in helping to secure bourgeois hegemony, the art museum can be understood as a crucial modernizing institution—a fact that was quickly grasped by ruling classes and elites throughout Europe and America. In *The Birth of the Museum,* Tony Bennett, a scholar deeply influenced by the work of Michel Foucault, takes up other aspects of the museum's modernizing role. Bennett argues that the art museum was a modernizing institution inasmuch as it "targeted the popular body as an object of reform." It aimed to "[screen] out the forms of public behaviour associated with places of popular assembly" such as the tavern and the fair. The museum, as "a technology of behaviour management," was thus designed to produce new forms of social cohesion.[18] Bennett gives a telling example from the writings of Sir Henry Cole, founding director of the South Kensington Museum (later the Victoria and Albert), who maintained that the chief lesson a museum "would teach the young child [would be] to respect property and behave gently."[19]

Inspired by national and civic pride, the American museum builders of the 1870s did their work. Art, they thought, would be a public good. An art museum was, in their view, a crucial instrument of reform. Not only would it provide inspiration and uplift, but it would also combat vice and promote virtue in the public at large. In his speech of November 1869, Bryant reminded his audience that "it is important that we should encounter the temptations to vice . . . by attractive entertainments of an innocent and improving character."[20] Works of art might provide one needed form of "innocent" entertainment. But note Bryant's use of the word "we." At this point I would like to turn to that "we"—to the bourgeois groupings that believed art museums were needed enhancements to American civic and cultural life.

High Art

Before the Civil War, upper-class Americans may have dreamt of an American Louvre, but American elites were for the most part far too weak and divided to cooperate in the creation of national cultural institutions.[21] Even on the local level, elite groupings generally lacked the power to achieve cultural dominance. Studies of elites in Boston, New York, Philadelphia, and Charleston demonstrate that factionalism and a concomitant political weakness were commonplace.[22] For example, in an analysis of the early years of the Boston Athenaeum, Ronald Story distinguishes between the Boston elite of the period 1800–50 and the "upper class" of the 1850s and 1860s, noting "the [latter's] greater cohesion of occupational, familial and generational components . . . and its greater consciousness of its interests vis-à-vis antagonistic social elements." By the 1860s, the Boston elite "seems to have achieved a unique cohesiveness and a singular cultural complexion,"[23] which in turn allowed for the foundation of the Museum of Fine Arts.

The history of the Boston Brahmins is in many respects unique; yet consolidation and increasing cultural awareness also characterized urban elites throughout the United States during the years following the Civil War. With the formation of what historians have described as a "national upper class" in the post-Civil War period, the bourgeoisie finally arrived at a point where it could achieve cultural hegemony.[24] Yet for the most part, hegemony developed through a network of local institutions. A national gallery representing the entire United States was out of the question until well into the twentieth century, but it might be argued that, in the interim, the Metropolitan Museum of Art took the place of a national gallery. My point is that the bourgeoisie's inability to create a national art institution comparable to the Louvre or the London National Gallery during the postwar period reveals the extent to which elite factionalism remained a persistent feature of American political and cultural life, and points to the far greater intensity of those divisions—the more or less fragmented character of American elites—during the years preceding the Civil War.[25]

The historical problem might be stated in terms of a history of institutions. But the historical issues should not be understood purely in institutional terms. There are also key questions that have to do with the sacralization of art, the definition of high art and its opposite, popular or low art, and the institutionalization of these categories. In a study of the founding of the Boston Museum of Fine Arts and the Boston Symphony Orchestra, the sociologist Paul DiMaggio suggests that three interlocking factors had to be present in order to establish institutions of high culture in Boston and, by implication, elsewhere in the United States. First, there had to be *elite entrepreneurship,* meaning the creation of organizational forms the elite group or faction could totally control. These organizational forms were invariably corporate and nonprofit, thus insulating them from the market and, to an extent, from the state. Second, *classification:* the erection of strong and clearly defined boundaries between art and entertainment, with the former appropriated by the elite as its own cultural property and, crucially, "the acknowledgment of that classification's legitimacy by other classes and the state." And third, *framing:* the creation of "a new etiquette of appropriation, a new relationship between the audience and the work of art."[26]

DiMaggio's three factors describe the organizational forms arrived at by not only the Museum of Fine Arts but also the Corcoran Gallery and the Metropolitan Museum. Boards of trustees were created to insulate the museum from the pressures of the market and the impositions of the state. This was a move that was of particular consequence in New York, where the Metropolitan's trustees, almost all of them Republicans, managed to pressure Boss Tweed, head of New York's Democratic Party machine, into accepting an arrangement in which the city would be responsible for the museum building and its maintenance, and the trustees would in effect own the collections and oversee the museum's operation.[27] This arrangement became a model for other American art museums where trustee-collectors focused on acquisitions, collections, and exhibitions, while municipal authorities shouldered the responsibility for heating, lighting, upkeep, and repair.

DiMaggio's second category—*classification*—describes what I earlier called "sacralization," or the way in which the museum as an institution assumed control of the meaning of the works it put on display. Questions of what was sacred dogged American art museums from their inception. Were plaster casts fit to be shown in the sacrosanct spaces of the museum? What, if anything, distinguished traditional forms of high art (oil paintings, say, or sculptures in marble and bronze) from objects associated with certain upper-class hobbies (collections of musical instruments, arms and armor, Chinese porcelains)? Yet the museum's sacralizing function, the way it attempted to establish a universally accepted definition of high art, was rarely in doubt. Indeed, one might argue, as I have elsewhere, that the category of high art—what we today simply call "art"—did not exist in the United States before the advent of the art museum.[28]

Finally, when it comes to DiMaggio's category of *framing,* or "a new etiquette of appropriation, a new relationship between the audience and the work of art," we encounter issues Bennett has explored in detail. In theory, the museum was to be a training ground for the lower as well as the middle classes, a place where suitable behavior might be learned through emulation. Yet questions of etiquette divided early museum directors and trustees, many of whom were not entirely resigned to the idea that the museum should be open to all. As a modernizing institution, the museum addressed a public made up of, in Bennett's phrase, "formal equals."[29] The claim of formal equality was crucial for an institution whose history coincided with the rise of bourgeois democracy. Yet in practice, as Bourdieu has insisted, the museum helped to constitute a hierarchy in which those who possessed the capacity to comprehend and enjoy works of art were superior to those who did not. Thus, as Bourdieu maintains, the "distinction" belonging to the former became an essential feature of modern, middle-class society.[30] In the nineteenth-century American art museum, the contradiction between the claim of formal equality and the reality of hierarchies of class and taste often played out around questions of the etiquette of appropriation. Could the masses be trusted to behave appropriately in the museum's galleries? Could the museum instill bourgeois decorum? In 1897, Luigi Palma di Cesnola, the Metropolitan's first director, defended the museum's decision to deny entrance on a weekday afternoon to a plumber dressed in overalls. "The museum is a closed corporation," di Cesnola told reporters. "We do not want, nor will we permit a person who has been digging in a filthy sewer or working among grease and oil to come in here, and . . . make the surroundings uncomfortable for others." Yet di Cesnola could also boast that the museum was succeeding in its efforts to improve the public's behavior. In a letter written in the wake of the incident with the plumber, he asserted: "You do not see any more persons in the picture galleries blowing their nose with their fingers . . . There is no more spitting tobacco juice on the gallery floors . . . There are no more nurses taking children to some corner to defile the floors of the Museum . . . No more whistling, singing, or calling aloud to people from one gallery to another."[31] In other words, the masses were learning to behave in a properly reverential manner—or so it seemed.

Models

Having an art museum was imperative—so elites in New York, Boston, and Washington believed. But what sort of museum? Although they could hardly hope to create an institution that would directly compete with the Louvre, at least not for the foreseeable future, the Louvre was, nonetheless, a major source of inspiration. On a visit to Paris in the summer of 1855, William Corcoran very likely spent time studying the Louvre, which Louis-Napoleon was then in the process of renovating and enlarging with the help of his architect, Hector Lefuel. Renwick, Corcoran's architect, was also in Paris that summer and may have gone with his patron to inspect a modernized Louvre. In any event, a few years later, Renwick produced for Corcoran a Louvre-like design complete with grand staircase and tribuna.[32]

The Louvre also inspired the founders of the Metropolitan Museum, at least initially. When, in Paris in 1865, John Jay called for the creation of "a National Institution and gallery of Art," his auditors would immediately have thought of the Louvre, the inescapable symbol of France and French civilization, as a model for a future New York art museum. However, by the late 1860s, the men who founded the Metropolitan had another model in mind. Henry Cole's South Kensington Museum, which had opened in 1857, became, in the words of the art historian Michael Conforti, "the most imitated and programmatically influential museum of the late nineteenth century."[33] Indeed, it is difficult to overestimate its influence on the formation and early development of American art museums. Unlike the London National Gallery, which opened in 1824 and was in the 1850s still a preserve of collectors and connoisseurs, the South Kensington Museum was devoted to the applied arts and popular education. As Conforti observes:

> With its historical roots in the liberal political philosophy of the nineteenth century and its early programs evolving from the publicly directed commercial spectacles that were the international exhibitions of the time, the [South

> Kensington Museum represented] a historical paradigm for public engagement through creative educational programming.[34]

For reform-minded American museum builders, the South Kensington's example proved irresistible. The 1869 dinner at the Union League Club that led to the foundation of the Metropolitan Museum featured a number of speakers, including Henry Cole's brother, who extolled the virtues of the South Kensington model. Eleven years later, at the opening of the Metropolitan Museum's permanent building in Central Park, Joseph Choate, an influential trustee, described a museum that, like the South Kensington, would gather together a great collection illustrative of the history of art. The collection, Choate asserted,

> should serve not only for the instruction and entertainment of the people, but should also show to the students and artisans of every branch of industry, in the high and acknowledged standards of form and color, what the past has accomplished for them to imitate and excel.[35]

In Boston, Charles Perkins caught the mood of many of his bourgeois contemporaries when he observed that any attempt to found an art museum in the United States would have to aim at "collecting material for the education of a nation in art, not at making collections of objects of art."[36] The Museum of Fine Arts would, in Perkins's words, someday rival "the great industrial museums at Kensington and Vienna."[37]

Thus we have two models. The Louvre was a treasure house, a repository for canonical works that represented the nation's unique cultural patrimony. The South Kensington Museum, although no less concerned with preserving its nation's cultural heritage, emphasized the practical goal of popular arts education. By imitating Lefuel's designs for an expanded Louvre, Renwick produced a building that symbolized Corcoran's ambition to create a national treasure house. By contrast, both the Metropolitan Museum and the Museum of Fine Arts closely modeled their earliest buildings on the South Kensington Museum. Ruskin Gothic emblematized their faith in social improvement, practical education, and moral uplift.

Thus, American art museums were from their inception in the 1870s torn between competing goals. Should museums devote themselves to popular education in the manner of the South Kensington Museum? Or should they focus their energies on amassing what Perkins called "objects of art"? Would the American art museum be a school of industrial arts, or would it be, like the Louvre, a treasure house of art-historical masterpieces?

And yet, although the Metropolitan Museum and the Museum of Fine Arts initially opted for the South Kensington model, their adherence to a program of popular and industrial arts education did not last for long. By the turn of the century, a new scale of industrial wealth had opened new possibilities. By then, the Museum of Fine Arts was abandoning its Venetian Gothic building on Copley Square for a neoclassical temple on Huntington Avenue while simultaneously modifying its aesthetic and pedagogical goals. About the same time, the Metropolitan Museum was, through its architecture, also signaling a new orientation, but it did not in the process desert its original neo-Gothic edifice. Instead, it surrounded and all but obliterated Vaux and Mould's design with Roman revival-style wings. Even the Corcoran, in 1897, forsook its mini Louvre for an up-to-date Beaux-Arts treasure house. A new age of imperial aspiration was at hand. Thus the museum boom of the 1870s represented the bourgeoisie's first, tentative step in the direction of the American art museum's later, unabashed claims to national greatness.

Notes

This essay is a revised and expanded version of Alan Wallach, "La naissance du musée des beaux-arts américain," in *L'art américain: Identités d'une nation,* ed. Veerle Thielmans and Matthias Waschek (Paris: École Nationale Supérieure des Beaux-Arts, 2005), 66–83.

1. See, for example, Nathaniel Burt, *Palaces for the People: A Social History of the American Art Museum* (Boston: Little, Brown, 1977).
2. See Pierre Bourdieu, *Distinction: A Social Critique of the Judgement of Taste,* trans. Richard Nice (Cambridge, MA: Harvard University Press, 1984).
3. For issues of class formation and consolidation, as well as the broader cultural context for the Metropolitan Museum, I have relied on Sven Beckert, *The Monied Metropolis: New York City and the Consolidation of the American Bourgeoisie, 1850–1896* (Cambridge: Cambridge University Press, 2001), esp. 1–14, 237–72.
4. Henry T. Tuckerman, *Book of the Artists: American Artist Life* (New York: H. Holt, 1867), 11–12.
5. Winifred E. Howe, *A History of the Metropolitan Museum of Art* (New York: Metropolitan Museum of Art, 1913), 1:99.
6. Cited in Howe, *History of the Metropolitan Museum,* 1:99.
7. Ibid., 1:100. On the Union League Club, see Beckert, *Monied Metropolis,* 130–31.
8. Cited in Howe, 1:101.
9. Ibid., 1:101–223; and Calvin Tompkins, *Merchants and Masterpieces: The Story of the Metropolitan Museum of Art,* rev. ed. (New York: Henry Holt, 1989), 11–59.
10. Cited in W. M. Whitehill, *Museum of Fine Arts Boston: A Centennial History* (Cambridge, MA: Harvard University Press, 1970), 1:9.
11. Ibid., 1:27.
12. For the museum's founding, see Whitehill, 1:1–39. *See also* Neil Harris, "The Gilded Age Revisited: Boston and the Museum Movement," *American Quarterly* 14, no. 4 (Winter 1962): 545–66.
13. The *[Washington] Daily Patriot,* February 21, 1871.
14. For the early history of the Corcoran Gallery, see Alan Wallach, "William Wilson Corcoran's Failed National Gallery," in Wallach, *Exhibiting Contradiction: Essays on the Art Museum in the United States* (Amherst: University of Massachusetts Press, 1998), 22–37.
15. Cited in Howe, *History of the Metropolitan,* 1:108.
16. See Andrew McClellan, *Inventing the Louvre* (Cambridge and New York: Cambridge University Press, 1994).
17. See Carol Duncan and Alan Wallach, "The Universal Survey Museum," *Art History* 3, no. 4 (December 1980): 448–69.
18. Tony Bennett, *The Birth of the Museum* (London and New York: Routledge, 1995), 100–01.
19. Ibid., 102. It is probably no accident that Cole's brother C. C. Cole played a role in the founding of the Metropolitan Museum; see Howe, *History of the Metropolitan,* 1: 114, 131.
20. Cited in Howe, 1:111.
21. The Smithsonian Institution is the one exception. Founded in 1846 under the terms of a bequest from James Smithson, a British subject who had never set foot in the United States, the Smithsonian was in effect forced upon a very divided American government.
22. See Frederic Cople Jaher, *The Urban Establishment: Upper Strata in Boston, New York, Charleston, Chicago, and Los Angeles* (Urbana: University of Illinois Press, 1982); Edward Pessen, *Riches, Class, and Power before the Civil War* (1973; repr. New Brunswick, NJ: Transaction, 1990); E. Digby Baltzell, *Philadelphia Gentlemen: The Making of a National Upper Class* (1958; repr. New Brunswick, NJ: Transaction, 1989); and Peter Dobkin Hall, *The Organization of American Culture, 1700–1900: Private Institutions, Elites, and the Origins of American Nationality* (New York: New York University Press, 1982).
23. Ronald Story, "Class and Culture in Boston: The Athenaeum, 1807–1860," *American Quarterly* 27, no. 2 (1975): 178. *See also* Story, *Harvard and the Boston Upper Class: The Forging of an Aristocracy, 1800–1870* (Middletown, CT: Wesleyan University Press, 1980), esp. 160–82, in which Story argues for Boston's preeminent role in the formation of a national upper class after the Civil War.

24. See Baltzell, *Philadelphia Gentlemen,* passim. Story, in *Harvard and the Boston Upper Class,* 220–70, analyzes in some detail the corporate and organizational bases for the emergence of a "national elite."
25. See Alan Wallach, "Long-Term Visions, Short-Term Failures: Art Institutions in the United States, 1800–1860," in Wallach, *Exhibiting Contradiction,* 9–21.
26. See Paul DiMaggio, "Cultural Entrepreneurship in Nineteenth-Century Boston: The Creation of an Organizational Base for High Culture in America," in *Media, Culture and Society: A Critical Reader,* ed. Richard Collins et al. (London and Beverly Hills: Sage, 1986), 194–211.
27. See Tompkins, *Merchants and Masterpieces,* 33–48.
28. See Wallach, "Long-Term Visions" and "The American Cast Museum: An Episode in the History of the Institutional Definition of Art," in Wallach, *Exhibiting Contradiction,* 9–21, 38–56.
29. Bennett, *Birth of the Museum,* 93.
30. See Pierre Bourdieu and Alain Darbel, *The Love of Art,* trans. Caroline Beattie and Nick Merriman (Stanford: Stanford University Press, 1990); and Bourdieu, *Distinction,* passim.
31. Both quotations in Tompkins, *Merchants and Masterpieces,* 84–85.
32. See Wallach, "William Wilson Corcoran's Failed National Gallery," in Wallach, *Exhibiting Contradiction,* 29–31.
33. Michael Conforti, "The Idealist Enterprise and the Applied Arts," in *A Grand Design: The Art of the Victoria and Albert Museum,* ed. M. Baker and B. Richardson (New York: Harry N. Abrams and Baltimore: Baltimore Museum of Art, 1997), 27.
34. Conforti, "Idealist Enterprise," 23.
35. Cited in Tompkins, *Merchants and Masterpieces,* 21.
36. Charles C. Perkins, "American Art Museums," *North American Review* 111 (July 1870): 7–8.
37. Cited in Conforti, "Idealist Enterprise," 42.

15
The Manufactured Patron: Staging Bourgeois Identity through Art Consumption in Postbellum America

John Ott

In his scholarship on art collecting in nineteenth-century Spain, Oscar Vásquez urges study of the philosophies of cultural philanthropy in conjunction with its key sites and practices in order to fully comprehend how art consumption articulates, consolidates, and perpetuates social identities. Through analysis of the cultural ecology of postbellum San Francisco, this essay argues that California's entrepreneurial elites reorganized the regional art world, particularly over the course of the watershed decade of the 1870s. For leading patrons, art gradually but dramatically changed its function from educational philanthropy to a mark of class distinction; its audience, from a democratic commonwealth of art lovers to a tight clique of connoisseurs; its location, from a public forum to a sacred precinct; and its scope, from local to national markets and beyond.[1]

In their attempts to reconcile the private consumption of luxury goods with a demonstrable commitment to the public good, elite collectors and their advocates initially staged patronage of the arts as a sensitive and versatile social instrument that could at once edify, rehabilitate, and placate industrial workers, forestall social revolution, promote the regional economy, and foster a unified and harmonious public culture. As the new economic order of industrial capitalism increasingly belied the widely cherished of ideal of an egalitarian nation of equals, elites turned to the disinterested, expressly noneconomic sphere of culture in order to forge more acceptable models of social union and harmony. Art and its delectation promised to smooth over discord where politics and work no longer could.

While the antebellum conception of art as a moral and educational force for a broad range of social classes both depended upon and served artists, markets, and audiences at the local level, the postwar art world exhibited the features of an exclusive domain of elites that was more well publicized, to be sure, but less public in terms of access and viewership. Where once patrons sought to edify and uplift diverse strata of their immediate communities through contact with the arts, they now targeted their collections farther afield to a smaller caste of fellow affluent cognoscenti. In California and beyond, entrepreneurial and managerial elites reconfigured patronage of the arts as the expression of class identity rather than as a contribution to a unified, harmonious, and necessarily local public culture. This nascent art community propounded a more elitist philosophy of and restricted audience for the arts. During the tempestuous 1870s, an art world more national in conception and scope gradually eclipsed a loose constellation of local art communities, thanks in large part to the cultural dominance of these nouveaux riches industrial capitalists. Most importantly, relationships between artists and patrons now depended less on either physical proximity or a shared civic identity.

The explanation for this revolution is twofold. First, this conversion occurred partly in reaction to critics who regularly challenged or negotiated the meanings imposed by these industrialists on their collecting practices and personal galleries. While entrepreneurs strove to distance their cultural activities from commerce and the marketplace, their critics worked to ascribe economic and materialistic motives to elite cultural philanthropy. Opponents' charges of bald self-interest trumped elites' claims of munificence and portrayed entrepreneurs' utopian republic of art lovers as a corrupt and barren feudal oligarchy presided over by a ruthless capitalist leadership. This social backlash effectively short-circuited patrons' claims of public service and benefaction, and helped catalyze developments toward exclusivity and away from public investment.[2]

Second, the distinctive character of leading California patrons' sources of wealth begat more pronounced distinctions in class identification. The emergence of a translocal class consciousness among California's entrepreneurial bourgeoisie at once accompanied, shaped, and best explains these cultural convulsions during an era of heated confrontation between workers and management. Peter Decker's book-length study has demonstrated that, by the 1880s, a nucleus of bankers and business executives who oversaw heavily capitalized and mechanized corporations quickly overshadowed the state's original leadership caste of wholesale merchants and importers. Most prominent art patrons in California hailed from this new dominant class fraction and boasted relatively high, inherited educational, vocational, economic, and social capital. The 1878 list of life members of the San Francisco Art Association (SFAA), to offer but one example, features precisely this species of corporate capitalist with interests in manufacturing, transportation, and finance: Charles and Edwin Bryant Crocker, Leland Stanford, D. D. Colton, James Haggin, Lloyd Tevis, William Alvord, Edward Bosqui, James Donahue, James Flood, Phoebe Hearst, D. O. Mills, I. M. Scott, and William Ralston. For clarity, however, this study highlights the five chief officers and owners of the Central Pacific Railroad (CPR): Charles Crocker, E. B. Crocker, Mark Hopkins, Collis Potter Huntington, and Leland Stanford.[3]

This composite portrait of San Francisco's major art collectors at once resembles and differentiates itself from national trends. After the Civil War, the most well-known collectors of domestic art production worked largely in manufacturing, transportation, and finance, in sharp contrast to antebellum patrons, who tended to draw their wealth from the mercantile sector.[4] Local historian Hubert Howe Bancroft boasted in 1890 that, proportionately speaking, San Francisco contained more millionaires than any other metropolis. Other studies from the period seem to bear out his claims; a roster of leading domestic fortunes published in 1889 enumerated Stanford and Charles Crocker among the ten richest Americans, and Huntington and Hopkins in the top 40.[5] Although New York and other metropolitan centers may have claimed more extensive and well-developed art worlds, San Francisco's artistic community matured in a city forged by and acutely dependent upon industrial capitalism.

Unlike many industrial elites back East, however, the economic power of these mining and railroad industrialists and financiers was unalloyed by an extant or "old money" elite; as one contemporary put it, San Francisco was "a New York that has got no Boston on one side of it and no shrewd and orderly rural population on the other to keep it in check."[6] It did, however, possess a vocal and often militant working class, and the city witnessed the most "spectacular" class conflicts during the turbulent year of 1877, in the estimation of social historian Mary Ryan.[7] Most notably, the sudden appearance of the short-lived but influential Workingmen's Party of California marked the first expression of a class politics explicitly framed in those terms. The Golden State's remarkable evolution even captured the attention of Karl Marx, who in 1880 asserted that "nowhere else has the upheaval most shamelessly caused by capital concentration taken place with such speed."[8] California's yawning chasm of class differences begat new and highly exclusive strains of bourgeois identity and affiliation.

Art Consumption as Disinterested Philanthropy

Through a variety of strategies, including the use of brokers, the support of art associations, and the practice of charity loan exhibitions, entrepreneurs strove to secure their cultural authority exclusive of the marketplace. Although numerous studies of bourgeois culture have underscored the importance of consumption patterns in the consolidation of class consciousness and authority, the central place of the "fine" arts in this regard depends upon their distinctive, rarefied status as extra-economic commodities. That is to say, in the case of art and other select luxury goods, elites distinguished themselves less as consumers of individual goods than as generous patrons and selfless supporters of art institutions. California industrialists' practice of accumulating art in specifically noncommercial settings downplayed the essentially economic character of collecting and transformed a private act of shopping into an expression of public virtue. By this they also dissociated class identities from simple differences in economic resources.

At first, during the 1850s and 1860s, San Francisco's art world was not only local in scope but also reflected the interests of local artists. The most important fora for the fine arts in early San Francisco were the Industrial Exhibitions of the Mechanics' Institute. Beginning in September 1857, the Institute hosted 32 of these annual events in a series of temporary pavilions before the conclusion of the century.[9] By contrast, early consumer-oriented organizations on the West Coast failed. Modeled after other, ultimately more successful subscription enterprises in cities like New York, Philadelphia, Boston, and Cincinnati, the California Art Union (CAU) opened its headquarters on the second floor above the Montgomery galleries of Wooll and Sutherland in early 1865. But despite extensive and generally favorable regional press coverage, the California Art Union folded within months. Years later, industrialist and former mayor William Alvord enumerated the causes for its failures: "the difficulty of varying the exhibitions by new pictures, the lukewarmness of the artists, and the materialistic character of our population."[10] Indeed, only two painters' names appeared in the directory of this pricey businessmen's club. The precipitous collapse of the CAU echoed the disintegration of the American Art-Union, in which an institutional leadership of New York merchants eventually foundered before disgruntled local artists and their advocates.[11]

During this initial phase of art world development, elite consumers needed to downplay the commercial aspects of buying art if they wished to mantle their purchases in the raiment of benevolence. Less than a year after the initial Gold Rush, art galleries had already began to blossom along the Montgomery Street corridor, the city's financial and mercantile center north of Market Street.[12] Generally speaking, however, the region's executive class eschewed these openly commercial emporia for less overtly mercantile milieu, such as artists' studios and volunteer associations. So, too, did New York's antebellum collectors favor direct patronage, as evidenced by the successful receptions at the Tenth Street Studios. Accordingly, collectors sought out professional and personal relationships with the painters and photographers themselves, many of who had cannily located their workspaces in San Francisco's mercantile district.[13] Sustained and well-publicized contact with artists, their studios, and other affiliated art venues greatly helped differentiate magnanimous patrons from mere acquisitive collectors.

If at midcentury most art transactions in the United States still took place in artists' studios, in the postbellum era art dealers became increasingly prominent. New York's commercial galleries, for example, waxed as studio receptions waned. Scholars examining European markets have documented comparable mutations from a system of patronage, in which clients worked directly with artists, to a system of collecting, in which an armature of middlemen intervened between producers and consumers.[14] This growing importance of cultural brokers, which included not only galleries and auction houses but also art critics and assorted advisors, presented both assistance to and an acute problem for would-be patrons of the arts. Even as these intermediaries made art more physically and intellectually accessible to the managerial elite, and further disassociated patronage from materialism and consumerism, they also threatened to expose these industrialists as cultural neophytes who relied on others' expertise and taste. The era of Bernard Berenson and the Duveen Brothers, in which brokers did most of the cultural legwork, had not yet arrived; but neither did art patrons act wholly independently.

Local industrialists regularly looked to friends, colleagues, and artists for advice, even as they often obscured or downplayed this dependence. A 1873 *Sacramento Bee* review of Edwin Crocker's new galleries in his Sacramento home divulged that the railroad executive had employed "selected agents of taste, skill and judgment" to assemble his European collections. In addition, Benjamin Parke Avery acted as a "broker" for Irving M. Scott, while Leland Stanford often consulted with Dr. J. D. B. Stillman about artistic matters.[15] A number of newspaper reports concerning one 1872 auction at the SFAA demonstrates how major patrons typically acquired artworks through intermediaries. But although one article discloses that "Dr. Stillman was the heaviest purchaser—acting, it is presumed, for Mr. Stanford . . . [and] W. C. Ralston also purchased through agents," other art columns suggest that these brokers may have concealed their employers' identities.[16] "Dr. Stillman, the ex-coroner . . . bought a considerable amount, and it was understood that his purchases were for Sharon; some said Ralston." This relative indeterminacy of attribution implies that many local businessmen preferred to collect anonymously, or at least wished to distance themselves from the actual act of economic exchange.[17]

At the same time, a reliance on consultants or agents risked both the loss of cultural cachet and condemnation as acquisitive rather than bountiful. In 1880, the *San Francisco Examiner* maintained that the interior furnishings of the city's "nouveaux riches" had been "selected by the liberally paid-for taste commissioned agents . . . In the contract system, pictures and all other works of art are simply so much necessary furniture, and are purchased in the full hanging capacity of the walls upon no greater higher principle of taste that that of the selection of a cooking range in conformity with the dimensions of the kitchens."[18] In these mansions, critics alleged, pragmatic and material considerations wholly obscured any aesthetic ones. At best, these oligarchs were avaricious collectors rather than true patrons; at worst, they were mere by-standers whose taste had been purchased outright. In like fashion, an 1874 editorial in the *San Francisco Post* drew a clear distinction between a "true" patron and a mere collector:

> A true patron of painting is not one who buys a picture at half its worth, and chuckles over the fact complacently. No! Those who watch the progress of young

> artists, find out what they have in them, drop in at their studios occasionally, and by and by, when the proper moment comes, give commission orders that show the artist he is understood and appreciated, such are the men who really encourage Art.[19]

This passage illustrates how industrialist consumers might have adapted their managerial roles to supervise artists in the same manner as their employees, corporations, and capital. It further elucidates how the honorific of patron helped entrepreneurs transcend the vulgarities of the marketplace and circumvent criticisms of materialistic motivations and behavior.

In the same way, the expressed support for art institutions usefully cloaked consumption in philanthropy, consolidated a public identity as a civic leader, and demonstrated a commitment to both the artistic community and the public welfare. The voluntary and nonprofit character of cultural organizations also effectively distanced patrons from more obviously self-serving spheres like the market and the workplace. In San Francisco, then, railroad managers and their industrial brethren devoted money and energy to art associations and institutions even as they amassed personal collections. As my introductory roster indicates, few entrepreneurial elites in California passed up the chance to underwrite cultural associations like the San Francisco Art Association.

Charity events at nonprofit organizations like the SFAA further packaged art collecting as public philanthropy. The exhibition of works from personal collections on behalf of benevolent societies began in force with the so-called Sanitary Fairs of the Civil War era; by loaning artworks, wealthy patrons could signal their loyalty to and support for the Union campaign. In San Francisco, painter William Jewett curated one such show for the Ladies' Christian Commission Fair in the summer of 1864 on behalf of the North, and many local collectors continued to farm their artworks out for charity for decades. In exchange for this recirculation of personal collections of painting and sculpture into public or semipublic exhibitions, patrons achieved a pronounced and highly favorable visibility. For example, in 1871, and to great acclaim, Edwin and Margaret Crocker displayed 179 of their newly purchased holdings in European art at the Snow & Roos gallery for four months, and directed all proceeds to the Howard Benevolent Society of Sacramento. The Crockers' plans to make their collections publicly available and to direct admission proceeds to orphans and "inmates of the asylum" impelled one *Sacramento Bee* reporter to observe that "the poor and the helpless have always been the objects of Judge Crocker's care."[20]

Art Consumption as Public Service

These practices legitimated art consumption as altruistic. By appearing to transcend more materialistic and selfish concerns, patrons of art could more readily figure their endeavors as an equal contribution to all members of society; as such, they also frequently defined them as quintessentially democratic pursuits that would unify disparate social groups. For example, at its first annual meeting, SFAA President William Alvord characterized the association as "a Society for the promotion of aesthetic tastes and the creation of a livelier interest in, and a more liberal patronage of, works of art." Soon the *San Francisco Bulletin* was predicting that the shows of the SFAA would "become one of the leading attractions and educational forces of the city." And in his stated aim of diffusing the appreciation of the visual arts, Alvord envisioned an ideal republic of art lovers: "[Art] seems especially to present an object of social union where there can be no rivalry, save in a generous desire to excel in improving its condition and extending the field of its usefulness."[21]

The intellectual platform of the San Francisco Art Association borrowed heavily from the program of art education advanced by Boston art critic and collector James Jackson Jarves. A millionaire who inherited wealth from the burgeoning manufacturing sector, Jarves urged his fellow moneyed industrialists to assume cultural leadership in manifestoes like "A Lesson for Merchant Princes," a chapter from his *Italian Rambles* that drew explicit parallels between fifteenth-century Florence and modern America. Like Alvord, Jarves presented patronage as a means of ameliorating class relations. Museums in particular promised to transmute the "selfish acquisitions of covetous amateurs" into "the inalienable birthright of the people," as he wrote in the *Atlantic Monthly* in 1860, and Jarves repeatedly characterized art collecting as the *ne plus ultra* of noblesse oblige. In *Art Studies* he maintained: "[I]f art be kept a rare and tabooed thing, a specialty for the rich and powerful, it excites in the vulgar mind envy and hate. But proffer it freely to the public, and the public soon learns to delight in it, and claim and protect it as its rightful inheritance."[22]

Yet for Jarves the support of arts institutions was more than either the mere laundering of ill-gotten fortunes or a heavy-handed public relations strategy; indeed, art education could both uplift and unite Americans from all walks of life. In *Art Thoughts,* for example, he touted "the educational advantages of galleries and museums, and their conservative and refining influence on society, in teaching respect for the past." In *Art Studies,* Jarves laid out in greater detail the program by which aesthetics would transform the lower orders of society: "At the best, prisons and punishments are an expensive means of but dubious efficacy for regulating society. Art tends to prevent crime, by proffering to the people new and exhaustless pleasures, which enlarge the faculties, stimulate their observation, and predispose them to brotherhood by a language intelligible to the entire civilized world." Proper public education in the arts could create a kind of an aesthetic commonwealth that erased differences of class, region, creed, and ethnicity. Painting and its sister arts could help one achieve membership in a "brotherhood" that spoke the same "intelligible language."[23]

Jarves's primary end goal, however, was less social welfare than social order: "The only permanent security for a republic," he argued in 1863, "is the enlarged culture of its citizens."[24] As numerous social and cultural historians have shown, this commitment to elite, privatized, and top-down legislation of morality was the hallmark of corporatist, managerial civics in Gilded Age America. In California, SFAA co-founder and perennial official Benjamin Parke Avery advanced similar arguments that art functioned as a moral tonic. "It is not enough that we persuade the gamester and the drunkard to drop cards and alcohol," he wrote "we must give them instead the means of innocent recreation. Just so far as we can increase the liking for books, pictures, statuary, music, oratory, fountains, parks, fine buildings, natural scenery, at the same time that we increase the faculties for obtaining the pleasures they afford, just so far we shall ennoble leisure and purify diversion."[25]

By and large, however, artworks were most often displayed and discussed in the context of private domestic galleries, instead of more public fora like the SFAA; the patently uneven and highly restricted distribution of art threatened to undercut high-minded goals of social transformation. Led by CPR executives Stanford, Hopkins, and Charles Crocker, California's entrepreneurial patrons housed their art holdings in prestigious urban neighborhoods and on expansive country estates. Like Prairie Avenue in Chicago, Beacon Hill in Boston, and Fifth Avenue in New York, San Francisco's Nob Hill claimed the majority of the region's postbellum manufacturing and financial elites. Their mansions forcefully broadcast their owners' sheer wealth and prestige.[26]

But despite their residence in tony enclaves, art patrons pledged their holdings to a large audience for high-minded goals of social transformation. Certainly, Edwin Bryant Crocker, if we take him at his word, originally envisioned establishing a public museum, as the *Bulletin* reported in 1872: "He is erecting at Sacramento a building a large proportions, intended as a gallery of art and museum of natural history . . . for the benefit, not alone of his family and friends, but of the community at large."[27] At first blush, the monied oligarchy of California did indeed situate their collections in spaces suitable for semipublic delectation. Collectors not only localized galleries within the more public zones of their houses but also created an inviting environment for their artwork in order to encourage sustained admiration. Flanked by reception and billiard rooms, galleries in the Charles Crocker and Leland Stanford houses occupied a locus of sociability and hospitality. Both executives provided visitors with upholstered chairs and sofas from which to soak up the paintings on display. A combination of skylights, windows, and artificial lighting amply illuminated these spaces of opulent gentility. Comparison with the major entrepreneurial New York discloses the relative uniformity of taste in domestic gallery decor in major American cities.[28]

Antibourgeois Responses

Many Californians challenged these efforts to articulate and valorize entrepreneurial bourgeois identity through art patronage. Amplifying in tone and volume over the course of the 1870s, most criticism grew directly out of larger challenges to the rise of the CPR monopoly. By and large, these dissenters simply translated their assertions of the railroad's greed and private interest to the rhetoric and practices by which the Central Pacific's managers organized their art collections. Critics also characterized art patronage by new-money industrialists as materialistic and self-aggrandizing in nature. These responses prove that patrons could no longer simply and disingenuously claim to promote the public good.

The most visible expressions of antibourgeois feeling occurred over the second half of 1877, the occasion of the United States' first national strike that began, significantly, in the railroad sector. In late July, a modest rally of socialist organizations held before San Francisco city hall in order to express sympathy with the striking workers soon overheated and boiled over into an anti-Chinese mob. Quickly, a number of Nob Hill residents active in the local Republican Party, including Charles Crocker and James Flood, formed the city's third Vigilance Committee. For less than a week, the rioters and the 4,000 or so members of the Committee's "pickaxe brigade" engaged in mostly bloodless street theater, although property damage to Chinese-operated establishments was hardly inconsequential.[29] The city soon returned to relative normality, but groups opposed to both railroad monopoly and the presence of Chinese laborers continued to conduct rallies, often in vacant sand lots near strategically-chosen locations: City Hall, the new U. S. Mint, and even the acme of Nob Hill. These public meetings eventuated in the creation of the short-lived Workingmen's Party of California, whose legacy was largely confined to a string of legislative measures aimed at Chinese immigrants.[30]

Vocal opponents of the railroad oligarchy nested their criticisms of elite cultural philanthropy within these broader condemnations of the political, economic, and social dominance of the Central Pacific. Ambrose Bierce, editor of the *San Francisco Illustrated Wasp,* took particular relish in cutting down the CPR president, whom he variously labeled "£eland $tanford" and "Stealand Standfirm." In a particularly astute editorial, Bierce combined criminal charges with the criticism that Stanford's cultural benefactions were wholly private in conception, purpose, and execution: "Mr. Stanford has not asked the public how it would be most agreeable to it to be robbed; he does not now consult it as to the method of restitution." And just as Bierce questioned Leland Stanford's commitments to the public welfare, so too did he try to discredit the alchemy of transmuting money into cultural authority. On the occasion of Stanford's appointment to the Golden Gate Park Commission, Bierce observed: "Governor Stanford of the Central and Southern Pacific is a pirate and a pig, but Governor Stanford of California Street is a gentleman and a philanthropist. In his dual character of malefactor and benefactor he somewhat resembles the ideal highwayman dear to the hearts of the novel writers, who sometimes bestows in charity as much as one half of one percent of his plunder." Bierce and other skeptics met each philanthropic gesture by the executives of the CPR with a reminder of the dubious business practices of the "rail rogues."[31]

In a parallel vein, other critics reduced the industrialists' hard-won cultural capital to simple economic capital by characterizing the motivations and taste of leading patrons as mercantile and materialistic at heart. The anonymous author of *The Monarch Philanthropist,* a barely fictionalized critique of "Eland Lanford," described the creation of a university not only as a ploy to "purchase the title of philanthropist" but also as "a great speculation, a boom like any other" that would merely and inevitably multiply "Lanford's" wealth through the inflation of real estate values near the school. Finally, during a brief period of estrangement from his employers, Central Pacific attorney Alfred Cohen publicly attacked Charles Crocker in like manner: "I will show the world how an intelligent patron of the arts and literature can be manufactured by the powers of wealth out of a peddler of needles and pins." For Cohen, not only was Crocker's metamorphosis into a cultured gentlemen a gaudy facade built up with sheer riches, but also the very process itself ("manufactured") was businesslike at heart.[32]

The Sacred Precincts of the Bourgeoisie

As if in response to this severe social and cultural backlash, leading California patrons increasingly interpolated a smaller constituency, and for less justifiably charitable purposes. The dual journey toward an art community and social authority soon exposed numerous gaps between patrons' rhetoric of public welfare and their practices of private consumption and display. In the end, California's entrepreneurial elites situated their holdings in spaces best described as publicly private. In essence, the executives of the CPR and other major patrons wished to make their collections known but not available to a larger audience. Decreased physical and social access helped draw sharper class distinctions, while increased accessibility through print culture broadcast and legitimated art patronage and consumption as the embodiments of a bourgeois class prerogative. Here I concur with sociologist Paul DiMaggio, who has argued that "it is important that their culture be recognized as legitimate by, yet be only partially available to, groups that are subordinate to them."[33]

Executive collectors contributed a handful of public statements about cultural patronage that attest to their competing and often contradictory aims. In an interview with historian Hubert Howe Bancroft, the CPR president and U.S. Senator Stanford prescribed the cultured medicine of the arts for America's materialism: "We are especially in need of art, culture, and a love of the beautiful in nature and in life. Now we are a material race, prizing what we own . . . [;] nevertheless we should be able to keenly enjoy whatever we see around us that appeals to the eye of taste."[34] Later, in an 1893 letter to Stanford University President David Starr Jordan, he synthesized platitudes about the aesthetic education of the masses with simple elitism:

> I believe in painting. I believe in having it possible for the masses to have their tastes cultured so that they can enjoy the finest art, and I think they should have public halls where of the masters might be found—painting, sculpture, and the fine arts generally—where the public could go and enjoy them, as persons with cultured tastes always will.

Here the railroad executive expansively offers fine art galleries to all, even while reserving art appreciation for those with suitably "cultured tastes."[35]

Stanford's equivocation between configuring art patronage as a private mark of distinction and as community service places him in the lineage of James Jackson Jarves. As with Stanford, Jarves's ideal of a nation united though the appreciation of the fine arts hardly disavowed its foundational Ruskinian notion of a sanctified elite charged with the dissemination and maintenance of artistic and ethical standards. These considerations were in part practical, since governmental patronage of the arts in the nineteenth century was illusory at best. From the outset of his career, Jarves averred that personal fortunes would have to suffice until the public taste had ripened and matured:

> In free countries, primary public efforts begin with individuals and their objects, be they railroads, hospitals, or colleges, and are subsequently sanctioned and aided by government, in accordance with their merits. With us, art must follow the same path. Private enterprise alone can be relied on, for the present, to initiate means of instruction, galleries, and to provide artistic adornment for public grounds. In time, however, the nation will charge itself with the "work."[36]

Here Jarves flatly advanced an aesthetic philosophy that was democratic in theory and elitist in practice. As collections and museums began to coalesce, Jarves's rhetorical republic—a kind of "imagined community" of art lovers—began to crack apart from strain.[37] In the wake of the turbulent 1870s, this underlying tension between the rhetoric of public improvement and the realities of private membership increasingly plagued advocates of art and its patronage.

The San Francisco Art Association, for example, exuded an aura of exclusivity even as it professed more egalitarian goals. In addition to the social barrier erected by its fee schedule, the association expressed its elitism through its location within the city's existing terrain of carefully demarcated social space. Significantly, the SFAA held its inaugural exhibition in the rooms of the Mercantile Library. Beyond its own art collection, this private businessmen's library possessed numerous features that necessitated a certain level of education: scientific displays, lecture series, and an intramural debating society. The inclusion of a "smoking and conversation room" reinforced this clublike atmosphere.[38] Moreover, proponents continually touted its elite constituency. Benjamin Parke Avery categorized SFAA exhibitions as "the most refined social events of the city" in a national arts magazine. And in the *Overland Monthly*, the regional journal he edited, Avery struggled to reconcile the paradoxes in organizational philosophy. When he celebrated the SFAA because it "tended to make art popular by making it talked about and fashionable," he extrapolated an audience that was simultaneously broad-based and narrow, and presupposed an aesthetics that was at once "popular" and sensitive to the nuances of high "fashion."[39]

Thus in practice the San Francisco Art Association staged the same kinds of social performances common to the city's many elite clubs, which rivaled their Eastern counterparts in their restrictiveness.

No single institution better demonstrates this marriage of the fine arts to the city's ruling class than its famed Bohemian Club. Initially chartered in 1872 as an informal meeting-group of journalists, the Club soon bragged San Francisco's most celebrated painters and writers, plus their most ardent supporters in the city's business class, such as Ralston and Alvord. Thus, the early membership of the Bohemian Club coincided with the leadership of the SFAA; in fact, the Association's School of Design initially inhabited rooms that had previously contained the Bohemians' art gallery. Over time, the maintenance of these hierarchies became more important than the day-to-day support of the local art community. In San Francisco, at least, the conventionally fraternal elements of the Bohemian Club soon dominated the original nucleus of painters, literati, and newspapermen. The number and frequency of artists among the Club's elected officers rapidly diminished over the course of the 1870s, so that in 1882 none other than Oscar Wilde, on tour in the States, could quip at the Club that he had never seen "so many well-dressed, well-fed business-like looking Bohemians."[40]

Even though major patrons physically arrayed their domestic galleries in a manner that intimated a desire to inculcate and amuse the general public, evidence strongly suggests that the vast majority of the public could only access these collections through print media, despite patrons' lofty and democratic rhetoric. As I hope to establish, industrialist elites did not so much make their private collections open to the California public as they simply publicized them to a larger audience. Unfortunately, little direct evidence survives as to who was allowed to view the collections on the Nob, or how often this might have occurred.

Yet in an apparent paradox, as the audience for art narrowed, its publicity rapidly mounted. As is already evident, regional print culture was the essential means by which the practices of collectors gained visibility.[41] In addition, press coverage increasingly figured art consumption as the province of elite taste. Always well reported in local newspapers, the purchase of a painting at a San Francisco Art Association event garnered highly favorable publicity. Loans also esteemed industrialist bourgeois patrons; SFAA shows typically borrowed "a large number of the best works from the private galleries of wealthy citizens," in the words of the *Alta California*.[42] A partial list compiled from period newspapers' art columns includes loans from Stanford, E. B. Crocker, Collis Huntington, Colton, Haggin, Alvord, Bosqui, Donahue, and Ralston. In fact, more often than not, wealthy patrons used the galleries of the SFAA for the purposes of display rather than for shopping. Several especially renowned or costly purchases of artworks often occurred *prior* to their display in the Association's rooms, which suggests that in practice the SFAA served less to promote the local art market than to showcase the munificence and taste of its leading members.[43]

A sympathetic local press regularly lauded the managerial caste's Nob Hill chateaus and the collections within. Beyond the usual coverage of home construction and society events, special newspaper editions, often issued in conjunction with a national event or festival, featured and celebrated the castles atop the Nob. By focusing at length on the region's most spectacular residences, booster publications like the special Centennial issue of the *California Spirit of the Times* elided the state's prosperity with that of its oligarchy. The most ambitious project in this vein appeared in 1888, when the *San Francisco Newsletter and California Advertiser* created a special serial insert, "Artistic Homes of California," that surveyed the stately manors of CPR executives and their industrial brethren. The honorific "artistic" and the medium of an expensive publication gilded the consumption of luxury goods with the venerable patina of high art.[44] Particularly in society columns, such as the *San Francisco Call's* report of one affair thrown by Charles and Mary Crocker in February 1882, art viewing emerges as but one of many diverting features of an evening out among California's nabobs.[45]

The simultaneously inclusive and exclusive character of cultural patronage was essential to social prestige; patrons required a rapt audience for their performances of bourgeois identity but not a true public with whom the terms of their collections would have to be negotiated. Writing about nineteenth-century Spain, Oscar Vásquez also identifies print culture as the crucial site for the consolidation of bourgeois identity and cultural authority through the fine arts: "Their *representations* through a host of documentary sources and publications made a reading and viewing audience aware of these private collections and helped transform them into public, contested repositories of knowledge . . . What was circulated as a 'collection' was most often not the artworks themselves but the listings, descriptions, reproductions, inventories, and other signs of the collections."[46] As the author notes, these cultural representations did offer critics a forum in which to articulate counternarratives and alternative philosophies of cultural philanthropy. And yet the mediation of art journalism and related practices filtered art patronage through a medium that was generally sympathetic to and indeed dependent upon the consent of affluent collectors.

Indeed, in many cases this art world publicity often touted the role of art consumers at the expense of art producers. In many catalogues for the SFAA and other societies, the name of the patron appears as prominently as the painter's. In the same fashion, many newspaper articles on the local art scene organized their discussion by individual collector rather than by artist.[47] Further evidence of a consumer-centered art world exists in the publication, both in specialized art journals and in multivolume encyclopedias, of numerous profiles of prestigious private collections, most notably, Philadelphia critic Earl Shinn's three-book *Art Treasures of America* (1879–82). Despite his East Coast bias, Shinn singled out the executives of the CPR for praise in his purview of California holdings. When enumerating individual artworks in these and other private galleries, Shinn printed the names of patrons in typeface as large as that reserved for the artists. Shinn's uncommon and rarefied view into the private boudoirs of the nation's wealthy collectors was, for the period, the usual vantage point from which Americans had access to elite domestic galleries. The general public was encouraged to bear witness to, but not participate in, the development of regional and national art communities alike.[48]

A National Art Market for a National Bourgeoisie

As the economic interests of postwar elites extended well beyond the boundaries of their local communities, so too did their conception of the art world. Numerous postwar developments point to a burgeoning national art world orbiting around New York: extralocal exhibitions drawn from geographically diverse collections; truly national art journals, histories of art, and compendia of art collections; private art collections more cosmopolitan in scope; and dealers with branches across the country and in Europe. California collectors increasingly directed their philanthropic efforts away from a geographically narrow but socially broad constituency and toward a geographically broad but socially narrow caste of art world insiders.

In terms of art consumption and social affiliation alike, these prominent collectors now largely addressed fellow elites around the nation.

In California, the most prominent collectors not only worked increasingly through dealers but also began to conduct these transactions outside the state. A few of them, like E. B. Crocker in Sacramento, acquired substantial collections during a European grand tour, but most of the California elite did not actively shop for art overseas and relied instead on intermediaries. Charles Crocker, Leland Stanford, and Collis Huntington all supported New York dealers and auction houses like Michael Knoedler's and the American Art Association as early as 1870. At the same time, Manhattan's cultural entrepreneurs extended their sales networks outward. By the 1880s, to offer another example, Pittsburg industrialist collectors were also patronizing Knoedler, and in 1897 he established a branch facility there.[49]

This period also saw the sudden fluorescence of postwar art texts explicitly national in scope. Published in 1882 and revised in 1884, S. R. Koehler's *United States' Art Directory and Year-Book* touted itself as "the first attempt to give a bird's-eye view of the organized efforts . . . in the United States in behalf of art."[50] Its inaugural volume, however, dedicated a scant three pages to national organizations and over 90 to local associations, so that while its broad prospect testifies to the possibility of conceptualizing a national art scene, its annals betray the lingering regional nature of art world institutions. Shinn's aforementioned *Art Treasures of America* more suitably exemplifies this consumption-centered view of a national art world. In this project, the Philadelphia critic undertook a rather selective but genuinely nationwide survey of many of the country's most prominent collections. In his preface, moreover, the author also announced ultimately unrealized plans for the serial *American Connoisseur*.[51] With a constituency that was necessarily smaller both in conception and in numbers, these specialty journals and publications not only served but helped to engender a close-knit but far-flung community of bourgeois cognoscenti.

A shift in bourgeois preference from a local to a national art scene is also evident in major California collections. As dealers and clients exerted greater control over the market, and as patrons increasingly frequented the same emporia and tastemakers, collections in San Francisco metamorphosed to become indistinguishable from their counterparts in other cities. The prewar proliferation of regional landscape, genre, and even history painting soon evaporated before a blitzkrieg of contemporary European academic canvases. The buying habits of the San Francisco elite were part of a national trend in which a spike of interest in domestic art production during Reconstruction immediately preceded a glut of purchases of European academic paintings. Patrons' abandonment of regional artists, in turn, precipitated familiar charges of materialism and self-interest.[52]

The influence of California's wealthy industrial magnates over the local art scene became so pronounced that many artists objected; on occasion they even tried to establish their own institutional terrain. In response to the California Art Union, artistic luminaries incorporated the San Francisco Artists' Union (SFAU) in late 1868. Like the CAU, it too imploded within months. Then, in 1884, landscapist Charles D. Robinson and painter Jules Tavernier spearheaded the formation of the California Palette Club, largely to protest the entrepreneurial management of the San Francisco Art Association. This splinter group of art professionals voiced complaints common to many Gilded Age artists: the SFAA's selection policies were too liberal, its admission fees too high, and the oversight of its exhibitions and auctions too authoritarian and heedless of artists' needs. The chief insult to the charter members of the Palette Club, however, was the SFAA's importation of some 50 works from New York painters for an impending show.[53]

The Palette Club's forceful seizure of the means of cultural production from their erstwhile manager-patrons exemplifies how art professionals shared many of the same concerns as other Bay Area laborers, although there is no evidence Tavernier and his confederates ever expressed solidarity with the city's working classes. Nonetheless, like the Workingmen's Party, the Palette Club protested most loudly against the importation of extralocal labor. Comparable trends emerged on the national level, as American artists began lobbying for tariffs on foreign art in 1867 and eventually prevailed in 1883.[54]

The gradual nationalization of the art market paralleled the development of a truly national elite. During the antebellum era, the American bourgeoisie articulated cultural hegemony at the local level. Only near the conclusion of the century could anything like a national elite be said to exist, either in fact, practice, or self-awareness. Capitalists who participated in nationalized economic sectors like the railroads abandoned transclass local or civic identities for a nationalized bourgeois class identity.[55] And, as the economic interests of postwar elites extended well beyond the boundaries of their local communities, their conception of the art world did as well. Most striking is the shift in patronage from local artists to European moderns. As corporate employers created greater "social distance" between themselves and the working class, and relied more heavily on cheaper immigrant labor, so too did their interest in and support of local artists wane.[56] Even as they increasingly proffered art patronage and art education as multifaceted means of social betterment, the entrepreneurial bourgeoisie in practice pulled away from more broadly conceived ideas about art's "public." Utopian proposals of an aesthetic commonwealth that would edify and unite Americans yielded, over time, to configurations of art as a more exclusive domain.[57]

Toward the Bourgeois Museum

In many ways, the genesis and evolution of the Leland Stanford Junior Museum, which eventually opened in 1894, epitomize the tensions between the public rhetoric of patrons, who claimed they wished to benefit the general welfare, and the ideologies of private cultural philanthropy and social distinction that actually defined their practices. Stanford University contained provisions for an art museum from its very inception, when its founding grant was drafted in late 1885. Early plans reported in the *San Francisco Call* suggested an educational institution easily accessible to a broad public:

> Leland Stanford Jr. . . . announced his intention frequently to establish a museum in Golden Gate Park so that California boys could see at home many things that rendered foreign travel a source of delightful pleasure and instruction. . . . Mrs. Stanford has decided to carry out her son's cherished ambition in this regard, and will establish a museum in the park. The museum project broadened into the grander one. The works of art which are now in the Stanford home are to be the nucleus of a museum in Golden Gate Park, independent of the University, but under the control of the trustees. . . . It is the intention of Mrs. Stanford to shortly open the mansion to art students.[58]

The conjunction of art museums and urban parks also manifested itself in New York (the Metropolitan in Central Park) and in Boston (the MFA in the Back Bay Fens), and even emerges in Jarves's many writings.[59] This kind of siting earmarked a faith in the ameliorative, environmental character of aesthetic education and in museums' capacity for moral uplift.

Over time, however, the Stanfords revised their plans and relocated the museum site from public to private land and from an urban to a rural environment: first to the remote Twin Peaks, then out of the city entirely and down the peninsula to their new university in Palo Alto.[60] In like manner, the fate of the Stanfords' art collection changed from a more public and urban locale to more private and exurban one. Up until Leland Sr.'s death in 1893, local newspapers reported that the couple's Nob Hill villa and its art treasures would eventually be "conveyed to the regents of the university to be either a picture-gallery or a public library for use of the citizens of the State when Governor and Mrs. Stanford have no further use for it." But within months, the *Collector* disclosed that Jane Stanford had transferred the art collection in San Francisco to Palo Alto, while the Great Fire of 1906 claimed the mansion before executors had finalized the particulars of Jane's will.[61]

Finally, the very architecture of the university museum eventually erected in Palo Alto suggests that Jane Stanford, who was most responsible for its conception, execution, and management, catered more to the small, international community of bourgeois art patrons than to a wider audience of Californians. First, Jane and Leland sought guidance from connoisseurs far afield, including Luigi Palma di Cesnola, the first professional director of the Metropolitan Museum of Art in New York, and officials at the National Museum of Athens, after which her museum was eventually modeled. Second, while the physical plant of the rest of the university campus synthesized the Richardsonian Romanesque with building traditions indigenous to California, the stark neoclassicism of the Stanford Museum expressed fealty to the Beaux Arts academicism of comparable institutions on the East Coast and in Europe.[62]

No doubt many other factors, both personal and practical, contributed to the Stanfords' retreat from local audiences, civic spaces, and public institutions; at the same time, examination of comparable cultural institutions in places like New York and Boston reveals a larger pattern of private governance and social exclusivity.[63] Many scholars have addressed this wide gap between the rhetoric and performance of cultural philanthropy, and conclude variously as to its underlying causes and broader significance.[64] But, however intentional or coordinated their efforts might have been, the entrepreneurial bourgeoisie widely advertised their cultivated domains of art consumption even as they carefully patrolled and barred others from them. The increasingly unfavorable public opinion about the cultural philanthropy of California's corporate managers had fueled these trends toward exclusivity and away from public investment. In the end, the economic downturn and outright class warfare of the 1870s in San Francisco and elsewhere not only helped to catalyze the corporate bourgeoisie's gradual withdrawal from Jarves's republic of art lovers, but also contributed significantly to the emergence of class-based consciousness, solidarity, and interest, both atop Nob Hill and at its foot.

Notes

1. "Acquisitions sites and procedures were inseparable from the discourses of collecting and, as such, helped to define differences among subject positions, that is, among individual and group identities" (Oscar E. Vásquez, *Inventing the Art Collection: Patrons, Markets, and the State in Nineteenth-Century Spain* [University Park: Pennsylvania State University Press, 2001], 31). I borrow the notion of an "ecology" of art patronage from Albert Boime, "Entrepreneurial Patronage in Nineteenth-Century France," in *Enterprise and Entrepreneurs*

in Nineteenth- and Twentieth-Century France, ed. Edward C. Carter II, Robert Forster, and Joseph N. Moody (Baltimore: Johns Hopkins University Press, 1976), esp. 181–84.

2. Ronald Story has likewise defined the rise of Boston Brahmins in this fashion: "An elite becomes an upper class, however, not only through internal development but through the attainment of class consciousness in the face of nonelite challenge for control over valuable resources" (Story, *The Forging of an Aristocracy: Harvard and the Boston Upper Class, 1800–1870* [Middletown, CT: Wesleyan University Press, 1980], 135).
3. See San Francisco Art Association, *Constitution, By-laws, List of Members and Catalogue of Library, and Rules of the School of Design of the San Francisco Art Association* (San Francisco: B. F. Sterett, 1878). On the "Big Five," see Cerinda W. Evans, *Collis Potter Huntington* (Newport News, VA: The Mariners' Museum, 1954); Oscar Lewis, *The Big Four* (New York and London: Alfred A. Knopf, 1938); K. D. Kurutz, "Sacramento's Pioneer Patrons of Art: The Edwin Bryant Crocker Family," *Golden Notes* 31, no. 2 (Summer 1985): 1–32; and Norman E. Tutorow, *Leland Stanford: Man of Many Careers* (Menlo Park, CA: Pacific Coast, 1971). "General" David Douty Colton was a Maine native who parlayed a law degree and political connections into a real estate fortune; in 1874 he became a substantial investor in and executive of the CPR. Another major player in the Central Pacific was Wells Fargo Bank President Lloyd Tevis. Together with Irving M. Scott, Peter and James Donahue owned and operated the prosperous Union Iron Works, whose profitability precipitated holdings in gas, transportation, mining, banking, and real estate. Equally diversified were William Alvord, president of the Risdon Iron Works and one-time San Francisco mayor; William Ralston, president of the Bank of California and owner of the lavish Palace Hotel; and banker Darius Ogden Mills. Finally, James Ben Ali Haggin, Lloyd Tevis, and George Hearst coordinated numerous investments in mining, financing, and real estate. Significantly, the few local plutocrats who could claim a true working-class background, mostly the Irish-born "Silver Kings" of the Virginia Consolidated Mining Company (James G. Fair, James C. Flood, John W. Mackay, and William S. O'Brien), engaged in collecting neither as extensively nor as early. Peter Decker, *Fortunes and Failures: White-Collar Mobility in Nineteenth Century San Francisco* (Cambridge, MA: Harvard University Press, 1978), esp. 170–95; Lewis, *Big Four,* 285–320; Evans, *Collis Potter Huntington,* 340–43; William Issel and Robert W. Cherny, *San Francisco, 1865–1932: Politics, Power, and Urban Development* (Berkeley and Los Angeles: University of California Press, 1986), 29–33; Gray A. Brechin, *Imperial San Francisco: Urban Power, Earthly Ruin* (Berkeley: University of California Press, 1999), 125–26, 211–12, 249–51; Judith Robinson, *The Hearsts: An American Dynasty* (Newark: University of Delaware Press, 1991); Oscar Lewis, *Silver Kings* (New York and London: Alfred A. Knopf, 1959); Richard H. Peterson, *The Bonanza Kings: The Social Origins and Business Behavior of Western Mining Entrepreneurs, 1870–1900* (Lincoln: University of Nebraska Press, 1977).
4. Prominent figures on the cultural scene included Washington, D.C., banker William Wilson Corcoran, New York railroad barons John Taylor Johnston and Robert M. Olyphant, New York department store tycoon Alexander Stewart, and Philadelphia manufacturing and railroad executive Joseph Harrison. Among this later group, only clothing wholesaler Thomas B. Clarke could boast a career comparable to his prewar mercantile brethren. W. G. Constable, *Art Collecting in the United States of America: An Outline of a History* (Toronto and New York: Thomas Nelson and Sons, 1964), 10–30, 141–43; Lillian B. Miller, *Patrons and Patriotism: The Encouragement of the Fine Arts in the United States, 1790–1860* (Chicago: University of Chicago Press, 1966), 148–59; Frederick Baekeland, "Collectors of American Painting, 1813–1913," *American Art Review* 3, no. 6 (November–December 1976): 121–48; Madeleine Fidell Beaufort and Jeanne K. Welcher, "Some Views of Art Buying in New York in the 1870s and 1880s," *Oxford Art Journal* 5, no. 1 (1982): 48–53; Ella M. Foshay, *Mr. Luman Reed's Picture Gallery* (New York: Harry N. Abrams, 1990), 11–17; Lance Lee Humphries, "Robert Gilmor, Jr.: Baltimore Collector and American Art Patron" (Ph.D. dissertation, University of Virginia, 1998); Carrie Rebora, "Robert Fulton's Art Collection," *American Art Journal* 22, no. 3 (1990): 40–63; Nicholas B. Wainwright, "Joseph Harrison, Jr.: A Forgotten Art Collector," *Antiques* 102, no. 4 (October 1972): 660–68; Alan Wallach, *Exhibiting Contradiction: Essays on the American Museum in the United States* (Boston: University of Massachusetts Press, 1998), 22–37; Barbara H. Weinberg, "Thomas B. Clarke: Foremost Patron of American Art from 1872 to 1899," *American Art Journal* 8, no. 1 (May 1976): 52–83.

5. Hubert Howe Bancroft, *The History of California* (San Francisco: The History Company, 1890), 7:693; see also Thomas G. Shearman, "The Owners of the United States," *Forum* 9 (November 1889): 262–73. E. B. Crocker may have not made this list because either he had died in 1875, or Sacramento was too small a city at the time, or his estate's value was less than $20 million.
6. Quoted in Carol A. O'Connor, "A Region of Cities," in *The Oxford History of the American West,* ed. Clyde A. Milner II, Carol A. O'Conner, and Martha A. Sandweiss (New York and Oxford: Oxford University Press, 1994), 543.
7. Mary P. Ryan, *Civic Wars: Democracy and Public Life in the American City during the Nineteenth Century* (Berkeley: University of California Press, 1997), 282.
8. Marx is cited in Philip J. Ethington, *The Public City: The Political Construction of Urban Life in San Francisco, 1850–1900* (Cambridge: Cambridge University Press, 1994), 242.
9. In its inaugural year, the Exhibition garnered almost 30,000 single admissions and twice as many season tickets in a little under one month; by the 1870s, daily attendance often approached 30,000. Ellen Schwartz, *Nineteenth-Century San Francisco Art Exhibition Catalogues* (Davis: Library Associates, University Library, University of California, Davis, 1981), 2; Birgitta Hjalmarson, *Artful Players: Artistic Life in Early San Francisco* (Los Angeles: Balcony Press, 1999), 24–25; B. E. Lloyd, *Lights and Shades in San Francisco* (San Francisco: A. L. Bancroft, 1876), 116–19; J. H. Culver, "The Building of a State: IX. The Mechanics' Institute," *Overland Monthly* 8 (September 1886): 314–24; John W. Wood, *75 Years of History of the Mechanics' Institute of San Francisco* (San Francisco: Mechanics' Institute, 1930); and the Mechanics' Institute annual Industrial Exhibition reports.
10. William Alvord, quoted in "San Francisco Art Association," *Alta California,* March 27, 1872, 1.
11. On the CAU, see Hjalmarson, *Artful Players,* 25; Schwartz, *Nineteenth-Century San Francisco,* 5; *Catalogue of the California Art Union* (San Francisco: Wade, 1865); "City Items," *Alta California,* January 12, 1865, 1; "Subscribers to the California Art Union," *Alta California,* April 15, 1865, 1; B. P. Avery, "Art Beginnings on the Pacific: II," *Overland Monthly* 1, no. 2 (August 1868): 113–19; Julian Dana, *The Man Who Built San Francisco* (New York: McMill, 1937), 93; and Raymond Wilson, "Painters of California's Silver Era," *American Art Journal* (Autumn 1984): 73.
12. Leading dealers include the picture and frame shop of Jones, Wooll & Sutherland (1850), M. D. Nile's (ca. 1850), the art gallery Snow & Roos (1853), and Gump's department store (1863). The Gumps bragged sizable accounts with Leland Stanford and Collis Huntington, among others. See Schwartz, *Nineteenth-Century San Francisco,* 4; Julia Cooley Altrocchi, *The Spectacular San Franciscans* (New York: E. P. Dutton, 1949), 155; Issel and Cherney, *San Francisco,* 27; "Days Gone By," *San Francisco Chronicle,* July 14, 1889, 2; "Art Notes," *San Francisco Bulletin,* January 29, 1869, 2; "New Art Gallery," *San Francisco Bulletin,* April 13, 1869, 2; "Snow and Roos Art Gallery," *San Francisco Newsletter and California Advertiser,* August 14, 1869, 14; Carol Green Wilson, *Gump's Treasure Trade: A Story of San Francisco* (New York: Thomas Y. Crowell, 1965 [1949]); and Janet Lynn Roseman et al., *Gump's since 1861: A San Francisco Legend* (San Francisco: Chronicle Books, 1991).
13. On the phenomenon of studio as showrooms, see Kenneth John Myers, "The Public Display of Art in New York City, 1664–1914," in *Rave Reviews: American Art and Its Critics,* David B. Dearinger (Hanover, NH: University Press of New England, 2000), 40; Annette Blaugrund, *The Tenth Street Studio Building: Artist-Entrepreneurs from the Hudson River School to the American Impressionists* (Southampton, NY: Parrish Art Museum, 1997); and Linda Henefield Skalet, "The Market for American Painting in New York, 1870–1915" (Ph.D. diss., Johns Hopkins University, 1980), 11–22.
14. On the domestic trade, see Myers, "Public Display," 47; see Skalet, "Market for American Painting," passim; and Malcolm Goldstein, *Landscape with Figures: A History of Art Dealing in the United States* (Oxford: Oxford University Press, 2000), 29. On Europe, see Dianne Sachko Macleod, *Art and the Middle Class: Money and the Making of Cultural Identity* (Cambridge: Cambridge University Press, 1996), esp. 38–40, 241–43; and Cynthia A. White and Harrison C. White, *Canvases and Careers: Institutional Changes in the French Painting World* (New York: Wiley, 1965).
15. Quotes come from "Judge Crocker's Fine Art Gallery," *Sacramento Bee,* December 27, 1873, 3.

16. "The Picture Sale," and "Art Sale," unsourced newspaper clippings, Edwin Deakin Scrapbook, p. 36 (reel 4201, frame 23), Archives of American Art.
17. The quote comes from an unsourced newspaper clipping, Edwin Deakin Scrapbook, p. 36. On advisers, see also Thomas Hill, "A History of the 'Spike Picture' and Why It Is in My Possession," repr. in Hardy Sloan George, *Thomas Hill (1829–1908)* (M.A. thesis, University of California, Los Angeles, 1963), 105–10.
18. "San Francisco Art: Probable Causes of a Current Depression," *San Francisco Examiner,* November 28, 1880, 3.
19. "Art Prospects," *San Francisco Post,* February 2, 1874, 2.
20. The quotes come from "Judge Crocker's Fine Art Gallery," *Sacramento Bee,* December 27, 1873, 3. See also "Art Items," *San Francisco Bulletin,* September 18, 1871, 3; "The Arts," *San Francisco Chronicle,* October 18, 1871, 3; "Valuable Paintings," *Alta California,* October 18, 1871, 1; "Local Art Items," *San Francisco Bulletin,* January 6, 1872, 3; and "Judge Crocker's Art Gallery on Exhibition," *Sacramento Union,* March 18, 1874, 3. Likewise, in the 1890s, a series of charity loan exhibitions, featuring pieces from the Bay Area's most feted collections, was organized on behalf of the Maria Kip Orphanage in Oakland. W. K. Vickery, *Catalogue of Paintings Exhibited for the Benefit of the Maria Kip Orphanage* (San Francisco, 1891); and *Catalogue of Paintings Exhibited for the Benefit of the Maria Kip Orphanage* (San Francisco, 1895). *See also* Society of Decorative Art, *Catalogue of the Art Loan Exhibition for the Benefit of the Society of Decorative Art of California* (San Francisco: The Society, 1881). On the Ladies' Christian Commission Fair, see Schwartz, *Nineteenth-Century San Francisco,* 2.
21. Alvord, quoted in "San Francisco Art Association," 1; "Art Notes," *San Francisco Bulletin,* January 25, 1873, p. 3
22. The still-essential guide to Ruskin's stateside reception is Roger B. Stein, *John Ruskin and Aesthetic Thought in America, 1840–1900* (Cambridge, MA: Harvard University Press, 1967). *See also* Mary Ann Stankiewicz, "'The Eye Is a Nobler Organ': Ruskin and American Art Education," *Journal of Aesthetic Education* 18, no. 2 (Summer 1984): 51–64; and Charles Colbert, "A Critical Medium: James Jackson Jarves's Vision of Art History," *American Art* 16, no. 1 (Spring 2002): 18–35. The quotations appear in James Jackson Jarves, "On the Formation of Galleries in America," *Atlantic Monthly* 6 (July 1860): 108; Jarves, *Art Studies: The "Old Masters" of Italy* (New York: Derby and Jackson, 1861), 13.
23. James Jackson Jarves, *Art Thoughts* (New York: Hurd & Houghton, 1869), 315; Jarves, *Art Studies,* 8–9.
24. James Jackson Jarves, "Art and Artists of America," *Christian Examiner* 75 (July 1863): 114–27.
25. Benjamin Park Avery, "Art and Its Uses," (unpublished manuscript, MSS C-H 61, Benjamin Park Avery Papers, Bancroft Library, University of California, Berkeley), 85–86.
26. On Nob settlement, see Decker, *Fortunes and Failures,* 215–33; Ryan, *Civic Wars,* 193; Gunther Barth, "Metropolitanism and Urban Elites in the Far West," in *The Age of Industrialism in America: Essays in Social Structures and Cultural Values,* ed. Frederic Cople Jaher (New York: Free Press, 1968), 158–87; Patricia Lawrence, "Four Mansions on Nob Hill in the 1870s" (M.A. thesis, University of California, Davis, 1976); Olive Palmer, comp., *Vignettes of Early San Francisco Homes and Gardens* (San Francisco: Garden Club, 1935); and Carol M. Osborne, *Museum Builders in the West: The Stanfords as Collectors and Patrons of Art, 1870–1906* (Stanford: Stanford University Press, 1986), 27–29.
27. "Local Art Items," *San Francisco Bulletin,* January 6, 1872, 3.
28. On the Stanfords, see Bertha Berner, *Mrs. Leland Stanford: An Intimate Account* (Stanford: Stanford University Press, 1935), 19–20; "Stanford's Home," *San Francisco Chronicle,* February 7, 1875, 4; "A Rare Collection," *San Francisco Chronicle,* May 14, 1882, 1; "A Brilliant Event," *California Spirit of the Times,* October 25, 1879, 41, 44; and "The Residence of Leland Stanford," *California Spirit of the Times,* July 1, 1876, 31. On the Crockers' mansion/museum complex, see Kurutz, "Sacramento's Pioneer Patrons," 1–32; Donald Clyde Ball, "A History of the E. B. Crocker Art Gallery and Its Founders" (M.A. thesis, College of the Pacific, 1955); Richard V. West, "The Crockers and Their Collection: A Brief History," in *Crocker Art Museum: Handbook of Paintings,* ed. Richard Vincent West (Sacramento: The Museum, 1979), 7–11; and Joseph A. Baird, "Judge Crocker's Art Gallery," in *Crocker Art Museum,* 13–16. Numerous New York galleries appear in Arnold Lewis, James Turner, and Steven McQuillin, *The Opulent Interiors of the Gilded Age* (New York: Dover Publications, 1987), passim.

29. Decker, *Fortunes and Failures,* 247–49; Ryan, *Civic Wars,* 284–86; Alexander Saxton, *The Indispensable Enemy: Labor and the Anti-Chinese Movement in California* (Berkeley: University of California Press, 1971), 114–15; Kevin Starr, *Endangered Dreams: The Great Depression in California* (New York and Oxford: Oxford University Press, 1996), 7–9.
30. William Deverell, *Railroad Crossing: Californians and the Railroad, 1850–1910* (Berkeley, Los Angeles, and London: University of California Press, 1994), 44–45; Ryan, *Civic Wars,* 286–92; Saxton, *Indispensable Enemy,* 116–21; Starr, *Endangered Dreams,* 9–15.
31. Ambrose Bierce, "Editorial," *San Francisco Illustrated Wasp,* May 31, 1884, 4; Bierce, "Editorial," *San Francisco Illustrated Wasp,* August 5, 1882, 2. On Bierce's *Wasp,* see Deverell, *Railroad Crossing,* 58–59; Lewis, *Big Four,* 156; Ernest Jerome Hopkins, *The Ambrose Bierce Satanic Reader* (Garden City, NY: Doubleday, 1968), 194–209; Kenneth M. Johnson, *The Sting of the Wasp* (San Francisco: Book Club of California, 1967); 1–15; and Daniel Lindley, *Ambrose Bierce Takes on the Railroad: The Journalist as Muckraker and Cynic* (Westport, CT: Praeger, 1999).
32. Anonymous, *The Monarch Philanthropist* (San Francisco: Cobery, 1892), 16; for Cohen's quote, see Lewis, *Big Four,* 144.
33. Paul DiMaggio, "Cultural Entrepreneurship in Nineteenth-Century Boston, Part II: The Classification and Framing of American Art," *Media, Culture & Society* 4 (1982): 303.
34. Hubert Howe Bancroft, "Biography of Leland Stanford," unpublished proofs (ca. 1888), p. 153, MSS C-D 807, folder 14, box 2, Bancroft Library, University of California, Berkeley.
35. "Mourning at Palo Alto," *San Francisco Examiner,* June 22, 1893, 1. This letter was also published in "Stanford's Ideas on Education," unsourced newspaper clipping, SC512, folder 7, box 2, Leland Stanford Collection, Special Collections and University Archives, Stanford University.
36. Jarves, *Art Studies,* 14.
37. My language here comes from Benedict Anderson, *Imagined Communities: Reflections on the Origin and Spread of Nationalism* (London and New York: Verso, 1983).
38. "Amusements, Etc.," *Alta California,* October 31, 1868. On the San Francisco Mercantile Library, see Joyce Backus, "A History of the San Francisco Mercantile Library Association" (M.A. thesis, University of California, Berkeley, 1931); and Bradford Luckingham, "Libraries and Museums in Emergent San Francisco: A Note on the Pursuit of Culture in the Urban Far West," *Pacific Historian* 17, no. 3 (Fall 1973): 4–11.
39. On the SFAA at the Mercantile Library, see "The San Francisco Art Association," *Alta California,* March 29, 1871, 1. Quotations appear in B. P. Avery, "Art in California," *The Aldine* 7, no. 4 (April 1874): 72; and Avery, "Etc.," *Overland Monthly* 9, no. 2 (July 1872): 91.
40. "Oscar Wilde," *San Francisco Examiner,* April 11, 1882; quoted in Hjalmarson, *Artful Players,* 63. Background on elite clubs in San Francisco comes from Lloyd, *Lights and Shades,* 483–86; *Annals of the Bohemian Club, Vol. 1: 1872–1880* (San Francisco: Hicks-Judd, 1898), esp. 247–50; and G. William Domhoff, *The Bohemian Grove and Other Retreats: A Study in Ruling Class Cohesiveness* (New York: Harper and Row, 1974). The Pacific Club exhibition is covered in "Local Intelligence," *Alta California,* April 16, 1869, 1. The Bohemian Club and SFAA collaboration is noted in Wilson, "The First Art School," 47.
41. Vásquez, *Inventing the Art Collection,* 7, has noted similar trends in Europe during the period of 1839–1860.
42. "Art Association," *Alta California,* February 9, 1877, 1.
43. Loans are discussed in "Art Association Exhibition," *Alta California,* July 29, 1872, 1; "Art Association," *San Francisco Newsletter and California Advertiser,* May 10, 1873, 4; and "Art Notes," *San Francisco Bulletin,* January 25, 1873, 3.
44. *Artistic Homes of California* (San Francisco: San Francisco Newsletter, 1888). This *California Spirit of the Times* supplement must have been inspired by *Artistic Houses* (New York: D. Appleton, 1883–84), a two-volume subscription affair issued by the creators of both *Appleton's Journal* and the popular illustrated book *Picturesque America*. See Lewis, Turner, and McQuillin, *Opulent Interiors*.
45. "The Social World," *San Francisco Call,* February 7, 1882, 5. As one example of journalistic hagiography, *Alta California* cooed that "the Stanford mansion is as purely a high work of art as a great historical picture" ("An Art Treasure," *Alta California,* April 7, 1876), 1.
46. Vásquez, *Inventing the Art Collection,* 10.
47. One such local example may be found in T. A. Barry, "Art in California," *California Spirit of the Times,* July 1, 1876, 14.

48. Earl Shinn [Edward Strahan], *The Art Treasures of America* (Philadelphia: G. Barrie, 1879–82). See also Emile Alix Durand-Gréville, "Private Picture Galleries of the United States," *Gazette des Beaux-Arts* 36 (1887): 65–75; and Walter Montgomery, *American Art and American Art Collections* (Boston: E. W. Walker, 1889). Dozens of articles on elites' personal galleries can also be found in the wave of new journals from the period, including *Art Amateur, Art Journal, The Collector,* and *The Studio;* see also Ruth Krueger Meyer and Madeleine Fidell Beaufort, "The Rage for Collecting: Beyond Pittsburgh in the Gilded Age," in Gabriel P. Weisberg et al., *Collecting in the Gilded Age: Art Patronage in Pittsburgh, 1890–1910* (Pittsburgh: Frick Art and Historical Center, 1997), 315–16.
49. On the Crocker's travels, see Kurutz, "Sacramento's Pioneer Patrons," 1–32. On Pittsburgh, see Goldstein, *Landscape with Figures,* 166; Charles R. Henschel, "A Personal History of Knoedler," in *The Rise of the Art World in America: Knoedler at 150* (New York: Knoedler, 1996), 10–11; and DeCourcy E. McIntosh, "Demand and Supply: The Pittsburgh Art Trade and M. Knoedler & Co.," in Weisberg et al., *Collecting in the Gilded Age,* 179–298.
50. S. R. Koehler, *United States' Art Directory and Year-Book* (New York and London: Garland, 1976 [1882–84]), iii.
51. Shinn, *Art Treasures,* 3:41.
52. One example of this criticism appears in "Art and Artists," *Californian* 3, no. 18 (June 1881): 572. On the preference for imported over domestic artworks, see Skalet, "Market for American Painting," 39–41, 128–30; Carol Troyen, "Innocents Abroad: American Painters at the 1867 Exposition Universelle, Paris," *American Art Journal* 16, no. 4 (Autumn 1984): 19–22; and H. Barbara Weinberg, "Cosmopolitan Attitudes: The Coming of Age of American Art," in *Paris 1889: American Artists at the Universal Exposition,* ed. Annette Blaugrund (Philadelphia: Pennsylvania Academy of the Fine Arts and New York: Harry N. Abrams, 1989), 33–34.
53. On the SFAU, see Schwartz, *Nineteenth-Century San Francisco,* 5; and Dana, *Man Who Built San Francisco,* 260–63. On the Palette Club, see Hjalmarson, *Artful Players,* 97–104; "California Palette Club," *San Francisco Call,* January 31, 1884, 3; and "Palette," *San Francisco Call,* May 15, 1884, 3.
54. On the tariff issue, see William J. Barber, "International Commerce in the Fine Arts and American Political Economy, 1789–1913," in *Economic Engagements with Art,* ed. Neil De Marchi and Craufurd D. W. Goodwin (Durham, NC, and London: Duke University Press, 1999); and Kimberly Orcutt, "Buy American? The Debate over the Art Tariff," *American Art* 16, no. 3 (Autumn 2002): 82–91.
55. Alfred D. Chandler Jr., *The Visible Hand: The Managerial Revolution in American Business* (Cambridge, MA: Harvard University Press, 1977); Chandler, *Scale and Scope: The Dynamics of Industrial Capitalism* (Cambridge, MA: Harvard University Press, 1990), esp. 51–94; Peter Dobkin Hall, *The Organization of American Culture: Private Institutions, Elites, and the Origins of American Nationality, 1700–1900* (New York: New York University Press, 1984); William G. Roy, *Socializing Capital: The Rise of the Large Industrial Corporation in America* (Princeton, NJ: Princeton University Press, 1997), 100–10, 122–43; Sven Beckert, *The Monied Metropolis: New York City and the Consolidation of the American Bourgeoisie, 1850–1896* (Cambridge and New York: Cambridge University Press, 2001), 239–42, 253–65.
56. Alternative interpretations of shifts in the postbellum art market appear in Beaufort and Welcher, "Some Views," 48–52; Skalet, "Market for American Painting," 129; and Goldstein, *Landscape with Figures,* 48.
57. In like fashion, Lawrence Levine figures high culture as a "cloak." Pierre Bourdieu has alternatively categorized the arts as symptomatic of the bourgeois "withdrawal from economic necessity" and their "denial of the social world." Lawrence W. Levine, *Highbrow/Lowbrow: The Emergence of Cultural Hierarchy in America* (Cambridge, MA: Harvard University Press, 1988); Pierre Bourdieu, *Distinction: A Social Critique of the Judgement of Taste,* trans. Richard Nice (Cambridge, MA: Harvard University Press, 1984), 53–54, 596.
58. "A Princely Design" *San Francisco Call,* November 15, 1885, 3.
59. The provision for a Stanford University Museum is noted in Osborne, *Museum Builders,* 17. In *Art Thoughts,* Jarves asserted that "Art creates a Central Park" (314).
60. Early reports from Leland include "Mrs. Stanford and myself have determined to locate this museum in San Francisco" (quoted in "The Academe," *San Francisco Examiner,* April 28, 1887, 1). *See also* Bancroft, "Biography of Leland Stanford," 153; "Stanford's Park Project," *Kansas Star* (ca. 1890), scrapbook 1, p. 110, Stanford Family Scrapbooks, Special Collections

and University Archives, Stanford University. "It was originally intended by [Leland Jr.'s] mother to place this museum in Golden Gate Park," wrote the *Argonaut,* "but, on further consideration, Palo Alto has been selected as its location" ("Editorial," *Argonaut* 27, no. 22 [December 1, 1890]: 1).

61. "Destined for the People," *San Francisco Examiner,* July 3, 1893, 3. The last report appears in "Notes and Novelties," *Collector* 4, no. 9 (1893): 144.
62. Paul Venable Turner, "The Architectural Significance of the Stanford Museum," in Osborne, *Museum Builders,* 93–97. Cesnola consoled the Stanfords for the loss of their 15-year-old son Leland Jr., lamenting that the young man's loss was all the greater since he had shown an early interest in antiquities and "the art-training of our American people"(quoted in Osborne, 15). On Cesnola, *see also* Calvin Tompkins, *Merchants and Masterpieces: The Story of the Metropolitan Museum of Art* (New York: E. P. Dutton, 1970), esp. 49–83.
63. On the Metropolitan, see Tomkins, *Merchants and Masterpieces,* 73–75; and Rachel N. Klein, "Art and Authority in Antebellum New York City: The Rise and Fall of the American Art Union," *Journal of American History* 81, no. 4 (March 1895): 1560. On Boston, see Story, *Forging of an Aristocracy,* 16–17; DiMaggio, "Cultural Entrepreneurship"; Neil Harris, "The Gilded Age Revisited: Boston and the Museum Movement," *American Quarterly* 14 (Winter 1962): 545–566; and Julia Rosenbaum, "Displaying Civic Culture: The Controversy over Frederick MacMonnies' *Bacchante,*" *American Art* 14, no. 3 (Fall 2000): 41–57.
64. Rachel Klein considers the trauma of the Civil War central to any understanding of the slow death of the idea of any commonwealth, whether held together by shared aesthetic philosophies or other means. In his book on urban and Victorian California, political scientist Philip Ethington attributes the erosion of republicanism and its attendant commitments to a broadly defined public to the rising dominance of economic liberalism, while Lawrence Levine's classic study finds the growth of mass consumer culture equally complicit. Most closely related to this study, Helen Horowitz's work has argued in a similar vein that financial and managerial elites explicitly adapted the Ruskinian notion of self-improvement through the arts in order to advance the country's new industrial order; as she writes, "cultural philanthropy . . . meshed with the laissez-faire ideology of these business men, who would limit the activities of government." Meanwhile, in her analysis of trends in Britain, Dianne Macleod regards regional merchants' project of uplift through art and art education as a self-serving self-deception rather than an active conspiracy to ensure the smooth transition to industrial capitalism. Klein, *Art and Authority,* esp. 1560; Ethington, *Public City,* esp. 287–344; Levine, *Highbrow/Lowbrow,* passim; Helen Lefkowitz Horowitz, *Culture and the City: Cultural Philanthropy in Chicago from the 1880s to 1917* (Lexington: University of Kentucky Press, 1976), 65; Macleod, *Art and the Middle Class,* esp. 107–109.

Contributors

Sven Beckert is Laird Bell Professor of History at Harvard University. He is the author of *The Monied Metropolis: New York City and the Consolidation of the American Bourgeoisie* (Cambridge University Press). Currently he is writing a global history of cotton.

Michael Broyles is Distinguished Professor of Music Emeritus from Pennsylvania State University and Professor of Musicology at Florida State University. His most recent book, *Leo Ornstein: Modernist Dilemmas, Personal Choices,* with Denise Von Glahn, won the Irving S. Lowens prize from the Society for American Music. He is currently writing a social-cultural study of Beethoven in America.

Alide Cagidemetrio is Professor of American Studies and Dean of the Faculty of Modern Languages at the University of Venice. Her research interests focus on the intersections between history and fiction, and she is currently writing a book on Henry James.

Paul DiMaggio is A. Barton Hepburn Professor of Sociology and Public Affairs and Director of the Center for the Study of Social Organization at Princeton University. He has written about the role of local elites in creating the nonprofit model for governing cultural institutions in the U.S. and the role of foundations in institutionalizing that model. He books include *Organizzare la cultura: Imprenditoria, istituzioni e beni culturali* (Il Mulino, 2009).

Peter Dobkin Hall is Professor of Public Affairs at Baruch College, CUNY, and Senior Research Fellow at the Hauser Center for Nonprofit Organizations, Harvard University. His publications include *Sacred Companies: Organizational Aspects of Religion and Religious Aspects of Organizations* (1998), *Inventing the Nonprofit Sector and Other Essays on Philanthropy, Voluntarism, and Nonprofit Organizations* (1992), and *The Organization of American Culture, 1700–1900: Institutions, Elites, and the Origins of American Nationality* (1982).

Katherine C. Grier is Professor and Director of the Museum Studies Program, Department of History, University of Delaware. She is the author of *Culture and Comfort: Parlor Making and Middle-Class Identity, 1850–1930* (Smithsonian Institution Press, 1997) and *Pets in America: A History* (University of North Carolina Press, 2006). Grier specializes in the history of everyday life in America in the nineteenth and twentieth centuries, with an emphasis on the study of material culture.

Anne Mendelson is a culinary historian with an interest in New York City food, past and present. A founding member of the Culinary Historians of New York, she is a contributor to *The Oxford Encyclopedia of Food and Drink in America* and the author of two books, *Stand Facing the Stove* (Holt, 1996) and *Milk* (Knopf, 2008).

Maureen E. Montgomery is a Associate Professor in American Studies at the University of Canterbury, New Zealand and author of *"Gilded Prostitution": Status, Money* *and Transatlantic Marriages 1870–1914* (Routledge, 1989) and *Displaying Women: Spectacles of Leisure in Edith Wharton's New York* (Routledge, 1998).

Francesca Morgan is a Associate professor of history at Northeastern Illinois University in Chicago. She is the author of *Women and Patriotism in Jim Crow America* (University of North Carolina Press, 2005), and has also published her work in the *New England Quarterly*. She is writing a book entitled *How Genealogy Became American, 1800–2000*.

John Ott is a Associate Professor of Art History at James Madison University and writes about art patronage, museums, institutions, and markets, and about social class and its intersections with ethnicity and gender. His scholarship has appeared in numerous journals, including *American Art, Oxford Art Journal*, and *Winterthur Portfolio*.

Ethan Robey is Assistant Professor of the History of Decorative Arts and Design at Parsons The New School for Design and the Associate Director of the Master's Program in the History of Decorative Arts and Design, jointly run by Parsons and Cooper-Hewitt, National Design Museum. His scholarship addresses issues of display, consumerism, and taste in the nineteenth and twentieth centuries. He holds a Ph.D. from Columbia University.

Mary Rech Rockwell is the Director of Studies at Nichols School in Buffalo, New York and author of *John R. Oishei: Buffalo Businessman and Benefactor* (The John R. Oishei Foundation, August, 2004). Her research interests focus on elite women and class formation. She was an American Memory Fellow at the Library of Congress, a Japan Fulbright recipient, and an NEH Seminar participant. She holds a Ph.D. in American history from the State University of New York at Buffalo.

Julia B. Rosenbaum is Assistant Professor of Art History at Bard College and has been a Visiting Research Fellow at The University of East Anglia in England. She is the author of *Visions of Belonging: New England Art and the Making of American Identity* (Cornell University Press) and her current work addresses new technologies and their impact on visual experiences in the nineteenth and twentieth centuries.

Anne Verplanck is a Associate Professor of American Studies at Pennsylvania State University, Harrisburg. She is the former Curator of Prints and Paintings at Winterthur Museum, where she also served as Interim Director of Museum Collections and Interim Director of the Research Fellowship Program. She co-edited, with Emma Lapsansky, the book *Quaker Aesthetics*. She is currently preparing a book on Philadelphia as a site of artistic production and consumption.

Alan Wallach is Ralph H. Wark Professor of Art and Art History and Professor of American Studies at the College of William and Mary. He writes frequently about American art and art institutions and is the author of *Exhibiting Contradiction: Essays on the Art Museum in the United States* (University of Massachusetts Press). Wallach was the 2007 recipient of the College Art Association's Distinguished Teaching of Art History award.

Index

GPSR Compliance
The European Union's (EU) General Product Safety Regulation (GPSR) is a set of rules that requires consumer products to be safe and our obligations to ensure this.

If you have any concerns about our products, you can contact us on

ProductSafety@springernature.com

In case Publisher is established outside the EU, the EU authorized representative is:

Springer Nature Customer Service Center GmbH
Europaplatz 3
69115 Heidelberg, Germany

www.ingramcontent.com/pod-product-compliance
Lightning Source LLC
Chambersburg PA
CBHW070949211125
35560CB00036B/544
* 9 7 8 0 2 3 0 1 0 2 9 4 1 *